THE THEATRICAL 'WORLD'
OF 1897.

THE

THEATRICAL 'WORLD'

OF 1897

BY

WILLIAM ARCHER

WITH AN INTRODUCTION

BY SYDNEY GRUNDY

AND A SYNOPSIS OF PLAYBILLS OF THE YEAR

BY HENRY GEORGE HIBBERT

BENJAMIN BLOM  New York/London

First Published 1898
Reissued 1969 by
Benjamin Blom, Inc., Bronx, New York 10452
and 56 Doughty Street, London, W.C. 1

Library of Congress Catalog Card Number 77-82818

Printed in United States of America
at Westbrook Lithographers, Inc.
Westbury, New York

CONTENTS.

————◆————

INTRODUCTION.

IF Mr. Archer had searched the world he could
hardly have found one less qualified than I am
to write a preface to this volume. My position
as a playwright scarcely entitles me to link my
name with his in relation to dramatic art; and
being by use and wont a writer for the stage, an
ordinary pen is in my hand an unfamiliar and
dangerous weapon, which, if by good luck it
does no harm to others, may very well recoil
upon myself. Another of my disqualifications
is the fact that my acquaintance with these
particular essays is limited to such of them as
have been forwarded to me by the interesting,
the irritating, the amusing, the depressing, the
indispensable Romeike. Under these circumstances, why have I taken up my pen? The
answer is simple. Mr. Archer has asked me to
do so.

Twenty years drop from my back, and I am
seated in a humble compartment on the London,

Chatham, and Dover Railway. Opposite to me
is a young Scotchman — Scotsman he calls
himself;* but I, possessing no literary style,
call him a Scotchman; because, though it may
be very bad Scots, it is excellent English. We
fall into conversation. We discover that we are
both profoundly interested in plays and players.
We discuss them eagerly; and I find myself,
almost for the first time in my life, in agreement
with one of my fellow-creatures. My companion was not then Mr. Archer, the eminent
critic, or I should not have presumed to address
him; he was only a young Mr. Archer, a law-
student, with a portrait of one Henrik Ibsen
hanging over his bedroom mantel-piece. How
we analysed those plays! How we dissected
those players! How we discussed that Ibsen!
And how we agreed! Our unanimity was
wonderful. Well, twenty years have passed,
and Mr. Archer is still an enthusiast. He has
not only been able to maintain his interest in
the theatre, but he has regarded it from new
points of view. I stand where I stood—a less
or more sympathetic spectator of a drama in

* No, never! *Scotsman*, except as the name of a newspaper,
I take to be a mere affectation.—W. A.

travail, not knowing what it may bring forth. But we agreed once ; and those were pleasant days. That is why Mr. Archer has invited me to write this preface, and that is why I write it.

When mortals disagree, such is the perversity of human nature that they seek to exaggerate their differences, and persist in regarding the points at which they diverge rather than those where they approach. During the year that is passing, Mr. Archer (so Mr. Romeike informs me) has returned to the attack upon Scribe (page 192), and *more suo*, does me the honour to associate my name with that of the French playwright. Great as my admiration is for the unapproached technique of Scribe, I have never cited any play of his as a masterpiece, nor have I ever held him up as a model in any other particular than the exquisite symmetry of his construction. I am willing to admit that in many other respects he is lacking. To bracket me with Scribe is to obscure the issue. My contention has ever been, that form is one of the most beautiful manifestations of art. I regard as a fallacy the proposition put by Mr. Archer into the mouth of a sort of Devil's advocate, that " Heaven is the arch-dramatist."

I deny that heaven is a dramatist. I contend that to put into dramatic form and shapeliness the confused tangle which we find in life is the very art and business of the dramatic author. Mr. Archer admits that there are no absolute truths in æsthetics; I have admitted that he has hold of half a truth; is he quite certain that I have not hold of another half? He has gone so far as to concede (page 222) "that the well-made play has its merits and is an art-form deserving of respect." This comforts me. And when he intimates (page 203) that deliberate formlessness and artful inartificiality may be pushed to extremes, I feel that he is on the high road to the discovery that they may be as puerile and irritating as the crudest machinery. The real question is not, and never was, "Has Eugène Scribe spoken the last word of theatrical technique?" That last word will never be spoken on this earth. The real question is: Is form an element of the highest art?

But what is the practical use of the discussion? While Mr. Archer is pioneering with laborious axe a hundred miles ahead of Eugène Scribe, the dear old simple-minded English play-going public is gathering buttercups and

daisies a hundred miles behind him. We will
dismiss Shakespeare ; he is the dramatic Bible ;
the touring manager puts him up on a Saturday
night, and proudly and truthfully declares that
he has drawn the biggest house of the week ;
but it has been said, "an actor cannot live by
Shakespeare alone." We will leave Sir Henry
Irving out of the question. He has become one
of our national institutions. His intense individuality, assisted by an unrivalled diplomacy
and a marvellous faculty of forgiveness, has
impressed itself upon a public which, however
flippant and frivolous, is always obedient to its
master. But genius is ever a thing apart. In
what has the production of *The Second Mrs.
Tanqueray, The Notorious Mrs. Ebbsmith, The
Benefit of the Doubt*, and the tremendous forward movement of psychology resulted ? In
the popular triumph of *The Prisoner of Zenda,
Under the Red Robe, Trilby*, and *The Little
Minister*. I have nothing that is not good to
say of these entertainments, and I rejoice that
an estranged audience has returned with gusto
to the theatre ; but do these financial pheno-
mena represent an advance in popular taste, do
they indicate a raising of the theatrical standard,

since the days when Sir Squire was Mr. Bancroft, and Mr. Hare and Mr. and Mrs. Kendal
played Sardou at the St. James's? Only Mr.
Wyndham remains at his old post. Sir Squire
and Lady Bancroft have retired from management; Mr. Hare has seen fit to resign the
Garrick Theatre; and Mr. and Mrs. Kendal have
long been exiles from London. Dost like the
picture? The theatrical situation will never be
realised until the fact is admitted that the
sober-minded, thoughtful mass of the English
public are not play-goers. Only a small
minority will take their drama seriously.

Can it be marvelled that an insignificant
dramatic author, who long ago abandoned all
idea of setting this naughty world to rights,
is unable to regard his vocation seriously? If
Mr. Romeike has not misled me, Mr. Archer
has publicly and very kindly regretted that
I devote so much attention to adaptation.
Indeed, of recent months, my adaptations
appear to have given a considerable number
of worthy persons grounds for great uneasiness.
If the matter is of any public interest, I am
quite willing to explain that I am in much the
same position as the proverbial Mr. Hobson.

The majority of the newspapers—in London, at any rate — cannot honestly applaud my original work ; and the public will not take the trouble to judge whether the newspapers are right. Its attitude I imagine to be this—and a very sensible attitude it is : This man—what's his name? Grumby—is a toss-up ; *The Geisha* is a certainty ; let's go to *The Geisha*. I have been original more often than is remembered ; but I am not sufficiently conceited to foist on play-goers an article which they do not require, simply because it is my own manufacture. Adaptation is an art in its way, and it has even some compensations. The adaptor has the opportunity of selecting his material from well-seasoned timber. He need only pick the best of a ·bundle. What does it matter to art who writes the play? One man, or two, or twenty? The play's the thing. If an author is original because he has something original and good to say, and there is an audience which wishes to hear him, he is right to be original ; but if he is original merely for the sake of originality, he is a coxcomb. Art is cosmopolitan, and one good adaptation is worth a score of indifferent originals. Moreover, as

I have contended of old time, an author who writes one original play and one adaptation is just as much an original author as he who writes one original play and adapts nothing. Would not thousands of play-goers have been deprived of the innocent amusement which Mr. Hare and Mr. Groves and Miss Kate Rorke have afforded them in *A Pair of Spectacles*, if I had not taken the original from the shelf where it had lain for thirty years and brushed the dust from its leaves? Labiche himself would have rejoiced over the success of his pet collaboration; and could he over-hear the rude ejaculations of a gesticulating French journalist, "English thief, you have robbed the fatherless!" would murmur, with a comedy twinkle of his eye, "Sarcey, I left no children."

There is a practical side to art which in public discussion is ignored, but which none the less helps to determine men's fortunes and reputations. The actual practice of any profession or calling has a wonderful knack of upsetting the theories and aspirations of the study, the dis-cussion forum and the critical bench. The stage has a voracious appetite, and somehow it must

be catered for. When one of the most uncompromising and enthusiastic of realists lays down
his critical pen and accepts a commission, he
adapts *The Prisoner of Zenda.* Another, *My
Friend the Prince.* If I am not mistaken, Mr.
Archer's own single contribution to the original
acted drama was of a most blood-curdling
description. There's a divinity that shapes our
ends, in the theatre as elsewhere. It has
happened to me more than once that a friend
has descended upon me like a bolt from the
blue; "I must have something in a fortnight,
and I must have a success. Can you help me?"
One may have a dozen original ideas in one's
mind, but they may not fit the occasion; and in
any case one can't do much with an original
idea in a fortnight. Adaptation was the only
resource. I am happy to say that in every such
case the desired result was achieved ; but it is by
one's successes that one is labelled, and again I
was "only a translator." In a workaday world
these rubs are inevitable.

Since I have never been able to accept my
own calling seriously, I cannot be surprised that
the majority of the critics find themselves in a
similar case. If I discuss their function as

though it were the mere apportionment of praise
and blame, it is not that I ignore its higher
aspects, its duties towards the public, and the
right of criticism to be considered a science
affording scope for the subtlest qualities of
the human intellect — a right which Mr.
Archer's essays have attested again and again
—but because the everyday theatrical "notice"
has not always reached the preliminary stage
of cultivating the judicial spirit; because the
dispensation of equal justice to all men and
to all women is so vastly more important than
the most brilliant analysis; and because I think
the concrete theatre suffers from being discussed in the abstract on too high a platform.
Professional criticism will always exist, and must
be accepted as an unalterable fact; but it would
be of absorbing interest if Mr. Archer, who does
take his vocation seriously, would devote one of
his luminous chapters to the consideration of its
net practical effect upon dramatic art.   On the
whole, is it gain or is it loss?   No doubt, in a
commercial sense, the theatre gains by the
publicity accorded to its doings; even unfavour-
able comment serves to keep it before the public
mind.   But what is the net effect on artists and

on art ?   I should very much like to hear Mr.
Archer's opinion.   Can he resist the testimony
of almost every author and artist in the past who
has left his views on record ?   Is it not a chorus,
an anthem of anathema ?   I can recall only one
instance, though no doubt there have been others,
in which a writer, or actor, or actress, has left
any memorial of indebtedness to professional
criticism.   Coming to our own time, Mrs.
Kendal's opinion is well known. Mr. W. S. Gilbert
has shaken the dust from his feet and departed.
Miss Winifred Emery, apparently as great a
favourite with the critics as with the public,
recently remarked to an interviewer that the
press had long ago crushed all her ambition.   I
know a score of such cases, but I must not name
them.   It has been said, "Oh, yes ! artists are
a conceited, sensitive set, who will swallow
butter by the pound, and resent the most
commonplace correction."   But is this a sufficient explanation ?   After making due allowance
for human nature and the artistic temperament,
it is a superficial cynicism to suppose that every
artist's views on a subject which equally con-
cerns his fellow-artists and his art itself are
absolutely dominated by his personal vanity
                                    * b

and limited by his individual experiences. The frequent lament, that those who have been most favoured are often the most dissatisfied, seems to point to something wider and deeper than mere egoism. Surely this is a most interesting and important matter, which deserves a more philosophical consideration than it has received. Even assuming that there is nothing in it but vanity and vexation of spirit, is it not unfortunate for art that such wide-spread dissatisfaction should exist? In artistic matters the personal equation counts for a great deal; and a paragraph of undue severity, or an injurious misstatement of fact, is not balanced by a column of fulsome adulation. Above all, no eulogy, however lavish, in the day of prosperity, can compensate for neglect or contumely in the day of small things. The diplomatist, the man of tact and of the world, affects to have forgotten these things; but I have heard diplomatists, when for a moment they have laid aside their diplomacy, and I have found them even more bitter than the rest. I have known that bitterness to affect the methods of an artist, the bearing, even the voice, and permanently to deteriorate his style.

We can all of us remember the time when no epithet was too contemptuous to be hurled at the acting of Sir Henry Irving.   Mr. Gilbert was recently taken severely to task for saying that criticism had a tendency to consider the author rather than his work, a statement which is absolutely true, and that the writer of an unsuccessful play was treated as though he were a malefactor.   I can recall the year—it was the year of *Low Water* — when Mr. Pinero was almost called a malefactor.   A long time ago, a leading theatrical journal devoted two whole pages to a scathing review of some published plays by a certain Mr. Henry Arthur Jones, citing them as samples of the hopeless trash with which managers were pestered.   And even to this day the name of the greatest English-speaking actress of our time is seldom mentioned without a reminder that she is past forty years of age — as though it were disgrace to have adorned so long the boards which her footsteps honour, and to be as pure and gracious an artist when over forty as when under twenty.

The only form of review which appears to me to be wholly admirable and wholly beneficial to art, to the criticised, and to the critic himself, is

that which has been introduced by Mr. T. P.
O'Connor in the columns of *The Weekly Sun,*
and I consider that for so happy an inspiration
literature owes him a debt of gratitude. Mr.
O'Connor writes appreciations of works other,
alas, than dramatic. If he does not like a book,
he is silent. When a book especially impresses
him, he endeavours not so much to criticise it
as to convey to his readers the aim of the
author and the measure of his accomplishment.
Such reviewing is nothing but wholesome.
Censure seldom served any good purpose, except
to relieve the liver of the censor. This, I take
it, was Mr. Pinero's meaning when he said,
" Praise, praise, praise ! " I am fully conscious,
and so no doubt is Mr. Pinero, that the press
errs quite as often in the direction of excessive
laudation as in any other direction ; but this
does not mend matters. The errors do not
cancel one another, and the resultant error is
doubled.

Be criticism good or evil, is there a more
melancholy spectacle under the sun than the
theatrical advertisements in the columns of the
daily newspapers ? This theatrical calling, which
is unduly discouraged by censure, no sooner

receives a word of commendation than it rushes
to the advertisement agent to have the tooth-
some adjectives reprinted in small type. I
myself object to be lectured by a man in a
mask, or by one to whom I am not permitted
to reply; and I have never been able to appreciate the manliness of submitting to an un-
provoked or unfair attack; but the moment
we quote the critic's praise we must accept his
censure, just or not. Here is where the theatre
commits its fatal indiscretion. It coquets with
the press. Instead of saying, " Go your way,
and I'll go mine; we will be friends, if you
like, but we can never be anything more," it
makes eyes, like a woman, and ultimately it
surrenders itself.

Nobody is more sensible than I am of the
delicacy, the difficulty — ay, the impossibility
of the critic's position. My dislike to him is
purely professional; as a human being he has
my sincere sympathy; though sometimes, when I
go to the play and see the sort of entertainment
which is too often set before him, I cannot repress
a chuckle of satisfaction that the whirligig of
time brings in his revenges. In any event, the
critic has come to stay; and if occasionally he

awards the race to the halt, the battle to the weak, the riches to the variety-artist, and the favour to his friends, is he not sometimes a pillar of strength himself and a cause of strength in others?   Such in my judgment is the author of this volume, beside whose name I esteem it a privilege to inscribe my own ; not because he is endowed with exceptional insight and a remarkable gift of literary expression, but because he fears no man and he favours no man; when he praises, he praises with sincerity ; when he uses the scalpel, he guides it with precision; and when he wields the sword, it is the sword Excalibur.

SYDNEY GRUNDY.

December 1897.

AUTHOR'S NOTE.

I BEG once more to thank the Trustees under the will of Mr. Edmund Yates for sanctioning this reprint of my criticisms in the *World;* and I gratefully acknowledge the courtesy with which the Editors of the *Daily Chronicle,* the *Westminster Gazette,* and *St. Paul's* have permitted me to include one or two articles which appeared in their columns. My friend, Mr. Sydney Grundy, has done me the honour of contributing an Introduction which must greatly enhance the interest of the volume; and my friend, Mr. H. G. Hibbert, continues that Synopsis of Playbills which will give a documentary value to these year-books when any critical vitality they may possess is long since dwindled and forspent. By way of rounding off the little group of five volumes, I have compiled an " Epilogue Statistical," in which the reader, if he care to turn to it, may, I hope, find matter of some novelty and significance.

PLAYS STILL RUNNING AT
PUBLICATION OF "THEATRICAL WORLD
OF 1896."

				Last Performance, 1897.
THE GEISHA	...	...	...	... Still running.
A NIGHT OUT	...	...	...	... October 9.
TWO LITTLE VAGABONDS		...	...	May 29.
				Revived October 4—December 18.
UNDER THE RED ROBE ...		...	...	June 2.
THE CIRCUS GIRL	...	...	...	Still running.
SWEET NANCY	...	...	...	May 8.
RICHARD III.	...	...	...	February 27 April 6.
BLACK EY'D SUSAN	...	...	...	May 8.
THE SIGN OF THE CROSS		...	...	February 3
				Revived August 21—October 23.

THE

THEATRICAL "WORLD"

OF

1897.

I.

"A MAN ABOUT TOWN"—"BETSY"—"THE HOLLY-TREE INN."

6th January.

THERE was one very funny scene at the Avenue
Theatre on Saturday evening, but it occurred, unfortunately, after the play was over. It was enacted
in dumb show, but with infinite spirit and expressiveness. The performers were the two authors of *A
Man about Town*,* who, coming forward in response
to the applause of the stalls and the groans of the
gallery, shook each other warmly by the hand,
expressed the liveliest mutual admiration, and, as
the curtain fell, fronted the angry gods in attitudes of
Ajax-like defiance. It was a thrilling spectacle, the
like of which has not been witnessed since Miss Olga

* January 2—23.

Nethersole and Mr. Henry Hamilton, before the curtain at the Gaiety, effusively congratulated each other on the fiasco of *Carmen*. While I applaud the gallantry which holds up its head against misfortune, I doubt the wisdom of the Ajax attitude. When I have a play damned, I shall bow and smile to my applauding friends, and shall loftily ignore the "organised opposition" of my enemies. Above all, I shall not let the manager come on and say, "Ladies and gentlemen, what is your verdict?" or "Do you like the play?" or "What message shall I send to the author?" That is the foolishest policy; it invites execration, and dots the "i" of failure. I have known several disasters that might quite well have passed as successes if the manager could only have been pinioned and gagged as the curtain fell. There is not the least use in defying or challenging an audience—in its inarticulate way, it will always have the last word. And there is always enough applause to cover a graceful retreat. At the Avenue, for instance, the applause was distinctly louder than the groans, to which the authors might perfectly well have turned a deaf ear. The British dramatist, like the British soldier, should never know when he is beaten—or at least he should never "let on" that he knows.

To tell the truth, I cannot quite make out what so enraged the gallery against *A Man about Town*.

Without affecting any personal enthusiasm for it, I must say that I have seen duller and more offensive productions rapturously applauded. The authors—who choose, for some inscrutable reason, to make themselves ridiculous by styling themselves "Huan Mee"—have perhaps acted unwisely in attempting to introduce plot into a musical farce. It is true they very soon drop it, and the piece becomes as incoherent as heart can desire; but it may be that the very fact of its beginning coherently made the public recognise and resent its lapse into inconsequence. In the initial idea of the "playwright in spite of himself" there are the makings of a tolerable farce of intrigue. To provide an excuse for club-haunting and late hours, a man pretends to his wife that he has written an opera. As a matter of fact, he has only translated it, and nothing is further from his thoughts than any effort to get it produced. Imagine, then, his consternation when his wife, without his knowledge, secures its acceptance; and the imbroglio is further complicated by the fact that the manager believes the play to be written by the wife, not the husband, and has accepted it because of his lively admiration, not for the play, but for the lady. From these elements it would be easy to work up a rattling farce; indeed, I should not be surprised to learn that some French or German playwright has already done so. The authors of *A Man about Town*, instead of

ingeniously developing their intrigue, obscure it by all
sorts of additional extravagances, and then let it slip
through their fingers altogether. They make a con-
vulsive attempt, indeed, within ten minutes of the
end, to gather up the threads again ; but by that time
we have forgotten all about them. Thus, if I read
the case aright, they fall between the two stools of
plot and no plot—of farce and " musical comedy."
I wish I could attribute the wrath of the gallery to
the utter vulgarity and frivolousness—to use a convenient euphemism—of the whole entertainment; but,
remembering what is applauded at other theatres, I
cannot take so optimistic a view. The lyrics are
somewhat laboured but not quite pointless, and the
score, by Mr. Alfred Carpenter, though dull enough
as a whole, contains some taking jingles. Mr.
Lonnen plays the playwright-in-spite-of-himself with
that conscientious hard-working whimsicality which is
the note of his manner. Some people find it oppres-
sive ; I do not. I can always laugh at Mr. Lonnen,
and I did even on Saturday night. On the other
hand, I cannot relish the rigid dancing of Miss Alice
Lethbridge, who played the wife. It was immensely
popular with the audience, however. Miss May
Edouin, who appeared as "an up-to-date parlour-
maid," has quicksilver in her veins, and makes up in
vivacity what she lacks in grace. Miss Alma Stanley,
regal as ever, was also amusing in her way, and Mr.

Sydney Howard made a clever caricature of the French librettist whose work the "man about town" has stolen.

With a devotion to principle which one cannot but admire, Mr. Charles Wyndham describes *Betsy** as "the Celebrated Comedy by F. C. Burnand." It would be unjust, in his opinion, to mention the French authors; and really, in this case, there is something to be said for that view. *Betsy* is one of those adaptations, much rarer nowadays than they were fifteen years ago, in which the meaning is eliminated with the "immorality," and the result is a violent hurly-burly about nothing at all. There is spirit, however, in this hurly-burly, and, being capitally played by the new cast, it thoroughly amused the Criterion audience. I am quite willing to believe that Mr. Aubrey Boucicault was very good as the personage who gives the French play its name, *Bébé*, but such characters are so repulsive to me that I am unable to estimate the merits of the actor who performs them. Miss Annie Hughes made an admirable Betsy, though it seemed to me that she and Mr. Boucicault grotesquely overdid the pinching and howling business of the first act, making it far more painful than comic. Mr. James Welch was extremely amusing as the accommodating tutor. I remember Saint-Germain in this part at

* December 29, 1896—February 13 (afternoon).

the Gymnase, and his performance was no better than Mr. Welch's. Mr. Alfred Bishop, too, was capital as the father of *Bébé*. His various attempts to hit upon the right tone in addressing his son showed genuine comic invention. Miss Carlotta Addison, Mr. Barnes, Mr. Kenneth Douglas, and Miss Sybil Carlisle all contributed to the success of the revival.

Mrs. Beringer's little dramatisation of *The Holly-Tree Inn*,* which precedes *Love in Idleness* in the afternoon bill at Terry's Theatre, affords an opportunity for two of the most delightful pieces of child-acting I ever saw. The story of the boy and girl who set off together for Gretna Green is in itself one of Dickens's most charming fancies, and it is rendered to perfection by Master Stewart Dawson and Miss Valli Valli. It is impossible, and if it were possible it would be ungracious, to say which of these little people is the cleverer. Neither could by any means be better—they have been most ably trained, and they enter into their parts with amazing and really touching spirit and intelligence. Mr. George Belmore and Miss Kate Mills are good as Jabez Cobbs and his wife, and altogether the little piece is an ideal

* December 28, 1896 (afternoon), and every Monday, Tuesday, Wednesday, and Thursday afternoon until week ending January 30. Then every Tuesday, Wednesday, and Thursday to February 18.

Christmas entertainment and a thing not to be missed.
At the same time I agree with the critic who protests
against the carrying off of Harry while Norah is
asleep; nay, I think it grossly inconsistent with Harry's
chivalry that he should take this base abduction so
quietly.

II.

"A PIERROT'S LIFE"—"THE SORROWS OF SATAN.'

13th January.

THE new "play without words," produced on Friday
afternoon at the Prince of Wales's, stands, in my
opinion, somewhere between *L'Enfant Prodigue* and
La Statue du Commandeur, both of which we have
seen on the same boards. There was a singular
charm about *L'Enfant Prodigue* which will not easily
be rivalled. It dealt with one of the simple, fundamental tragedies of life; a tragedy that needs no
words; a tragedy so inherent in the very nature of
things, that a great psychologist, whose first aim it
was to be understanded of the people, made it the
subject of the most popular of his similitudes.
Moreover, it was full of a charming humour, most
ingeniously dramatised, and illustrated with truly
inventive music. And, to crown all, it was very
cleverly acted by the whole company, and quite

perfectly by the three essential personages — the
Father, the Mother, and the Prodigal Son.   If *A
Pierrot's Life* * can be said to possess these advantages
at all, it is certainly in a minor degree.   The story
has nothing like the typical value of its predecessor.
Pierrot's debauchery is much more wanton and heartless than the wild-oats-sowing of the Prodigal Son;
and while no one can refuse to sympathise with a
mother's inexhaustible tenderness for her erring child,
the instant relenting of a woman towards a man
who has treated her with the utmost brutality is a
different and much more questionable matter.   The
fact that they are husband and wife is not essential
to the issue.   What is essential is that he steals her
savings and elopes with another woman at the very
moment when he has learnt that she is soon to be
the mother of his child.   To make this child the
instrument of their reunion is to apply the good
old "coup de l'enfant" almost paradoxically.   Perhaps you think I am taking Pierrot much too
seriously, and justifying the pleasant parodist † who
made me indite a ponderous analysis of the tragedy
of *Punch and Judy.*   Well, I am going to justify
him still further, and insist that, whether we are
conscious of it or not, we do instinctively analyse
any situation which appeals (as this does) to our
rudimentary sympathies, and that the greater or less

* January 8—May 11. See Art. XII.   † Mr. Max Beerbohm.

enjoyment of an audience depends on the whole-
heartedness or half-heartedness with which its sympathies go out to the personages. There is a term
in mental science—I am not sure that I can spell
it, but I believe it is "cœnæsthesis"—which, though
one naturally shrinks from using it except on the
severest provocation, would really be of great service
to criticism if it could only get itself translated into
a less abhorrent form. It implies, as I understand
it, the sum of those myriad sensations which do not
rise into consciousness, and yet are, at any given
moment, the factors which mainly determine our
comfort or discomfort, our well-being or ill-being.
Especially does the individual "cœnæsthesis" determine the individual temper; and the collective
"cœnæsthesis" of an audience determines its tem-
perature towards a play. Ninety-nine people out of
a hundred are absolutely unconscious of the real
reasons why they applaud more, or less, or not at
all, or hiss, or "boo," or throw things, or tear up
the benches; but in nine cases out of ten the
mercury rises or falls in the thermometer of approval
or disapproval in accordance with some such analysis
as I have attempted above, instinctively performed
either in the recesses of the brain or in that extension of the brain which we call the nervous system.
We critics are for ever picking at our "cœnæsthesis"
(when we are not dogmatically asserting it), and

generally, of course, we give a quite mistaken—
always and necessarily an imperfect—account of it.
Perhaps it is a mistaken account of mine that I am
now giving; but as I look back upon *A Pierrot's
Life,* I fancy the lukewarmness of the pleasure with
which I saw it was largely due to an (as yet un-
reasoned) sense that the story was common rather
than typical, and the clearly foreseen conclusion a
piece of somewhat immoral sentimentality.

Furthermore, the humour of the play is much less
happy than that of *L'Enfant Prodigue,* and much
less ingeniously interpreted in the orchestra.   There
was only one thing that really and irresistibly
" brought down the house," and that was Pochinet's
miming of Lafontaine's fable of the " Two Pigeons."
This was done with admirable cleverness by Signor
Egidio Rossi, a born pantomimist, who, indeed, was
very good throughout.   But the best pantomimist
cannot do more than the author has invented for
him ; and, this one episode excepted, none of
M. Boissier's inventions is so clever as at least half-
a-dozen of M. Carré's in *L'Enfant Prodigue*—for
instance, the reading of the newspaper, in which
M. Courtès was so admirable, and the love-scene
between the banker and Phrynette, with its delightful
inweaving of the Wedding March.   With the exception of Signor Rossi, it did not seem to me that
any of the performers showed a real genius for the

art. Mdlle. Litini was graceful and expressive as
Pierrot, Madame Germaine Ety was expressive but
commonplace as Louisette, and M. Jacquinet, as the
villain Julot, was energetic and comprehensible; but
Signor Rossi alone got hold of me, and carried me
away. Let me add that though I cannot think that
the enjoyment of the public was as spontaneous as
it might have been, any lukewarmness they felt
remained entirely in their "cœnæsthesis," and did
not rise into their consciousness. They applauded
liberally at the ends of the acts, and would no doubt
have sworn that they enjoyed themselves immensely.

On the whole, I am inclined to fancy that a
thoroughly delightful play without words is the result
of a happy combination of circumstances that is not
likely to occur more than once in a decade—if so
often. Unless the invention and execution are
altogether exquisite, the silence soon becomes oppres-
sive, and ultimately irritating. Dramatic expression
with the chief organ of expression eliminated is at
best a curiosity, a virtuosity, a feat. As a means of
education in acting, I should think voiceless miming
must be invaluable. Some practice in it would be
of great assistance to young English actors and
actresses. If I were director of a dramatic school,
I should set the pupils to act *Romeo and Juliet* in
dumb show; and then, to make the balance true, I
should get them to speak the text with all the passion

they could muster, but sitting with arms folded in their chairs. Under competent direction and criticism (which, needless to say, would not be mine), such analytic exercises would do them a world of good; but I do not think I should invite the public to be present. And yet—who knows?—I should not wonder if *The School for Scandal*, cleverly acted in dumb show, were to prove exceedingly entertaining.

A dramatic version, by Messrs. Herbert Woodgate and Paul M. Berton, of Miss Corelli's romance, *The Sorrows of Satan*,* was produced at the Shaftesbury Theatre on Saturday evening. The audience seemed to like it; they applauded loudly, and the applause had a quite genuine ring in it. I am at a loss to imagine what they found entertaining; but I gladly bear witness that, although the play is no doubt an outcome of the boasted reconciliation between religion and the stage, it is devoid of the two great attractions of "religious drama" as hitherto exemplified— brutality and sensuality. So far as I could hear it (for I was very badly placed) there seemed to be nothing in *The Sorrows of Satan* that called for any vehemence of protest. In a half-educated age, it is not at all surprising that there should be an immense public for pinchbeck imagination and spurious intellectuality; and in one way or another this public will be provided for. I am not sure, indeed, that

* January 9—February 27.

even puerile theology and ethics, so long as they are not eked out with more deleterious matter, may not be wholesomer dramatic fare than empty yarn-spinning or epileptic "musical" tomfoolery. The play is not even aggressively or offensively vulgar; or, more precisely, the vulgarity lies rather in the fundamental conception of life, death, and the scheme of things, than in the surface sayings and doings of the characters. It is simply a stupid play for stupid people—that is the worst (and the best) that can be said of it. The adapters, so far as I can judge without having read the novel, have done their work judiciously enough. It appears that they have followed Miss Corelli very closely—rather too closely, perhaps. I certainly had not the smallest notion of what the dramatic conflict was really to be, until the play was more than half over. About the middle of the third act it began to dawn on me that Lady Sibyl was in love with Prince Lucio, and by the end of the fourth act she had confessed her passion, and taken her quietus, so that the drama was practically over. An act and a half of drama to five acts of play does not seem a large allowance; but if the adapters' reverence for their author forbade them to depart from the lines she had laid down, I do not see how this proportion was to be amended. The mounting was lavish, and the acting, without being brilliant, was adequate. Mr. Lewis Waller was most happily chosen for the part of Prince Lucio, that roaring lion who goes about the world seeking whom he may *not* devour. He spoke well, as he always does, and there was about his whole personality something of that steelly glitter which one associates with a modern Mephistopheles. Talking of "steelly glitter," by-the-bye, it was rather a shock to me when he appeared among the icebergs of the last act in a cuirass of shining mail. I should not have thought armour a desirable costume either for "thrilling regions of thick-ribbèd ice" or for that other element which we are apt to associate with "the sorrows of Satan." But perhaps I should apologise for alluding to such antiquated superstition in the presence of this new and improved Safety Satan, who, like the Swedish Lucifers of bygone years, is non-sulphureous —"utan Svåvfel och Fosfor." He deals only in the more refined pyrotechnics of electricity, being accompanied on his path through life by irrelevant and disconcerting "fuffs" of lightning. Mr. Yorke Stephens made as much as could be expected of the flaccid character of Geoffrey Tempest, but Miss Granville left something to be desired in the part of Lady Sibyl. It is a pity the management could not, or at any rate did not, secure Mrs. Patrick Campbell for this character, which would have suited her to a nicety.

III.

"THE FREE PARDON"—"OLIVIA."

3rd February.

IT was quite refreshing on Thursday night to find good, honest, unbedizened, unbedevilled melodrama in the ascendant at the Olympic. For my part, I have a keen relish for popular drama, so long as it keeps to its own theatres and frankly wears its own colours. It is when melodrama goes a-masquerading in historical, philosophical, spiritual frippery, and imposes itself upon the intellectual incompetence of the half-educated masses as something new and noble—then it is that I cannot away with it. Mere simple-minded vulgarity is inevitable and respectable ; tawdry pretentiousness is equally inevitable, it would appear, but no amount of press or pulpit puffery can induce me to respect it.

Nothing could be more unpretending than the work of Messrs. F. C. Philips and Leonard Merrick. Their story is told in their title, *The Free Pardon.** We all know that quaint form of English law by which a convict who is found to be innocent receives a free pardon for the crime he has not committed. It was clear, then, from the outset, that the hero was not only to be wrongfully accused of the murder com-

* January 28—February 18 (?).

mitted by the villain, but was to be actually convicted and sentenced. The more usual plan is to turn the tables at the very trial, and simply transfer the handcuffs from the hero's wrists to the villain's; but there is excellent precedent, of course, for sending the hero to Portland, and an escape from that establishment is always popular. It is varied in this instance by a situation of some ingenuity. The innocent convict takes refuge in the house of a warder, whose wife conceals him in her room. The husband returns, and the feeble devices by which his wife tries to keep him from entering the room arouse first his suspicions and then his furious jealousy. Meanwhile the hero might have made his escape; but, overhearing the discussion between husband and wife, he realises that the woman is sacrificing her reputation for his sake, and bursts open the door and gives himself up rather than suffer her to do so. This is, in its way, a strong effect, and it gives rise to an interesting question of casuistry as to what course the warder ought now to take. Our authors, however, are not in a moment's doubt on the point— the warder throws duty to the dogs and helps the fugitive to escape. Then arises a further question : Is it entirely heroic on the hero's part to let the warder betray his trust in this fashion? It is a little like straining at a gnat and swallowing a camel; for the wife's reputation, after all, could very easily have

been re-established, whereas nothing can undo the
warder's flagrant breach of duty. These scruples,
however, do not trouble the authors. It is half-past
ten, and the villain is waiting to be checkmated, so
there is no time for contests of generosity. It will be
seen that novelty is not one of the merits of *The Free
Pardon*, nor, to tell the truth, is it a particularly skilful
or spirited working-up of the old material. It served
its purpose, however, and fairly entertained a good-
humoured but not very impressionable audience.

Mr. Harrison Hunter and Miss Esmé Beringer
made a pleasant enough hero and heroine. Mr.
Edward O'Neill, as the villain, might have been
more plausible, but could scarcely have been more
sinister. Mr. George Cockburn and Miss Cicely
Richards were capital as the warder and his wife;
and Mr. Courtenay Thorpe, as the hero's father, who
is murdered in the first act, played not unimpressively.
The manageress, Miss Vane, contented herself with
the subordinate part of the villain's accomplice, and
played it well. Mr. Abingdon for once put off the
villain and put on the comic man, in the person
of an American reporter who mightily amused the
audience. I daresay he might equally amuse an
American audience—but it would be in a different
way.

The late W. G. Wills had in him an undeniable
strain of the poet, and even of the dramatic poet.

The fact that he has not very notably enriched our dramatic literature must be ascribed, I think, to two reasons: he followed bad models, and his taste was very uncertain, his sense of form defective.   His ideal of dramatic composition was too much influenced by German sentimentalism and English fustian.   His style suggested, at times, the last dying echo of that pseudo-Elizabethan rodomontade which reverberated through the century and a half between Otway and Sheridan Knowles.   But even in verse he sometimes struck a purer and more individual note, while in prose he now and then did work of real strength and distinction.   Why does not one of his friends—Mr. Joseph Knight for example—edit for us a couple of volumes of his best plays?   In such a collection, *Olivia*,* revived on Saturday at the Lyceum, would certainly take an honourable place.   It is a most sympathetic transcript of *The Vicar of Wakefield*, true to the spirit of its original, yet owing curiously little to the actual text of Goldsmith's narrative.   It is full of pleasant touches which might very well be in Goldsmith, but are not.   In other words, Mr. Wills did not merely paste-and-scissor a play out of a novel, but imbued himself with Goldsmith's humour and sentiment, and then proceeded to an almost independent act of invention and creation.   Read *The Vicar* after seeing *Olivia*, and you will be

* January 30—February 20 (afternoon).

astonished to find how unlike they are in the midst
of their likeness. One defect of construction Mr.
Wills has too faithfully transferred from the book
—he omits to provide any semblance of a motive
for Sir William Thornhill's persisting so long in his
disguise, and not locking the stable-door till the steed
is stolen. Otherwise I do not see how the dramatist
could have done his work better. It would be absurd
to quarrel with the simple-minded way in which Olivia
is held to be highly praiseworthy or deeply blame-
worthy according as the parson who married her to
Thornhill was or was not in holy orders, although no
one has the least doubt that in any case she believed
the ceremony to be perfectly genuine. This belongs
to the manners of the book and of the time, and it
would be a flat anachronism to represent the Vicar's
family as sensible of the slightest drawback to the joy
with which they learn that Olivia is an "honest
woman" in virtue of being tied for life to a heartless scoundrel.

Mr. Hermann Vezin's portraiture of the Vicar is a
very delicate and artistically subdued piece of acting,
full of humour and feeling, yet never straying into
over-emphasis. Miss Ellen Terry was obviously
suffering from a severe cold on Saturday night,
and was therefore not quite at her best. The
lighter scenes she played rather perfunctorily and
from the outside; but when the situation took hold

of her, she showed all her old depth of feeling.
Olivia is certainly one of the real creations of her
career. Miss Julia Arthur made a pleasant Sophia,
and Miss Maud Milton was good as Mrs. Primrose.

———

POSTSCRIPT.—I append an extract from an article
(*St. Paul's*, May 1, 1897) upon the influences
which tend to make critics, and theatrical critics in
particular, readier to condemn than to praise a new
production :—

"Of one thing I am sure—to wit, that on a first night
of any importance, when we feel that something more
than conventional phrases will be expected of us, we
are apt to get into a condition of hyperæsthesia, and
scan the play with an intentness which throws
blemishes into exaggerated relief. Our eyes, as Sam
Weller would say, become 'patent double-magnifying
gas microscopes.' Not once, but fifty times, have I
found a second visit to a play take the edge off my
first-night criticisms. The faults I had noted might
be real enough, but, somehow—mainly because I
was prepared for them—they would bulk far less
largely in proportion to the merits of the piece. A
curious instance of this gradual softening towards a
play occurred in my own experience not long ago.

"When *Olivia* was revived at the Lyceum in
February last, I went to see it in a somewhat passive
and somnolent frame of mind—the very opposite of

an alert first-night mood. Apart from the acting of
Miss Terry and Mr. Vezin (and Miss Terry had a
cold that night, and was not at her best), the play
bored me exceedingly. It was only the sternest
sense of duty that made me sit it out, and yet, as I
did sit it out, the workmanship of it, without giving
me positive pleasure, distinctly satisfied me. Point
after point my intelligence approved, even though
my emotions remained untouched. In writing of the
production I expressed this sense of approval with
some warmth. My article was sent to me in proof, and
as I read it there came over me a vague sense that
though I had more than once criticised the same play
before, I had never treated it in this spirit. I looked
up the essay on W. G. Wills in a book I had
published in 1882 and compared my opinion of that
date with my feeling of to-day. Let me print the
passages side by side :—

1882.

" *Olivia* has been praised
much above its deserts. It is
by no means the best dramatic
version we possess of *The
Vicar of Wakefield.* It contains some beautiful touches,
but also several errors of
taste, and the last two acts,
especially the last of all, are
extremely faulty."

1897.

" *Olivia* is a most sympathetic transcript of *The Vicar
of Wakefield.* . . . Mr. Wills
did not merely paste-and-
scissor a play out of a novel,
but imbued himself with Goldsmith's humour and senti-
ment, and then proceeded
to an almost independent act
of invention and creation."

"How has this change of view come about? Is it simply that I am older and wiser? or older and foolisher? Has my standard become debased in the course of fifteen years' journey-work? Or has the play improved with keeping? In 1882 I seem to have had clear in my memory some other version of the story, which has now vanished and left no trace, so that I no longer subject *Olivia* to the ordeal of comparison. But that is only part of the explanation. The real fact, probably, is that the placid and indifferent mood in which I went to the Lyceum was more conducive to tolerant receptivity than the high-strung and exacting temper in which I studied the play when it was new. . . .

"What, then, is the moral to be deduced from these reflections? In the first place, it appears that we should often do well, in giving our first impressions of a play, to moderate the trenchancy of our judgments—"to praise as though one day we might blame, to blame as though one day we might praise." In the second place, we are put on the track of a theory which I have not space at present to develop: namely, that the classic or masterpiece is not the faultless play, but the play which has sufficient vitality to hold its own, until, by process of time, its faults come to seem, if not absolute merits, at least unalterable facts, as far beyond the range of criticism as Mont Blanc or the Atlantic Ocean."

IV.

"THE DAUGHTERS OF BABYLON."

10th February.

IT is pleasant to meet Mr. Wilson Barrett once more on ordinary human terms. Before *The Sign of the Cross,* criticism could only stand aghast, and protest that this brutal and vulgar spectacle at no point touched the confines of its province. All rational discussion presupposes some common standard to which reference may be made, explicitly or tacitly; and for my part I felt that I had not only no principle but no perception in common with any one who could tolerate *The Sign of the Cross.** If you put coarse brandy on the table and tell me it is the finest burgundy, and hold it up to the light, and smack your lips over it, and pronounce it an exquisite and exhilarating beverage, it is useless for me to argue against your delusion: I can only push my glass away, and wonder what has befallen your eyes, your nose, and your palate. Nor can you persuade me that bad spirits are good wine by showing that up to a certain point the chemical composition of the two things is the same. I have been reproachfully reminded that there are torture scenes and massacres and orgies in other plays besides *The Sign of the Cross,* to which

* *Theatrical World of 1896,* p. 9.

I have made no special objection; nay, that I have even defended the torture scene in *La Tosca*. To argue thus is merely to ignore the first principle of criticism, which is, broadly speaking, that matter is nothing and manner everything—that it is of very little moment what you do, while everything depends on how you do it. Any one who, knowing the two plays, does not discern the world-wide difference between the torture scene in *La Tosca* and that in *The Sign of the Cross*, is flatly incapable of artistic perception. Moreover, I never pretended that the torture of Mario (or *La Tosca* as a whole) was a piece of high or admirable art. I only said that, accepting it as a link in a rather ingenious chain of make-believe, I did not find it cause me the intolerable anguish of spirit with which it seemed to afflict some other critics. This is qualified praise, at best. *La Tosca* is low art, certainly; bad art, perhaps; but there is sufficient intellectual competence and manipulative skill in it to bring it within the range of rational criticism. *The Sign of the Cross*, in my judgment, never for a moment came within that circle. It is neither low art nor bad art, but no art at all. Do not tell me that in thus writing of it I abandon my position. I mention it, because the stage is my subject, and this thing exists on the stage—ay, on a hundred stages. But it remains, as aforesaid, beyond the range of criticism. Nothing that I have written now or at any other time, has affected, or will affect, any one who is capable of admiring this play. Such a person does not know what art is, in the sense—a wide sense enough, in all conscience—in which the word is used in these pages. On the other hand, readers with whom I stand on common ground, who share my general conceptions of art and sense and decency, do not require any demonstration, from me or any one else, that *The Sign of the Cross* is, artistically speaking, a thing beyond the pale. Its popularity is a phenomenon of a certain interest to all who concern themselves about the stage. It is a fact, like any other; and it is useless to close our eyes to facts. But there is a vast difference between recognising the fact and criticising the play. Its admirers and champions complain bitterly that I have never criticised it—and they are right. I have simply denounced it from the first.

Quite different is the case of *The Daughters of Babylon.** Here we have a play which comes well within the range of criticism. It is an entirely innocent, rather tedious, singularly well-mounted melodrama of the second or third order. Not comparable for a moment with good French work—such, for instance, as *Two Little Vagabonds*—or with the best English work of its class, such as *The Silver King*, it ranks decidedly above the average Adelphi

* February 6—April 10.

melodrama, in respect both of aim and of execution. It stands, in short, very much on the level of the inferior plays of the old Princess's series—such plays as *Claudian*, *Hoodman Blind*, and *The Lord Harry*. So marked is its resemblance to the dramas in which Mr. Barrett collaborated with Mr. Henry Arthur Jones, that I feel I owe both these gentlemen an apology. I used to suspect that this collaboration was merely nominal, or at any rate that Mr. Barrett's share in it consisted mainly in staging the plays. This was evidently quite a mistake. His must have been the inspiring spirit if not the shaping hand. Mr. Jones, even in those distant days, had a knack of infusing a certain vigour into individual scenes, which we miss in *The Daughters of Babylon;* but otherwise this melodrama of Mr. Barrett's own invention bears the strongest family resemblance to its predecessors. Thus we may safely attribute to Mr. Barrett a determining share in the manufacture of *Hoodman Blind* and *The Lord Harry;* and this partition of responsibility is eminently to the advantage of both collaborators. Mr. Barrett can no longer be suspected of not having done his part of the work, and Mr. Jones stands acquitted of having done the whole.

The first act of *The Daughters of Babylon* is by a long way the best. It announces a very interesting conflict between passion and law—an essentially dramatic theme—and it is put together with a good

deal of skill. In the second and third acts, the drama,
as drama, falls to pieces, and becomes an arbitrary
series of adventures, with no necessary coherence and
no effect of climax. There is a great appearance of
movement and excitement about some of the situations, but they all come to nothing, neither compli-
cating nor unravelling the dramatic skein. For
example, the auction scene, which is the great
"effect" of the third act, is not only ludicrous in
itself—dragged in simply because a passage of bidding
or betting always produces a certain thrill in an
audience—but is absolutely annulled the minute it
is over by the opportune rebellion which sets the
hero and heroine free. Why all this fuss as to who is
to own Lemuel and Elna, when, as a matter of fact,
they are to escape from bondage altogether the
moment the hammer has fallen? The position of
affairs would have been precisely the same if the
revolt of the Jews had occurred before instead of
after the sale, which is therefore a mere excrescence
on the action. The same may be said, in a minor
degree, of the whole second and third acts, and the
first scene of the fourth. The drama really consists
of the first act and the last scene. The intermediate
passages serve no essential purpose except to give
Ishtar a motive (such as it is) for threatening to
accuse Jediah, and so forcing him to renounce his
vengeance upon Lemuel and Elna. This practically

means that the whole of the second and third acts might be expunged, except one scene to account for Ishtar's interference. Of character, of course, we have no trace—the personages are the seraphic hero and angelic heroine, the saturnine villain, and the sentimental courtesan, purified and ennobled through her hopeless passion for the hero. Thus the piece fulfils to the letter the definition of melodrama—dolls and declamation. On the other hand, Mr. Barrett has been notably sparing of comic relief. What there was of it was mainly unintentional—for instance, the collapse of the villain when he is outbidden at the auction, and his docile repetition of the judgment dictated to him from the well of the court by his ex-mistress, Ishtar.

I have said nothing, you observe, of the great and masterly originality of the play—its biblical diction. I have said nothing, because really it is not my affair. If Mr. Barrett's friends the clergy approve, who am I that I should object? There is a story of an old Scotchwoman reproving her grandson for reading the newspaper with the snuffle and chant which she regarded as exclusively applicable to the Scriptures. "Eh, Jock!" she cried, "ye mauna read it in that holy way!" To tell the truth, I incline to this good lady's opinion—I should probably have liked Mr. Barrett's melodrama better if he had not written it in "that holy way." For one thing, it is so much the longer way ; "well stricken in years" is five times as long as "old," "peradventure" is twice as long as "perhaps," and "he goes to Babylon," compared with "he goeth unto Babylon," shows a gain in brevity of just twenty-five per cent. But, after all, it matters very little, and by making his dialogue a mosaic of biblical phrases—the Jews of the Captivity were apparently quite familiar with the New Testament as well as the Old—Mr. Barrett manages to get some touches of beauty into it. If only he could at the same time keep out the frequent touches of modern commonplace! Without pitting my knowledge of the Scriptures against Mr. Barrett's, I should be curious to learn the biblical authority for "I claim that these two are adulterers," or "For the first time in all her short wicked feverish life she knows a good man's pure love," or "I do it all for one kind thought from him, one pulsation of pity, one gleam of gratitude," or again, "It is not good for woman to lose her faith in man." All these phrases, except the first, are placed in the mouth of the Babylonian *Dame aux Camélias*. I need scarcely give further specimens of the linguistic tact and historic sense displayed by this dramatist. In his care for local colour, he has filled his very dialogue with Assyrian bulls.

But oh! it is a relief to be in vague, far-off Babylon, which nobody knows or cares anything about, and not in imperial Rome. If *The Sign of the Cross* had been in every other respect as inoffensive as *The Daughters of Babylon*, it would still have been hard to forgive Mr. Barrett for taking the great name of Rome in vain.

The mounting is exceptionally beautiful. The pastoral scenes of the first and last act, painted by Mr. Telbin and Mr. Ryan respectively, are real works of art; and Mr. Hann shows a grandiose, Martinesque imagination in his pictures of Babylon. Mr. Barrett plays the hero in that staccato, peremptory style which has won him such hosts of admirers, and is not quite so aggressively statuesque in his costumes as he is wont to be. He appreciably protracted the performance by what I take to be a "holy" way of pronouncing the names of his lady friends—"Elllll-na," "Ishshsh-tar"—with the first syllable dragged out like a languishing concertina. Miss Maud Jeffries played Elna very gracefully, and Miss Lily Hanbury was vehement and effective as Ishtar. Mr. Franklin McLeay's Jediah was a remarkably picturesque and forcible piece of acting. It was not Mr. McLeay's fault that one or two of the things he had to do were irresistibly ludicrous.

V.

"NELSON'S ENCHANTRESS"—"MY FRIEND THE
PRINCE"—"A MERRY CHRISTMAS"—"THE
PRODIGAL FATHER"—"TWELFTH NIGHT."

17th February.

ALTHOUGH I am an uncompromising believer in the
right of the paying public to express disapproval in
theatres: although I often envy those sturdy en-
thusiasts in the gallery who can give immediate
utterance to their disgust and irritation, and are
sometimes even privileged to relieve their feelings in
a hand-to-hand tussle with the acting manager and
his myrmidons: although I think the gallery, as a
rule, too tolerant rather than too captious: yet I
own myself at a loss to defend or understand the
sounds of hostility which mingled with the applause
at the close of *Nelson's Enchantress.**   That some
people may have been mildly bored I readily understand; I myself was not more than mildly interested;
but there was nothing base, nothing offensive, nothing
pretentiously inept in the play—nothing, in short,
that could possibly merit a sterner verdict than
silence.   And even that, in my judgment, would have
been unduly harsh.   Had I been in the gallery I
should certainly have applauded, not only the actors,

* Avenue Theatre, February 11—March 17 (?).

but the play. It is not a work of dramatic genius; there is no trace of invention or construction in it; but there is a fine literary tact, a delicacy, a sobriety which ought to be recognised even by those who prefer drama in the narrower sense of the word to idealised biography. "Risden Home" may never be a playwright, but she has written very agreeable text to a series of quasi-historic tableaux. She has read, I take it, not only the actual documents of the case, but Miss Burney and Miss Austen to boot, so that her diction, without labour or strain, smacks pleasantly of the period. And if the arrangement of the tableaux shows no definite dramatic inspiration, neither does it show unintelligence or incompetence. To hoot at such work, simply because another style of work happens to be more to your taste, is clearly to abuse the privilege of free comment.

For my part, I am all for widening our definition of drama so as to include these tableau-plays. Ever since the company of the Théâtre-Libre acted *La Mort du duc d'Enghien* at the Royalty, I have felt convinced that there are fine effects to be got from the faithful reconstruction and transference to the stage of certain episodes of history. "Risden Home," it is true, is by no means pedantically faithful to fact. She frankly idealises Lady Hamilton, and if she does not precisely idealise Nelson, she makes no attempt to get in the subtler lights and shades of his character.

She stipples away the nodosities and seams of his physiognomy. She dwells on the pathos of the empty sleeve, but shirks the grotesqueness of the blinded eye. Well, the time has not yet come for a real Nelson on the stage. When another hundred years have elapsed, and brought a new technique and a new public, it is quite conceivable that a genuine study of that extraordinary character may be cast in dramatic form. In the meantime we must be content with the traditional hero, who was quite near enough to the actual man to pass muster, if tactfully presented, without flagrantly offending our sense of reality. And in this case there is nothing blatant or blusterous in the presentation. The real Nelson, if I am not mistaken, was a good deal more given to bragging than the Nelson of "Risden Home." He was certainly not averse from posing as a hero. There is a curious picture in Macready's *Reminiscences* of Nelson and Lady Hamilton visiting the Birmingham Theatre during the Peace of Amiens. After the play (*Henry IV.*) there was "a sort of divertisement in honour of the illustrious visitor." One item of the "divertisement" was a song with the refrain:

> " We'll shake hands and be friends ; if they won't,
>   why, what then ?
>   We'll send our brave Nelson to thrash 'em again,
>   Derry down," etc.

" The crowded house was frantic in its applause at

this sublime effusion. Lady Hamilton, laughing loud and without stint, clapped with uplifted hands and all her heart, and kicked with her heels against the footboard of the seat, while Nelson placidly and with his mournful look bowed repeatedly to the oft-repeated cheers." Such a scene reminds one that it is possible to be a hero and at the same time to know it, and even to court the vulgar rewards of heroism—for no doubt Nelson could have avoided such demonstrations had he cared to. But the fact remains that when it came to the pinch he did "thrash 'em again," and to some purpose; that he was a man of unique genius for the work he had to do; a man who inspired his adoring followers with something of his own magnanimity; and a man, to conclude, who laid down his life simply and greatly for the welfare and greatness, as he understood it, of the country we call ours. That scene in the cockpit of the *Victory*, here placed upon the stage, not irreverently or ineffectively, casts its light backwards upon such garish passages as that in the Birmingham Theatre, and makes them pathetic rather than ludicrous. Moreover, he was capable of an intense personal devotion which, from his own day even to ours, has overborne and almost put to silence British morality. The very fact that Lady Hamilton, even partially whitewashed, should figure after a hundred years as the sympathetic heroine of an English play,

is a curious testimony to the abiding magic of the
name of Nelson. And surely we cannot regret
this magic, or resent having it brought home to us
once more in this tasteful and graceful fashion. In
no instance, probably, is national hero-worship saner
or better justified. Nelson was a great man, if ever
there was one, not because his character was flawless,
but because he was pre-eminently and magnificently
the right man in the right place. And, though no one
who knows me will, I hope, suspect me of Jingoism,
I cannot but reflect that the future, not only of
England but of democratic civilisation, may at no
distant day depend on our finding another Nelson
(with or without a Lady Hamilton), and knowing him
when we have found him.

It seemed to me that the audience, as a whole,
was charmed and moved by the play. It relished
(or so I imagined) the very absence of drama, in the
narrow, not to say the vulgar, sense of the word.
Drama, in that sense, essentially and inevitably falsifies
history; whereas here we had simple and plausible
glimpses of the past, which kindled the imagination
without insulting the intelligence. What matter
though this Lady Hamilton was not the Emma Hart
of the scandalous chronicle? It was Nelson that we
cared about, and we were quite content to see Lady
Hamilton with his eyes rather than with those of
history or gossip. After all, there was nothing to

show that these events—the meeting after the Nile, the parting before Trafalgar, the arrival of the splendid and terrible tidings—did not take place very much as we here saw them ; and it certainly pleased me, for the moment, to conceive that they did. I even found something singularly touching in the idea of that chilly dawn, the woman fevered with hope and dread, the murmur from the street, the gathering roar, and flashing out of it, like forked lightning from a thunder-cloud, the phrases " Glorious victory ! " and " Death of Nelson ! " But my colleagues, it appears, were not to be so childishly amused. The play was not a play ; it was neither history nor fiction ; it was naught, and must come to naught. I am sorry ; I believe the public would have thrilled to these echoes of great days and deeds if the press had given it half a chance. As it is, I fear the canons of criticism have outroared the cannon of Trafalgar.

Mr. Forbes Robertson, marvellously made up, played Nelson with sympathetic tact. Mrs. Patrick Campbell's Lady Hamilton was beautiful and touching throughout, but especially admirable in the first act. The scene of the rupture with Greville is, in my view, the best piece of real acting Mrs. Campbell has ever done. It enlarges my conception of her powers. Other parts are well played by Mr. Nutcombe Gould, Mr. Elwood, Mr. Ben Greet, Mr. Sydney Brough, Mr. Frank Dyall, Mr. C. M. Lowne, and Mrs.

E. H. Brooke; and the mounting is careful and tasteful.

If *My Friend the Prince*,* at the Garrick, achieves the success predicted for it in some quarters, it will be in virtue of the excellent acting of Mr. James Welch, Mr. Fred Kaye, Mr. Aubrey Boucicault, Mr. Paul Arthur, and Miss Juliette Nesville, to say nothing of the superb beauty of Miss Miriam Clements, whose apparition in the last act, in a robe of regal splendour, simply took our breath away. The play, adapted from the American by Mr. J. H. McCarthy, is one of those which subsist on the indulgence of audiences greedy of laughter and determined that nothing shall baulk them of their feast. The initial idea is good, and promises a lively and ingenious comic romance. But the developments soon become arbitrarily fantastic and inconceivable, straining our power of make-believe out of all proportion to the effect attained. From the moment when Mr. Pinning undertook to impersonate Prince Maurice of Pannonia in order to drive the other impostor from the field, I confess that I lost all interest in the incoherent fable, and laughed solely at the whimsicality of the comedians, without reference to either dialogue or situations. This, I fancy, is very much what the average audience always does, even when the dialogue and situations happen to be

* February 13—August 6.

good; so that it is quite possible *My Friend the Prince* may succeed.   It is preceded by *The Man in the Street*, with Mr. Welch as the clarinet-player—a painfully able character study.

The new programme at the Strand is empty but inoffensive; and, as things go, that is no slight praise. It opens with an old-fashioned French comedietta, entitled *A Merry Christmas*,* in which Miss Florence Gerard, condemned to an outrageously farcical part in the subsequent play, reminds us in advance that farce is not her native element.   She acts very agreeably, and should certainly find openings for her talent in work of a higher order than *The Prodigal Father*,* by Mr. Glen Macdonough.   This three-act farce, another importation from America, is a piece of unmitigated nonsense, with no pretence to wit or ingenuity, but now and then amusing in virtue of its sheer, reckless extravagance.   Miss Gerard here played a music-hall star, the point of whose character consists in its aggressive vulgarity.   Her performance was clever, but somewhat self-conscious and calculated.   It lacked the impetus essential to such a personage.   Mr. Charles Collette put impetus enough and to spare into an antiquated "patter" part; Mr. Harry Paulton was stolidly amusing as an African traveller who has never been nearer Africa than Margate; and other parts were filled by Mr.

* February 1—17.   † February 1—March 26.

Charles Weir, Mr. Hargreaves, and little Miss Lulu Valli.

The performance of *Twelfth Night** by the Elizabethan Stage Society in the Middle Temple Hall did not greatly differ from their previous rendering of the comedy,† but was on the whole better. Apart from the particular tenets they seek to enforce (to which I can give but a qualified adhesion), this society now forms a capital company of amateurs. There was not in the cast of *Twelfth Night* a single obtrusively square peg in a round hole. The scene in the noble old hall was altogether picturesque and interesting.

VI.

A STUDY OF ECHEGARAY.

Daily Chronicle, 19*th February.*

DON JOSÉ ECHEGARAY has written fifty or sixty plays, and of these I have read four—in translations. Evidently, then, I am in no position to estimate his genius as a whole. The four which have been translated, *The Great Galeoto*, *Folly or Saintliness*, *The Son of Don Juan*, and *Mariana*, are all dramas of modern life; but in a list of his works before me I note "dramatic legends," "tragic legends,"

* February 12. † *Theatrical World of 1895*, p. 219.

a "dramatic picture of the sixteenth century," a
"trilogy," a "tragic study," various comedies, and
at least one proverb. We may take it, however,
from the very fact of their having been selected for
translation, that the four plays above mentioned are
fairly characteristic of one side of his manifold
activity. Certain it is that they all exhibit some
salient and admirable qualities which, in my judgment, give the author a very high place among the
living dramatists of Europe. The performances of
Mariana, to take place next week at the Court
Theatre, will not be, strictly speaking, his first
introduction to the English stage. Mr. Malcolm
Watson "discovered" him ten years ago, and produced an adaptation of *El gran Galeoto*. In the
meantime, however, his fame has spread through
Europe; he has been acted in Paris, and several
of his plays have achieved some popularity on the
cosmopolitan stage of Germany. He is now to be
reintroduced to us in a translation, not an adaptation,
so that we may hope to get nearer his true artistic
individuality, which is above all things national.

His name has been linked with Ibsen's on the
prospectus of the Court performances; but the two
poets have scarcely anything in common. There
is more of Björnson than of Ibsen in the facile,
voluminous, sanguine Echegaray. But in truth he
is to be contrasted rather than compared with all

northern dramatists whatsoever. He is essentially southern. Even a Provençal like Daudet—even an Italian like Paolo Ferrari—appears staid and cold-blooded by the side of this ebullient Spaniard. In his fertility, his copious rhetoric, and his love of vivid, romantic situation, he proves himself a true descendant of Lope and Calderon. Many of his plays, indeed (*El gran Galeoto* for one), are written in the assonant verse, with passages of rhyme, used by the classic dramatists of his country. How unlike are his methods to Ibsen's is proved by the fact that, though he took to play-writing late in life (after having been a distinguished mathematician, an engineer, a statesman and Minister, and a political exile), he has in twenty years produced two or three times as much work as Ibsen in his whole career of nearly forty-five years. Ibsen is essentially reflective, Echegaray essentially impetuous ; Ibsen's dialogue is a mosaic, Echegaray's a lava-stream. Difficult as Ibsen is to translate (I speak feelingly), Echegaray must be far more difficult. Norwegian, after all, is a cognate language to our own ; the time and rhythm of Norwegian conversation are not so very different from the time and rhythm of English. The Spaniard, on the other hand, speaks three words to our one, and I am not without a suspicion that Echegaray's excitable heroes speak six words to the average Spaniard's three. The consequence is that volubility in Spanish becomes prolixity in English, and what is probably picturesque rhetoric in the original is apt to seem amazing fustian in the translation.   That is the reason, I take it, why the dramatist's extraordinary power has hitherto met with scant recognition in England.   His plays have to be read *through* rather than *in* the literal versions published in this country; and I am not surprised to find that Mr. Graham's stage version of *Mariana* is much less literal than the printed book.

Mariana will speak for itself on Monday next. While it is the most beautiful, it is perhaps the least characteristic of the four plays, inasmuch as it has no theme or thesis, but is a love tragedy pure and simple. The drama which established the poet's fame, both in the Peninsula and throughout Europe, was *El gran Galeoto*—as who should say "The Great Go-between." Quite devoid of technical fastidiousness, Echegaray shrinks from no device by which he can clearly strike the keynote of a play in the opening scenes.   Sometimes he begins with a little essay, either in monologue or dialogue, and to *El gran Galeoto* he actually prefixes what the Elizabethans would have called an " Induction," in which the leading characters discuss the theme before the drama begins.   Ernest, a young poet, is sitting at his desk, in despair because he cannot give form to a dramatic idea which possesses him. To him enters his friend and benefactor, Don Julian, and asks what is the matter. "Why this," replies Ernest, "that the principal personage of my drama, who creates, develops, and animates the action, and brings about the catastrophe, cannot possibly be brought on the stage." This personage, it appears, is none other than *todo el mundo*—all the world—everybody—with their whispers, innuendos, questions, suggestions, significant smiles, raised eyebrows, and shoulder-shrugs. To concentrate this "everybody" into one or two types, says Ernest, is necessary to falsify the picture, and make it seem as though malicious scandal-mongering were the subject; whereas *todo el mundo* is "listless and absent-minded, acting without passion, without anger, without guile, often for mere distraction's sake." His drama, too, can have little external action; it "evolves within the personages; it advances slowly; to-day it takes hold of a thought, to-morrow of a heart-beat, until little by little the will is undermined." To place this explanatory and deprecatory prologue in the mouths of the leading actors in the drama seems to me a grievous artistic error; but one understands the author's despair of fully conveying the subtlety of his intention within the limits imposed by the dramatic form.

The play, when we reach it, is nobly and classically simple. Don Julian, a man of forty, has an adoring and devoted young wife, Teodora. Ernest, the only son of a man who founded or restored Don Julian's

fortune, has rooms in his house, and is treated as his
adopted son. The situation at the outset is made
abundantly clear. Ernest and Teodora are good
friends, but have absolutely no thought of anything
beyond friendship. Teodora is passionately attached
to her husband, while Ernest feels for him the most
whole-hearted gratitude and affection. All would be
well, if only *todo el mundo* would let well alone ; but
that is impossible, for " people will talk." The world,
in this case, is represented by Don Julian's brother,
Don Severo, his wife Mercedes, and their empty-
headed son, Pepito. They are not bad or malicious
people by nature, but they think it their duty (and
perhaps it *is* their duty) to report to Don Julian and
Teodora " what people are saying." And now the
dramatist's art is shown in the delicate degrees by
which the poison works in the mind, not only of Don
Julian but of Teodora and Ernest as well. Don
Julian indignantly repulses the suggestion ; he feels,
he knows it to be untrue and degrading. But the
very effort of rejecting the doubt disturbs his mental
equilibrium. He begins to watch Teodora and Ernest,
and he sees that they are self-conscious and embarrassed. This is only natural under the circumstances;
but who knows ?—it may be an unconfessed feeling
on their part that has wakened to consciousness.
Don Julian may say, with Othello, " Farewell the
tranquil mind," and except in the third act of *Othello*,

I know not where to find a parallel for the inevitable-
ness of the process by which, without the intervention
of any Iago, he is swept through all the shades of
feeling between the serenest faith and the wildest
jealousy.

At the opening of the second act he is still resolved
to live down the tittle-tattle. Ernest has insisted on
leaving his house, and is going to start for Buenos
Ayres. Don Julian comes to his lodging to beg him
to remain; he does not find Ernest, but learns that
he is to fight a duel that day with a man about town,
who has spoken slightingly of Teodora. This, of
course, Don Julian cannot permit; he himself must
seek out and chastise the traducer of his wife. He
goes off, Ernest returns, and presently Teodora enters.
She, too, has heard of the intended duel, and has
come to implore Ernest not to fight, pointing out to
him that to do so will make the scandal ten times
worse. This is obviously true; but what can be
done? Every movement they make plunges them
deeper into the maze of misconception. Some one is
heard approaching; if it is Don Julian, Teodora will
stay and meet him; he will not misunderstand her
presence. But it is not Don Julian, it is the
chattering Pepito; and Teodora conceals herself in
the adjoining bedroom. Pepito has come with the
news that Don Julian has met Ernest's antagonist,
they have fought, and Don Julian has been seriously

wounded. The duel has taken place close by, and the wounded man is being brought to Ernest's rooms. He appears, and so genuine is Ernest's love and sorrow that for a moment he forgets Teodora. Then those who are supporting Don Julian make a move towards the bedroom, and Ernest has to bar the way against his dying benefactor. They push past him and throw open the door, discovering Teodora; and on this terrible situation the curtain falls. In the last act the hapless Ernest and Teodora writhe helplessly in the toils of calumny, which, against their own will, draw them ever closer and closer together. Don Julian dies, after having summoned up his last strength to strike Ernest in the face; and the curtain falls upon Ernest taking Teodora into his arms and facing the representatives of *todo el mundo*. "She is mine," he says; "the world has so willed it, and I accept its decision. . . . Come, Teodora; my mother's spirit kisses your pure brow. Adieu all! And let heaven choose its day to udge between me and you!" Such, says the poet, is the work of "The Great Go-between."

I hope that even this slight sketch may show how ably the play is conceived. But no narrative can convey any idea of the extraordinary vigour of the scenes. Echegaray has a rare genius for wringing every drop of effect out of a situation. His technique is often clumsy and careless (according to o ur ideas)

his mechanism antiquated; but in the thoroughness
with which he works out all the various aspects and
potentialities of a given conjuncture, he has scarcely
a rival. His *Son of Don Juan* is, to my thinking, a
very inferior play. It is confessedly suggested by
Ibsen's *Ghosts*, and is, in fact, the play Ibsen did *not*
write, the play of which Ibsen's is simply the sublima-
tion and the catastrophe. Echegaray, moreover, gives
us a mere diatribe against debauchery, in place of
Ibsen's stern arraignment of social conventions.
But there is one scene in *The Son of Don Juan*
of extraordinary strength and originality. Lazaro, the
Oswald of the play, a " degenerate " of genius, has
learnt that his mother has returned greatly disturbed
from a conversation with a celebrated specialist in
nervous disease.   By chance he meets this doctor,
who mentions in an off-hand way that his mother has
been consulting him about a nephew whose health
causes her great uneasiness. Lazaro is well aware
that no such nephew exists; but by pretending to
know all about the case, with a cunning which is
half genius and half insanity, he worms out of the
doctor his mother's terrible indictment of his father's
life, and the sentence of approaching paralysis and
idiocy which the doctor, judging from the mother's
statement, has passed upon the son himself.   The
scene is painful in the extreme, but is worked up
with amazing ingenuity and power.   Every facet of

the situation is presented in turn, and each is more appalling than the last.

Far stronger as a whole than *The Son of Don Juan* is an earlier play, *Folly or Saintliness*, which ought rather to be entitled *Madman or Saint*. Don Lorenzo is a man of great wealth, and of the most scrupulous honour. We find him, when the curtain rises, delivering a little essay in monologue upon *Don Quixote*, and defending the sanity of the Ingenious Hidalgo. His only daughter, the apple of his eye, has set her whole heart upon marriage with a young man of the bluest blood, and will die if she is thwarted. Just as everything is on the point of being arranged, Lorenzo learns that he has been "changed at birth," or rather that his supposed parents never had any children, but passed off the child of a servant as their own. His real mother, now dying, reveals this fact to him, and produces in proof a letter from his supposed mother, long since dead. Hereupon, to the horror of his wife, his daughter, and every one, he insists on giving up not only the inheritance to which he has no right, but also the name which is not his. This will render his daughter's marriage impossible, and his heart is agonised at the thought; but his will is immovable. The marriage might still be arranged if he would agree to a compromise, retaining the name and finding some pretext for handing over the fortune to the rightful heirs. He wavers, but finally stands firm; and this obstinacy, accompanied by transports of frenzied grief, comes gradually to wear the aspect of madness in the eyes of his family. The old woman who has worked all the mischief by her untimely revelation is most of all distressed. It was by no means her purpose to drag her son down from his high estate; so she manages to abstract from its envelope the letter proving her story, replaces it with a blank sheet of paper—and then dies. The result is that when Lorenzo, to prove his sanity, produces the letter —behold! it is no letter at all; and while the others conclude that the whole thing was a hallucination, he himself, in his overwrought condition, furiously accuses his wife and friends of conspiring against him. The play ends in his being led off to a madhouse, his daughter alone clinging to her belief in his sanity.

Thus, out of threadbare melodramatic materials, Echegaray has woven a psychological tragedy of great intensity. And he is an actors' poet. He always sees his scenes in action, and gives his actors every possible opportunity. His great parts, indeed, such as Julian, Ernest, Lazaro, Lorenzo, call for a volcanic fervour, a hysterical impetuosity, quite foreign to the northern temperament. That is probably the reason why these magnificent acting parts have not as yet attracted any leading English or American actor. But I own it surprises me that Salvini has never added such a part as Don Lorenzo to his repertory. *Mariana*, as aforesaid, is of these four plays the one in which the author's peculiarities appear with least exaggeration. How its Spanish colouring may strike an English audience it is impossible to predict. But I am much mistaken if we do not feel ourselves face to face with a dramatist who may be a little antiquated in his methods (he would be no Spaniard else), but whose passion and poetry are in their way unique.

VII.

" MARIANA "—" ROSEMARY "—" A BIT OF OLD CHELSEA."

24th February.

As a subscriber to the as yet anonymous Fund,* to which we owe the production of *Little Eyolf,* and which promises us *John Gabriel Borkman* and *Admiral Guinea,* I have been present to-day (Friday, February 19th) at a dress-rehearsal of Echegaray's *Mariana,* a romantic love-tragedy in modern dress, very happily interposed (to my thinking) between the two Ibsen plays. Until a play is brought face to face with the actual public, it is impossible for any one to predict its effect. In France, where a dress-rehearsal before an invited audience is a recognised institution,

* Afterwards known as the New Century Theatre.

the auguries of the *répétition générale*, whether for good or ill, are often flatly contradicted at the *première*. Thus I cannot even guess how *Mariana*, as an acted play, will strike the critics and the public; but I know very well how, as a piece of dramatic literature, it struck me when I read it years ago, and how it again impressed me when I saw it acted to-day by Mr. H. B. Irving, Miss Elizabeth Robins, and their comrades. It has certainly one of the marks of great literature— it bears the test of familiarity.

"Romantic love-tragedy" is the exact description of *Mariana*. It is a love-story, pure and simple. It deals with no social problem, no ethical dilemma, no general idea of any sort, political, philosophical, or moral. There is no symbolism in it and no thesis. It preaches nothing and teaches nothing. It exists for no other purpose than to show how wonderful and terrible a thing is love. "But hold!" says the reader. "Surely you are describing, not *Mariana*, but *Romeo and Juliet*." The truth is, I am describing both. *Mariana* is of the family of *Romeo and Juliet*—one might almost say its nearest living relative. Love, indeed, is the motive, or a motive, in most plays, but it is usually complicated by all sorts of other matters. Even in the plays which come under the simple formula "two lovers and an obstacle," the interest, as often as not, resides rather in the obstacle than in the lovers, or at least in the general considerations to which the obstacle gives rise. A common obstacle is caste-prejudice and difference of station; another, almost equally common, is great wealth on the lady's side, deterring a poor and high-minded suitor. In Mr. Jones's *Michael** the obstacle was a sacerdotal ideal of celibacy; in Mr. Pinero's *Profligate* it was the past life of the lover. In all such cases there is a moral or casuistical interest in the obstacle. Ought fond hearts to be more than coronets? Ought a poor man to accept wealth at the hands of his wife? Ought an inward vow of celibacy to bind action when it can no longer bind impulse? Ought a "good woman" to insist on similar and equal "goodness" in the man to whom she gives her life? Upon our instinctive answer to these questions depends our sympathy with the lovers, our interest in their fate. But in *Romeo and Juliet* and in *Mariana* no such questions arise; the interest resides wholly and solely in the beauty, the intensity, and the tragic issues of the passion represented; and that is why I call these two plays love-tragedies in a peculiar and eminent sense. The Montague-Capulet vendetta, which is the obstacle in *Romeo and Juliet*, raises no moral question whatever. No one but a German professor ever dreamed of blaming or praising the lovers for ignoring it. We feel that they have no choice; that their passion is their destiny. The beauty, and nobility,

* *Theatrical World of 1896*, p. 16.

and awe of the thing lie precisely in the sense that we are beyond the sphere of will, of morality, and that these two creatures of air and fire are the playthings of elemental forces crossed by inauspicious stars. So, too, with Mariana and Daniel; it is their love simply *as* love that appeals to us and moves us. There is nothing to approve, condemn, or even discuss in their conduct. They love, under circumstances which, to one of them at least, make happiness in love impossible; and as they cannot live without love, they die.

It needed an out-and-out romanticist to handle such a theme. José Echegaray is a romanticist of the original stock, not of the collateral or Gallic branch of the family. He descends in a right line from Lope and Calderon; he is closely akin to our own Elizabethans, and claims but a distant cousinship with the Parisian romantics of 1830. His technique he has borrowed, in the main, from the realists; but he is too impulsive to be a scrupulous technician. It is clear that he works more by instinct than by reflection; but he has a splendid instinct for the three essential elements of drama—character, passion, situation—and he flings characters and situations upon the scene with the prodigal facility, but also with the energy and conviction, of an earlier age.

The strength of *Mariana*, to my thinking, lies not so much in Mariana herself as in Daniel. Mariana is a complex and admirable creation, but she is not unique, even on the modern stage; whereas Daniel stands alone among lovers. He is passion itself, passion incarnate. Echegaray has the romanticist's love for dealing in prodigies; his Ernesto in *El gran Galeoto* and Lazaro in *El Hijo de Don Juan* are magnificent geniuses from the first. Daniel is nothing of the sort; he is a quite commonplace, simple-minded young man. It is love, and love alone, that lends him poetry, eloquence, genius. There is no art in his wooing; it is even touchingly artless; its strength lies in its intense, overwhelming sincerity. He has this advantage over Romeo himself, that he has a certain amount of resistance to overcome. Mariana loves him from the first—it would be a mistake to interpret her coquetry otherwise—but the experiences of her childhood and girlhood, which she relates with such exquisite pathos in the second act, have made her shrink from love and cling desperately to her liberty of heart. Thus Daniel, during the first two acts, has to battle with a deep-seated dread, veiling itself in coquetry and sometimes in deliberate cruelty. She is ten times as clever and quick-witted as he; she is mistress of all the arts which he hates and despises. But what is that to him? He seizes on her irony and sends it back to her palpitating with conviction; her lightest jest awakens reverberations that awe and subdue her; when she wounds him, he makes a weapon of his sufferings. You cannot fence with a

thunder-storm; the bright steel of Mariana's wit only
brings down upon her the lightning of his passion.
At the end of the second act she confesses herself
vanquished; and at this point I rather fear that
inattentive spectators may feel their interest flag for
want of a clearer prevision of what is to follow. It
may be a mistake, or it may be a justified audacity on
Echegaray's part, to leave the audience so long in the
dark as to the true nature of the barrier between the
lovers. There can be no doubt that it heightens the
interest of the third act, in which the scene of the
Mexican pendent is, in a lower order of art, extra-
ordinarily ingenious and effective. I shall respect
Echegaray's reticence, and only say that at the end
of this act it appears quite clearly that, though there
is no formal or legal barrier between Mariana and
Daniel, and although they themselves are innocent
of all wrong, it is impossible for a woman of her
sensitive imagination to be happy in his love—"the
daughter cannot drink the dregs of her mother's
shame." Therefore she seeks to raise an insuperable
wall between them; but "stony limits cannot hold
love out." In spite of her horror of the name he
bears, in spite of the formal bond she has now contracted, "her heart goes out of her body to Daniel."
They cannot love each other, and they cannot live
without each other's love; so she deliberately calls
down death upon their heads. There is no more

poignant scene in modern drama than this fourth act
of *Mariana.*

That delightful comedy, *Rosemary*,* seems to have
taken a new lease of life at the Criterion.† Last
Thursday night—the fifth night of its reproduction—
I found a full house enjoying it to the top of their
bent. And I myself enjoyed it even more than when
I saw it first. It is a most amiable piece of humour
and sentiment, delicately written and admirably acted.
Mr. Wyndham is as good as ever; Miss Mary Moore
and Miss Carlotta Addison are charmingly old-
fashioned; Mr. Alfred Bishop caricatures the irascible
Captain, to the huge delight of the audience, and Mr.
Barnes, as the Professor, is quiet, artistic, and excellent. Mr. A. E. George replaces Mr. Welch as the
postboy, and Miss Mary Jocelyn is remarkably clever
as Priscilla.

Sentimental realism is the note of Mrs. Oscar
Beringer's little play, *A Bit of Old Chelsea,*‡ which
precedes *Sweet Nancy* at the Court. It is clever,
amusing, not entirely pleasant. The young artist who
befriends the flower-girl makes a great deal too much
of his own chivalry, and pats himself on the back
obtrusively and unnecessarily because he refrains from

* *Theatrical World of 1896*, p. 156.

† February 13—March 20 (192nd performance).

‡ February 8—May 8. Reproduced at the Royalty, October
5 —November 20.

converting an impulse of hospitality into an act of blackguardism. The passage about the flowers and the Bible struck me as singularly false and unpleasing. Still, the play is much above the average of first pieces, and, being very cleverly acted by Miss Annie Hughes, Mr. Edmund Maurice, and Mr. Martin Harvey, is well worth seeing. Its title is curiously inapt. It is in reality a sort of counterpart or companion piece to *The Man in the Street;* but a title which should indicate this might doubtless be open to misunderstanding.

VIII.

THE O.U.D.S. PERFORMANCES—"THE MACHAGGIS" —"MARIANA."

3rd March.

IT is on record that Colonel Newcome read Cæsar and Tacitus "with a translation, sir, with a translation." My acquaintance with the Greek dramatists is even more distant : I have to read (for instance) Hookham Frere without Aristophanes. Whether this is an advantage or a disadvantage to a spectator of the O.U.D.S. performances, I must leave the learned to decide. All I can say is that I keenly enjoyed the *Knights* last Saturday afternoon ; whereas it is conceivable that persons familiar with Aristophanes and with Greek prosody might have found

certain drawbacks to their enjoyment. What little
Greek there ever was in my mind has evaporated
years ago; but it has left a sparse sediment of roots
and vocables, just sufficient to enable me, with the
aid of an interleaved crib, to follow the recitation
and know where the actors are. Taken in this
way, and regarded simply as an extravaganza in the
abstract, the *Knights* is highly entertaining. How
far the actors realised the poet's intention in their
embodiment of the different characters, I cannot even
guess; but several of them displayed unmistakable
comic talent, and the stage-management was inventive,
spirited, and amusing. The Chorus was perhaps
the weak point. It is necessarily less picturesque
than that of the *Birds;* but a little more care
might with advantage have been expended on its
costuming and wigging. The Knights looked rather
like the classic heroes depicted by a schoolboy on
the fly-leaf of his grammar — spirited, but out of
drawing. They fell between the two stools of
grotesqueness and grace. So long as they rode (or
wore) their hobby-horses, they were naturally grotesque enough; but when they dismounted, they
were only unintentionally comic. It struck me, too,
that if they could not, as Dick Swiveller would phrase
it, " do the light fantastic," they might at least have
attempted " the mazy." A little more movement and
evolution would have given life to the picture, and

might, moreover, have taken the rough edge off their
singing.   Of the individual actors the least successful,
to my mind, were the Demosthenes and Nicias.
Demosthenes, I take it, should have been a burlier,
more highly-coloured personage, and Nicias more
varied and perhaps less abject in his timidity and
superstition.   The same performers (Mr. F. Stevens
and Mr. A. N. Tayler) played Lucentio and Gremio
in *The Taming of the Shrew* very cleverly indeed, but
they made (or left) the opening scene of the *Knights*
a trifle dull.   The Sausage-Seller, on the other hand
(Mr. H. M. M. Woodward), proved himself a genuine
comedian in the first five minutes, and was vastly
entertaining throughout.   If he lacked anything, it
was volubility.   There was more stolidity than effrontery in his acting.   Perhaps he would be even better
as Bottom or Bardolph than as the Sausage-Seller;
but a genuine comedian he is, beyond a doubt.   The
Cleon (Mr. P. A. Rubens) played with excellent
vigour and conviction, and with a good deal of
dramatic instinct.   He was justly applauded in the
passage of burlesque tragedy at the close, where
(like Macbeth) he learns that the oracles on which
he relies in reality make for his adversary.   The
thwacking and buffeting he undergoes at the hands
of the Chorus were surely overdone.   The text,
indeed, suggests something of the sort; but if Cleon
is to be so pitilessly mauled at the outset, the effect

of his final overthrow is discounted. Demos was conceived by Mr. L. R. F. Oldershaw in an eccentric and niggling rather than a broadly comic spirit, but the performance was clever in its way. The mounting was simple but beautiful, and the musical setting, by the Rev. F. W. Bussell, was at least ingenious in its in-weaving of popular airs. What an amazing state must that have been in which such an onslaught was possible upon a man who was at the same time so powerful that the mask-makers feared to represent his features! It would be affectation to envy the Athenians their licence of scurrility; but are we never to find a middle course between that and the imbecility of current extravaganza?

Necessarily less interesting than the *Knights, The Taming of the Shrew* was scarcely less creditable. I have already mentioned the Lucentio of Mr. F. Stevens, which was a really graceful and charming performance. I do not know that I ever saw the part better played. Mr. P. Comyns Carr made a capital Petruchio. He is as yet rather a light-weight for the character, but acted with ample spirit and discretion. Mr. A. R. Mackintosh was a quietly amusing Grumio, and Viscount Suirdale showed a good conception of Christopher Sly, though he played it far too slowly. Miss Marion Morris was really clever as Katharina, and Miss Mabel Terry Lewis made an agreeable Bianca.

Of *The MacHaggis*,* by Messrs. Jerome and Phillpotts, produced last week at the Globe Theatre, only
one thing need be recorded, and that is that Mr.
Weedon Grossmith is exceedingly funny in it. The
story is simply delirious—but Mr. Grossmith is funny.
The part of Eweretta is ugly and repulsive—but Mr.
Grossmith is funny. The authors have hashed up
Ireland with their so-called Scotland in this quite
indigestible haggis—but Mr. Grossmith is funny.
Charley's Aunt is a work of coherent inventive
genius in comparison with this sheer tomfoolery,
which bears no sort of relation to life and never
deviates into common-sense—but Mr. Grossmith is
funny. As the piece goes on, he becomes extremely
and excruciatingly funny; and as he is not one of
the self-sufficient buffoons who require no material
to work upon, it is to be presumed that he is in some
measure indebted to the authors' invention for the
effects he produces. He is well supported, especially
by Mr. H. Reeves Smith, Mr. George Shelton, and
Miss Beatrice Ferrar. Mr. Blake Adams's Scotch
accent (Lowland, not Highland) is so unimpeachable
that it is strange he should not rebel against the
amazing vocabulary the authors place in his mouth.

The statement that I "conducted" the rehearsals
of Echegaray's *Mariana*† at the Court Theatre is

* February 25—April 24.
† February 22—26 (afternoon performances).

ludicrously wide of the truth.   Heaven help any
rehearsals "conducted" by me!   Modern stage-
management is as complex and difficult as chess-
playing, and I never had any head for chess—it is
not my affair.   Still, I saw so much of the preparations for the performance that, under ordinary
circumstances, I should scarcely think myself justified
in criticising it.   I have generally abstained from
more than a formal mention of such pieces of acting
as I have watched in the process of growth.   But in
this case I feel it impossible to confine myself to curt
phrases of compliment, however sincere.   In very
different ways, the Daniel of Mr. H. B. Irving and
the Mariana of Miss Elizabeth Robins seem to me
to call for the most serious attention that criticism
can bestow.   When a new actor of unmistakable
power and passion springs suddenly to the front, the
event is not one to be passed over in a stereotyped
sentence.   Hitherto we have known Mr. Irving as a
young man of picturesque appearance and promising
intelligence, but have had no opportunity of really
estimating his powers.   In Daniel he saw his chance,
and he seized it.   The part, as I said last week, is
a superb one, but exceedingly trying for a man of
northern race.   There is scarcely an actor on the
stage—none, certainly, of his own generation—who
could have played it with half the fire and vitality
that Mr. Irving threw into it.   Many critics, I note,

have called his acting "undisciplined." They are
right enough ; Mr. Irving has still a good deal to
learn in the way of self-control and mastery of his
means. But what a thing it is, in these days, to find
an actor with any real passion to " discipline "!—an
actor who can let himself go, even if he cannot
always hold himself in ! Most of our stage-lovers
can do that to perfection, and nothing else. Mr.
Irving's voice is at once his strength and his weak-
ness. It is a fine, resonant organ, but as yet it lacks
tenderness and flexibility. These qualities will doubtless come in time, for Mr. Irving is an earnest worker ;
and, in any case, he has shown that behind his handsome presence, and gallant if not graceful bearing,
there lie depths of genuine feeling and a true power
of imaginative self-abandonment. The stage stands
sadly in need of new blood with a little warmth in it ;
and here it has found what it wanted.

It has been my good fortune to work with Miss
Elizabeth Robins in the preparation of five or six of
Ibsen's plays, in which her performances have given
me the keenest pleasure. But Ibsen stands by
himself. To an actress of sympathetic intelligence
he offers such unique opportunities that it is hard to
bring her work into perspective, and see it in its true
relation to the general work of the stage. Thus I
have never been able quite to "place" Miss Robins
among her fellow-artists. Outside the Ibsen circle,

she had shown (in *Karin*, for example) a rare and admirable gift of pathos ; but in dealing with commonplace parts she was apt to appear to less advantage than more commonplace actresses.   After Mariana, I have no longer any doubt where to place her.   This is far from a commonplace part, indeed; but neither is it a creation of super-subtilised thought and feeling, like Ibsen's Hedda or Hilda or Rebecca. It is not one of the parts which demand a peculiar intellectual equipment, and give what may almost be called an unfair advantage to such artists as happen to possess that equipment.   In playing it, Miss Robins was measuring herself with the general run of emotional actresses, from Eleonora Duse downwards ; and it seemed to me that her performance placed her very high in the scale.   It was not flawless; there were subsidiary passages, minor transitions, individual phrases, which the actress had not perfectly worked out.   The first act especially, though full of beautiful touches, was not quite fused into a convincing whole.   But from the beginning of the second act onwards the flaws were few and far between, and the beauties varied and manifold.   The scene in which Mariana tells Don Felipe the story of her mother's life and her own showed not only Miss Robins's exceptional gift of pathos, but also a rare talent of composition and diction.   It was not only finely inspired but admirably accomplished acting.

In the remaining scenes of the second and third acts,
the actress kept well up to this high level; but here
the great effects really belong, not to Mariana, but to
Daniel. It was in the last act that Miss Robins
achieved her great and decisive triumph. Her acting
was no longer merely "emotional," but tragic in the
highest sense of the word. Throughout that magnificent scene she let slip no finest shade of Mariana's
agony of soul. Her dignity of action, her variety,
intensity, and justness of expression, were beyond all
praise. She seemed to live the scene rather than
to act it; and yet every motion and intonation was
informed and controlled by vigilant art. It was a
great opportunity, and Miss Robins rose to it greatly.
The other parts were more than sufficiently—in some
cases excellently—filled. Mr. Herman Vezin's tact
and refinement, Mr. Edward O'Neill's impassive
sternness, Mr. James Welch's garrulity, and Mr.
Martin Harvey's frivolity, all contributed greatly to
the general effect. Miss Beverley Sitgreaves and
Miss Mary Keegan were good in small parts, and
even Mr. George Bancroft and Miss Mabel Hackney,
as the two servants, contrived to make something of
their little scene.

IX.

"ANTONY AND CLEOPATRA" IN MANCHESTER.

10th March.

MR. LOUIS CALVERT has chosen for his second
Shakespearian season at the Queen's Theatre, Manchester, the greatest, in some respects, of Shakespeare's historical plays, *Antony and Cleopatra.* This
was a harder task than his last year's venture, the
first part of *Henry IV.** The play is considerably
looser in structure, and therefore calls for more
skilful curtailment; the style is far more compressed
and difficult, with frequent passages of that intellectual
shorthand to which Shakespeare became more and
more addicted as years went on; and the two leading
characters present much more complex problems to
the actors than the straightforward rhetorical personages of the English chronicle-play. It would be
too much to say that Mr. Calvert has grappled quite
as successfully with the world-historic as with the
national theme; but he has made a more than
creditable effort, and, so far as popular appreciation
goes, he has met with a generous reward. Though
the play has now run three weeks—no inconsiderable
run in a provincial city—the theatre on Saturday
night was crowded and overcrowded. It was a

* *Theatrical World of 1896*, p. 29.

pleasure to see how intently the vast concourse
of people followed the unfolding of the vivid and
majestic action.   Mr. Calvert, as a stage-manager,
has that art of making Shakespeare live and breathe
which is so often conspicuous by its absence from
our more sumptuous metropolitan solemnities.   One
may guess with tolerable assurance that this production has not cost one-fifth part of the money
expended on Mrs. Langtry's revival of the play at
the Princess's some years ago; but it is certainly
five times as vital and interesting.   Not that money
has been spared; considering that the prices at the
Queen's Theatre range from three shillings to sixpence, one can only wonder at the completeness of
the costumes, accessories, and scenic effects.   But
Mr. Calvert is much more bent on enchaining the
attention than on dazzling the eyes; and in this, with
the help of Miss Janet Achurch and a company full
of intelligent pleasure in their work, he succeeds to
admiration.

The text presented is in the main that arranged by
the late Charles Calvert for his revival in 1866.   In
the earlier acts the excisions and re-arrangements
are not immoderate, and on the whole judicious; but
in the closing scenes the pruning-knife is much
too freely used.   It is especially disastrous to
run together Act III. Sc. 11 and Act IV. Sc. 2.
This deprives both Antony and Cleopatra of one of

their greatest effects—the rekindling of hope, courage, and passion in the midst of disaster—and actually docks Cleopatra of the lines which are perhaps, from the theatrical point of view, the most effective in the whole play :

> " It is my birthday :
> I had thought to have held it poor ; but since my lord
> Is Antony again, I will be Cleopatra ! "

As it is, no sooner has Antony said

> " Fill our bowls : once more
> Let ò mock the midnight bell,"

than his mood sinks again and he goes off into the elegiac strain of the farewell address to his servants, which, in Shakespeare, belongs to another day and scene.   This is a pitiful anticlimax.   In the last scene of all, again, which includes the substance of Shakespeare's Act IV. Sc. 13 and Act V. Sc. 2, a striking and really imaginative scenic effect is attained, but at far too great a sacrifice of the text, and especially of the part of Cleopatra.   I am not purist enough to object to the arrangement by which Antony's body remains to the end at the foot of Cleopatra's throne; nay, I positively applaud it, and appreciate the effects attained by the simple shrouding and uncovering of his face.   But if these effects necessarily involve the excision of some of Cleopatra's very greatest speeches, then I say they are

too dearly bought.   Nothing can atone for the sacrifice
of such lines as these :

> " Ah women, women ! look,
> Our lamp is spent, it's out.—Good sirs, take heart;
> We'll bury him; and then, what's brave, what's noble,
> Let's do it after the high Roman fashion,
> And make death proud to take us; "

or these :

> " I dreamt there was an Emperor Antony !
> O, such another sleep, that I might see
> But such another man ! "

or, again, these :

> " Nay, 'tis most certain, Iras.   Saucy lictors
> Will catch at us, like wantons; and scald rhymers
> Ballad us out o' tune: the quick comedians
> Extemporally will stage us, and present
> Our Alexandrian revels.   Antony
> Shall be brought drunken forth, and I shall see
> Some squeaking Cleopatra boy my greatness."

These and several other passages ought certainly to
be restored.   That done, I, for my part, should
admire without scruple or reserve the no less
poetical than pictorial impressiveness of the final
scene.   The entrance of Augustus is of truly magnificent effect; we seem to breathe the essential air
of this great epoch; and it is a fine tact which

brings down the curtain on the phrase: "*And then to Rome!*"

Mr. Calvert's Antony is rugged, forcible, ánd effective. It lacks elevation, and is not very strong in diction; but it has plenty of impetuosity and vitality. Cleopatra is perhaps the most overwhelming character in all drama—not, indeed, the most difficult to *act*, but the most impossible to *be*. The imagination of ages has dwelt upon this woman until it has not so much idealised as deified her. Not Helen herself has assumed in our thoughts such superhuman proportions. In defiance of reason and even of history, we endue her with the greatness of her great lovers.

> " Did I, Charmian,
> Ever love Cæsar so?"

is a terrible phrase to live up to; and yet the greatest of her lovers was not Cæsar, not Pompey, not Antony, but the man who said of her:

> " Age cannot wither her, nor custom stale
> Her infinite variety,"

and who put on her dying lips such incomparable words as:

> " Show me, my women, like a queen :—go fetch
> My best attires;—*I am again for Cydnus*,
> *To meet Mark Antony.*"

How simple they are—how obvious, one might almost

say—and yet how utterly beyond the reach of any
other poet than Shakespeare! As the actress spoke
them on Saturday night, they took me by the throat,
as it were, with a sense of absolute beauty and
miraculous fitness that comes only with the greatest
things in literature. To say, then, that Miss Achurch
is not the Cleopatra of the imagination is only to say
that she is human. But I think she might, in the
earlier acts, come nearer the ideal, if she would seize
upon the poetry of the part, and let the comedy take
care of itself. It is true that there is warrant, and
more than warrant, in the text for all her comedy,
except one or two touches of by-play which seem to
me founded on verbal misconceptions. It is true
that the actor who "boy'd her greatness" in Shakespeare's own day probably went much further than
Miss Achurch in the direction of the ludicrous. But
just because this side of the part is so plainly marked,
I think a modern actress would do well to lay no
unnecessary stress upon it, and to concentrate her
thoughts on the dignity, the fascination—in a word,
the poetry of the character. Miss Achurch seemed
to me quite at her best in the last act, where she gave
a haggard nobility to the figure of the dying Queen
that was original and memorable. Some of her
emphases she should either study more or not so
much; they are either unconsidered or paradoxical.
Why, for instance, should Cleopatra say

> " I am fire and air; my other elements
> I *give* to baser life "

—as though it were likely that she should sell or lease them? And finally I implore Miss Achurch not to be led astray by a mere misprint in the ordinary editions, but to follow the Folio and the metre and say

> " Rather make
> My country's high pyrámidës my gibbet."

" Pyramids " is impossible. The effect of this scene, by the way, would be heightened if the Clown who brings the asps were made a frankly comic personage. Shakespeare knew what he was about in introducing this grim jester. Among the subordinate characters, those which struck me most were the Octavius Cæsar of Mr. G. F. Black, a very able performance, and the curiously devoted and almost dog-like Iras of Miss Maria Fauvet.

X.

MR. MEREDITH ON COMEDY.*

Westminster Gazette, 16*th March.*

MR. MEREDITH'S *Essay on Comedy* may without

---

* *An Essay on Comedy and the Uses of the Comic Spirit.* By George Meredith. (Westminster: Archibald Constable & Co. 1897.)

hesitation be set down as one of the subtlest, wittiest, and most luminous pieces of criticism in the English language. It has lain twenty years in the files of a forgotten magazine, and now comes to most of us— to me for one—as an unexpected and delightful gift. I wish I had known it all these twenty years; it would have been a thing of light and leading to me. Perhaps, however, its long eclipse has been providential. Perhaps it was the Muse of Comedy herself that hid it away in 1877, and prompted its resuscitation in 1897, when we are riper, if not for Comedy according to the critic's definition, at any rate for the appreciation of " fine shades and nice feelings " in dramatic art. If a play of Menander's were to be unearthed in the archives of some Russian or Spanish monastery, we should rejoice in it all the more for its unexpectedness; and similarly the feeling that this little gem of criticism "was lost and is found " gives an added zest to our pleasure in it.

The Comic Spirit, according to Mr. Meredith, is "the first-born of common sense," "the genius of thoughtful laughter." It hovers over civilised society, "luminous and watchful."

" It has the sage's brows, and the sunny malice of a faun lurks at the corners of the half-closed lips, drawn in an idle wariness of half tension. . . . Men's future upon earth does not attract it : their honesty and shapeliness in the present does ; and whenever they wax out of proportion, overblown, affected, pretentious, bombastical, hypocritical, pedantic, fantastically delicate; whenever it sees them self-deceived or hoodwinked, given to run riot in idolatries, drifting into vanities, congregating in absurdities, planning short-sightedly, plotting dementedly; whenever they are at variance with their professions, and violate the unwritten but perceptible laws binding them in consideration one to another; whenever they offend sound reason, fair justice; are false in humility or mined with conceit, individually or in the bulk—the Spirit overhead will look humanely malign, and cast an oblique light on them, followed by volleys of silvery laughter.   That is the Comic Spirit."

Comedy is essentially distinct, according to this definition, from Satire, from Irony, which is "the humour of satire," and from Humour itself, which "embraces contrasts beyond the scope of the Comic poet."

" Byron had splendid powers of humour and the most poetic satire that we have example of, fusing at times to hard irony. He had no strong comic sense, or he would not have taken an anti-social position, which is directly opposed to the Comic."

In such passages as these Mr. Meredith seems practically to identify the Comic Spirit with that regulative or restrictive Sense of Humour on which we are all so apt to plume ourselves.   This faculty is essentially critical, and has scarcely anything in common with creative Humour; so that there have been great humorists of whom it might without paradox be said that they had no sense of humour, in our peculiar acceptation of the term.   Says Mr. Meredith:

" If the Comic idea prevailed with us, and we had an Aristophanes to barb and wing it, we should be breathing air of
Athens. . . . There would be a bright and positive, clear
Hellenic perception of facts. The vapours of Unreason and
Sentimentalism would be blown away before they were pro-
ductive.   Where would Pessimist and Optimist be?   They
would, in any case, have a diminished audience."

In a thousand such delicate touches of exposition
and discrimination, Mr. Meredith stipples in, as it
were, his conception of the Comic Spirit. It is
neither scornful nor brutal, neither cynical nor inhuman. "A perception of the Comic Spirit gives
high fellowship. You become a citizen of the selecter
world. . . . Look there for your unchallengeable
upper class ! . . . Sensitiveness to the comic laugh is
a step in civilisation. To shrink from being an object
of it is a step in cultivation."

Here, however, one cannot but pause and reflect.
For my part, I am all anxiety to be a citizen of the
selecter world, and a member of the unchallengeable
upper class ; but if it be one of the statutes of this
freemasonry that one must " shrink from being an
object of the comic laugh," I despair of becoming an
adept. Not but what I "shrink" with ready instinct;
the trouble is that in many cases I am heartily
ashamed of so doing. This proves, no doubt, that an
incorrigible Sentimentalist lurks somewhere in my
composition ; but even if, by prayer and fasting, I

cast him out, could I any the more reasonably hope
to avoid being an actual or potential " object of the
comic laugh "?   And where the matter is so hopeless,
would not common sense counsel one rather to overcome the instinctive shrinking than to regard it as
" a step in cultivation "?   He was a profound (though
hapless) philosopher who said, " Vulgarity is the
behaviour of other people " ; and if we substitute
" comicality " for " vulgarity," the epigram suffers,
but the truth remains.   It is scarcely a mark of
sanity to believe, or even hope, that one is fault-
lessly sane ; and if the Comic Spirit ever broadens
its " finely tempered smile " into a sardonic grin, it
is perhaps in contemplating the man who believes
himself exempt from its animadversions.

Mr. Meredith is at his best in his rapid flash-light
survey (the paper was originally a lecture) of the
comic poets.   The ideal " comic poet," according to
this critic, is a very rare bird ; he does not hesitate to
say, "We count him during centuries in the singular
number."   The centuries he has in mind are those of
modern literature, and the solitary poet is, of course,
Molière.   A finer and juster panegyric of Molière than
that which runs through this whole essay is nowhere
known to me.   For the English comedy of manners
Mr. Meredith has scant tolerance.   He riddles it
with epigrams.   It is " comedy of the manners of
South Sea islanders under City veneer."   Its realism

is crass and primitive; and "it is unwholesome for men and women to see themselves as they are, if they are no better than they should be." Congreve's style he admires, the poise of his sentences; and he takes off his hat to Millamant. Otherwise he will have little to say to our "blowsy Hoyden" of a Comic Muse. Even *She Stoops to Conquer* he writes down, perhaps not quite happily, "an elegant farce." I should rather call it an inelegant comedy; but the difference is merely verbal. Mr. Meredith's brilliant passage on Aristophanes I can only commend to the attention of scholars; suggesting, with all diffidence, a doubt as to whether he may not have over-estimated, not his genius, but his wisdom. German "attempts at comedy" remind Mr. Meredith of " Heine's image of his country in the dancing of Atta Troll." Heine himself "has not been enough to cause his compatriots to smart and meditate. Nationally, as well as individually, when they are excited they are in danger of the grotesque." But surely (apart from a possible application near home) these words apply even more directly to the countrymen of Molière than to the countrymen of Goethe. Gregarious folly takes no account of frontiers, and flouts the Comic Spirit in every language under the sun.

One could wish that Mr. Meredith had said more of the relation between the comedy of types and the comedy of individual character. He has himself drawn the great type-figure of modern fiction—I mean, of course, *The Egoist*—fusing, in that master-piece, the two methods of art, and making of a colossal type a complete individual. Has it ever occurred to Mr. Meredith that the decline, not to say the impossibility, of pure comedy on the modern stage is due to the fact that the broad types are exhausted, and that individuals, if they live at all, touch our sympathies so nearly as to interfere with the free play of the Comic Spirit? It may be too much to say that the types are exhausted; but in any case the centring of all attention upon one vice or foible strikes us, in modern drama, as an expedient of farce. (Mr. Meredith, by the way, does not mention Labiche, who, with all his extravagance of action, was surely impregnated with the comic spirit.) I am inclined, however, to foresee a revival of pure comedy (as dis-tinct from farce on the one hand and drama on the other) so soon as we shall have got over that itch for action and intrigue with which Scribe inoculated us. We are gradually expelling it from our blood; but it takes time. Fancy *Le Misanthrope* or *Les Femmes Savantes* produced for the first time before an audience of to-day! How the critics would cluster together in the entr'actes and button-hole each other to explain that "there's no action," that "nothing happens," that "we don't get any forr'ader," that "it's all talkee-talkee," and so on through the whole

litany ! Which of us, I wonder, would pluck up heart
to cry, like the legendary man in the pit, " Courage,
Molière ! Voilà la bonne comédie ! "

XI.

"Saucy Sally "—" The Mariners of England."

17th March.

ADAPTED by Mr. Burnand from *La Flamboyante*, and
entitled *Saucy Sally*,* the new farce at the Comedy
Theatre places me in an awkward dilemma. I
laughed at it very much ; I think, as things go, it
thoroughly deserves to succeed, and I have every
wish to lend it a helping hand ; yet I can find
nothing to say of it that does not sound disparaging.
Every question you can ask about it, except one, I
must answer to its disadvantage. Is it novel ? Not
in the least ; the idea is as old as the hills ; we met
it last in *The Prodigal Father*, now running at the
Strand. Is it ingenious ? Why, no ; it replaces
ingenuity by sheer effrontery ; I can remember
nothing more audacious in farce than the appearance in the second act of a real " Saucy Sally " with
a real Captain Jocelyn, unless it be the coincidence
which brings Mrs. Jocelyn and her mother, in the
third act, to Cecile's apartments. Is it witty ? Oh

* March 10—June 5. Reproduced July 26—August 20.

dear, no; there is not a single line in the dialogue
that any human being would care to remember; the
best one can say of it is that Mr. Burnand has
heroically abstained from puns and word-plays.   Is
it edifying?   Quite the reverse; Mr. Burnand has
thrown a very flimsy veil over the profligacy implied
in the original plot; and even if we close our eyes to
the meanings that stare at us through this veil, the
piece remains one long apotheosis of imperturbable
mendacity.   Where, then, does its merit come in?
Upon my word, I haven't the slightest idea.   But if
you ask me, finally, "Is it amusing?" I can only
reply, "Yes, very amusing, and, with all its reckless
irresponsibility, not base or offensive.   Go and see it
if you want a good laugh, and don't mind holding
both your common sense and your moral sense in
temporary abeyance."   The real merit, of course, lies
in the acting.   Mr. Hawtrey finds in Herbert Jocelyn
the biggest liar in his whole brazen gallery, and is
therefore quite delightful.   One may call him,
without paradox, a story-teller in whom there is no
guile.   Mr. Ernest Hendrie, as the too grateful Old
Man of the Sea, shows a genuinely humorous
fantasy; Mrs. Charles Calvert is most amusing
as the disillusioned mother-in-law; Miss Jessie
Bateman as Rosie, and Miss Maud Abbott as
Cecile, are bright and intelligent; indeed, there is
no part that is not cleverly filled.

As I can find nothing praiseworthy in the conception, construction, or writing, and nothing noteworthy in the acting, of *The Mariners of England*,* by Mr. Robert Buchanan and "Charles Marlowe," and as, on the other hand, it is too puerile to call for serious condemnation, I prefer to pass it over in silence. It was certainly rather painful to see the death of Nelson treated as a limelit scene of vulgar melodrama; but fortunately one had long ago ceased to associate, even in make-believe, the figure on the stage with the name in the playbill.

XII.

"THE PHYSICIAN"—"A PIERROT'S LIFE."

31st March.

WHATEVER else Mr. Henry Arthur Jones may or may not be, he is a first-rate theatrical story-teller. Even when his story seems inacceptable and unpleasing, he does not bore us; and when he gets a good story to tell, he holds us like a vice. In his new Criterion play, *The Physician*,† he has a capital story to tell, and tells it with really admirable skill. He shows no scrupulous over-refinement of technique;

* Olympic, March 9—April 3.

† March 25—June 15. Followed by *David Garrick*, June 16 —July 17.

his methods are straightforward and frankly theatrical. He gives his hero a confidant, and he introduces an elaborate piece of scenic architecture so that his heroine may comfortably overhear a somewhat uncomfortable conversation. But even these things he does with dexterity; the confidant is decently disguised, and the eavesdropping scene is so prettily led up to, and, in a sense, so inevitable, as to disarm the veriest pedant. For the rest, the play is little short of a masterpiece in the art of exciting and sustaining interest. I echo the entreaty of the management that the audience should be seated before the rise of the curtain, for late comers will not only miss for their own part, but spoil for others, one of Mr. Jones's ablest inventions. Not many opening scenes in drama put one's curiosity so keenly on the alert as this. The classic instance of the "introductory chord," as Gustav Freytag calls it, is the incomparable first scene of *Hamlet*. Mr. Jones's introductory chord, firmly and crisply touched, serves the same purpose of showing that there are ghosts abroad, and setting us wondering what they portend.

Ghost-like indeed is this pale and nervous young man who, left alone in Dr. Lewin Carey's consulting-room, searches out a chapter in some medical handbook, and scans it feverishly. He has refused to give the servant his name, but we recognise Mr. Thalberg and turn to the playbill : he is called Walter Amphiel.

To him enters Dr. Brooker, Dr. Carey's friend.
" Surely we have met before?" he says to Amphiel.
" No, no," is the reply. " Didn't you come to
consult me——?" " No, no—you are mistaken.
I must go. I shall call again and see Dr. Carey"—
and the pallid creature takes flight. Dr. Brooker's
eye falls on the open book ; he looks at the heading
of the page, raises his eyebrows, and says "H'm!"
The curtain has not been up three minutes, scarcely a
hundred words have been spoken, and already we
have had two sensations : the sensation of life, for the
scene in itself is a grim little everyday drama ; and
the sensation of mystery and vaguely impending
fate. Having thus got hold of us, the author may
proceed at leisure to the development of character
and circumstances. He posits the character of his
hero, Dr. Lewin Carey, and shows how he is at a
loose end, as it were, in his emotional life, and
prepared to set forth in search of adventure. Be his
character-drawing true or false, shallow or profound,
Mr. Jones at this point takes still firmer hold on our
interest. In fiction, at any rate, however it may be
in life, adventures are to the adventurous, and when
we see a man set forth in search of them, be it
Haroun al Raschid, Don Quixote, or Prince Florizel
of Bohemia, we know that they will make all haste to
present themselves. And in this case our confidence
is justified : for behold ! Miss Edana Hinde comes to

beg for Dr. Carey's interest in the case of her
betrothed, a young man whose enthusiastic devotion
to the cause of temperance is killing him; and the
young man's name, already famous in philanthropic
circles, is—Walter Amphiel.   Dr. Carey promises to
interest himself in Mr. Amphiel, and evidently does
interest himself deeply in Mr. Amphiel's betrothed.
She has scarcely gone when the pallid young man of
the first scene reappears, gives a name which is not
famous in philanthropic circles, and consults the
doctor on the case of "a friend" who suffers from
intermittent attacks of uncontrollable dipsomania.
If this is not an interesting first act—interesting in
itself and in its possibilities—I know not where to
look for one.

The second act contains much less movement.
Only at the very end does Dr. Carey learn that the
lover of the saintly Edana, to whom he himself is
by this time deeply and silently devoted, is none
other than the miserable being who detailed to him
the case of his "friend."   Mr. Jones reserves all his
strength for the third act, which is really absorbing
from first to last, and remarkably well written to boot.
Dr. Carey has for six months devoted himself to
Amphiel for Edana's sake, all the time loathing his
task and his patient.   But Amphiel has broken loose
again and disappeared.   Will he ever return?   Carey
confesses to his confidant that he hopes not.   He

does return, however, having got through his bout of
debauchery; and it is the colloquy between him and
Carey that Edana overhears. The scene is intensely
painful and intensely powerful; the encounter of the
two men would in itself be both painful and powerful
enough, even if there were no wretched girl behind
the curtain (yet, thanks to the architectural device
before mentioned, in full view of the audience), to
whom it brings perhaps the ghastliest of conceivable
revelations. We have had subtler and more ingenious
situations in recent drama, but for sheer crushing
force, for downright hard hitting, I do not remember
its equal. And we have vaguely known it impending
all through the act. In that art which is half the
secret of theatrical story-telling, in the art of foreshadowing without forestalling his effects, Mr. Jones
is really a master. The fourth act brings the play
to an acceptable enough, but tame and indifferent,
conclusion. In this, however, Mr. Jones perhaps
shows wisdom and even taste. Professor Murray, in
his recently published *Literature of Ancient Greece*—
in which the drama is treated with singular and very
suggestive insight—remarks that "the gradual slack-
ening of the interest till the 'pity and terror' melt
away in gentle artistic pleasure was one of the
essential principles of Greek art," and that "Shakespeare was with the Greeks." This principle might
conceivably have been modified had the Athenian

or the Elizabethan stage possessed the mechanism necessary for what we call a "quick curtain." Not to insist on this (perhaps impious) suggestion, I grant that Mr. Jones may cite Æschylus and Shakespeare in proof of the artistic value of anticlimax. For myself, I am so rabid a modern that if I had written the third act of *The Physician*, I should have racked my brains and perhaps spoilt my play in the attempt to devise a still stronger fourth act. It is all very well to be in the same boat with Æschylus and Shakespeare, but the distinction seems dubious when you find it shared by every half-baked amateur that ever lived.

The discerning reader who studies the theatrical advertisements may by this time have noticed that, whereas Miss Marion Terry and Miss Mary Moore are both appearing nightly at the Criterion, my account of Mr. Jones's plot shows only one lady concerned in it. The truth is that another lady adorns the stage at intervals, but is totally unconcerned in the action, and might as well, nay, much better, have been omitted. Much better, I repeat; for this sandwiching of the hero between cynicism and candour, between worldliness and other-worldliness, between the pagan and the saint, between porphyry and alabaster, reduces the play from the psychological tragedy it might have been to the intellectual melodrama it is. The character-drawing,

in a word, is by no means on a level with the story-
telling. There is no character whatever in Edana;
she is a figure of pure convention; and the temptress,
Lady Valerie, is sadly inferior to her first cousin,
Audrey Lesden, in *Michael and his Lost Angel.* Her
share in the action is inessential and painful. Except
as a means of getting Dr. Carey off the stage for
ten minutes in the third act, she is of no use whatever. The play would really be much better if we
never heard her name, and knew no more about her
than what Carey tells his confidant in the first act.
The scene in which she dismisses Carey unnecessarily
humiliates him, and the scenes in which she tries to
resume her empire over him degrade both herself and
(by implication) her lover of bygone days. Never
was siren so innocent of subtlety; or rather, to put it
in plain English, never was woman so devoid of tact.
Her clumsy coquetries have not one ha'porth of
allurement in them; and, as they only bore Dr.
Carey without producing one ha'porth of effect, it is
hard to see what possible purpose they serve. The
worthy doctor himself is somewhat romantically conceived. Does one, I should like to know, find
eminent nerve specialists buttonholing their colleagues to bewail their lack of "faith," and bemoan-
ing to maidens in white muslin the inapplicability
of the microscope to metaphysics? When I have
chanced to roam through Harley Street and Cavendish

Square, I have not found the air rent with these
ululations. Some doctors, it seems to me, never
dream of bringing their microscope into touch with
their metaphysics, or say, adapting the poet, "the
undevout anatomist is mad." Others get through
life very comfortably without any faith to speak of—
even in the Pharmacopœia. But the variety studied
by Mr. Jones—the physician in trouble about his
soul, or his lack of soul—has somehow escaped my
observation. I should have more belief in him if
he did not talk so much about "curing" people,
and if, on meeting the dipsomaniac lover of the
lady he himself adores, he did not seize him by
both hands and cry "Whilst Nature holds out one
little rushlight of hope, I'll never leave you till I can
set you upright before all men and before her!"
This is distinctly unprofessional language. I know
that doctor—he comes from the Princess's. And he
brings with him a harmonium to play hymn-tunes
at appropriate cues (for instance, "He passed away
peacefully, begging you to forgive him"), and a
chintz-walled vicarage, and a procession of comic
and pathetic rustics, and, in brief, an atmosphere
of melodrama which lowers, not the interest and
power, but the artistic status of the play.

Mr. Wyndham's Dr. Carey is an admirable piece
of acting, perhaps the most striking thing he has
done in serious drama. If anything, he plays the

part with too studious self-restraint, and makes
certain passages gloomier than is strictly necessary.
Mr. Thalberg's Walter Amphiel is exceedingly clever,
especially in the consultation scene of the first act.
There is not enough character in the part to give
room for variety; Amphiel is a dipsomaniac in the
abstract. Mr. Alfred Bishop's Parson Hinde is an
accomplished and beautiful performance, which, more
than anything else, lights up the somewhat sombre
play. Mr. Jones's conception of the character is
delightful; the scene in which the old man "preaches
a sermon, tells a story, and sings a song," shows a
touch of the true humorist; and it is not often that
an author finds an actor to collaborate with him as
Mr. Bishop does. Miss Marion Terry makes a
charming Lady Valerie; the shortcomings of the
character are in no way attributable to the actress.
Edana is not at all a part for Miss Mary Moore.
Mr. Jones has given his heroine little enough individuality, yet a great deal more than Miss Moore
put into it. The enthusiasm which is Edana's one
definite quality nowhere appeared in the acting.
When Dr. Carey said "The girl's face glowed like
a live coal," we could almost have suspected him
of sarcasm. Perhaps, if Edana had been more real
to us, we should not have found the last act so
much of an anticlimax. Minor characters are
capitally played by Mr. Leslie Kenyon, Miss Carlotta

Addison, Miss Mary Jocelyn, Mr. Kenneth-Douglas, and Mr. J. G. Taylor.

The Physician is *Rosemary* writ large and brought to a "happy ending." It might have been a great play had Lady Valerie been suppressed, and Edana made a character instead of a muslin doll. Even as it stands, it is thoughtful and skilful, absorbingly interesting, and eminently alive.

Mlle. Félicia Mallet, who now plays Pierrot in *A Pierrot's Life** at the Prince of Wales's, is certainly an accomplished pantomimist, and puts abundance of movement and expression into the part; but it seems to me, I own, that in the substitution of Mlle. Mallet for Mlle. Litini what is gained in vivacity is lost in charm. The truth is, I have at best but a moderate relish for this form of art, and am apt to prefer grace to virtuosity. Miss Ellas Dee is clever as Louisette, and Mlle. Litini is curiously effective in the small part of Fifine.

XIII.

"LE TRAGIQUE QUOTIDIEN."

St. Paul's, 6th April.

"IT's a lonely thing to be a champion," says the prize-fighter hero of one of Mr. Bernard Shaw's

* See p. 8.

novels. In the same plaintive rhythm I am moved
to exclaim, "It's a dismal thing to be a specialist."
How one's sympathies dwindle! How one's vision
narrows! Take my own case, for instance: having
put on the blinkers of theatrical criticism, I have no
eyes for the world outside the theatre. Crete and
Rhodes, the Famine and the Jubilee, the Education
Bill and the Lincolnshire Handicap—all these, and
a hundred other topics of national or mundane
interest, solicit my attention in the daily papers; yet
to what do I turn first? Why, to "Green Room
Gossip," or "Footlight Flashes," or "The Drama
Day by Day." Similarly, when M. Maeterlinck's
essays come into my hands, on which of them do
I pounce with instant avidity? On "The Awakening of the Soul"; on "Mystic Morality"; on "The
Deeper Life"? No, on none of these—not even on
"Women"—but on "The Tragical in Daily Life";
because I know that it is more or less concerned with
the theatre.

Was it in Laputa or in Gotham that the proverbial
philosopher was bent on extracting sunbeams from
cucumbers? Imagine the converse process—extracting cucumbers from (say) moonbeams—and you will
have some idea of the difficulty of disengaging any
solid doctrine from M. Maeterlinck's fascinating essay.
What M. Maeterlinck aims at is the negation of the
theatre—a drama which eschews volition and passion,

conflicts and crises—a drama in which nothing is done, and whatever is said must be studiously irrelevant. Tolstoï issuing a "Soldier's Pocket-book" on non-resistance principles would not be a more paradoxical spectacle than M. Maeterlinck constructing an æsthetic of the drama or the theory that the most interesting moments in life are those in which we are doing nothing, saying nothing, and thinking nothing.

If you suspect me of caricaturing M. Maeterlinck's position, read Mr. Sutro's smooth and sympathetic translation of the essay in question, and you will see : "The true tragic element of life only begins at the moment when so-called adventures, sorrows, and dangers have disappeared. . . . Is it not tranquillity that is terrible—tranquillity watched by the stars? And is it in tumult or in silence that the spirit of life quickens within us? . . . Is it not an ancient error to imagine that it is at the moment when passion possesses us that we live our truest lives? . . . An old man seated in his arm-chair, waiting patiently, with his lamp beside him, giving unconscious ear to all the eternal laws that reign about the house . . . submitting with bent head to the presence of his soul and his destiny . . . does yet live, in reality, a deeper, more human, and more universal life than the lover who strangles his mistress, the captain who conquers in battle, or 'the husband who avenges his honour.'"

The fact is, M. Maeterlinck himself caricatures his

own creed; and that is why I read with a certain
regret these utterances of a great poet and an
exquisite spirit. There are deep and essential truths
in this very paper, but their practical efficacy is to
a great extent marred by the mystical vesture in which
they are enveloped. Here, as in so many other cases,
mysticism means sheer over-statement. You take a
poor little truth, often subtle and valuable in itself,
and you distend it like a soap-bubble until it seems
to fill the whole vault of heaven, and, having lost all
proportion to other truths, is itself a truth no longer,
but a filmy monstrosity. Of course, you attain a
certain effect by this isolation and exaggeration of
your idea; but it is a cheap effect, unworthy of a
thinker and an artist.

The truth which M. Maeterlinck has portentously
overblown in this essay, he himself has stated with
incomparable simplicity and felicity in one of his
dramas—*Intérieur*, if I am not mistaken. "*It is in
the soul that things happen*"—that is the inmost
secret of his dramatic theory and practice. External
happenings are of no interest save as they express and
interpret what happens in the soul; and when the
soul-states they interpret are barbarous or bestial, the
interest we feel in them is not strictly artistic, but
rather archæological or pathological. "When I go
to a theatre," says M. Maeterlinck, "I feel as though
I were spending a few hours with my ancestors, who

conceived life as something primitive, arid, and brutal; but this conception of theirs scarcely even lingers in my memory, and surely it is not one that I can share." Clearly, M. Maeterlinck would not enjoy *Richard III.*; he betrays a certain distaste even for *Othello*, and what he likes in *Hamlet* is that "he does not act."

With certain qualifications, all this can be accepted readily enough.   One very important qualification M. Maeterlinck himself suggests : "It is not in the actions but in the words that are found the beauty and greatness of tragedies that are truly beautiful and great. . . . The only words that count are those that at first seem useless, for it is therein that the essence lies."   To the devotees of the well-made play this must seem the most damnable of heresies.   But if there is one thing more certain than another, it is that the great plays of the world are not the well-made plays, and that Sophocles and Shakespeare live precisely by the things which Monsieur Scribe, had they had him for a collaborator, would inexorably have cut.   Give us poetry, and we can put up with a good deal of archaic psychology.

It is certain, however, that archaic psychology, like any other anachronism, is out of place in modern drama.   So far M. Maeterlinck carries us with him. But when he leaps from the assertion that some passions are primitive, to the theory that all passion is vulgar and insignificant, and the implication that the highest drama would consist of an old man sitting beside a lamp and silently "submitting to the presence of his soul and his destiny," then we feel that the truth is getting a little filmy. It is all very well for an old gentleman, in the words of Whitman, to "loaf and invite his soul," but drama is not the medium, and the theatre can never be the place, for such solemnities. In the ideal drama, according to M. Maeterlinck, "it is no longer a violent exceptional moment of life that passes before our eyes—it is life itself." Yes, but how is the thing to be managed? At this rate the ideal theatre would be a Trappist monastery, and we should go to a Quaker's meeting for rattle and devilment.

Fortunately for the world, M. Maeterlinck, the poet, does not act up to his critico-mystical theory. It is in the souls of his personages that things happen, but things *do* happen in their souls. His romantic scenery and dateless time are mere devices for the isolation of the soul, its abstraction from all narrowing influences of custom, tradition, religion, race, nationality. But things *do* happen, I repeat. His dramas are dramas because conflicts and crises occur in the souls he bodies forth. They love and they hate; they are tossed to and fro on waves of rapture, and terror, and anguish :—

> "In their heart is a blind desire,
> In their eyes foreknowledge of death."

Turn from "The Tragical in Daily Life" to *Aglavaine et Sélysette*—one of the profoundest and most beautiful dramas in existence—and you will find it contradict in every scene the excesses of M. Maeterlinck's theory. It is not "static" but irresistibly dynamic.

XIV.

"THE PRINCESS AND THE BUTTERFLY."

7th April.

THERE had been rumours that in his new play at the St. James's Mr. Pinero was not pursuing his recent line of advance, but beating a temporary retreat. The production of *The Princess and the Butterfly** has proved these rumours groundless. Mr. Pinero has turned a little aside, indeed ; he has got out of a rut, or what threatened to become one ; but, far from retreating, he has made, I venture to say, a distinct and decisive advance. More than any of his previous works, this one brings home to us the conviction that, after all these years, or centuries, we are again within measurable distance of possessing, not a "literary drama," but a dramatic literature.

That is the one vital aspect of the matter, the

* March 29—June 30. Nine performances of *The Prisoner of Zenda* brought the season to a close on July 9.

aspect on which criticism ought to insist. Let us
hold in check, for once, our habit of confounding
criticism with fault-finding, until we have clearly
realised and affirmed that with such a play as this the
English theatre takes an independent, honourable,
even conspicuous place among the theatres of Europe.
I do not mean that *The Princess and the Butterfly* is
certain to be greatly successful abroad. It may or
may not be ; if fitness for exportation were the test of
merit, *Charlie's Aunt* would be the greatest play of
the age. What I do mean is that this largely conceived, thoughtful, delicate, delightful comedy deserves
to be judged not by a merely local, but by a
European standard, and more than confirms Mr.
Pinero in his position among the first half-dozen of
living dramatists. Nay, more—if we try to place it
in another dimension, not looking abroad over contemporary Europe, but looking back along the record
of the English stage—we shall have to go I know not
how far to find work in which intellectual and scenic
qualities are so happily blended. Mr. Pinero has
imposed upon himself conditions not hitherto accepted by any English playwright. He has written
what may be called a realistic comedy, nowhere
availing himself of the traditional licence of the
English theatre in the direction either of rhetoric or
of farce. For *Caste*, immeasurably the best of T. W.
Robertson's works, I have a great affection and

respect.   There is perhaps more racy humanity in it than in *The Princess and the Butterfly*, which turns on a subtlety of sentiment, not on an obvious contrast of manners.   But how trivial is the wit of *Caste*, how grossly farcical its technique, compared with the exquisite style and workmanship of Mr. Pinero's play! Going a generation further back, we come upon *Money*, that intolerably artificial farrago of pinchbeck wit, Byronic sentiment, and conventional "business." Here, surely, we need not pause—any more than at the Fondloves and Wildrakes of Sheridan Knowles, the Silkies and Sulkies of Holcroft and Morton.   Not till we come to Sheridan and Goldsmith do we find work of anything like the calibre of Mr. Pinero's ; and here, again, the conditions, the conventions, are so different that it would be absurd to suggest any order of merit.   Sheridan and Goldsmith continued and consummated a long tradition.   They were the lineal descendants, respectively, of Congreve and Farquhar.   They worked in ready-made forms ; they did over again, with brilliant success, what others had done before them.   The interest of Mr. Pinero's work lies in the fact that he is not the transmitter, but rather, we may hope, the originator, of a tradition. He is essentially a pioneer.   His method is not local, but eclectic, European ; and he adapts and applies it with original genius to the portrayal of English life.

Though a comedy pure and simple, steering as

exact a course between melodrama on the one hand
and farce on the other as any play in the language,
The Princess and the Butterfly scarcely comes under
Mr. Meredith's now famous definition. The comic
spirit, in this play, is not "the first-born of common-
sense;" or, if it is, it turns and rends its parent in
most unfilial fashion. The whole action is a genial
satire upon worldly wisdom. I cannot guess what
Mr. Pinero means by his sub-title, *The Fantastics*, for,
until within five minutes of the end, his hero and
heroine are fantastic only in their devotion to
common-sense. They seem to have been reading
Mr. Meredith on Comedy, and to have laid to heart
the maxims that "Sensitiveness to the comic laugh is
a step in civilisation. To shrink from being an object
of it is a step in cultivation." It is because Sir
George Lamorant and Princess Pannonia fear "the
comic laugh" that they are bent on "going to meet
old-age half-way." Comedy has always sanctioned
their initial cowardice and derided their ultimate
daring. The Princess strives to act up to the counsel
of Orsino in *Twelfth Night :*

> " Let still the woman take
> An older than herself; so wears she to him,
> So sways she level in her husband's heart."

Sir George, in like manner, shrinks from playing
Arnolphe to his elvish Agnès. Nay, it is perhaps

Mrs. Tanqueray that has put Sir George on his guard against the marriage of a middle-aged man with a woman young enough to be his daughter, *Mrs. Ebb-smith* that has warned the Princess of the danger of fixing her affections on a man who was still in the nursery at the time of her first marriage.   But if it is the duty of comedy to illustrate the rules of worldly wisdom, it is its privilege now and then to plead for the exceptions.   Mr. Pinero has in this case turned round upon common-sense with such ingenious casuistry that our sympathies are entirely with the lovers who, in the end, so flatly defy its dictates.   And indeed it would be a prosy world if common-sense always had the laughter all on its side.   Prudence, no doubt, prescribes a due respect for the almanac ; but it is well to be reminded now and again that love laughs at almanacs no less than at locksmiths.

Some time ago, I defined the technical movement of recent years as an advance from the well-made play to the better-made play.   *The Princess and the Butterfly* does not exactly bear out this description. Mr. Pinero recognised, I fancy, that close structure and elaborate intrigue are hostile to the equanimity of comedy, tending always towards drama or farce. He consequently gave more thought to his idea than to his story, and allowed himself ample canvas for his social picture.   Perhaps he gave rather too little thought to his story, and somewhat neglected that foreshadowing which is of no less importance than momentary clearness of presentation. This remark applies especially to the part played by Fay Zuliani in the third act. Looking back, we see a reason for her coldness to the Princess, and the "exceptional" perversity of her conduct, in a vague and instinctive jealousy of the friendship between Sir George and this great lady; but at the time her attitude is quite enigmatic. This renders the end of the third act practically ineffective. We so little foresee what is to come of Fay's midnight escapade that we take no particular interest in it, and are rather disconcerted by the care with which it is led up to and the prominence assigned it. This I regard as the one serious error in the play.

For the rest, its large, easy, undulant, and yet never languid movement is, to my sense, delightful. It obeys no hard-and-fast rules, yet is far from purposeless or lawless. On the contrary, we can trace in it a clear and even symmetrical design. The first two acts are introductory: they place the personages in their environment and state the theme. The first shows us the woman mourning her wasted youth and shuddering on the verge of middle age. Every incident and every character is germane to the central idea and throws a side-light upon it. How admirably imagined, for instance, are the blunders of Oriel, the old young man, and of Lady Chichele, the young old

woman, so serenely happy in her husband's love, even
with the bulk of the world between them, that she
quite forgets what terrors the lapse of years may have
for the "girls" her friends! The second act paints a
companion picture, with the man for its central figure.
The "broken butterfly" is bidding farewell to his
youth; and the bitterest thing of all is that he can no
longer "see any gaiety in this sort of racket"—in
Levan's laboured puerility, in Mylls's affectation of
obsolete vices, in Denstroude's cynical Don Juanism,
or in the shrieking parrot-laugh of Perceval Ord.
The picture of the St. Roche household and its
melancholy head is a superb piece of work.   True, it
reduces the tragedy of middle age to a mere episode
in the satyr-play of brainless idleness, and is thus,
perhaps, not quite in the scheme of the piece; but it
is so actual, so vivid, and so intensely interesting as
to silence all merely theoretical objection.   In the
third act the drama proper sets in, and takes the form
of a quite symmetrical quadrille-figure, though the
symmetry is disguised with delicate art.   There is
more real originality and poetry, to my thinking, in
the scenes between the Princess and Oriel in the
third act than in the scene between Sir George and
Fay in the fourth act, though Fay being admirably
acted, and the Princess (a more difficult part) but
moderately, the more commonplace passage produced
the greater effect.   The comparison, however, is really

uncalled for. All four scenes—the Princess's rejec-
tion of Oriel, her provisional acceptance of Sir George,
her recalling of Oriel to "play, for a month, at
happiness and youth," and the quarrel and reconciliation between Sir George and Fay—all these scenes,
while conceived in the truest spirit of comedy, are at
the same time delicately poetical. Mr. Pinero has
never before attained such distinction of workmanship. The two kisses in which the two acts culminate
sufficiently forecast the course of the final scene. Sir
George and the Princess each thinks that the other is
marrying to escape a purely hypothetical danger. So
soon as each discovers that the other's danger is as
real and imminent as his or her own, they see that
their marriage is impossible, and the compact is at an
end. It is a foregone conclusion, but Mr. Pinero
works it out with a graceful and inventive touch
which makes the last act perhaps the most delightful
of the five. With its atmosphere of spring and sun-
shine, it vaguely recalls the last act of the last play we
saw on these boards—*As You Like It*—and even that
reminiscence does not rob it of its savour.

Immortal though they be, Rosalind and Celia,
Jaques, Touchstone and Orlando are airy and evasive
essences compared with Othello or Lear, Cleopatra
or Lady Macbeth. We cannot demand that comedy
should probe into the depths of character. "In the
reproof of chance" (that is to say, in serious or tragic

situations) "lies the true proof of men"—and women.
The Princess and the Butterfly is comedy unalloyed;
the worst "reproof of chance" with which the characters are even threatened is a marriage of reason
thwarting two marriages of love.   In a word, it ends
in marriage—where tragedy begins.   Therefore we
must not look to it for soul-searching analysis or
extreme solidity of character-projection.   It contains
in abundance all that we have any right to demand—
observation, wit, humour, tenderness, scenic and
literary skill, an animated picture of society, and a
kindly criticism of life.

The acting is good, without surprising merit, except
in one case.   Even Miss Fay Davis, as Fay Zuliani,
though she made, and deserved, a very great success,
did not seem to me in the earlier acts quite the
irrepressible will-o'-the-wisp of Mr. Pinero's imagination.   Her freakishness did not seem temperamental,
bred in the bone.   I saw more in the part on reading
the second act than I had seen in the performance.
It was when the fourth act brought with it a series
of strong emotions that Miss Davis's refined and restrained yet perfectly expressive acting carried all before
it.   She was equally admirable in the fifth act—graceful,
tactful, sincere.   In emotional comedy, if not in
drama, she has certainly a future before her.   Miss
Neilson, as the Princess Pannonia, did more justice
to the majesty than to the tenderness of the character.

Some scenes she played very effectively, but the crucial passages of the third and fifth acts demanded a more supple and sensitive art. Mr. Alexander, polished and graceful throughout, was at his best in the fourth act, where he showed genuine feeling. Mr. H. B. Irving was clever as Edward Oriel; Mr. Esmond was delightful as the luckless Ronald St. Roche; and Miss Rose Leclercq and Mr. Arthur Royston were particularly good as Lady Ringstead and Max Demailly.

XV.

" MADAME SANS-GÊNE "—" OUR HOSTESS."

14th April.

WE are apt to pay Sir Henry Irving the embarrassing compliment of regarding him as a privileged person, and instinctively imposing on him correlative obligations. The Lyceum has for so long been proclaimed, and justly, our leading theatre, and its manager holds by common consent so pre-eminent and representative a position, that we find it difficult to think of the theatre as a commercial enterprise like any other, and the manager as a mere dealer in entertainments. Drury Lane has been ridiculously entitled "the National Theatre" without a shadow of reason, historic or actual. We do not openly apply any such term to the Lyceum, but we involuntarily think of it as a sort of national institution which Sir Henry Irving simply holds in trust. As a matter of fact, the Lyceum is no more a national institution than the Gaiety over the way. Sir Henry Irving enjoys no privileges and is under no obligations. His eminent position has not been conferred upon him, but created by his genius, industry, and tact. If it involves certain advantages (as distinct from privileges), it entails corresponding drawbacks. He is not the depository of any national trust, but simply the inventor and owner of a complex and enormously expensive machine, which he works at his own risk and peril. Thus we have not the smallest right to confront him with what Gregers Werle calls "the claims of the ideal." He has an exceedingly difficult game to play, and he plays it with great spirit and liberality. We may question the wisdom of this move or that; but why assume a tone of reproach, as though in descending to considerations of filthy lucre he were in some way betraying our sacred confidence? If he chose to put on *A Night Out* or revive *Charley's Aunt*, we might wonder, but we should have no cause to complain. The Lyceum is no sacred precinct, dedicate from of old to poetic drama ; and it is absurd for us to feel injured, humiliated, or even surprised if we find Shakespeare, for a season, supplanted by Sardou.

In all probability, *Madame Sans-Gêne** will prove a most attractive entertainment for the Jubilee public. It gives Miss Ellen Terry a rollicking part, through which she gambols delightfully, with a richness of humour and breadth of comic effect which remind one at intervals of Mrs. John Wood. It presents Sir Henry Irving in a great historic character, for which he has obviously no physical fitness, so that people are curious to see how he effects the incredible transformation. It involves a lavish display of costumes and uniforms, and a great deal of scenic movement and bustle. In short, it is quite the play for holiday-making pleasure-seekers, and may very well fill the gap left by the departed *Prisoner of Zenda* and the departing *Red Robe*. It may even be said to take its place with a certain appropriateness among the "record reign" solemnities, for it exemplifies in high perfection the technique of sixty years ago, and is therefore, so to speak, a timely anachronism. Sardou alone, of living men, could have written that deadly last act, in which the worst methods of Monsieur Scribe are resurrected in all their ruthless unreality; and this reflection brings vividly home to us that

* April 10. *The Bells* was played every Saturday evening, beginning May 8. On July 15, 17, and 22 (afternoon), *The Merchant of Venice* was performed. The season closed July 23, with *Madame Sans-Gêne* (first three acts) and *A Story of Waterloo*.

sense of progress which is, I take it, the basis of our jubilations. So long as the intrigue is kept in the background, the play is amusing enough, and the scene between the washerwoman-duchess and the sub-lieutenant-Emperor may rank as one of the most ingenious and amusing pieces of quasi-historic comedy ever written. It is not unworthy of the elder Dumas. But the preparations for the Fouché-Neipperg-Rovigo intrigue cause a tedious break in the fun of the first act, while the working-out of the miserable invention simply devastates the last act. It seemed to me that the actors were as much bored as I was by the childish futility of this scene, the plots and counter-plots that lead to nothing at all, the perpetual movement without the smallest advance. Might not Mr. Comyns Carr, I wonder, have spared us some of this tedium ? He seems to have followed his original ·with a fidelity which would have been most com-mendable had he been dealing with a piece of genuine dramatic literature, but which is perhaps over-scrupulous as applied to a mere vaudeville. I could not but think, too, that he had been over-conscientious at one or two points in reproducing the vulgarities of Madame Sans-Gêne. A vulgarism which may be redeemed in its original language by its racy reality, loses that reality when expressed, even by a carefully-selected equivalent, in another tongue, and is apt to seem frigidly offensive. On the whole, however, Mr. Carr has done his work with tact. He was probably not free to attempt any radical modification of the precious intrigue. When Miss Ellen Terry is perfectly at home in her words, the prologue and the first two acts, in which the intrigue is kept fairly in abeyance, will be very well worth seeing; for Miss Terry is a born comedian and throws herself with immense gusto into this sympathetic part. Sir Henry Irving has reproduced Napoleon's figure with astonishing success; but the head has proved more refractory. The peculiar cut of Napoleon's hair shows the actor's own physiognomy to disadvantage without giving it any plausible resemblance to that of the Emperor. The subordinate parts offer very slight opportunities, but are well enough acted according to the established Lyceum standard. Miss Gertrude Kingston and Miss Julia Arthur look truly magnificent as the Queen of Naples and the Princess of Piombino.

Miss Irene Vanbrugh appeared at the Kilburn Theatre last week in *Our Hostess*, an adaptation by Mr. A. O'D. Bartholeyns of Goldoni's *La Locandiera*. I was curious to see how this charming comedy would come out in English, and therefore devoted an evening to the "Farthest North" of the theatrical world. The adaptor had transferred the action to England and to modern life, with what seemed to me disastrous results; but Miss Vanbrugh showed

agreeable vivacity in a part so unlike the Mirandolina
of the original that it awakened no crushing reminiscences of Eleonora Duse's incomparable creation.

XVI.

" ON LEAVE "—" DR. JOHNSON "—" THE FRENCH MAID."

28th April.

THERE are fashions in buffoonery as in everything
else, and undressing on the open stage has, for the
past two or three years, formed the staple device of
French farce-writers.   These ingenious gentlemen
have outbidden each other in the daring display of
underclothing, and the sansculotte has run riot on the
comic stage, as he did a hundred years ago in the
political arena.   Our adaptors have been surprisingly
tardy in following suit. In *A Night Out*, indeed (as
we are reminded on every hoarding), braces and a
chest-protector play a prominent part; but it has been
reserved for the intrepid Mr. Horner to proceed to
extremities in the way of disrobing.   I was not present
at the first performance of *On Leave** at the Avenue,
when the audience, it appears, showed scant appreciation of the latest Paris fashions as exhibited on the
stage.   Some modifications had been introduced

* April 17—30 (?).

before I saw the piece, and the double exchange of
trousers between Mr. Arthur Playfair and Mr. W. H.
Denny was no longer effected at the very footlights.
Mr. Denny, indeed, was in both instances concealed
from the public gaze, and even Mr. Playfair dissembled
in a certain measure the processes of his toilet. The
incidents were distasteful enough, but not more so,
to my thinking, than the rest of the play. Perhaps I
should blush to confess it, but the fact is that I resent
insults to my intelligence more than outrages upon
my sense of propriety. Had there been any merit in
the clowning, one might have put up with the panta-
loons. The French play, *Le Sursis*, by MM. Sylvane
and Gascogne, seems to have been fairly amusing in a
rough, second-hand way; but to force it, neck and crop,
into an English mould, without the smallest tact or
ingenuity, was to deprive it of all meaning and reduce
it to rank ineptitude. More offensive and malodorous
farces have been applauded in their day by both
press and public. It was the sheer silliness of *On
Leave* that got on the nerves of the audience, and
made them cry out upon the deliberate vulgarity of
the trouser incidents In Paris, where there was
some sort of coherence in the intrigue, the first exchange of clothes went well enough, and the moment
the second was foreseen the audience shrieked with
laughter. There, the repetition of the incident re-
duplicated its comic effect; here, it was justly regarded

as adding insult to injury. Adaptors and managers would do well to take note that the day for sheer imbecility is over. There must be some unusual ability in a French farce (as in *A Night Out*) or some exceptional cleverness in the acting (as in *The Saucy Sally*) if it is to attract the public. We can no longer live on the mere dregs of the French stage.

"Foote," says Boswell, "had resolved to imitate Johnson on the stage, expecting great profits from his ridicule of so celebrated a man. Johnson being informed of his intention, and being at dinner at Mr. Thomas Davies's, the bookseller, from whom I had the story, he asked Mr. Davies 'what was the common price of an oak stick;' and being answered sixpence, 'Why then, sir' (said he), 'give me leave to send your servant to purchase me a shilling one. I'll have a double quantity; for I am told Foote means to *take me off*, as he calls it, and I am determined the fellow shall not do it with impunity.' Davies took care to acquaint Foote of this, which effectually checked the wantonness of the mimic" And again—BOSWELL : "Foote has a singular talent of exhibiting character." JOHNSON : "Sir, it is not a talent; it is a vice; it is what others abstain from." BOSWELL : "Did he not think of exhibiting you, sir?" JOHNSON : "Sir, fear restrained him; he knew I would have broken his bones." If Johnson could come to life again, I should be sorry to insure the bones of

Mr. Leo Trevor, author of the "episode in one act" which now precedes *The Queen's Proctor** at the Strand Theatre. Nor should I greatly care to stand in the shoes of Mr. Arthur Bourchier, who does what Foote feared to do. Both these gentlemen are probably guiltless of intentional irreverence; but between them they do grave injury to a man who holds a unique place in the affections of all who care for literature. It would need the rarest tact, indeed, to give an acceptable stage-portrait of Samuel Johnson; but then, no one is bound to make the attempt. Mr. Trevor has done "what others abstain from," and he has done it with a total absence of tact. Johnson, on arriving at Boswell's house in Edinburgh, is first made to conduct himself with puerile petulance to his host and hostess. Then, being irritated by the sarcasms of a young officer, Mrs. Boswell's cousin, he takes his revenge in a base and abominable innuendo, saying to Boswell, "It seems you have not returned too soon—the soldiery has been making free in your absence." For this he afterwards apologises; but scarcely has he done so when he picks up a letter on the floor, and, though the first word shows him that it is not for him, reads it without a moment's hesitation. Armed with the knowledge thus obtained, he proceeds to an act of gratuitous intermeddling in other

* Revived April 17. *Dr. Johnson* produced April 24. Last night of both, June 8.

people's business, which might have had the most disastrous effects. Of course all comes right in the end ; but none the less has Johnson played the part of an intolerable boor and a shameless and reckless busybody. Rude he was, no doubt, but not childishly and vulgarly brutal; and a busybody he can never have been. We know, as a matter of fact, what occurred on that memorable evening—memorable as the opening scene of the never-to-be-forgotten Tour to the Hebrides : " My wife had tea ready for him, which it is well known he delighted to drink at all hours, particularly when sitting up late. . . . He showed much complacency upon finding that the mistress of the house was so attentive to his singular habit ; and as no man could be more polite when he chose to be so, his address to her was most courteous and engaging; and his conversation soon charmed her into a forgetfulness of his external appearance." How delightful to imagine the scene ! And how impossible to imagine in its place the painful and humiliating episode which Mr. Trevor would substitute for it !

The dialogue contains one or two of Johnson's recorded sayings, but is for the rest hopelessly un-Johnsonian. Any one can use long words feebly ; what Johnson did was to use them forcibly, and sometimes superbly. Modernisms, too, abound. How little Mr. Trevor realises the period is shown in

Johnson's reference to "the laureateship" as the summit of literary ambition. Mr. Bourchier's make-up was ingenious, and there were touches of ability in his acting. For instance, his way of screwing up his eyes in reading, while holding the paper almost against his nose, was cleverly imitated from a well-known portrait. But, influenced no doubt by Mr. Trevor's conception, he made Johnson far too querulous, peevish, and ill-conditioned. His temper was not that of Ursa Major, but of a surly and snapping cur. Miss Sidney Crowe, as Mrs. Boswell, played with delicacy and feeling, but Mr. Fred Thorne's Boswell was an intolerable libel upon that coxcomb of genius. Boswell was vain, pompous, childish, anything you please, but he had the air and address of a gentleman. Mr. Thorne gave him the accent of a pedlar and the appearance of a broker's man.

The new musical farce at Terry's Theatre, entitled *The French Maid*,* is a very fair specimen of its class. There is ingenuity, and even wit of a sort, in Mr. Basil Hood's lyrics; "The Twin Duet," for instance, contains some word-plays that the other Hood would not have disdained. Mr. Walter Slaughter's music, too, is rather more ambitious than is usual in works of this class, without being less tuneful. The plot is exceedingly involved; but we soon give up all hope of following it, and simply take the situations as they

* April 24—still running.

come.   The chief successes in the way of acting were
made by performers whom I presume to have been
members of the country company—Mr. Joseph
Wilson, Mr. Murray King, and Mr. H. O. Clarey,
clever comedians all.   Mr. Eric Lewis and Mr.
Herbert Standing, who have no doubt been imported
into the cast for the London production, either had
inferior parts, or had not found time to work them up.
Miss Kate Cutler played the title-part pleasantly
enough.

XVII.

"The Seats of the Mighty"—"Lost, Stolen,
     or Strayed"—"Mr. Sympkyn"—"John
     Gabriel Borkman."

5th May.

No doubt Mr. Beerbohm Tree merely intends *The
Seats of the Mighty** to "dry the plaster" of his new
and spacious and comfortable theatre ; and no doubt
it will serve that purpose well enough.   If it does
more, all I can say is that chaos has come again,
and that I renounce all hope of ever reading the
riddle of public taste.   I make every effort to place
myself at the right point of view ; I transport myself
in spirit to the balcony, the upper circle, the pit, the

* April 28—June 5.

gallery; and from whatever angle I regard it, I find
The Seats of the Mighty equally empty and equally
dull. This is not a question of liking or disliking a
particular class of play. It would be idle to pretend
that cape-and-sword drama is the one thing of all
others for which my spirit yearns; but when it is
good of its kind it interests and amuses me. *The
Prisoner of Zenda* I liked very much; *The Red Robe*,
though it pleased me less, had obvious elements of
attractiveness; but what *The Seats of the Mighty*
has to commend it, I am at a loss to imagine. It
is not good of its kind, but very much the reverse.
The Prologue, though tedious in itself, promises well
enough. It is like the opening of a second-rate play
of Scribe's. There is even something piquant in the
prophetic Doltaire, who, in 1758, foretells the French
Revolution, even to the tumbrils, the guillotine, and
the head-basket. He is first-cousin to Rameau's
Nephew, with whom, through the intervention of
Brachvogel and Grundy, we made acquaintance in
The Pompadour; but that need not specially dis-
courage us. He sets off to achieve the adventure
of the compromising papers, and though we seem to
have heard of those papers before, we wait in hope
of thrilling developments. But in the succeeding
acts the prophetic Doltaire has become the most
commonplace of villains, the situations have no
ingenuity or necessary sequence, the interest is

frittered away by the introduction of another and
blacker villain with two irrelevant imbeciles in his
train, the scenery becomes gloomy, the effects
mechanical and malodorous, and the whole thing as
flagrant a compilation of pasteboard and saltpetre as
ever, under the guise of " military melodrama," stirred
and half-stifled a transpontine audience. For sheer
effrontery of effect-hunting, it would be hard to beat
Doltaire's searching the pockets of the barber Voban.
He has not the smallest assignable reason for imagin-
ing that Voban is in possession of the papers ; the
inspiration, so far as we can see, must be the result
of clairvoyance; and if we are to take it as another
instance of the occult powers manifested in the
Prologue, how comes it that these powers fail him
in the nick of time, so that Voban is enabled to
transfer the papers from one pocket to another?
In short, there is neither rhyme nor reason in the
incident—the effect is attained (if attained it is) by
the simple process of setting common-sense at defiance. The situation at the end of the act was thrilling
enough to the eye, but had not the least real strength
or interest ; and up to this point I think the audience
quite shared my feeling of profound boredom. The
wildly improbable and theatrical starts and surprises
of the second act seemed to arouse them to interest
and even enthusiasm, and they apparently relished
the sulphurous and explosive catastrophe ; so that,

on the whole, the play passed as a success. It is possible, indeed, that romantic drama is gathering momentum as it rolls downhill, and that *The Seats of the Mighty* may prove all the more popular in virtue of its inferiority to its predecessors of the same school. How it makes one sigh for *Trilby!*

I have not read Mr. Gilbert Parker's novel, but I can quite well see that it may be, and probably is, vastly superior to the play. The old idea that no novel could make a good play has been superseded by an equally mistaken notion that any novel which has run through a certain number of editions can be adapted to the stage. In this case, not only does the play bear unmistakable traces of its narrative origin, but it has not even the redeeming quality of presenting good opportunities to the actors. It is long since we have seen Mr. Tree do anything so commonplace as his Doltaire—the part really gives no scope for intelligent acting. Mrs. Tree is good in a character of very limited opportunities, and Mr. Lewis Waller and Miss Kate Rorke are conventionally effective in parts in which nothing more could possibly be expected of them. The best performance of the evening, to my mind, was Mrs. Tree's clear and graceful delivery of a rhymed address by Mr. Alfred Austin.

In *Lost, Stolen, or Strayed*,* a musical farce pro-

* Afterwards called *A Day in Paris.* April 27—July 10.

duced last week at the Duke of York's Theatre, Mr. J. Cheever Goodwin has so faithfully imitated all the characteristics of the peripatetic school of French vaudeville, of which Labiche's *Chapeau de Paille d'Italie* is the accepted type, that one instinctively ransacks one's memory for a French original. The playbill, however, forbids any such "recherche de la paternité" by applying the term "original" to the piece itself; and in any case the matter is of no possible moment. Whatever its origin, the production is a genuinely comic piece of buffoonery, absolutely without refinement, ingenuity, or any intellectual merit whatever, yet free from deliberate coarseness, and (though it deals with a baby) not even offensively vulgar, as such things go. It makes one laugh mechanically, just as a pinch of snuff makes one sneeze; and in both cases the mere physical spasm is not unrefreshing. In the reckless extravagance of its methods and effects the piece resembles and rivals *A Night Out.* It is lavishly mounted, and cleverly acted by Mr. Frank Wheeler, Mr. J. H. Barnes, Mr. Robb Harwood, Mr. H. De Lange, Mr. Arthur Styan, Miss Ethel Sydney, and Miss Decima Moore.

In the two acts of *Mr. Sympkyn,** by Messrs. A. J. Flaxman and William Younge, which I sat out at the Globe on Saturday night, I could not discover

* May 1—21 (?).

a gleam of cleverness or of reason. It seemed to me unmitigated nonsense, like a nightmare begotten by a surfeit of French farces; but the pit and gallery dutifully laughed at it. Even the acting was third-rate, though Mr. George Shelton contrived to be amusing at points, in a part obviously designed for Mr. Penley.

By the time these lines are published, *John Gabriel Borkman** will have been presented at the Strand Theatre, and the public will doubtless have been assured by a dozen critical authorities that "the last blow has been struck at the Ibsen craze," and that it may be "conveniently buried and consigned to oblivion." I have quite lost count of the number of "last blows" which have been struck at this "craze," and of the deeps within deeps of oblivion to which it has been consigned. Of course such prophecies no longer impose on the meanest intelligence—not even on the prophets themselves. How *John Gabriel Borkman* may affect English audiences I cannot pretend to foresee. A tragedy of wasted lives, it certainly cannot be called inspiriting or recreative; but to my thinking it is much less painful than *Little Eyolf*, and its intensely imaginative and poetic quality gives it a peculiar place in my affections. The second act, with the exquisite humour of the Foldal scene, and the thrilling passion

* May 3—7 (afternoon performances).

of the colloquy between Borkman and Ella, seems
to me one of the greatest things Ibsen has ever
done; the first half of the third act is superb; and
in the last scene of all the poet of *Brand* recaptures
the lyric impetus and fervour of his youth.   Con-
troversy will no doubt rage around the cynical speech
with which Mrs. Wilton bids adieu to the house of
Borkman.   Most people will profess themselves un-
utterably shocked and scandalised, while some will
proclaim it an incomparable stroke of genius.   Both
views seem to me excessive.   I regard the touch as
an artistic error, and regret its presence in the play.
My theory of the matter is that the poet has here
introduced an "anecdote," an incident he has seen
or heard of in real life, and has failed to harmonise
it with its surroundings.   That is the danger of darn-
ing patches of reality upon a fabric of fiction—their
reality is only relative, and unless you exactly reproduce all the antecedents and conditions of the case
(and this is almost always impossible) the anecdotic
fact becomes artistic falsehood.   I have no evidence
to allege in support of my theory, but it seems to
me not improbable.   As for the acting, I must leave
praise or blame to critics who can see the production
in the true, or rather the normal, perspective.   My
occasional attendance at rehearsals, however, while
it disables me from criticising, enables me to bear
emphatic testimony to the unwearying labour and

thought bestowed upon their work by all the artists
concerned—Mr. W. H. Vernon, Mr. James Welch,
Mr. Martin Harvey, Miss Geneviève Ward, Miss
Elizabeth Robins, Mrs. Beerbohm Tree, Miss Dora
Barton, and Miss Marianne Caldwell.

XVIII.

"'CHAND D'HABITS"—"VIRGINIUS."

12th May.

THE really significant "play without words" at Her
Majesty's Theatre on Saturday night was enacted
before, not behind, the curtain.   As episode after
episode of *'Chand d'Habits** passed before our eyes
without for a moment thrilling, touching, or amusing
us, our faces grew gradually longer and longer, until
they wore an expression of utter blankness which
Pierrot himself might have envied.   Then we looked
at each other with a wild surmise, each wondering
whether he alone was devoid of sense for this exquisite form of art.   But, no! like Douglas Jerrold
when he found that his wife understood *Sordello* no
better than he did, we were reassured as to our sanity
by finding our own blankness of expression reflected
in the countenances of all around.   Then those of us
who were not bound by stern duty to our stalls began

* May 8—June 5.

softly and sadly to vanish away, until, at the end of
the second scene, the retreat became a stampede, and
I mentally set it to the music of one of Mr. Henley's
refrains, "Into the night go one and all." This
melancholy exodus was by far the most expressive
piece of pantomime of the evening.

The fate of *'Chand d'Habits* confirms me in my
belief that our alleged taste for French pantomime is
almost entirely an affectation, and that the critics who
write it up are practically (not altogether) in the
position of those who went into ecstasies over the
Emperor's New Clothes. Not altogether, I say; for it
is a very stupid pantomime indeed in which there are
not one or two ingenious and amusing passages to
leaven the mass of dulness. For instance, Signor
Rossi's miming of Lafontaine's fable in *A Pierrot's
Life* gave us three minutes of real and appreciable
pleasure in the course of a long afternoon; we recognised the (quite genuine) cleverness and grace of a
great deal of the remainder; and as the thing was
French, and not to be amused by it might argue us
insular and obtuse, we omitted to note that, cleverness
and grace notwithstanding, we had, on the whole,
been horribly bored by a fundamentally irrational
form of entertainment. Consequently we wrote it
up—"we" collectively, not I personally—and the
management bolstered it up with piquant changes in
the cast, and the thing ran I don't know how many

weeks. A long run, however, may or may not mean
a popular success. All I can say is that I never
met or heard of a single human being to whom *A
Pierrot's Life* had given anything like keen and con-
tinuous pleasure. The case of *L'Enfant Prodigue*
was different. The designers of that piece, by chance
or inspiration, had strung together an almost un-
broken series of ingenious and amusing incidents, so
that it was unique in its kind. The worst one could
say of it was that it had its dull moments : the best
one can say of its successors is that they are not
without their amusing moments. Even of *'Chand
d'Habits* this might have been said if the piece had
gone crisply and the tricks had succeeded. As
was, the mechanism creaked and all the illusions
missed fire. The appearances and disappearances of
the ghost were arranged with a total absence of
ingenuity, and executed with a fatal lack of precision.
It was pitiful to see so expert a pantomimist as Mr.
Lauri, when the cue came for the ghost to vanish,
solemnly stationing himself upon the trap he had
come up by a moment before, and stamping his foot
as a signal to the powers below. The trick which
should have brought the second scene to a close did
not come off at all, and was left to the imagination.
And still less, in another sense, did the sword business at the end "come off." Poor Mr. Lauri's
struggles with the waggling point of steel on which

Pierrot was to be impaled were truly painful to behold. If we are to be entertained with child's-play, at least let it be neat and ingenious of its kind.

But in dwelling on mechanical imperfections and defects of rehearsal, I feel that I am obscuring my real point. If the tricks had gone well, and the thing had been briskly and brightly played, it might, like *A Pierrot's Life*, have passed as a success ; but it would have been thoroughly tedious none the less. It was not the dragging and bungling that bored us ; they merely gave us courage to confess our boredom ; the tedium lay in the miming itself. Pray do not think that I went to the theatre prejudiced against this form of entertainment, and determined to find my prejudice justified. Oddly enough, the reverse was the case—I went with the liveliest anticipations, fully expecting to find *'Chand d'Habits* another and better (because shorter) *Enfant Prodigue.*   I had heard great things of the play and of M. Séverin ; the name of the inventor, Catulle Mendès, excited my interest ; and, above all, I could not doubt that it must be a truly remarkable work which Mr. Tree went out of his way, as it were, to bring into prominence at his new theatre.   Thus my frame of mind, when the curtain rose, was all that author, actor, or manager could possibly desire ; but it had not been up five minutes before the old familiar boredom began to steal over me.   As Pierrot lay on the bench and

Musidora pranced and curvetted around him, I began
to feel that here was an infinite deal of miming to an
infinitesimal modicum of meaning ; and that feeling
grew upon me all through the action.   M. Séverin, to
be sure, is graceful and agile, despite his girth, and
has ample play of feature ; but, frankly, I should as
soon think of calling Mr. Arthur Roberts or Mr. Dan
Leno a "great poetical mime."   In a rough-and-
tumble comic action, lasting twenty minutes at the
outside, M. Séverin would no doubt be vastly
amusing ; and that, I take it, is Pierrot's proper
sphere.   I have not gone into the history of this
branch of pantomime, but I am much mistaken if
the tragic Pierrot—Grimaldi playing Hamlet—be not
a recent development, or corruption, of the pristine
idea.   The French seem to find some subtle irony in
sending Pierrot, with his floury visage, through all
possible scenes and conjunctures of life ; but this
irony does not exist for us.   The whole art-form is
an exotic which cannot really take root here ; and
(except in the rarest instances) the relish we pretend
for it is an affectation and a provincialism.   It is
part of the superstition which declares French acting
better than English, simply because the French have
more gesture and external expression than we have.
It may be true that this renders acting easier to
them ; but I cannot see that an English artist is to
be despised because, if he is to keep within the limits

of nature, he must deny himself some of the means of expression which his French colleague is free to employ. We have dozens of actors (in theatres and music-halls) who, with equal licence of grimace and gesticulation, could rival and perhaps outdo the "great poetical mime" of '*Chand d'Habits.*

If we are to judge by persistence of applause and number of recalls, Mr. Wilson Barrett's Virginius* (at the Lyric Theatre) is a creation beside which Salvini's Othello and Duse's Magda must pale their ineffectual fires. In truth, Mr. Barrett's performance is effective enough in its dry, staccato way; and no doubt this dryness has its advantages as compared with the "fruitiness" of the minor tragedians of a bygone generation. Miss Maud Jeffries made a graceful and pathetic Virginia, and Mr. Franklin McLeay a good Dentatus; but Mr. Edward Irwin's Icilius was curiously spiritless.

XIX.

"SECRET SERVICE"—"A DOLL'S HOUSE"— "HAMLET."

19th May.

LAST Saturday evening brought with it a conflict of duties, or rather—what is much rarer in the

* May 8—20.

experience of a theatrical critic—a competition of pleasures. I wanted to be at the Court, to join in welcoming Mr. Hare back to London after his too long absence; but I wanted no less to be at the Adelphi, where an American company was to present an American drama of the Civil War. Not having acquired the art of disengaging my astral body, I was compelled to make my choice between Chelsea and the Strand; and, truth to tell, the choice was not long a-making. Mr. Hare was secure of his welcome ; my seat would probably be occupied by a louder, though not a heartier, well-wisher ; and *The Hobby-Horse*, after all, was not a new play. At the Adelphi, on the other hand, there was a new play to be seen, a new company and new method to be studied, perhaps a new departure in artistic intercourse with America to be inaugurated. For we see too little of American art on this side of the Atlantic. In exchange for a dozen companies and combinations, the Americans, as a rule, send us only one company, Mr. Daly's ; and individual American artists, when they appear among us, make haste to become Anglicised as much as possible. Thus we are confirmed in that illusion of metropolitanism which is, in fact, the worst form of provincialism. We do not even take the trouble to know what is going on beyond the Atlantic. I myself unreservedly plead guilty to this sin of incuriousness; yet I had somehow gathered—

mainly through my friend Professor Brander Matthews
of New York—that American authors were doing
remarkable work, especially in the domain of popular
drama.   It was under this impression, then, that I
went to the A'delphi, where, for once in a way, the
event more than justified my most sanguine expectations.

  In dealing with *Secret Service*,* we must get rid from
the outset of Adelphi standards.   To call it the best
play we have seen at the Adelphi for many years,
would be to assign it to a wrong class.   It is simply
the best thing of its kind, the best drama of adventure and situation, written within my recollection in
the English language.   Mr. Gillette shows throughout a gift of invention that would do Sardou no
discredit ; he piles situation on situation with almost
too lavish ingenuity ; and he writes with such sobriety,
delicacy, and feeling as to transpose what would
otherwise be crude enough military melodrama into

  * May 15.   Transferred to Comedy Theatre, June 14.   Returned to Adelphi Theatre, July 15.   Last performance of
American company, August 4.   On the following evening it
was acted by an English company (Mr. William Terriss, Miss
Millward, Mr. Harry Nicholls), and ran until September 4.   It
was revived, with the English company, November 24, but the
run was cut short on December 16 by the assassination of Mr.
Terriss.   On the afternoon of Boxing Day (December 27), it
was revived with Mr. Herbert Waring and Miss Mary Whitty
in the leading parts, and ran till January 20, 1898.

the key of literature, almost, one might say, of poetry.
The play is compounded entirely after the popular
formula. There is no character in it—only heroism.
The villain, as in duty bound, is a discarded suitor of
the heroine. At the prescribed point in each act
the stage is cleared for the duet between the comic
lovers. A happy ending is mechanically tagged on
to a tragic theme. All the rules of the game, in
short, are punctiliously observed. But the heroism is
quiet and gentlemanlike, not rampant and robustious.
The villain (and this we may almost call a touch
of realism) is conscientious and virtuous. The
comic lovers are pleasantly imagined, entirely inoffensive, amusing, and even touching. The happy
ending is not insisted on, and is not so very happy after
all. And within the limits imposed by his popular
form, Mr. Gillette shows consummate technique. The
time of action is as compressed as in *John Gabriel
Borkman* itself; the entrances and exits are plausibly,
if not pedantically, motived; there are no soliloquies
or asides; the workmanship throughout is careful,
skilful, finished. Accepting the play for what it is—
a drama of situation devised for popular audiences—
one can scarcely point to a blemish in it, whether of
technique or of taste.

It is true that, in order to make a popular play,
Mr. Gillette had to mar a really fine theme   There
is no more tragic situation conceivable than that of

the man (or woman) detached upon " secret service."
It may be necessary, it may be heroic ; but it belongs
to the " dirty work " of the world, and, for poetic
purposes, death alone can purge the stain it leaves
on character. Mr. Gillette, indeed, seems to have
felt this ; for, throughout his play, one little word
trembles on every one's lips, and no one, so far as
I heard, dares to utter it—the scathing monosyllable
" Spy." All that Colonel Dumont says to Edith in
his own defence is true enough, and admirable in its
sober brevity. True, the spy takes his life in his
hands, renounces glory, and affronts a shameful
death. True, he requires the rarest courage, resource, and devotion. But the fact remains that
part of his courage is the courage to be base, and
that the height of his devotion is to be measured by
the depth of his treachery. Any personal advantage
he may reap through his mission must be tainted,
like the thirty pieces of silver which repaid a piece
of secret service nineteen hundred years ago ; and
a " happy ending " to his saga is, as it were, a personal advantage which the traitor-hero of romance
ought not to allow himself. We see, indeed, that
even Mr. Gillette's ingenuity cannot secure a happy
ending except at the cost of making his hero doubly
a traitor. When the actual crisis comes, at the end
of the third act, he betrays the North for no better
reason than that it is the woman he loves who has

placed it in his power to betray the South. This is paltry sentimentality on his part, and President Lincoln would have been justified in shooting him simply because President Davis had spared his life. No! the logic of the theme demanded that he should send the false telegram, and should then, in the fourth act, confess to Edith and expiate his fidelity to the Stars-and-Stripes by refusing to take advantage of the chance of escape she offers him. The incident of the cartridges is moving and beautiful, but I confess I am bloodthirsty enough to wish that, having reloaded, the corporal's guard had marched him off and done their duty. Edith would then have had the consolation of reflecting that "His honour rooted in dishonour stood," and the play would have been a work of art, and not a popular drama. Sardou, in *Fédora*, realised the artistic necessity of giving a tragic end to a drama of treachery—or was it merely the business necessity of giving Sarah Bernhardt a death-scene?

But I must not end on a note of disparagement. A fortnight ago, speaking of *The Seats of the Mighty*, I protested that I had no theoretical dislike to romantic drama, if only it was good of its kind. Here, then, is a case in point. Here is an admirable play of its kind, and I desire to say so with all possible emphasis. There are occasions when comparison, however ungracious, affords the only means

of showing a thing in its due proportion and perspective. Therefore I do not disguise my feeling that
no home-made romantic drama within my recollection shows anything like the originality of invention
or delicacy of touch displayed in *Secret Service*. It
is by no means a play for the Adelphi public alone.
It ought to be seen by every one who cares for
skilful and tactful dramatic story-telling.

The acting, too, is most interesting, and in the
case of Mr. Gillette himself, quietly original and impressive. Miss Blanche Walsh is good as the heroine,
Mr. Campbell Gollan shows real skill as the villain,
and the juvenile lovers are delightfully played by Mr.
Henry Woodruff and Miss Odette Tyler. There is
perhaps rather too much " snap " and precision in
the stage-management ; it smacks too much of the
drill-sergeant ; but this is at least excusable in a
military drama.

Many people thought that Miss Achurch's performance in last week's revival of *A Doll's House** by
the Independent Theatre was the finest she had ever
given. Perhaps it was ; but I must own to a rooted
prejudice in favour of the old Nora, the Nora of
1889. So clear and detailed is my remembrance of
that creation, that it necessarily renders me unjust
to the Nora of to-day. Every divergence from the
old reading, were it never so great an improvement,

* May 10—14 (afternoon performances).

would jar on me simply as a thing new and unexpected. I shall say nothing, then, except that in
the last act there were some admirable passages in
which the Nora of the Novelty lived again. In the
first act, at the moment when Nora realises that
Krogstad has discovered the forgery, I thought—
but surely my ears deceived me—that Miss Achurch
gave a long, low whistle. Seriously, the thing seems
impossible; and I shall be more relieved than surprised to learn that I was mistaken. If not—if Miss
Achurch has deliberately selected that method of
interpreting Nora's emotion—let me beg her to reconsider the point. Excellent as was Mr. Waring's
Helmer in the original production, I think Mr.
Courtenay Thorpe's was, or with a little more preparation might have been, even better. Mr. Thorpe
was very uncertain in his words, so that it was hard
to tell when his pauses and hesitations were intentional, and when they were merely devices to cloak a
lapse of memory. I am inclined to think that a
certain measure of undue deliberation belonged to
Mr. Thorpe's conception of the character, and I am
sure that he overdid the very well-conceived simper
of self-satisfaction with which he endowed the
egregious Torvald. Otherwise, his performance was
excellent, an original character-study, and, in the
last act, luminous and daring. It justified Nora's
action more thoroughly than did Mr. Waring's; one

felt it really impossible for her to come to terms with this weakly violent egoist. Mr. Charrington resumed his old part of Rank, and played it effectively; but the music which accompanies his last scene with Nora is a great mistake. Mr. Fulton's Krogstad promised excellently, but became too rough and loud as his scenes went on. The children were very cleverly played by Misses Ethel Rayner and Maud Evelyn, and their scene went admirably.

Mr. Ben Greet's "cheap Shakespeare" season at the Olympic opened last week with a highly meritorious performance of *Hamlet.** Mr. Nutcombe Gould is an imposing and quite intelligent Hamlet, by no means brilliant or poetical, but equally remote from ill-taste or eccentricity. I know how hopeless it is, but, simply to unburden my own conscience, I would beg him to give more attention to verbal and syllabic accuracy in his delivery of the text. He found in Miss Lily Hanbury an Ophelia of proportionate stature and talent. Her rendering of the part was competent rather than exquisite, but competent it was; and her mad scene, if not pathetic, was distinctly clever. Mr. Courtenay Thorpe again distinguished himself as the Ghost; Mr. Ben Greet made an amusing Polonius, and Mr. G. R. Foss was a spirited Laertes. I did not notice any very striking talent in the other performers, but they were all well up to their work.

* May 10—25.

XX.

"THE HOBBY-HORSE"—"A COURT OF HONOUR"
—"BELLE BELAIR"—"THE WILD DUCK"—
FRENCH PERFORMANCES—"OTHELLO."

26th May.

THERE is only one word for Mr. Hare's revival of
The Hobby-Horse* at the Court Theatre, and that word
is—delightful. I don't know when I have spent so
refreshing an evening in the theatre. It is just the
play for this season, keeping the audience in a cool
ripple of amusement, not plunging it, like a roaring
farce, into a vapour-bath of gross laughter. Here is
an instance—they are not infrequent—of a play that
has improved with keeping. When it was new, eleven
years ago, I fancy we treated it rather churlishly.
What I myself said of it I do not remember; but
certainly the impression I had retained of it did not
lead me to anticipate the pleasure with which I saw it
again. We came to it, probably, with too definite
and exacting expectations. It was called a comedy,
and thus distinguished from the farces with which
Mr. Pinero had just been regaling us; it purported,
moreover, to have a satiric purpose; but we somehow
could not refer it to any known class of comedy, and
the satiric purpose seemed to be, like Mr. Chevy

* May 15—June 4.

Slime in *Martin Chuzzlewit*, always "round the corner," but never visible and tangible. Now that we are no longer bound to classify it and make up our minds about it, these troubles vanish. If a docket it must have, let us call it a fantastic comedy or comic fantasy. The fable is certainly improbable, the long arm of coincidence intervening rather obtrusively; and the dialogue is distinctly tinged with deliberate quaintness. Its wording is ingenious and admirable; Mr. Pinero's literary skill has never, perhaps, been more happily manifest; but the conscious humorist has throughout the upper hand of the conscientious dramatist, so that the play, though decidedly not a farce, must be called a comedy with a difference. As for the satiric purpose, it escapes me as much as ever; but I now do not care a jot about it. There seems to be some intention of satire either upon philanthropy in general or upon philanthropy as restricted to a particular class, the philanthropist's hobby. But all that is really shown, so far as I can make out, is that a lady who cannot endure bad smells ought not to try slumming, and that "decayed jockeys" and deserving jockeys are not always synonymous. I prefer, then, to ignore the satiric purpose (of which, after all, Mr. Pinero may be quite innocent), and simply to enjoy the pleasant embarrassments arising from a conjuncture of self-will and unwisdom with mischievous chance.

The whole fabric of the play glisters and sparkles with happy humour. You are sorry when it is over, and you have to bid good-bye to these whimsical creatures of a genial fantasy. And it was actually called cynical when it was new!

Oddly enough, it distinctly gains by being not quite so well played as it was at first. Mr. Waring, as the Rev. Noel Brice, and Mrs. Kendal as Mrs. Jermyn, made the "clerical error" on which the second and third acts turn a little too serious and distressing. Mr. Waring excited our sympathies too vividly, and Mrs. Kendal's dignity and feeling were out of place in so fantastic a situation. Mr. Frank Gillmore and Miss May Harvey play these parts well, yet not too well. They do not make them painfully real to us. Mr. Fred Kerr's Pinching is a capital piece of comedy, and Miss Mona Oram, being less subtle and more straightforward than Mrs. Tree, makes Constance Moxon less real and more agreeable. Mr. Hare's Spencer Jermyn was delightful from the first, and is as good as ever; Mr. Charles Groves is excellent as Shattock; Mr. Gilbert Hare is bright and pleasant as Tom Clarke. Mrs. Porcher alone— a creation which would render *The Hobby-Horse* memorable if it had not another point in its favour —has fallen on evil days. Miss Susie Vaughan makes her a conventional caricature; in the hands of the late Mrs. Gaston Murray she was a portrait from the life.

The British Drama has been enriched during the past week with two original plays: *A Court of Honour*,* by Messrs. John Lart and Charles Dickinson, at the Royalty, and *Belle Belair*,† by Mr. Ralph Lumley, at the Avenue.   In each case well-known and doubtless well-paid actors have been engaged; in each case the management has evidently gone to great expense in mounting and dresses; and in each case it ought to have been manifest to any one of ordinary competence, on merely reading the manuscript, that nothing short of a miracle could make the play a success.   And every year sees at least a score of such productions. The regret is foolish and unprofitable, I know; but I cannot help thinking now and then what a magnificent Endowed Theatre we could have if only we could somehow impound the money squandered year by year on enterprises which have not from the outset a glimmer of hope in them.

Let me hasten to say that, in so classing these two plays, I am recklessly backing my own judgment. They were both received with unmixed and unstinted applause by the first-night audience, or, in the consecrated phrase, "produced with every appearance of success."   I have not happened to see what other critics have said of them.   I rely entirely on my own feeling that there is not enough matter in them, not enough attractiveness of any sort, legitimate or

* May 18—June 5 (?).   † May 19—29.

illegitimate, to enable them to compete with other entertainments. It is not precisely that they are bad plays. Worse plays, not only morally but artistically, have oftentimes succeeded. The trouble is simply that there is no vitality in them. They mean nothing, and are nothing. They do not really exist.

Messrs. Lart and Dickinson evidently started out with the best intentions, even, one may say, with a highly creditable ambition. They wanted to write a serious, elevated, emotional drama, culminating in a scene of great power and originality—for so they no doubt described to themselves the "Court of Honour" which gives the play its name. Unfortunately, their way of working up to this effect was to pile psychological inconsequences on physical improbabilities, to animate their characters with the conventional idealisms and cynicisms of fourth-rate fiction, and to make them talk a strange high-flown jargon, probably intended for "literary" dialogue. And when the Court of Honour was at last reached it proved to be novel enough, indeed, but only in virtue of its solemn absurdity. The authors, in short, had gone to the theatre, not to life, for their material, yet, in their studies of the theatre, had not even learnt the trick of theatrical effect. Mr. Fred Terry and Miss Calhoun, Mr. Abingdon and Mr. Fulton, entered heart and soul into their parts, and the first-night success was entirely due to their sincerity and fervour.

Mr. Lumley's *Belle Belair* is a much less ambitious and, in some ways, a more able piece of work. Its fault is its exceeding tenuity both of motive and of workmanship. The story of the children changed at birth is incalculably ancient, violently improbable, and inexpressibly uninteresting. Never was a more trumpery theme hammered out over four acts. Mr. Pinero once defined a comedy as "a farce by a deceased author;" Mr. Lumley's definition seems to be, "a farce which is not funny." True, he calls his play simply a "play," not a comedy; but a trick of nomenclature, though it may baffle criticism, cannot allay boredom. There are, however, some amusing scenes and episodes in the nondescript production, and Mrs. John Wood and Mr. Weedon Grossmith, two of the best, if not the two best, comedians of our day, seize upon every opportunity offered them. Mr. Martin Harvey, a young actor of versatile talent, is excellent in a colourless part; and Mr. John Beauchamp, Mr. Athol Forde, Miss Irene Vanbrugh, and Miss Louise Moody are all good.

If they have done nothing else, the Independent Theatre Ibsen performances at the Globe have brought into prominence the remarkable intelligence and originality of Mr. Courtenay Thorpe. His Gregers Werle in *The Wild Duck** was a very spirited sketch

* May 17—21 (afternoon performances). See *Theatrical World of 1894*, p. 136.

of a very difficult part. It suffered, like his Helmer, from hasty preparation, and there were touches in it which seemed to me misconceived; but, whatever its defects, it was a most able effort at character-creation. Mr. Laurence Irving showed a very intelligent appreciation of the humour of Hialmar Ekdal, but his technical resources are as yet scarcely adequate to such an exacting part. Mr. James Welch was good as old Ekdal, but did not bring out the character so clearly as I should have expected. Mr. Charrington gave a marked physiognomy to Relling, and Mr. Leonard Outram was good as old Werle. Miss Kate Phillips was rather out of her element in the part of Gina, but Miss Ffolliott Paget was excellent as Mrs. Sörby, and Miss Winifred Fraser repeated her pathetically beautiful rendering of little Hedvig. The whole production suffered, on the first afternoon, from insufficient rehearsal, the last two acts in particular dragging deplorably.

Though I have not been able to follow Mlle. Jane May's performances at the Royalty* so assiduously

---

* In the course of her season (May 17—June 12), Mlle. Jane May produced *La Petite Fadette*, *À ce Soir*, *Comme elles sont toutes*, *Le Corbeau et le Renard*, *Le Monde où l'on s'ennuie*, *Monsieur et Madame Pierrot*, *Pauvre Petit*, *Le Gamin de Paris*, *Un Mari dans du Coton*, *Les Amours de Cléopatre*, *Les Premiers Armes de Pierrot*, *Si jamais je te pince*, *En bonne Fortune*. The Censor vetoed *Le Fiacre 117*.

as I should have wished, I can testify that this charming actress has lost none of her freshness and piquancy. Her imitation of Sarah Bernhardt in *À ce Soir!* is by no means the best we have seen, but the burlesque as a whole is gay and amusing, and M. Didier is excellent as the Director. Of *Le Monde où l'on s'ennuie*, I saw enough to assure me that the performance was good all round, and that Mlle. Jane May was still an ideal Suzanne. On the other hand, I cannot say that her two performances in dumb show —*Le Corbeau et le Renard* and *Monsieur et Madame Pierrot*—have cured me of my heresies regarding this form of art.

Mr. Wilson Barrett appeared as Othello* at the Lyric Theatre on Saturday evening, amid the usual scene of enthusiasm,—treble and quadruple recalls, speech, and all the rest of it. His treatment of the part was devoid of poetry or elevation, but sufficiently intelligent and dramatic to interest the uncritical spectator. One must gratefully admit, indeed, that there is life and movement in the whole revival. A distinguished performance it is not, either on the part of Mr. Barrett or of his comrades; but at least it is not a dead-alive spectacular solemnity. One could forgive the dry superficiality of Mr. Barrett's emotional expression, if his diction were not so painfully faulty. He inordinately elongates one syllable

* May 22—29.

in a line—generally an unimportant one, a preposition or a prefix—and huddles all the rest together, as though he felt he had lingered too long over his favourite *on* or *un*, and must needs make up for lost time. These meaningless retardations and accelerations are very distressing when applied to Shakespeare's verse, and complicated by the hollow throat-voice which Mr. Barrett assumes in emotional passages. He speaks the words of the part with tolerable accuracy; I presume "Away at once with *either* love or jealousy" was a momentary slip of the tongue. But it cannot have been a slip of the tongue that led him to spoil the most magnificent dramatic invention in all Shakespeare, by saying—

> " I took by the throat the circumcised dog
> And smote him—thus—*thus !* "

This reduplication is quite indefensible. The whole point of the thing lies in the lightning-like suddenness *and singleness*, so to speak, of the word and the blow. Miss Maud Jeffries made a pleasant but not very poetical Desdemona ; Mr. Franklin McLeay was a rather too straightforward Iago (but that is a better fault than over-subtlety) ; Mr. Ambrose Manning was a capital Roderigo ; and Miss Frances Ivor played Emilia with force and discretion.

XXI.

THE HUMOUR OF "THE WILD DUCK."

St. Paul's, 29th May.

OF all the amazing delusions that ever entered mortal brain, the most astounding, surely, is the idea that Ibsen has no humour, and that, when he writes a comic speech or scene, he does not intend it to be laughed at. It is true that many people pretend to be under this delusion simply because they find it the most convenient way of keeping up the Anti-Ibsen superstition. They are not by any means such fools as they look. Hating Ibsen with the utmost sincerity, they think it their bounden duty to discredit him by every means in their power; and one of the easiest methods, and quite the astutest, is to pretend that they triumph over him when they laugh at his comic characters and scenes. The trick is rendered to some extent plausible by the fact that Ibsen blends the comic and the tragic elements of life more intimately than other dramatists.

Take for instance *The Wild Duck*, acted last week by the Independent Theatre Society. If there ever was a comic character in literature, or on the stage, that character is Hialmar Ekdal. He is comic to the point of caricature. Ibsen has concentrated in his single person every ridiculous feature of naïve and pretentious egoism, and has deliberately placed him in a series of the most ludicrous situations. He is as comic as Sancho Panza, or Malvolio, or Mr. Micawber. The actor who should fail to keep the theatre in a roar at his monstrous selfishness and laziness, and posing self-pity, would be a bungler indeed.

Here are one or two of his traits : He has promised to bring home some sweets for his little daughter from the dinner-party he has been at, and having forgotten them, he thinks to make up to her by producing the menu of the feast. "Sit down and read it," he says, "and I'll describe to you how the dishes taste." He tells how his father, when confronted with disgrace, put a pistol to his head, but had not the courage to fire. "Can you understand it?" he cries : "he, a soldier! He who had shot nine bears, and was descended from two lieutenant-colonels—one after the other, of course!" Then in the next breath he goes on to tell how, when his father was condemned, he, Hialmar, pointed the same pistol at his own breast. "But you didn't fire?" says Gregers. "No," he replies: "at the decisive moment I won the victory over myself. I remained in life. I can assure you it takes some courage to choose life under those circumstances." These are fair specimens of his sayings and doings throughout the play. I think the caricature is laid on a little too thick, especially about the lieutenant-colonels. But can anything be more obvious than their comic intention?

Here, now, is the *Daily Telegraph* criticism of the Independent Theatre performance : "Why was it that an outburst of irreverent laughter unduly disturbed the reverential attitude of the Ibsenites? But so it was, and as ill-luck would have it the 'Master' laid himself out all the afternoon for ribald jests. . . . No one was able to decide if *The Wild Duck* is the very funniest play ever written, or a desperately serious problem. Has Ibsen any sense of humour at all, or is he the funniest fellow who ever put pen to paper? Is he poking fun at us all as is done in the most brilliant fashion by his very cleverest supporter? For our own part, since Mr. W. S. Gilbert wrote *Engaged* and *Tom Cobb*, no play was ever written so exquisitely ludicrous as *The Wild Duck*. We shrewdly suspect that Mr. Laurence Irving shares our opinion, for he played Hialmar Ekdal, the sublime egoist, so magnificently that the house pealed with laughter."

Of course, as I said before, the writer of this notice is not nearly so stupid as he pretends to be. He is simply carrying on the Anti-Ibsen campaign with what he regards as fine tactical address. The day for foul-mouthed abuse is past, and a subtler policy is now demanded. What can be simpler, and with the great public more effective, than to give out that the laughter, for which Ibsen is bidding all through with almost inartistic emphasis, is "ribald" laughter at "the Master's" expense? Simple the method is, undoubtedly; but what should we think of a critic who wrote of *Henry IV.*: "Has Mr. Shakespeare no sense of humour at all, or is he the funniest fellow who ever put pen to paper? We shrewdly suspect that Mr. Beerbohm Tree shares our opinion, for he played Sir John Falstaff, the sublime egoist, so magnificently that the house pealed with laughter." Do not accuse me of burlesquing the critic's deliverances. The substitution of Falstaff for Ekdal does not make the criticism one whit more ridiculous.

The simple fact is that *The Wild Duck*, as this gentleman quite justly says, is one of the most "exquisitely ludicrous" plays ever written. Its humour is bitter and brutal, if you like. Tell me that the laughter which Ibsen here wrings from you is disagreeable and depressing, and I don't for a moment deny it; but tell me that you are laughing not at Hialmar Ekdal but at Henrik Ibsen, and you place me in the painful dilemma of having to doubt either your candour or your intelligence. To me, I own, the play would be almost intolerably Swiftian were it not for the pathetic figure of little Hedvig, a creation of absolute beauty and tenderness. Yet Hedvig serves rather to emphasise than to relieve the grim comedy of her surroundings, and in the ultimate effect of the play, laughter—the harsh laughter of disillusionment—largely predominates.

This strange idea that one must never laugh at the work of a man who is nothing if not a great humorist, crops up in the strangest quarters. Not long ago a most intelligent and able comedian was studying a part in one of Ibsen's plays, which he ultimately played to perfection, and with great applause. In the course of the rehearsals he came to me with a good deal of embarrassment, mentioned one of the most delightfully humorous lines in his part, and said, "Aren't you a little afraid of this? Don't you think they'll laugh at it?" "Good heavens!" I said, "I should hope so! What do you expect them to do? It's a deliciously funny line, and if they don't laugh at it you'll miss your effect altogether." "Oh!!" he said, relieved, but at the same time surprised. The line, as a matter of fact, "went" exceedingly well; it was one of the gems of the part; but the actor would have been quite content to have had it altered or cut out, no doubt because the Anti-Ibsenite critics had industriously dinned in his ears that laughter at "the Master's" plays must necessarily be "ribald" and "irreverent."

I am far from meaning that at Ibsen performances the public never laughs in the wrong place. Details of Norwegian manners are apt to strike people as comic, for, globe-trotters though we be, we English are full of that provincialism which cannot

distinguish the unaccustomed from the ludicrous.
There are cases, too, no doubt, in which things
beautiful and touching in themselves strike a chord
of vulgarity in the public and are greeted with guffaws.
At the moment I can think only of Mrs. Solness and
her dolls; other instances may perhaps occur to my
readers. But as a matter of fact, inopportune laughter
is far less to be dreaded at Ibsen performances than
the absurd notion so carefully fostered by the Anti-
Ibsenite faction that they are solemnities at which it
is profanation to smile. I would beg playgoers to
take heart of grace and believe that when Ibsen
draws a comic character he intends him to be
laughed at.

XXII.

SHAKESPEARE AT THE OLYMPIC.

2nd June.

IT is curious to note how Lyceum methods are
penetrating — not to say vitiating — our treatment
of Shakespeare on every hand. One might have
imagined that Mr. Ben Greet, being, by the very
nature of his enterprise, dispensed from the obliga-
tion of scenic display, would revel in his freedom
and seize the opportunity to let Shakespeare tell his
own story after his own fashion. But not a bit of
it ! We must have all the drawbacks of a spectacular

Lyceum setting without its beauties. The first two acts must be remodelled so that almost their whole action may pass in one "set," a roughly effective but topographically absurd representation of the Piazzetto and a corner of the Riva, with the Doge's Palace in the background. To this end, all the Belmont episodes are crowded together in the third act, in which Portia makes her first appearance; while the precious scene for which so much is sacrificed becomes as conventional as the "street" of a classic comedy, and it finally appears that Shylock is the Doge's next-door neighbour! And then, because Sir Henry Irving at the Lyceum fills up pauses in the action with living pictures of street life—gondolas coming and going, fruit-sellers, maskers, and what not—Mr. Greet, with a handful of supers and ballet-dancers, must needs essay the same effects. Even at the best, with all Sir Henry Irving's resources and stage-management, these interludes are of questionable advantage. To fill a street-scene with life and bustle for a moment is merely to emphasise its emptiness when the stage is cleared for action, and some necessary question of the play is then to be considered. But Mr. Greet, with his small resources, cannot even for a moment attain any real effect of life and bustle. After Antonio, Shylock, and Bassanio have had the whole scene to themselves—the very central point of

Venice, be it noted—for as long as they require it, the Venetian populace heaves in sight in the persons of two small boys! What can be the use of this, save to throw into relief the unreality of the whole thing? And the hopelessly unconvincing revels of the very limited ballet-corps serve precisely the same purpose. Mr. Greet doubtless knows his business, and has found that this aping of the Lyceum impresses country audiences; all I can say is that the effects are childish in themselves, and afford no artistic compensation for the reckless rearrangement of the text which they involve. Similarly, in mounting *Romeo and Juliet* at Camberwell last year, Mr. Greet carefully reproduced the Lyceum setting of the tomb-scene, placing Juliet on a lofty bier in front, and making Romeo enter from the back. This setting is, to my thinking, bad at best, and obviously the reverse of what Shakespeare had in mind. It may be defensible, however, on a large stage and when Mrs. Patrick Campbell is the Juliet. On a smaller stage, and with a less exquisite Juliet to occupy the obstructive bier, there is absolutely nothing to be said for it. Mr. Greet would do very much better for art, and no worse, I am sure, for himself, if he frankly accepted the situation and said to his public: " I cannot give you Lyceum archæology and luxury, but I can give you what is not to be had at the Lyceum—Shakespeare's

scenes, not more than necessarily abridged, and in
the order in which he wrote them."

Apart from this scenic pretentiousness, the rendering of the *Merchant of Venice* * is by no means a
bad one.   Mr. Nutcombe Gould's Shylock is more
impressive to the eye than thrilling to the dramatic
sense.   His physique assigns him to the Kemble
rather than the Kean school of actors, the school
of dignity rather than of passion.   It is not for
a moment imaginable that Shakespeare pictured
Shylock at all as Mr. Gould presents him.   The
red-haired comic Hebrew of pre-Macklin days was
liker Shakespeare's conception of the man.   The
brutality of Antonio's conduct to Shylock becomes
doubly incredible when that eminent financier wears
the aspect of a prophet from the Sistine Chapel.
But Mr. Gould speaks his lines like a man of
intelligence and culture (with a slightly defective
ear for verse), and does not offend us by affectations
or vulgarities.   Whether purposely or not, he indicated a piece of "business" which struck me as
good.   In addressing Antonio shortly before he
proposes the bond, he happens to touch him on
the breast, and Antonio draws away with a marked
gesture of disgust.   The idea conveyed to me was
that it was this which suggested to Shylock the
"merry sport" about the pound of flesh.   Mr.

* May 26—29; June 9 (afternoon); and June 11 and 12.

Gould had probably no such design, or he would have timed the touch differently and brought out the idea more clearly; but it struck me as a possible and not ineffective method of giving a little greater plausibility to the incident.   Miss Lily Hanbury made a stately Portia, and delivered her speeches with just emphasis.   Charles Macklin and his daughter are said to have been estranged for years by a quarrel as to the correct way of speaking one phrase in the address on Mercy.   Miss Macklin insisted on saying, "'Tis mightiest in the *mightiest;*" her father maintained that it should be, "'Tis mightiest *in* the mightiest."   Miss Hanbury follows Macklin, and in so doing she has superficial logic as well as authority on her side.   But, to my thinking, this is a case in which poetic feeling should override logic.   There is a petty rationalism about "'Tis mightiest *in* the mightiest;" it is argumentative, not emotional; it has a tone of retort, not of appeal; it almost implies some previous allusion to "the mightiest," expressed or understood.   If Miss Macklin spoke the words smoothly, with an equal emphasis on the two "mightiests," I think hers was the better way. The phrase would arise in Portia's mind, I take it, "full-formed, like Venus rising from the sea," and she would not trouble about its anatomy and articulation, but simply make the most of its beauty.

Portia, after all, was a woman ; her rhetoric came from the heart, not from the schools ; so that in this case Miss Macklin's instinct was perhaps more to be trusted than her father's logic.   But I must apologise for discussing at such length a mere point of diction—an art in which no one nowadays takes the slightest interest.

I spoke some weeks ago of Mr. Louis Calvert's production of *Antony and Cleopatra*,† which has now been transferred from the Queen's Theatre, Manchester, to the Olympic.   The most important change in the cast is the substitution of Mr. Alfred Kendrick for Mr. George Black as Octavius.   Mr. Kendrick (who also makes a very pleasant Bassanio in *The Merchant of Venice*) gives us no cause to regret the change ; but he speaks much too loudly the last words of the play, "And then to Rome !" Miss Achurch, as Cleopatra, seemed to me to have improved a good deal in the earlier scenes ; if her performance as a whole does not quite rise to the ideal of the character, let her remember that Eleonora Duse herself fell equally short of it.   Miss Achurch, by-the-bye, like Duse and Miss Rehan,

† May 24, 25, 27, 28, 29, and June 5 (afternoon performances). June 1—5 (evening performances).   *Macbeth* was also performed (Macbeth, Mr. Louis Calvert; Lady Macbeth, Miss Laura Johnson) on May 31 and June 7—10, with afternoon performances on June 2 and 12.

indulges very daringly in inarticulate noises. I wish
—forgive the jingle—that she would let us substitute
"sparingly" for "daringly." These audacities are
seldom felicities. The scenery (painted by local
Manchester artists) comes out very effectively on
the Olympic stage. Even Mr. Calvert, I think,
succumbs to the Lyceum influence towards the
close of the production, and sacrifices Shakespeare
to spectacle and that "incidental music" on which
Sir Henry Irving has been discoursing so pleasantly.
There were times, in the later acts, when we seemed
to have been transported from the Olympic and
Antony and Cleopatra to Covent Garden and *Aïda*.
Even Cleopatra's "business" was timed to the
music, and one would scarcely have been surprised
if Miss Achurch, who is always rather inclined to
chant her words, had broken out into a "recitative
and aria."

XXIII.

"Settled out of Court "—"The Maid of
Athens "—" Les Amours de Cléopatre."

9th June.

Miss Estelle Burney, who evidently possesses a
good deal of dramatic instinct, has conceived the

idea of confronting in the same play two antagonistic
types of feminine character—bringing the impenitent
Mrs. Tanqueray face to face with the penitent Mrs.
Haller. The title she has chosen, *Settled out of Court*,*
does her work some injustice. It is quibbling and
frivolous, whereas the play is tragical or nothing; but
we feel at the same time that a really good title, a
durable title, so to speak, would have been wasted on
work which is certainly tentative and immature. Miss
Burney has both observations and ideas, but she does
not yet know how to present and marshal them.
Her central character, a morbidly passionate and
morbidly conscientious woman, is well conceived.
There is even a touch of poetry in the idea of making
the moral phantoms which beset a narrow and ill-
regulated intelligence assume the guise of physical
hauntings and hound their victim into madness. It
is not only on deeds of violence that the Eumenides
attend. They are the emanations of a sickly conscience, and it matters little whether the offence
which nominally engenders them be great or small,
real or imaginary. Moyra's fate, then—and this is
subtle and true—is of her own making. She conjures
up the disaster that finally descends upon her. If
she could take a sane view of things, and dismiss
from her mind the superstition of punitive forces,
stealthy and inexorable, reducing life to a goody-

* Globe Theatre, June 3 (afternoon).

goody anecdote, with the moral printed in red, she might quite well retain her husband's love (such as it is) and live and die as happy as any one else. In the larger sense, no doubt, life *is* a moral anecdote; but the sins which are punished in this case (if Moyra could only be got to see it) are not her individual misdeeds, but the sins of her ancestors, who gave her an ill-balanced brain, and of her pastors and masters, who, to say the least of it, did nothing to restore equilibrium. Moyra, of course, cannot be got to see it on this side of the grave; but the main defect of the play is that we cannot even tell whether Miss Burney sees it. At some expense of imagination, I have disengaged what I take to be her theme; she has not had the art to make it, what it ought to have been, evident yet not obtrusive. I say her theme, be it noted, not her thesis; there is all the difference in the world between the two things. No dramatist is bound to teach a lesson; but we inevitably require that he or she should indicate a point of view. Miss Burney having failed to do so with any distinctness, we have at times an uneasy feeling that she is painting these sordid scenes for their own sake, and taking pleasure in exhibiting a knowledge of the world which is little more than cynical knowingness. This suspicion, I am sure, is quite unjust; it arises simply from the fact that Miss Burney stands too close to her characters and has not the art to see them, and make us see them, in a truly significant perspective.

Again, Miss Burney has not achieved the very difficult feat of lending variety to a monotonous character. It is essential that we should realise how Moyra's eternal self-torturing depression gets upon her husband's nerves, but it is no less essential that it should not get upon our nerves. Only a highly-skilled dramatist could achieve this paradoxical task; Miss Burney may one day acquire the skill, but as yet she has it not. She fails, indeed, in a very much simpler point of technique—the carrying on of the interest from one act to the next. Her first and second acts are little plays in themselves; in each case, after the curtain has fallen, there is no imperative reason for it to rise again. We feel a general interest in the further fortunes of the characters, but so we do at the end of most plays, unless the stage is strewn with corpses. The particular crisis or train of events on which our attention has been concentrated is over and done with, and we are not made to divine or desire any inevitable development. Between the third and fourth acts the transition is inevitable, the interest is duly carried forward. If Miss Burney will consider how much greater is the momentum of the action at the end of her third act than at the ends of her first and second acts, she will realise the defect at which I am aiming. It may or may not be necessary that the action of a play should be complete and rounded off at the end of the last act, but it is essential that at the ends of the earlier acts it should be obviously (and if possible tantalisingly) incomplete. Miss Burney's dialogue is sometimes witty, sometimes crude, sometimes stilted, never quite easy and natural. That, too, is an art to be acquired.

The acting was fair without great distinction. Miss Janette Steer as Moyra played with intelligence and force, but her voice in the more emotional passages proved very intractable. Miss Granville seemed rather embarrassed (and no wonder) by the audacities of Mrs. Alleyn, but played the part, if one may say so without paradox, agreeably. Mr. Lewis Waller was good as the sketchily-drawn Sir Gerald Delacourt, and Mr. Charles Fulton threw a good deal of sincerity into the dumbly devoted Lord Mottram. Mr. Sydney Brough was excellent as the Hon. Bobby Haigh, and Mr. Holmes-Gore played a philosophic valet with point and discretion.

"Maid of Athens, ere we part," sang Byron, "Give, oh give me back my heart!" Had I been one of the paying public at the Opera Comique on Thursday night, I should have been inclined to adapt Byron's distich, and sing "Give, oh give me back my money!" That was not the feeling of the majority, however, for, though the first act fell flat, and one indescribably silly episode was received with groans, the second act was loudly applauded.   The authors of *The Maid of Athens*,* Messrs. Charles Edmund and Chance Newton, have not even that happy knack of rhyming which in some measure redeems the better sort of musical farces; and, having poor material to work upon, Mr. Osmond Carr is not at his best in the music.   It was rumoured at the end of the first act that one of the comedians had forgotten his part at the critical moment, and omitted a speech which should have explained the plot of the play.   Heavens ! what a speech that must have been !   No wonder the poor fellow's brain reeled.   In the absence of the cosmic word that should have shed light and order through chaos, *The Maid of Athens* may fairly claim to hold the record for incoherence.   Not for a single moment was the smallest connection discoverable between any two incidents, or the faintest glimmer of reason in anything that was said or done.   In point of vulgarity, too, the production takes an eminent, if not a solitary, position, and may thus be said to combine in a unique degree the characteristic qualities of this class of work.   Mlle. Louise Beaudet and Miss Claire Romaine shared almost equally the honours of the evening, both showing cleverness of the most pronounced music-hall type.   Miss Constance Collier made a very handsome " Maid of Athens," and Miss Cicely Richards bestowed her genuine comic talent on

* June 3—July 3.

a thankless part. Of the male performers Mr. Fred Storey chiefly distinguished himself, by agility not unseasoned with humour. Mr. Lonnen worked hard to very little purpose, and Messrs. W. Elton, Charles Weir, and Cecil Ramsey did all they could with the scantiest opportunities.

Of Mlle. Jane May's productions I have been able to see only *Les Amours de Cléopatre*,* an old-fashioned but exceedingly amusing farce by M. Marc Michel. Its humour is purely fantastic, without any of the satiric sub-intention which ran through even the wildest extravagances of Labiche. There is not even any constructive ingenuity in the farce, as in the elaborate pigeon-hole vaudevilles of which Hennequin established the type. We simply see a number of people doing extravagant things for no better reason than that they are laughable; and so genuine is the author's comic spirit that, despite the extreme simplicity of his method, one cannot refuse to laugh, and that heartily. Mlle. Jane May is delightful as the lady who takes such heroic measures to vindicate her property in the gentleman who ought to be her husband; and M. Le Gallo, as that luckless personage, is comic in his somewhat mannered way.

* See note, p. 143.

XXIV.

"A MARRIAGE OF CONVENIENCE"—"THE COUNTY
FAIR"—"AN IRISH GENTLEMAN"—"CASTE"
— "FOR THE HONOUR OF THE FAMILY"
REVIVALS AT HER MAJESTY'S.

16th June.

MR. SYDNEY GRUNDY has produced at the Haymarket a spirited translation of a comedy by the elder Dumas, *Un Mariage sous Louis XV.* I am told by those who have read the original that Mr. Grundy has followed it very closely; and therein he has done well. One can take a rational interest and pleasure in seeing a play of Dumas's done into English by a man who thoroughly understands the art of terse and pointed dialogue. Of course one would rather see him exercising that art on his own account; but since, for the moment, he prefers not to do so, he does the next best thing in placing his literary skill at the service of Dumas. If we cannot have English literature, by all means let us have French literature; this gay and graceful trifle was well worth translating. I am sometimes thought to be prejudiced against this class of work, but that is quite a mistake. Translation I applaud; and by translation I understand, not necessarily a word-for-word rendering of the original, but such a tactful transcript of it as shall best convey the author's meaning to an English audience. It is adaptation that I deplore, except in the rarest instances—the attempt to force foreign character and manners into an English dress. Had Mr. Grundy, for instance, tried to transmogrify *Un Mariage sous Louis XV.* into *A Marriage under George II.* he would have been wasting his own art on spoiling Dumas's. There are exceptional cases, indeed—farces like *The Pink Dominoes*, fairy-tales like *A Pair of Spectacles* —in which adroit adaptation rather improves the original. But to adapt a play which pretends for a moment to be a serious picture of manners is simply to produce a monstrosity, all the more deplorable if it happens to be clever; for it dulls people's sense for just observation and delineation, and makes them expect and almost demand that theatrical manners and character shall be quite unlike those of real life. "But," say the champions of adaptation, "most French plays are so frankly and flagrantly sexual that they *must* be adapted in order to be possible on the English stage." In Heaven's name, then, let them remain impossible! It is a curious instance of the force of habit that people should argue at this time of day as though it were a law of nature that every French play should in one form or another find its way to the English stage. There is no *must* in the matter. If a French play is untranslatable that is an excellent reason for letting it alone.

A Marriage of Convenience,* then, is a pleasant, graceful, insubstantial comedy, which shows the great Alexandre in one of his happiest moods. Sardou has rather taken the gloss off it by calmly annexing its motive in *Divorçons!;* but, on the other hand, the costumes (which, at the Haymarket, are gorgeous beyond words) give it a new gloss of the very glossiest. The acting is more than adequate—Miss Winifred Emery altogether delightful, Mr. Cyril Maude highly entertaining, Mr. William Terriss a little lacking in the grand manner, but handsome and effective in his way, Mr. Sydney Valentine humorous and forcible, Mr. Holman Clark good, and Miss Adrienne Dairolles excellent. Altogether, a bright and agreeable entertainment for a summer evening.

There is a good deal of ability in the acting of Mr. Neil Burgess, an American comedian who has brought to the Princess's a "picture of New England life" by Mr. Charles Barnard, entitled *The County Fair.*† Mr. Burgess plays Abigail Prue, a maiden lady "prim, prudish, and practical," and redeems the inherent unpleasantness of the travesty by his strongly marked but quite inoffensive humour. The

* June 5—July 24. Reproduced September 4—November 4.
† June 5—18 (?).

play is a sort of go-as-you-please variety drama, unsophisticated, but at the same time unpretentious, and far more human and entertaining than the spectacular melodrama of commerce. Mr. Edward S. Metcalfe shows a genuine sense of character in the part of the stolid and inarticulate New England farmer; and Miss Emma Pollock as the waif, "Taggs," is cleverly elfish and uncanny. The quartettes introduced in the "Husking Bee" scene are curious and effective; and curious, but not effective, is the horse-race which brings the play to a close. The horses run on a rotating stage, so that they move at a considerable rate without really advancing, while the background moves in the opposite direction to produce the illusion of progress. But as the scenery in the foreground remains stationary, there is no illusion whatever, and the effect is simply nightmare-like. In order to produce any sort of illusion, everything on the stage would have to move; and even then I doubt whether American ingenuity would wrest from the late Sir Augustus Harris the blue ribbon of the (stage) turf.

A harmless but quite puerile play entitled *An Irish Gentleman*,* by Messrs. D. Christie Murray and J. L. Shine, was produced at the Globe Theatre last week. It is an ordinary melodrama, plus some reminiscences of Charles Lever, and minus the

* June 9. Ran about five nights.

scenic effects. A recklessly extravagant Irish squire, a pair of plotting villains, and a lovely heiress to marry the squire and baffle the spalpeens—out of these familiar ingredients the authors have concocted three absolutely vapid but not impossibly tedious acts. Mr. J. L. Shine manages to keep the play going by means of his expansive and infectious geniality; Miss Eva Moore makes a charming heroine, taking the best advantage of her small opportunities; and Mr. J. B. Gordon, as a Scotch villain—a fabulous animal, of course : as who should say a snake in Iceland—speaks an authentic dialect and plays with unobtrusive skill.

Mr. John Hare has revived *Caste* * at the Court Theatre with exactly the same company with which he played it at the Lyceum in October last.† His Eccles is a masterly performance, fully compensating in finish of detail for what it lacks in breadth and unction. It is in itself true, consistent, and delightful; its only fault is that of not being first in the field ; and to the majority of playgoers that is no fault at all. It is only we old fogies who are haunted by other—certainly not better—incarnations of the character. Miss May Harvey and Mr. Gilbert Hare make a capital Polly and Sam, and Mr. Frank Gillmore and Miss Mona Oram a passable George and Esther. Mr. Frederick Kerr frankly modernises

* June 10—July 9.   † *Theatrical World of 1896*, p. 293.

the part of Hawtree, and thereby takes a good deal of the point and colour out of it. The day is fast approaching when *Caste* will have to be played in the costumes of the 'Sixties.

A "comedy-drama" in three acts, adapted from Augier's *Mariage d'Olympe*, and produced at the Comedy Theatre last Thursday afternoon, exemplified to the full the above remarks on the futility of adaptation. The anonymous adapter, though not devoid of a certain ingenuity, has simply obliterated the merits of a strong and interesting play. *For the Honour of the Family* * (so he calls his work) represents nothing and resembles nothing. It is not even a bad copy of a good picture, but rather the picture itself painted over, smudged, distorted, mutilated, a thing painful and pitiful to behold. All that is best in the French is necessarily omitted, and all that remains loses its meaning until we have mentally replaced it in France. The scheme of the original is pretty closely followed, except that the adapter has made his courtesan, in the first act, sincere in her love for her husband, so that the wanton cruelty of her conduct at the last becomes a grave inconsistency instead of a logical development of character. This, however, is only one among a host of distortions. Even where he has kept most faithfully to his original he has done it cruel injustice. In Augier's play, for instance, a

* June 10 (afternoon).

parvenu enters into a compact with a well-known duellist, of good family but bad character, that he (the parvenu) is to be allowed, for a consideration of fifty thousand francs, to call the duellist out and inflict a slight wound upon him, so that, having thus "given his proofs" of courage, he may in future be exempt from the necessity of fighting duels. Such an arrangement is at least conceivable in France. It may be improbable, it is not absurd. In the English play the parvenu, Wickslow, bargains with Sir Vincent Grisedale, a man about town, that he (Sir Vincent) is to accept a horse-whipping in Hyde Park, and so to establish Wickslow's position in London society. The thing is too absurd for comment; it would serve no purpose whatever; we can only regard the pair as lunatics, until we re-translate the scene into French, and remember that this preposterous "horse-whipping" is to be taken as the equivalent of a duel, in a society where duelling is an established institution. This flagrant unreality vitiates every trait of manners in the play, and, among other things, deprives the catastrophe of all meaning. Miss Eleanor Lane, who played the Anglicised Olympe Taverny, has the advantage of a good appearance and presence, but is as yet deficient in force and variety of expression. The production, by the way, demolishes once for all the absurd notion that *Le Mariage d'Olympe* has anything to do with *The Second Mrs. Tanqueray*.

Energetic as ever, Mr. Tree has revived at Her Majesty's, in the course of one week, *Trilby*,* *The Red Lamp*, and *The Ballad-Monger*, and in each case the revival went quite smoothly, and with excellent spirit. Clever as it is, I cannot regard Svengali as one of Mr. Tree's really great performances. His Demetrius, on the other hand, is a masterpiece of what is rather loosely termed character-acting. We ought to draw a distinction between creating a character and imitating the external peculiarities of a physical type. The author has in this case given Mr. Tree no real character to work upon, so that the merit of the performance lies almost entirely in the actor's admirable observation and reproduction of physical traits and mannerisms. It is a most able piece of acting in an amusingly preposterous play, and the two together delighted the audience. Mrs. Tree's Princess Claudia is a powerful and memorably picturesque performance, and Miss Kate Rorke is good as the somewhat insignificant Olga. Miss Dorothea Baird appeared as Trilby and as Loyse in *The Ballad-Monger*. She has made Du Maurier's heroine her own in right of a sort of predestination, for it amounts to nothing less ; but her Loyse, which is graceful, sincere, and unaffected, proves that her talent is not to be measured by her fortuitous fitness

* *Trilby*, June 7—11. *The Red Lamp* and *The Ballad-Monger*, June 12—July 8.

for a single part.   Miss Rosina Filippi's Madame
Vinard is, as it was from the outset, one of the very
best pieces of acting in *Trilby*.   Her sister, Miss
Gigia Filippi, succeeds her as the maid, Félise, in
The Red Lamp, and plays the part brightly and
cleverly.

XXV.

THE DRAMA OF THE REIGN.

23rd June.

ONE of the poetic playwrights of the Victorian Era
has remarked that

> " Gratulation plays the hypocrite
> Rejoicing in an unknown jubilee."

This distich (treasured in the first instance as a marvel
of style) recurs to me with a warning note as I sit down
to review the theatrical history of the past sixty years.
Is the Jubilee, in this particular sphere, an occasion
for jubilation?   Or must one ignore the facts of the
case in order to keep in tune with the world-wide
chorus ?

On the whole, as it seems to me, there is no need
for gratulation to play the hypocrite.   There has
been loss as well as gain during these sixty years, and
they leave the stage in a chaotic and somewhat pre-
carious condition ; but the general movement of the

past thirty years, at any rate, has been upward, and, instead of mourning a decline, we have at worst to fear that adverse conditions (which it would be folly not to recognise) may prove strong enough to cut short our advance.

It may help us to see things in their proportions if we contrast the sixty years of Queen Victoria with the sixty years of her grandfather, King George the Third.   A critic of 1820, reviewing the history of the theatre since 1760, would have had some difficulty in giving a reasonably cheerful account of things.   At the beginning of the reign Garrick was at his zenith, surrounded by a company of actors almost as great, though not as versatile, as himself—Mrs. Cibber, Mrs. Pritchard, Mrs. Clive, Mrs. Abington, Barry, Macklin, Palmer, King.   This generation had all, of course, disappeared long ago.   Gone, too, were John Kemble, Mrs. Siddons, Mrs. Jordan, Miss O'Neill, George Frederick Cooke.   The one pride of the tragic stage—Edmund Kean—was scarcely its hope. Indubitably a great genius, he had never been a self-respecting artist, and was already visibly on his decline.   Macready had as yet scarcely made his mark, and there was no sign whatever of a worthy successor to Mrs. Siddons or Miss O'Neill.   In acting, then, the end of the reign showed a notorious falling-off as compared with the beginning or the middle ; and in authorship there was no one to bear a moment's comparison with Goldsmith or Sheridan. So low had the drama fallen that Sheridan Knowles, who made his first essay in this very year (1820), was hailed as its regenerator.

There is no doubt that 1897 can look back to 1837 more complacently than 1820 could look back to 1760. Take it all in all, the theatre was then on the down-grade : take it all in all, the theatre is now on the up-grade. But it must be clearly understood that "the theatre" in the second clause means a totally different thing from "the theatre" in the first clause. The latter half of the Queen's reign has seen, not a revival or resuscitation either of the drama or of acting, but a renascence in the strict sense of the word. The theatre has been "hatched over again and hatched different." In 1837, in 1840, even down to 1850, the terms "tragedy," "comedy," "tragedian," "comedian" meant very much what they had meant ever since the Restoration ; now they have either become obsolete or entirely altered their connotation. We no longer write tragedies or comedies, but "plays." The tragedian is as extinct as the candle-snuffer, and the comedian, except at the music-halls and music-hall theatres, has become a " character-actor." The objects and methods of Macready were very much the same as those of Betterton ; the objects and methods of Sir Henry Irving, even when he deals with the same material,

are utterly dissimilar.   Think of the times when Mrs.
Siddons and Mrs. Jordan were hailed as the Tragic
and the Comic Muse, and each reigned supreme in her
own sphere !   Nowadays, our Mrs. Jordan plays Lady
Macbeth, and if we had a Mrs. Siddons we should
not know what to do with her.   She would either
starve or star the provinces.

During the first twenty years of the Queen's reign
the tradition of two centuries—the rhetorical tradition, we may call it, both in tragedy and comedy—
was in its death-throes.   Macready strove hard to
keep it alive, but his two periods of management
(Covent Garden 1837-39, and Drury Lane 1841-43)
were honourable failures.   It died, I think, partly of
its inherent vices, for there is no doubt that the
second- or third-rate actor of the rhetorical school
was a terrible personage.   But the chief forces which
made for its destruction were social and literary : the
growth of London and the invention of stage realism.
During the first forty years of the century the population of the metropolis had more than doubled, and
in a city of nearly two million inhabitants it was
obviously absurd that the privilege of playing the
"legitimate" drama should be confined to the two
patent theatres.   A host of minor theatres had arisen,
and it was inevitable that their position should be
legalised and their disabilities removed.   This was
done by the Act of 1843, which (though it enabled

Phelps to make a last stand for the old order of things, at Sadler's Wells, 1844-62) in reality hastened the disintegration of the rhetorical drama.

The free competition of an unlimited number of theatres in a great centre of population necessarily tends to beget the Long Run. "Man kommt zu schaun, man will am liebsten sehn," says the Manager in *Faust;* and as soon as there is a public large enough to make spectacle remunerative, spectacle becomes the inevitable card to play. Along with the growth of population came improved methods of lighting ; and in the struggle of the eye for supremacy over the ear and the intelligence, it found invaluable allies in the newly-invented gas and limelight. It is a significant fact that limelight was first introduced about 1837 and perfected about 1851. As the public increases, moreover, and the claims on its attention multiply in (or out of) proportion, the claim which is to make itself felt must become ever louder and more insistent. In other words, advertisement is found to be the great secret of success ; and it soon appears that lavish display is the best advertisement. Until well on in the present century, I believe (the fact is certain, but I cannot lay my hand on the exact dates), the newspapers inserted theatrical advertisements for nothing, and eagerly competed for them ; to-day, his advertising bill is one of the most formidable items in a manager's outlay. But the advertisement which is directly paid for is never the most effective. The great thing is to make people talk, and, above all, to surround any given production with the opinion, the rumour, of extraordinary popularity. So long ago as 1838, Mr. Vincent Crummles had discovered that if you want people to flock to a theatre, you must persuade them that they have no chance of getting in ; and, in a large community, the only way to beget this sheep-like rush is, as it were, to make a play its own advertisement, and keep it going night after night. Thus a great many influences concurred to force managers to gamble with large stakes for large returns—to invest great sums of money in one production, and then play it for all it was worth.   All these influences were obviously hostile to the Shakespearian drama and to rhetorical acting.   In the first place, other and far inferior plays were better suited to spectacular treatment.   In the second place, the addition of spectacular attractions to Shakespeare tended to obscure the faults of bad performances and distract attention and appreciation from really fine acting.   In the third place, the conditions of really fine acting were still so far realised by the leading actors themselves that they would not undertake to play the same exhausting part six times a week the whole season through.   It was because he stood out against the long-run system that Macready failed as a manager.   He spent large sums of money on

mounting his "revivals" (a term then ridiculed as
pretentious), and when one or other of them caught
the public fancy he was again and again urged to drop
everything else and (as we should now say) to "boom"
it. But Macready did not see, or would not admit,
that the "boom" was a necessity of the age. He
disdainfully left such methods to the Poet Bunn,
who, being an ignorant man, and still hampered,
moreover, by tradition, made little enough of them.
But the tendencies of the time were with Bunn, not
with Macready.

The retirement of Macready in 1851 marked the
extinction of the great dynasty founded by Betterton,
or rather by Burbage, and, in his person, consecrated
by Shakespeare himself. The tradition lingered on at
Sadler's Wells, in the provinces, and in America,
where it died only the other day with that fine actor,
Edwin Booth. In Phelps, in Booth, and in one or
two stray survivals of minor note, we men of middle
age have seen enough of the methods of this school
to assure us that they must, in part at least, be
recovered if Shakespeare is really to live on the stage.
Physical grace, elegance and force of diction, freedom
of passionate expression, can, and must, be attained
by study, without the vices of exaggeration and
mannerism which often accompanied them in the
past. With Charles Kean, who entered upon his
Princess's management in 1850, began the reign of

spectacular Shakespeare, intermingled with French melodrama, which endures to this day. A man of dramatic instinct and some intelligence, but notoriously deficient in physique and voice, Charles Kean had to elude the problems of Shakespearian acting instead of grappling with them—to substitute for the effects Shakespeare obviously intended, other effects, scenic and histrionic, which he as obviously dreamed not of. In this he has been followed by Sir Henry Irving, a Charles Kean of greater genius and stronger character, who has carried Kean's methods, both of acting and of mounting, to their logical and artistic perfection. But the main significance of the twenty years that intervened between Macready and Irving lay, not in Kean's application to Shakespeare of the spectacular long-run method, but in the growth of what I have called scenic realism, under the influence of France, and especially of Scribe. Adaptation from the French was no new thing; it was as old as Wycherley and Dryden. But the trick of invention and manipulation which, rightly or wrongly, we connect with the name of Scribe, was, in its way, a new thing, and during the early years of the Queen's reign it made the French stage an inexhaustible storehouse of readily adaptable dramatic material. To some extent we adapted and imitated the romantic drama of the period—witness those Early-Victorian masterpieces, *The Lady of Lyons* and *Richelieu*—but Victor

Hugo and the Dumas of *Henri III. et sa Cour* produced little permanent effect in England.   It was the
bourgeois comedy of Scribe and his school that was
destined to revolutionise the stage.   The literary
parentage of this group could no doubt be traced,
but it would be a dismal task.   Who was Scribe's
father I do not know, but Scribe was the father of
the modern drama.   He analysed dramatic effect far
more minutely than any of his predecessors, and
recombined its elements in a thousand new forms.
Through adaptation and imitation of his methods, we
got rid of our essentially rhetorical conception of
comedy (which is last represented in *Money* and
London Assurance), and learned to make our domestic
dramas technically interesting.   Broadly speaking
(though the statement requires much qualification),
Scribe taught us to photograph the surfaces of life,
leaving it to his successors to develop " X-ray "
methods and get below the surfaces.   And in the
meantime the influences which were making for
spectacle at the larger theatres were promoting at the
smaller houses the accurate reproduction of costume,
furniture, and the outward accessories of modern
life.   Charles Mathews and Madame Vestris at the
Olympic and Lyceum, and Mr. and Mrs. Alfred
Wigan at the Olympic, made great strides towards
realism in the dressing of modern plays and setting
of everyday " interiors " ; yet when the Bancroft

management began at the Prince of Wales's, it was still regarded as matter for admiring remark that the doors in the scenes should be provided with handles. Such trifles are not really trivial, but typical. In 1837 a room on the stage was represented by a roughly painted back-cloth, three "wings," and a couple of flapping "borders"; forty years later, a room on the stage was built and cieled, to all appearance, as solidly as any room in Mayfair or Belgravia, and upholstered, not only with liberality, but with ostentation. In all externals, the stage realised the ideal of "a room with one wall removed," and it followed as a matter of necessity that authors should aim at a corresponding ideal—at natural groupings and movements and "overheard" conversation. Conventions of action and speech which passed unnoticed on an empty stage, with three chairs painted on the backing, became intolerable in a setting of absolute reality. Thus, through action and reaction between authorship and stage-management, we gradually developed a totally new ideal (however imperfectly realised on the literary and histrionic side) of "holding the mirror up to nature." It is this ideal which differentiates the theatre of to-day from that of the two centuries between 1660 and 1860. The initial impulses to the change are to be found (I suggest) in the French comediettas and vaudevilles, which called for an elegantly realistic

setting, and in the multiplication of the theatrical
public, which brought with it the long run and made
elaborate mounting possible.

The upward movement, which enables one to
bring this survey to a more or less cheerful close,
definitely set in, beyond a doubt, with the Bancroft
management at the Prince of Wales's, just midway in
the Queen's reign.   Until T. W. Robertson came to
the front, the predominance of Scribe and his school
had been absolutely paralysing to original authorship.   Robertson was not technically a disciple of
the French school, but applied to ends of his own
the scenic mechanism which had been evolved mainly
through French influence.   He possessed a strain of
original genius, narrowed by defective culture and
a very limited knowledge of the world.   Finding
in Mr. and Mrs. Bancroft accomplished actors
and sympathetic managers, he created a new form
of English drama : new, because it ignored the
rhetorical convention of our classic comedies ;
English because—if I may be allowed the truism
—it was not bastard-French.   At Robertson's death
his mantle was divided between Albery and H. J.
Byron ; the poetico-sentimental side of it falling to
the former, the lining of verbal flippancy to the latter.
Byron was deficient in talent, Albery in character, so
that the movement seemed for a time to have ended
in sheer puerility.   The Bancrofts, with the younger

managers, trained in their school — Mr. Hare, Mr.
and Mrs. Kendal, Messrs. Clayton and Cecil—were
forced to fall back in the main upon adaptations from
the French.   But the dramatists of the Second
Empire in France, while faithful to the methods of
Scribe, had vastly enlarged the scope of their application, and even the comparatively bloodless works of
Sardou, which were the most adaptable and the most
adapted, suggested a larger type of social drama than
the Scribisms, original or adapted, of the 'fifties, or
the Robertsonian idylls of the 'sixties and early
'seventies.   After an interval, then, in which we
seemed to be relapsing into sheer servitude to France,
there arose a group of writers who took their methods,
indeed, from the French, but applied them to original
and thoroughly English ends.   Mr. Sydney Grundy
remains an ardent and militant apostle of the gospel
according to Scribe, but has shown himself capable of
throwing a strong individuality into the forms imposed by his religion.   Mr. Henry Arthur Jones and
Mr. A. W. Pinero have, as some of us think, acted
more wisely, in studying the methods of the Scribe-
Sardou school in order *not* to practise them.   They
have realised that "those move easiest who have
learned to dance," but do not make this a reason for
waltzing down Regent Street.   Both have gone straight
to life for their material, have observed sincerely and
reproduced thoughtfully ; while Mr. Pinero in parti-

cular has so perfected his inborn gifts of invention
and style as to stand well on a level with the foremost
dramatists of Europe.   Younger men, or at any rate
younger playwrights—Messrs.Carton, Parker, Esmond,
Shaw—are developing unmistakable talent, while such
managers as Mr. Hare, Mr. Wyndham, Mr. Alexander,
Mr. Tree, are following, more or less consistently, a
progressive policy.

What, then, are the dangers of the situation? Is there
any justification for the cry, which is raised from time
to time, that the drama is "marching to its doom "?
At the first blush, it seems wildly absurd ; for the
very men who raise it have made their fortunes out of
this moribund art, and are probably from five to ten
times richer than the most successful playwright of
thirty years ago.   But it may possibly prove that in
this very fact there lurks a danger to art.   Just about
the time when the Bancroft-Irving movement had
awakened a new interest in the London theatres, it
happened (partly from the same causes) that the
provinces and America became unexpected sources
of wealth.   The profits of successful managers
and authors increased enormously; the salaries of
actors went up in proportion ; the whole theatrical
world remodelled its life on a greatly augmented scale
of expenditure.   The necessity which this system
involves of continuously appealing to an enormous
public, in London and beyond it, must very soon

place a limit to possible advance upon our present lines. "Plain living and high thinking" is not possible to the dramatist, however much he may desire it, for there is practically no middle course between a huge success and a disastrous failure. Unless such a middle course can be discovered or devised, our Victorian Drama will come to little enough.

XXVI.

" LORENZACCIO "—" LA DAME AUX CAMÉLIAS "— " ALL ALIVE, OH ! "

30th June.

THERE is no doubt that Alfred de Musset's *Lorenzaccio** is one of the most Shakespearian plays outside Shakespeare. I have long dreamt of the possibility of putting it on the stage—and I dream of it still. The performance at the Adelphi neither realised nor demolished my dream. It was not good; it had better have been left alone; but that was because Madame Bernhardt had not gone about the thing in the right way. The play, or rather the dramatic

* Madame Sarah Bernhardt's season at the Adelphi lasted from June 17 to July 14. She appeared in *Lorenzaccio* seven times; in *Magda,* thrice; in *Frou Frou,* four times; in *Fédora,* twice; in *Spiritisme,* thrice; in *La Tosca,* four times; in *La Dame aux Camélias,* five times; and in *L'Etrangère,* twice.

romance, ought to have been differently adapted and differently cast. Madame Bernhardt ought to have played the Marchesa di Cibo, and De Musset himself, as he was at twenty-three, when he wrote this astonishing poem, ought to have been summoned from the shades to re-create Lorenzino. This is simply to repeat that Madame Bernhardt ought to have left the play alone; for my two recommendations—that the poet should be recalled to life, and that the actress should play a minor part—are equally fantastic. Nevertheless, if a youth with the grace of a tiger-cat and the genius of Edmund Kean should one day appear on the French stage, he will find a triumph awaiting him in Lorenzaccio. No young ladies need apply.

The coming Lorenzaccio will certainly not be content with M. Armand d'Artois' version of his adventures. De Musset used a more than Shakespearian licence of scene-shifting; M. d'Artois sticks at nothing in order to make a single scene serve for each act. Thus the drama is quite unnecessarily deprived of all its freedom and suppleness of movement. Large curtailment was necessary, no doubt, and could have been effected without serious injury to the play; but the sequence of the scenes should have been left as nearly as possible intact. The simple devices known as a "cloth" and a "carpenter-scene" appear to have slipped not only out of use but

out of recollection. We act on the assumption that
scenery is not made for the drama, but the drama for
scenery. Even if less actual violence had been required to compress the action into four scenes (the
second and fifth acts both pass in Lorenzo's chamber),
the general effect of the play would still have been
injured; for the one-act-one-scene system suggests
and demands a method of construction totally different
from that which the poet deliberately adopted. The
compression gives De Musset the air of trying and
failing to do a thing which in fact he did not dream
of attempting. He aimed at and attained an effect of
sequence, a lithe, snake-like movement; he is made
to appear as though he had aimed at symmetry,
balance, architectural dignity and strength, and had
hopelessly missed his mark. It would take too long
to give adequate instances of the mutilation to which
the text has been subjected in order to force it into
the four-scene mould. The most amazing trans-
position, perhaps, is that of the scene between the
two pedants and their charges, the young Strozzi and
Salviati, which is lifted bodily out of the fifth act and
placed in the first! I did not very clearly catch the
dialogue, so cannot tell whether it was altered to suit
its altered position, before instead of after the murder
of the Duke. If not, it must have made pure
nonsense. Again, in the stage version the Duke is
present at the conversation between Lorenzo and

the painter Tebaldeo (Act ii. Scene 2 of the original text), in which Lorenzo most clearly reveals his hatred of the Medici tyranny. His Highness listens blandly and does not move an eyebrow—the incident has become a sheer counter-sense.

Madame Bernhardt speaks De Musset's beautiful prose very prettily, and at times with what may be called abstract dramatic force—that is to say, dramatic force unconditioned by any care for appropriateness to the particular character to be portrayed. She is never for a moment Lorenzaccio, that "lendemain d'orgie ambulant," as the Duke calls him; she is much liker Hamlet, and likest of all to Madame Sarah Bernhardt in a highly becoming male costume. She is a dignified, languid, eminently respectable personage, as diverse as possible from the vicious stripling De Musset has drawn for us, hollow-eyed and hectic with debauchery, his lip curled with a perpetual sneer at the world and himself, fanatical idealism and sick self-contempt seething like a hell-brew in his brain, and spurting forth in vitriolic jibes at all that in his heart he holds sacred. Hamlet may or may not be mad—Lorenzaccio certainly is. He has worked himself up into a delirium of cynicism. He revels morbidly in dissimulation for its own sake, and almost loses sight of the end with which he first entered upon it. His machinations are absurdly disproportionate to their object. They remind one now and then of

Tom Sawyer's plots for getting Jim out of prison in strict accordance with the rules of art. At the last moment, he wantonly endangers the success of his designs out of sheer defiant cynicism. The thing would be childishly easy if he were capable of acting with sane resolution ; as a matter of fact, he conducts himself so insanely that his success seems a miracle. There is a great problem here for a character-actor of the rarest physical and mental gifts. Should he ever appear, he will certainly not end the play with the murder of Alessandro de' Medici, but with that admirable scene between Lorenzo and Filippo Strozzi which immediately precedes Lorenzo's own assassination.

"At Drury Lane," wrote George Henry Lewes in April 1853, "we were threatened with a version of *La Dame aux Camélias*, but the Lord Chamberlain refused a licence to this unhealthy idealisation of one of the worst evils of our social life. Paris may delight in such pictures, but London, thank God ! has still enough instinctive repulsion against pruriency not to tolerate them. . . . If any Lord Chamberlain be supine enough to license it—but there is no fear !" And now the play is familiar to satiety in London no less than in Paris, is recognised as the starting-point of the serious modern drama, and formally claims its place as a classic by reverting to the costumes of its date of origin ! Could there be a more trenchant

commentary on the uses of the Censorship? The
supporters of that institution are in a cleft stick.   If
the play is not harmful, why was it vetoed at the
outset, and England in so far shut off from the
dramatic movement? If it *is* harmful, why has the
Censorship been false to its trust, and permitted, any
time the last seventeen years, this pollution of our
chaste boards? There is no escaping from the
dilemma; either the Censorship was vexatious and
tyrannous in 1853, or it was culpably lax and com-
pliant in 1880. It may perhaps be alleged that the
absolute merits of the play are of secondary importance, and that the fact of its being *commonly reputed*
immoral in 1853 was sufficient to justify the action of
the Censorship.   In that case the office resolves itself
into a patent mechanism for keeping the English stage
thirty years behind the rest of the world; for it is
clear that every enlargement of the dramatist's domain
will always shock timidity and outrage hypocrisy.

Well, well—time works wonders, and even official
omnipotence grows less ignorant and arrogant as the
years roll on.   Logically, the Censorship ought to kill
the drama; practically, the drama is rapidly killing
the Censorship.   Certain it is that *La Dame aux
Camélias*—that somewhat mawkish but irresistibly
touching idyll of passion in the midst of pollution—
now conveys to no mortal hearer any suggestion of
that "pruriency" which stirred Lewes to such a

surprising outburst of British pharisaism. It gains
greatly, in my opinion, by confessing its date in its
costumes. The manners date, the language dates,
the wit and the sentiment date—why should the
dresses contradict them? Madame Bernhardt looked
better as Marguerite, and played the part much more
charmingly, to my thinking, than she has done of
recent years. Her art was absolutely consummate.
It is my own misfortune, no doubt, that I have
become so keenly alive to her art as to have no eyes,
or no feeling, for anything else. There is such a
thing, surely, as too great virtuosity: an artist can
have his or her means of expression too completely
under control. If we have no sense of momentary
effort, of struggle to subdue and fashion more or less
resistent material, our admiration is apt to be un-
thrilled by sympathy. The gentleman who rides
eight horses round the circus ring pretends (if it be a
pretence) to rein them in with mastery indeed, but
not without effort. Very likely the animals are so
accustomed to do their turn that they would keep
pace and place as though by clockwork if the rider
held no reins at all; but if he is a wise artist he will
not allow us to suspect this. The effort after perfection, in a word, is more interesting and real than
its mechanical reproduction. "You mean," the
enthusiast for French acting may say with a sneer,
"that bad acting is better than good!" Where-

upon I retort, with disdain, that caricature is not argument.

Mr. Arthur Bourchier has produced at the Strand a farce named *All Alive, Oh!** adapted (by Mr. Ralph Lumley, says rumour) from *Le Disparu*, by MM. Bisson and Sylvane. Most of the action becomes quite meaningless in English, but the dialogue is inoffensive and the situations fairly amusing. Mr. Bourchier, Mr. Fred Thorne, Miss May Palfrey, and Miss Phyllis Broughton play the leading parts with spirit; Mr. Mark Kinghorne is capital as a servant; and Mr. James Leigh, as an auctioneer, puts life into the preposterous auction-scene of the third act.

XXVII.

PROVIDENCE AND THE WELL-MADE PLAY.

St. Paul's, 3rd July.

"WHAT is good enough for God is good enough for me!" Thus spake Mr. Sydney Grundy the other day to an irrepressible interviewer. The piety of the sentiment we must all applaud, but the practical merits of the proposition can scarcely be estimated until we have ascertained what *is* good enough for God and Mr. Grundy. If you know Mr. Grundy you will have no difficulty in guessing; otherwise you may

* June 16—July 9.

as well give it up at once. It is nothing more nor less than the "well-made play" for which Mr. Grundy thus claims divine sanction and approval. Scribe, it would appear, is a prime favourite in even higher spheres than those in which Miss Marie Corelli's genius is said to find august admirers. And how has Mr. Grundy arrived at this knowledge? Has he read it in the stars? For Mr. Grundy, as all the world knows, is an astronomer in his leisure hours, studies the stage-management of the heavens, and keeps a critical eye upon the planetary exits and entrances. But no! it is not through his telescope that Mr. Grundy has taken the opinion of the Almighty. It is by way of anatomy, not astronomy, that the revelation has come to him.

"The 'well-made' play," said Mr. Grundy, with decision, "is the play which *is* well made. I'll take the human body as my analogue. Is that 'well made'? Are we a conglomeration of bones, and muscles, and electric nerves huddled together any-how? Or did the Creator build us with design? There is the framework of bone, the covering of muscle, the filigree of exterior beauty. What is good enough for God is good enough for me." Mr. Grundy might have driven home his pronouncement with a quotation from James Russell Lowell:

> " God hez sed so, plump an' fairly,
>   It's ez long ez it is broad :

> An' you've gut to git up airly
> Ef you want to take in God."

The worst of such an appeal to headquarters is that the same device is open to your adversary, and that he is equally sure of a decision in his favour. The answer that comes to us from the vault of heaven is simply the echo of our own voices. If I were an opponent of the well-made play (I am not; Mr. Grundy thinks I am, but he has not, as he puts it, "read me aright"), I could, with the greatest ease, enlist the Creator on my side. The argument would run somewhat like this: Why dabble in false analogies when Heaven pronounces, not analogically, but with the utmost directness, against the well-made play? The human body is the sculptor's theme and gives the sculptor, not the dramatist, his laws. Heaven is the arch-sculptor; all the human artist can do is to study and reproduce its masterpieces. But Heaven is also the arch-dramatist, at once author and stage-manager of the popular tragi-comedy known as Life. The playwright's business is to study and reproduce scenes from this tragi-comedy; but the first thing that strikes him when he looks at it critically is that it is *not* well made, in the Scribe-Grundy sense. The marvellous articulation and equipoise of the human body—the sculptor's object—find no analogy in Life, which is the playwright's theme. Therefore the two artists work by different laws to a different end.

What should we think of a sculptor who should produce formless lumps of marble in place of statues, on the plea that Life is formless? Hear his argument: " I'll take Life as my analogue. Is Life 'well-made'? Does it present a clear, symmetrical, jointed, and rounded design, with everything in its place, and nicely adapted to its end? Certainly not; if there is any design at all in the matter, any plan in the 'mighty maze,' it is so sedulously and successfully concealed that only theologians and philosophers can divine it at all, and each of them divines it differently. Well, then, what is good enough for God is good enough for me. If Life is amorphous, why should sculpture strive after form? Here is a chunk of marble, chiselled at random; you will find just as much design in it as I, or any one else, can find in Life."

" Preposterous nonsense!" you say; but if it is preposterous for a sculptor to deduce the rules of his art from the dramaturgy of Heaven, why should a dramatist go for his canons to the sculpture of Heaven? Mr. Grundy will find, I think, that in argument on sublunary themes "God" is always a treacherous ally, and metaphor a two-edged sword. " Nec deus intersit, nisi dignus vindice nodus." Let us leave God out of the question—a point of policy on which the Decalogue is at one with the *Ars Poetica* —and try whether an analysis of terms may not possibly help us forr'ader.

There is nothing so fatal to lucidity as a question-begging term, and especially one which implies a false opposite. In municipal politics, for instance, I have often wondered why one party should have allowed the other to grab the designation " Moderate." Once accept this description of your opponent's measures, and how can you argue against them ? What is not moderate is immoderate, and what is immoderate is unwise, reprehensible, vicious. Such is the unrealised influence of words, that the fallacy involved in this mere designation is, I am convinced, an appreciable factor in London politics. In the same way, the term " well-made play" obscures the point at issue by suggesting as its opposite " ill-made play," which is absurd. The true question—the only question worth a moment's discussion—is between the well-made play and the better-made play. " Hold ! " says Mr. Grundy. " You are now begging the question in your own favour ! " Very well, I have re-established the balance. The two fallacies having cancelled each other, we can make a fresh start on equal terms.

The real question is this : Has Eugène Scribe spoken the last word of theatrical technique ? Is every departure from his principles and practice a change for the worse ? Has not his art, which, in its novelty, was immensely interesting and attractive, come to seem, through sheer familiarity, a somewhat tedious artifice? Is there not an art beyond his art, an art which conceals art, a higher skill which minimises the mechanical element in drama, and so leaves more room for character, thought, emotion, humour, the essential components of life? When last Mr. Grundy went a-theorising, he compared the well-made play, not to the human form divine, but (more modestly) to a mechanical rabbit.* Well, accepting the comparison, I suggest that it is possible, by simplifying the mechanism, to make our mechanical rabbits a good deal more like real ones than those of the Scribe-Sardou warren.

If the interviewer is to be trusted, however, I am preaching to the converted. "There *is* something in the jeer at the well-made play," Mr. Grundy is represented as saying, "but the fact is the critics are the victims of only half a truth." Why, then, what more would you have? If the critics have got hold of a half-truth, they are greatly to be congratulated. There are no absolute truths in æsthetics. In this sphere, half the truth is the utmost that any human mind is capable of apprehending. If Mr. Grundy can see— and much more if he can utter—a critical whole-truth of any moment, his vision and faculty must indeed be god-like.

One word more. "I sometimes think," says Mr. Grundy, "that the public of these days will only go

* *Theatrical World of 1896*, p. 41.

to see the plays it doesn't like." This is a really
profound and suggestive observation, though I am
not sure that Mr. Grundy himself realises all that it
suggests. He goes on to quote the following conversation as illustrating his point : " ' Have you been to
see So-and-so ? ' ' No ; but it seems the rage.' ' Oh,
you must go ; but for my own part it bored me to
death.' " You do hear people talking in this strain ;
but if the play is really a successful one, they mis-
represent their sensations when they say " It bored me
to death." What they mean is, " It interested me in
spite of myself. I disliked it, and it puzzled me ; but
it bored me much less than the trumpery pieces I like
and understand." If Mr. Grundy would take his own
wisdom to heart, and write a play which should
fascinate and irritate the public in about equal proportions, it would probably be the success of his
career.

XXVIII.

LES DEUX FROU-FROU—" LA DOULOUREUSE "— THE VIENNESE COMPANY.

7th July.

LONDON is becoming the Belgium of the theatrical
world—its recognised duelling-ground. The leading
actresses of Europe have contracted an agreeable

habit of popping across the Channel every summer to exchange a few shots, and we lucky dogs of critics have the privilege of sitting by and seeing fair. This year, like the shepherd of Mount Ida, we have three goddesses to choose between; but fortunately there is no law against trisecting the apple. We can assign a solid wedge to each; it is their own fault if they insist on measuring and weighing to determine which is the largest—and the smallest.

Madame Bernhardt appeared as Gilberte in *Frou-Frou* on Wednesday evening, Madame Réjane* on Thursday; and the comparison thus forced upon us was not only interesting but pleasant, inasmuch as both actresses came out of it with credit. Madame Bernhardt's first performance of Frou-Frou, at the Gaiety some fifteen years ago, dwells in my memory as one of the most brilliant pieces of acting I ever saw—an exquisite, iridescent creation. It has suffered somewhat by sheer lapse of time; it has suffered still more from the actress's gradual coarsening of effects in the effort to bring them home to audiences which do not understand her language, and therefore look for and applaud what may be called

* Madame Réjane's season at the Lyric Theatre lasted from June 28 to July 17. She appeared in *La Douloureuse* five times, in *Frou-Frou* five times, and in *Madame Sans-Gêne* ten times. *Amoureuse* and *La Maison de Poupée* (*A Doll's House*) were announced, but not performed.

the athletics of acting.   Where Sarah is content to be
beautiful and subtle, she is quite as subtle and almost
as beautiful as ever.   In the lighter and more subdued scenes, were it not for the signs of wear-and-tear
in her voice, one could almost imagine oneself back
in the early 'eighties.   Here she still shows a mastery
which is all her own.   But in the scenes of storm
and stress she has lost all restraint, all temperance,
all truth and beauty.   Her quarrel with Louise, and
her parting from De Sartorys before the duel, are
painful examples of what, in any other actress, we
should call unmitigated rant.   True, Sarah is not
"any other actress"—these paroxysms of fury, in
which her words come seething forth through her
clenched teeth at the rate of five hundred to the
minute, are peculiar to herself alone.   If they were
as admirable as they are wonderful, they would be
triumphs indeed.   But as a matter of fact they stand
in no relation to nature, and in a false relation to art.
They are, as I have said, feats of vocal and physical
athletics designed to impress spectators on whom
delicate acting and even articulate speech are thrown
away.   Perfect as Sarah's diction can be when she
chooses, I defy any one to follow her words towards
the close of the scene with Louise; whereas every
word of Madame Réjane's, though she plays the
scene with ample vehemence, reached the ear as
clear-cut as a jewel.   In the frantic effort to detain

De Sartorys both actresses transgressed all measure, and the transgression was more painful, because less physically skilful, in the case of Madame Réjane. For a single moment, she became positively ludicrous. If this passage cannot be more artistically regulated, so as to avoid the monotony of clutch and clamour, it ought to be cut as short as possible, and the combatants ought, like Macbeth and Macduff, to " fight off." Madame Réjane's performance, as a whole, was fresh, vivid, delightful, and in the last two acts genuinely pathetic. Perfect distinction is not within this actress's scope, and her performance is not so rich in opalescent light and colour as Sarah's. Her smile, too, is so irrepressibly joyous as to be almost discordant now and then with the tone of the final scenes. On the other hand, her acting is perfectly accomplished and delicately artistic, without over-emphasis, except in that one passage of the fourth act, and without mannerism. A hundred little points might be singled out for praise ; but space is precious this week. Let me merely note, as symbolising the difference between her performance and Sarah's, the little incident of the glass of water which Gilberte offers to De Sartorys and he will not accept. Réjane puts down the glass simply and naturally, trusting to her face to bring out the meaning of the point ; Sarah must needs shatter the glass in putting it down ; and this *proportion* holds throughout. The general per-

formance at the Lyric is much better than at the
Adelphi, where M. Brémont alone, as De Sartorys,
rose above mediocrity. At the Lyric, M. Calmette
was a good De Sartorys, M. Nertann a capital
Brigard, and M. Magnier the best Valréas I remember to have seen.

It is curious to compare *Frou-Frou*, that eminently
well-made play (despite the conventionality of the last
two acts), with the opening play of Madame Réjane's
season, *La Douloureuse* by M. Maurice Donnay.
This is a sentimental comedy of the new school,
deliberately formless and artfully inartificial. I earnestly counsel Mr. Grundy not to go and see it; he
would probably rise up in the stalls and protest, like
Mr. Tomlins at *It's Never Too Late to Mend*, or Lord
Queensberry at *The Promise of May*. To think that
the very century and the very city which received the
revelation according to Scribe should thus have relapsed into heathenism! I am myself a noted backslider, and in the very worst odour with the orthodox;
but I think M. Donnay goes a little too far. He has
written a four-act play, as it seems to me, for the
sake of a single scene. It is a superb scene when
we reach it (in the third act); but the author has
apparently taken pains to prevent us from foreseeing
or desiring it. The play is compounded in this wise:
Act I. gives us an amusing picture of shady society
in Paris, the splendours and miseries of fraudulent

finance. Though helplessly stage-managed, this act is good enough in itself; but only five minutes of it have anything to do with the drama which is to follow. Its whole practical purpose is to show us that the wife of the dishonest banker has a lover, and to inform us that by her husband's suicide she becomes a widow. It is not pretended that the environment so elaborately painted in this act has any particular effect upon her character or upon the subsequent course of events. An absolutely different first act, in a wholly dissimilar environment, might be substituted for this one, without entailing any change in the remainder of the play. I agree with Mr. Grundy that this is not good policy. Why concentrate our attention on the Bohemia of the Bourse if it is to be neither the subject nor the general setting of the play ? A first act ought not to be an irrelevant frontispiece— that is one canon to which I subscribe with all my heart. The second act opens with an abstract discussion of the theory of an equal moral law for the two sexes. The characters, like those of Molière and Moore & Burgess, sit in a semicircle and speak their pieces. We almost wonder that they do not elect a chairman and put the matter to the vote. A new personage—the heroine's mother—is introduced to champion the old-fashioned morality, who, when she has said her say, goes home, and is out of the saga. The discussion, however, is not so undramatic as you might suppose, for we feel that the interest of the play is to turn on the application of the principles here enunciated. The stage is then cleared for a love-scene between hero and heroine—Philippe and Hélène—an admirable, modern, unconventional love-scene, admirably acted by Madame Réjane and M. Calmette. But we ask ourselves at its close where the drama is to come from, where the obstacle is to crop up and the struggle to begin? We are nearing the end of the second act, and nowhere on the horizon can we discern a cloud as big as a man's hand. Hélène's year of widowhood is nearly over; she and Philippe are presently to be married; all is harmony, adoration, and security. In the last scene of the act a cloud does begin to gather, for we find that Gotte des Trembles, Hélène's bosom friend, is also in love with Philippe, and is determined to let him know it. But Philippe resists her blandishments with melancholy austerity, and when the curtain falls on the second act things seem perfectly safe and in order. Hélène a widow, and Philippe austere—what harm can Gotte possibly do?

The fact is, M. Donnay is carefully keeping a secret from us, which Mr. Grundy, had he been treating the theme, would as carefully have revealed to us early in the first act; and I think Mr. Grundy would have been right. Philippe is not Hélène's first lover; her son, Georges, is not the child of her

late husband; and Gotte, and Gotte alone, knows
the truth.   Had we also been initiated from the
outset (and nothing could have been easier or more
natural—three words exchanged between Gotte and
Hélène would have done it) we should have been at
no loss whatever to foresee the impending drama,
and the sense of irony would have tripled the interest
of the intervening scenes.   In renouncing this effect,
M. Donnay abjures the most precious birthright of
the dramatist.   The chief attraction of the theatre is
that there we can sit like gods, knowing the past,
foreseeing the future, and watching poor purblind
humanity dreeing its weird in ignorance, bewilder-
ment, "a general mist of error."   If we ourselves are
in the mist, and know no more than the actors in the
drama (in this case, indeed, no more than the most
ignorant of them), we lose that complexity of realisation and that sense of superiority which the whole
mechanism of the theatre is designed to afford us.
And we have no compensating gain.   The effect of
M. Donnay's third act is not a whit more forcible
because it comes upon us unprepared.   We learn at
the beginning that Philippe's austerity has not after
all been proof against Gotte's seductions; but it has
now returned upon him embittered by remorse, and
he treats Gotte with sternness approaching to contumely.   She takes her revenge by revealing Hélène's
secret; he tells Hélène that he knows it; and

Hélène, putting two and two together, divines how it has come to his knowledge. This long scene of mutual reproach and remorseful misery is in reality the whole drama. A magnificent scene it is, and magnificently acted. In its agonising hesitancies and despairing brutalities, it is the most poignantly life-like scene I can remember in French drama. And here I chop round and side with M. Donnay against Mr. Grundy. Mr. Grundy would certainly have ended it with a bang, so to speak—a swoon or a scream, a tableau, or, at the very least, a piece of rhetoric. M. Donnay does nothing of the sort. He lets Philippe and Hélène unpack their hearts with words until they are exhausted, broken, dazed with misery, and have nothing more to say. Then Hélène asks, "What o'clock is it?" Philippe looks at his watch, "Nearly seven." "I must be going"—and she dries her eyes, smoothes her hair, pulls herself together, in a word, to face the world again. The mechanical round of life re-asserts its hold upon them. She entered the room happy and confident, she leaves it heart-broken—but she must bear up somehow. "Help me with my cloak," she says; and he holds her mantle for her, and tucks in the puffed sleeves of her blouse. Then he takes up the lamp and lights her out—and the curtain falls. The fourth act consists rightly and inevitably of the reconciliation. Their cup of life is embittered, but they will make shift to drink it with the best face they may. M. Donnay did right in not trying to wind up his play in the third act; but in removing the scene to the Riviera, and giving an elaborate pictorial setting to the five minutes' dialogue of which the act consists, I think he sinned against the law of artistic economy. The re-union might much more naturally and effectively have taken place in the studio which witnessed the parting.

M. Donnay's play afforded such a tempting opportunity for an endeavour to strike the balance between the old and the new dramaturgy, that I have exceeded my space and cannot possibly do justice this week to our Viennese visitors at Daly's Theatre.* They have given us two most interesting specimens of the work done at the Vienna Volkstheater, evidently an admirable and enviable institution. Nothing could be more modern and alert than *Untreu*, a translation of an Italian comedy by Roberto Bracco, in which Madame Odilon, Herr Christians, and Herr Nihl made their first appearance. *Die Goldene Eva*, on the other hand, by Von Schöntan and Koppell-Ellfeld, seemed a trifle old-fashioned, but was redeemed from commonplace not only by the excellent acting, but by the literary grace and sparkle of the ingenious rhymes

* The company of the Vienna Volkstheater appeared at eight afternoon performances, playing *Untreu*, June 28 and 29; *Die Goldene Eva*, June 30 and July 1; and *Renaissance*, July 5—8.

(*Knittelverse* is the technical term for them) in which the dialogue is cast. Madame Odilon showed remarkable ability and charm as the Francillonesque heroine of *Untreu*, and Herr Christians played the hero of *Die Goldene Eva* with such grace, fervour, and force as we look for in vain, at the moment, on the English stage. He is not only a well-graced, but a well-trained actor. Nothing could have been better, in its way, than his really moving delivery of the lyric tirade at the end of the second act. I shall return next week to the subject of the Vienna company, when I hope to have seen more of their very interesting work. In the meantime, let me say emphatically that they are well worth seeing, and that the spirited enterprise of Herr Kadelburg, the manager, deserves all encouragement.

XXIX.

An Ideal Popular Theatre.

Daily Chronicle, 10th July.

A LONG and interesting talk with Mr. Henry Kadelburg, of the Vienna Volkstheater, has, I own, left me profoundly humiliated, and disposed—

> " In spite of jubilation,
> To renounce the British nation,
> And become an Aus-tri-an."

They do as a matter of course in Vienna everything that we ought to do here and can't. Observe that Mr. Kadelburg represents, not the Hofburg Theater, the most magnificent playhouse in Europe, financed by the Emperor and managed by the Court, but the Volkstheater, a private enterprise, founded indeed by public spirit, but self-supporting and profitable. We need not envy the Viennese their palatial Burgtheater, the outcome, doubtless, of a system which has its drawbacks; but it is hard to see what drawback attaches to such an institution as the Volkstheater. One such playhouse in London would be the salvation, if not of the British drama, at any rate of English acting.

"It is nine years since the theatre was founded," says Mr. Kadelburg in his excellent English. "The Stadttheater had been burnt down, and was rebuilt as a sort of music-hall. The need for a new popular theatre made itself felt; the Emperor presented a splendid site near the Ringstrasse, of an estimated value of £80,000; and a number of wealthy citizens subscribed the building-fund. Contractors and furnishers did their work on the lowest possible terms, yet the building cost £60,000. This money was subscribed in 500 florin (say £42) shares, but no one could hold more than ten shares, so that there was no possibility of the whole property being concentrated in one or two hands. More precisely, it is possible to hold more than ten shares, but additional shares above ten give no additional voting power."

"Well, the theatre being built, what did the proprietors do with it?"

"They established a constitution, and, subject to that constitution, let it to the present manager, Herr von Bukovics, whose second in command I am.   The yearly rental is over £4,500, and pays the proprietors four and a half per cent. on their shares.   In addition to this, they have the right of booking seats in advance without the extra booking fee, which the general public has to pay; and this privilege, being exercised through a system of transferable coupons, is equivalent to an extra two and a half per cent."

"Now, as to the constitution, Mr. Kadelburg— of what is its nature?"

"In the first place, our prices are regulated, and are very low.   A stall costs 2½fl. (4s.), a box from 7fl. to 15fl.   The cheapest seats in the house cost 50 kreuzers (about 10d.), and for 60 kreuzers you can reserve a numbered and comfortably upholstered seat.   On no account are we permitted to raise the prices; but they are reduced by thirty per cent. on the classical nights—for we are bound to give one night a week (Thursday as a matter of fact) to the classical repertory—Shakespeare, Lessing, Goethe,

Schiller, Kleist, Grillparzer, etc.   On these classical
Thursdays, and at afternoon performances on Sundays
and holidays, we last season played Shakespeare's
Hamlet, *Taming of the Shrew*, and *Comedy of Errors*.
Next season, we shall do *Richard III.*   These
classical evenings and afternoons are largely attended
by school children with their parents, and once a
year, on the Emperor's fête, we give a free performance for school children alone."

"Then, on non-classical evenings, you can play
what you please?"

"Within limits, yes.   We cannot play operettas,
extravaganzas, or sheer farces."

"How you must pine under that restriction!"

"Our modern repertory consists for the most part
of light comedies, but we do not shrink from plays
of the most serious order.   For instance, we produced
Sudermann's *Die Ehre* and *Sodom's Ende*, while
Heimat, *Die Schmetterlingschlacht*, and *Morituri* were
done at the Burgtheater.   We have acted five of
Ibsen's plays, *The Pillars of Society*, *A Doll's House*,
Ghosts, *The Wild Duck*, and *Rosmersholm*."

"Certainly not the lightest of his works."

"No, but next season we may possibly produce
the lightest of his works, *The League of Youth*.
Then, as you know, one of Madame Odilon's chief
successes has been made in *Madame Sans-Gêne*, and
of other recent French plays, we have produced

Porto Riche's *Amoureuse*, and Donnay's *Amants*—
both great successes."

"What do you reckon a success? How many
performances in a season?"

"Well, a successful play will probably be repeated
from sixty to eighty times in its first season. *Madame
Sans-Gêne* has been performed 108 times in three
seasons."

"How many performances of a successful play do
you give in a week?"

"We are not allowed to act any play more than
twice running. On the third night we must change
the bill."

"Do you find it any disadvantage to be debarred
from running a play continuously?"

"No, we are under no temptation to do so."

"Don't you find that one success kills another—
that the public flocks to one play at a time, to the
exclusion, or marked disadvantage, of others?"

"Not at all; we have frequently three successful
plays running together. Last season, for instance,
our chief successes were *Die Goldene Eva*, which you
have seen at Daly's, a local play, *Das grobe Hemd*,
and Donnay's *Amants*. These ran abreast, as it
were, neither interfering with the success of the
other."

"With whom lies the choice of plays?"

"There is a 'Dramaturg' attached to the theatre,

whose business it is not only to read plays sent in to us, but to keep an eye on the French and Italian drama for plays likely to suit us. We now do a good many Italian plays. The great majority of our pieces, however, come to us from well-known Austrian, German, and French authors. During the nine years of the theatre's existence, 6000 plays have been submitted by unknown outsiders, and of these only four have proved worth production."

"And how many 'Dramaturgs' have succumbed in the process of winnowing the 6000?"

"One only—he went mad, poor fellow! If the 'Dramaturg' reports favourably on a play, I read it. If I think well of it, Herr von Bukovics reads it; and if he approves, it is accepted. Then it is assigned to one of the four *régisseurs*, or stage-managers, of whom I am one. He is responsible for the *Inscenierung*—the mounting and acting of it. He has much more authority and influence than a stage-manager in England."

"That is because most of our actor-managers do their own *Inscenierung*, and the nominal stage-manager merely carries out their orders. Now tell me—with your frequent changes of programme, you must have a large company of actors?"

"We have a company of sixty, and a working staff of sixty more."

"And how do salaries range?"

"From 50fl. to 2000fl. a month. That means that a 'utility' lady or gentleman will receive about £80 a year (including payment for extra performances), while a 'leading lady' will make from £2500 to £3000 a year. A young 'leading man' we probably engage at about £600 a year, rising gradually to as much as £1500. Then I must tell you that we have a pension fund. Every actor, after five years' service, is entitled, if disabled from playing, to retire with a pension of 40 per cent. of a third of his salary. After ten years' service he is entitled to 80 per cent. of a third of his salary; and after thirty years' service he can retire upon the full third."

"And how is the pension fund constituted?"

"The proprietors of the theatre are bound to pay 2000fl. a year towards it, the management 3000fl., and the actors themselves 6000fl. But this is raised not by deductions from their salaries, but by an annual benefit performance. Last year we mounted a Chinese play, *The Chalk Circle*, for this benefit, acting it exactly after the manner of the Chinese stage, with no scenery or properties. If A. said, 'Give me a cup of tea,' B. poured from an imaginary teapot into an imaginary cup, and handed the imaginary cup to A., who raised it to his lips, and went through the pantomime of tasting, approving, and drinking—and so on throughout.

The play deals with a story not unlike that of the Judgment of Solomon. It was quite a success. We took one of the largest theatres in Vienna for the occasion, and charged special prices. The receipts were 9000 florins, the expenses about 2000 florins; so that a net profit of 7000 florins, or 1000 more than the actors are required to contribute, went to the pension fund."

"How many people does the Volkstheater seat?"

"About eighteen hundred—and at ordinary prices a full house means a gross receipt of £200, while our nightly expenses are about £125. The Emperor, I may say, pays £500 a year for his box. Let me add that we have practically no advertising expenses. The newspapers insert our brief announcements simply as news, and we never dream of placarding the town with posters."

"Now tell me about the training of your actors. I was very much struck the other day with the admirable diction and delivery of Herr Christians in the part of Peter in *Die Goldene Eva*. He would make an ideal Prince Hal in *Henry IV*. We have scarcely any one on the English stage who could approach him in the part, simply because our actors have not learned their business as Herr Christians has. Where does such an actor get his training?"

"Of course we have a Conservatorium in Vienna, supported by the Government, where the leading actors of the Burgtheater and the other theatres officiate as professors. Many of the foremost actors take private pupils as well; but at least three-fourths of our actors have been through the Conservatorium. The pupils give trial performances from time to time; we note those who seem to show promise, engage them, or at any rate pay them a retaining fee, and send them for a couple of years to one of the provincial theatres, to gain experience as members of the stock company. We find this system answer very well."

"It seems to me an ideal system. Nothing could possibly be better. Here—but you can see for yourself what the effects of the long-run system and the lack of competent instruction are, and must be."

"What I cannot understand," said Mr. Kadelburg, "is why you have not here a popular Shakespeare Theatre, where Shakespeare and the classical drama should be regularly performed at moderate prices."

"You do not quite realise," I replied, "the difficulties of such an enterprise. Still, it would be possible, if only we could find a man with the requisite knowledge, energy, enthusiasm—and capital —to found such a theatre and carry it on. At the same time, it would be neither possible nor desirable to rely exclusively on the classical drama. But to return to Vienna. I have heard some rumour of a new theatre to be subsidised by the municipality. Is there such a project?"

"Yes; an Anti-Semitic theatre is to be started by the town."

"What a droll idea! And how is it to manifest its Anti-Semitism?"

"By having no Jews in its company and excluding from its repertory plays written by Jews."

"It will not open, I presume, with Lessing's *Nathan der Weise?*"

"Probably not."

"Now, tell me, Mr. Kadelburg—I hope the result of your present too short season at Daly's has been such as to encourage you to revisit us?"

"Nothing could have been more gratifying than the artistic success with which we have met, and I certainly hope to repeat the experiment. And do not be too much surprised if you were one day to see Madame Odilon, who speaks excellent English, in an English translation of one of her popular parts."

"An excellent idea! I wish her—and you— every success. And now—many thanks, and *auf Wiedersehen!*"

XXX.

"SPIRITISME"—GERMAN PLAYS—"THE SILVER KEY."

14th July.

AGAIN the theory of the well-made play! Last week we had its negation in *La Douloureuse;* this week its affirmation in *Spiritisme.** The fact that M. Sardou's latest play made a very doubtful success in Paris, and has by no means taken the European stage by storm, shows how genuinely and universally the current is setting against the well-made play, in the narrow sense of the word. Twenty-five years ago *Spiritisme* would have been the event of the theatrical season, and every manager in Europe and America would have been struggling and scrambling for the rights of it; to-day, it is pooh-poohed in Paris and regarded abroad as a very doubtful property. True, it does not show Sardou quite at his best. It is to some extent marred by its controversial episodes and its curious illogicality. But it is amusing throughout, and the second act is one of the strongest Sardou ever wrote —an interesting and poignant situation worked out with a master-hand.

The inconsistency of M. Sardou's position is manifest. He obviously believes in spiritualism—in the

* See note, p. 185.

existence of disembodied intelligences, and their power
of communicating with the living—yet he has not the
courage to assign them an essential part in his drama.
The spirits hover round the outskirts of the action,
but do not really or effectually mingle in it. The
hero's *belief in* them, indeed, helps to bring about
the conclusion ; but the apparition which so potently
works upon him is an admitted imposture, a pious
fraud. Whatever the rights and wrongs of spiritualism,
the play would certainly have been a better one had
it been written by a disbeliever. We should then
have escaped the argumentation—amusing, but too
evidently biassed to be really dramatic—and we
should not have been disconcerted by the three or
four trivial and unnecessary miracles which M. Sardou
introduces by way of clinching his profession of faith.
For instance : Towards the close of Act I. Madame
d'Aubenas has gone off, nominally to take the night
train for Poitiers, in reality to pay a visit to her lover,
M. de Stoudza. When she has gone, her husband
and his guests arrange a séance and evoke a spirit.
No sooner have preliminaries been settled than the
spirit spells out the word "O-u-v-r-e-z." They open
the window, and behold ! the sky is red with a glare
which proves to proceed from the burning of the
train in which Madame d'Aubenas is supposed to have
started. The incident is effective enough and a little
creepy ; but its effect is quite incommensurate with the

strain upon our powers of belief. The thing is supposed to be a miracle, of that there can be no doubt ; but it has not the smallest influence on the course of the play, except to bring on the hurry-scurry and alarm a few minutes earlier than might otherwise have been the case. Now if the spirit, instead of merely announcing the accident, had informed M. d'Aubenas that his wife was not in it—if, for example, it had rapped out " Gilberte chez Stoudza "—it would have been an honest ghost (though indiscreet), and we should not have felt that our credulity had been taxed to no purpose. Or is it M. Sardou's deliberate intention to hint that, though spirit communications are genuine enough, they are never of the slightest use ?

Into the second act no spirits intrude, and the drama is really potent and superb. Gilberte has passed the night with De Stoudza and is preparing to proceed on her journey. A clamour outside alarms them, and De Stoudza's servant arrives with the news of the catastrophe, and with a paper containing an account of it. Gilberte's gradual realising of the situation is in itself highly dramatic. The friend and maid with whom she was to have travelled have both met a horrible death, and her own name appears in the list of the missing, with an account of her husband's agony and despair. Then there comes a violent ringing at the bell ; she hides in an adjoining room, and her husband and three other men rush in,

still in their evening dress of the night before, now
torn and begrimed with their frantic search among
the charred ruins of the train. There is some hope
that Gilberte may have caught an earlier train, and it
is thought that De Stoudza may have information on
the point. The husband's anguish and despair are
of really thrilling effect, while we know that Gilberte
is only a few paces off, hearing, and writhing at,
every word he utters. He is called away by the
intelligence that his wife's body has been found; but
her cousin and friend Valentin (a naval officer, if I
understood aright) has got an inkling of the truth,
and remains in De Stoudza's room when D'Aubenas
and the rest go off. In spite of De Stoudza's denials,
Valentin summons Gilberte from her concealment;
and the scene which ensues is altogether masterly.
What is Gilberte to do? Confess that she is alive?
In that case she changes the tragedy of the situation
into a grotesque, humiliating, loathsome farce. France
is ringing with the news of her dreadful death; to-
morrow it will be shaking with cynical laughter at her
escape. Her husband must either give the jest its
final relish by forgiving her; or "la femme au chemin-
de-fer" must be dragged through the Divorce Court
amid a notoriety a thousand times augmented by her
adventure. No! she is dead and she will remain
dead; she will bury herself with De Stoudza in the
recesses of his native Roumania. But this does not

at all suit Monsieur de Stoudza. What he has all along been aiming at is a divorce which should enable him to marry her—and her fortune. But a dead woman cannot be divorced; a dead woman cannot carry her fortune with her to her grave—in Roumania. Little by little, the absolute baseness of the adventurer's nature betrays itself; and on the top of her horror, remorse, and penitence towards her husband (whose despair has touched her profoundly) Gilberte has now to pile contempt for her seducer and loathing for the degradation she has undergone. I know few scenes so complex in their emotional substance, and at the same time so dexterously developed and worked up. Undoubtedly the well-made play has its merits, and is an art-form deserving of respect. It does not go deep, and it does not wear well ; but, at its best, it is enormously amusing.

Let me illustrate what I mean by saying that it does not go deep. These people of Sardou's, who fret their little hour before us so entertainingly, are not characters at all, and have no existence apart from the particular action in which they are engaged. Imagine trying to transport this Gilberte into another play, and construct another action around her ! You would find there was nothing to take hold of, no temperament, no organism, nothing but a name. She exists in and for these incidents; they, and nothing else, are, as it were, her differentia ;

take them away, and she merges indistinguishably in abstract conventional humanity. You could (if you were Shakespeare) write a totally different play from *As You Like It*, in which Rosalind should re-appear and be as clearly and convincingly Rosalind as the Fat Knight of the Second Part of *Henry IV.* is clearly and convincingly Falstaff. You could (if you were Molière) take Célimène out of *Le Misanthrope* and place her in a totally different action, while keeping her individuality intact. You could (if you were Dumas) write a new play around Francillon ; you could (if you were Ibsen) write a new play around Nora or Hilda. But though you were Shakespeare and Molière and Dumas and Ibsen in one, you could not take Gilberte out of *Spiritisme* and place her— that very woman, and no other—in a different story. She is literally a nonentity. To build another play round her would be like making a cannon according to the well-known recipe—you take a hole and you surround it with metal. Madame Sans-Gêne, on the other hand, *is* a character, so far as she goes ; you could easily write another play around her. But note, in the first place, that Sardou found the character (or something like it) ready made ; in the second place, that the action is sacrificed to the development of character, and that, as soon as intrigue takes the upper hand, the play becomes tedious.

Madame Bernhardt was admirable in the second act of *Spiritisme;* she has done nothing better of late years. . M. Brémont, too, made a very sincere and dignified D'Aubenas.

The performances of the Viennese company,* which has just departed after a too short visit, gave us a very interesting glimpse into the popular drama of the German-speaking world. The first play produced, indeed, was not German, but Italian—*Untreu*, by Roberto Bracco. It was a clever piece of pure dialogue—one might describe it as two acts of *Francillon*, with the Screen Scene from *The School for Scandal* sandwiched between them. The originality lies in the treatment, which is fresh, vivid, and daring. Much less modern, but at the same time more interesting as indications of the trend of popular taste in Germany, were the two rhymed costume-comedies by Franz von Schönthan and Franz Koppell-Ellfeld, *Die Goldene Eva* and *Renaissance.* One scarcely knows whether to envy the Germans this peculiar dramatic form. It is essentially commonplace and bourgeois in inspiration, superficial in its psychology, conventional in its criticism of life. It reminds one strongly of the excellent but unendurable Sheridan Knowles, in his moods of elephantine merriment. This painful association occurred to me when I saw *Die Goldene Eva ;* and when, in *Renaissance,*

* See note, p. 207.

I found the famous Helen-and-Modus scene in *The Hunchback* repeated with a difference, my suspicion of an intellectual kinship between the German authors and their English predecessor was fully confirmed. But the difference aforesaid is important and all-pervading. Not only have the Germans a more ingenious turn of fantasy than that of the worthy Knowles, but their literary form is infinitely lighter and brighter. Instead of dull and stodgy blank-verse —a measure which is either the divinest or the deadliest form of human speech—they write in free, various, graceful and witty rhymes, which give point and sparkle to the shallowest humour, and a certain tender charm even to commonplace sentiment. It is the vivacity of its rhymes alone that lends any merit to *Die Goldene Eva ;* but the conception of *Renaissance* —the awakening of narrow puritanism and pedantry at the touch of art—is really poetical, and the execution is ingenious and delightful. It is said that the German Emperor went five times to see this play. If so, I venture *unterthänigst* to applaud his Majesty's taste. One may say of this form of comedy what M. Faguet says with malicious wit of the belated romanticism of the Odéon, that it presents "un aliment littéraire très distingué, très délicat, et d'une incontestable originalité rétrospective." The company which presents these plays is strong both in individual talent and in ensemble. Madame Odilon

is an expert and well-graced actress, with keen intelligence and ample powers of expression. She has
not the marked individuality of Madame Réjane or
Miss Rehan, but all that she does is able and interesting. Herr Christians and Herr Nihl have polish and
grace in comedy, force, feeling, and technical skill in
rhetoric. The broad humour of Herren Eppens and
Kramer in *Die Goldene Eva* was very clever indeed.
They would be excellent as Sir Toby Belch and Sir
Andrew Aguecheek. As for Herr Wallner's performance of the old monk in *Renaissance*, it was one of
the most amiable and accomplished pieces of comedy
I have ever seen on any stage. I trust this company
will one day give us a fuller taste of its quality.

At Her Majesty's Theatre, Mr. Sydney Grundy has
produced a skilful rendering of *Mlle. de Belle-Isle*
under the title of *The Silver Key.** The play is one
of the classics of its school, and is very alert and
entertaining. I have seen it so often at the Français
in the old days that it no longer thrills me very
deeply ; but the majority of the audience, to whom
ignorance meant bliss, were evidently enraptured
with it. The changes introduced by Mr. Grundy are
inessential, except that, by running the first two acts
into one, he has upset the balance of the play and

* July 10—August 11. The season closed with two performances of Hamlet, August 12 and 13. *The Silver Key* was
reproduced November 1—26.

emphasised the impossibility of the time-scheme. The acting is good all round, Mrs. Tree being quite admirable as the Marquise, Miss Millard very beautiful and not unpathetic as Gabrielle, Mr. Tree graceful and polished as Richelieu, Mr. Lewis Waller sincere and forcible as the Chevalier.

XXXI.

"ARDEN OF FEVERSHAM"—"EDWARD III."

21st July.

THE time has come for an earnest remonstrance with the Elizabethan Stage Society. Perhaps the Society is of opinion that I have all through its career been apter at expostulation than at eulogy, and has come to class me among its adversaries. In that case it does me wrong. It has only to be true to its ideals, and exert a reasonable modicum of intelligence in the effort to realise them, in order to command my warmest sympathy. Far from approaching *Arden of Feversham** with any hostile prejudice, I went to St. George's Hall full of pleasurable anticipation, feeling that here the Society had undertaken a task well within the scope of its powers and purposes. Marlowe's *Faustus*† had proved a little beyond its powers ; but this extremely

* July 9.   † *Theatrical World of 1896*, p. 204.

interesting domestic tragedy was easier to handle
and likely to prove more effective. At any rate,
the Society was much more usefully employed in
reviving a play which was practically unknown,
except to professed students, than in giving costume
recitals of more or less familiar plays of Shakespeare.
These were my sentiments when I entered the hall.
How could one possibly foresee that a society which
aims at restoring the conditions of the Elizabethan
stage, and, above all, dispensing with the mutilations
of text necessitated by modern scenery, would not
only mutilate but break on the wheel, dismember,
shatter, bray as in a mortar, a drama whose artless
perspicuity of narration is one of its greatest charms?
The ordinary vocabulary of criticism is inadequate
to describe the process of disintegration to which
these reverent Elizabethans had subjected the un-
offending play. They had quite literally made a
hash of it, or rather a mash, a senseless stirabout.
They began by deliberately sacrificing the one great
advantage, or at any rate characteristic, of the
Elizabethan stage — its innocence of hampering
Unity of Place—and contrived to concentrate into
one interior an action which demands at least
twenty changes of scene, and shifts from Feversham
to London, and all up and down the north coast
of Kent. Then they began the action—incredible,
but true—exactly in the middle, with the fourth

scene of the third act. Black Will, Shakebag, and
Michael are the first characters we see; who they
are, or what they are about, no one can possibly
tell. It is just as though we were to begin *Macbeth*
with the scene in which the murderers are lying in
wait for Banquo. Then we skip back to the last
scene of the second act, whence we take a flying
leap into the middle of the first scene of the first
act. When we reach Alice's first soliloquy, she
speaks two out of its twelve lines, and ekes them
out with six lines from another soliloquy in the fifth
act. It would be tedious and impossible to follow
our Elizabethans in their game of hop, skip, and
jump backwards and forwards through *Arden of
Feversham*. They are for all the world like grass-
hoppers in a hay-cock—there is no guessing where
they will pop up next. Never, never, have I seen
a hapless play so muddled and stultified. Monsieur
d'Artois' treatment of *Lorenzaccio* was comparatively
reverent. And these are the purists who protest
against the methods of the modern stage, and talk
about "enlisting public interest in the erection
of an Elizabethan playhouse in London, as a
Shakespearian memorial!" What interest can the
public possibly take in exhibitions of presumptuous
foolishness like this (so-called) performance of *Arden
of Feversham*? The acting was very feeble, only
one gentleman (who played Black Will) showing

any real talent; and the stage-management was
utterly helpless. Such exploits can only bring
discredit upon the scholarship, the intelligence,
nay, the common-sense of the Elizabethan Stage
Society.

"On this occasion," says the programme, in
English which is neither Elizabethan nor Victorian,
"the object of the performance is to show, side by
side, those portions of two plays that are associated
with Shakespeare's name, and which differ widely
in their versification, their dramatic treatment and
characterisation." The unwary might gather from
this that Shakespeare's hand was to be traced in
those "portions" of *Arden of Feversham* which
were presented, and not in the rest. But no one
has put forward such a theory, nor does the writer
mean to imply anything of the sort. He is only
explaining (in his own graceful way) that *Arden*
had to be unsparingly cut in order to fit into the
same programme with the scenes from *Edward III.*
But practically the whole of it could have been
given if the performance had begun at eight instead
of nine; or, if that was impossible and the pruning-
knife had to be called in, the order of the scenes
might at least have been retained, and the story
comprehensibly set forth. The idea of placing
Arden in contrast with the Roxborough Castle
scenes from *Edward III.* was in itself a good one,

and, as the latter episode was acted with spirit and intelligence, the evening was not, after all, entirely wasted.

The juxtaposition was really very curious. While *Arden of Feversham* was being recited, a still, small voice in the background of one's consciousness kept up a running protest against the theory that this was the work of Shakespeare. Even in the mangled remains of the tragedy, one could feel not only the short-windedness of its versification, but the absolutely un-Shakespearian quality of its psychological method. Then came the scenes from *Edward III.* I blush to confess that I had not read this play; and yet I cannot regret the ignorance which procured me a keen and unexpected sensation. Before twenty lines had been spoken, the still, small voice aforesaid was whispering "Shakespeare!"— and ever as the recitation proceeded the whisper grew louder and more emphatic: "Shakespeare! Manifestly Shakespeare! Shakespeare all over! Shakespeare without the shadow of a doubt!" It was a curious and memorable experience thus to stumble, as it were, upon an unknown page of Shakespeare—to hear the familiar, incomparable voice uttering, in characteristic profusion, these unfamiliar but fascinating and delicately "conceited" things. Not altogether dissimilar must have been the thrill with which two Oxford scholars the other day deciphered on a shred of papyrus the words *Legei Iesous*, and after them the sentence, "Raise the stone, and there ye shall find me ; cleave the wood, and there am I." Take, for instance, these lines of Edward's after the Countess of Salisbury has repulsed his advances :

> " Whether is her beauty by her words divine ;
> Or are her words sweet chaplains to her beauty ?
> Like as the wind doth beautify a sail,
> And as a sail becomes the unseen wind,
> So do her words her beauty, beauty words."

Who could have written this but Shakespeare, the young Shakespeare in the springtide of his poetical, as opposed to his dramatic, power? But single lines and detached sequences are always treacherous evidence. Here we have (in Act I., Scene 2, and in Act II., Scenes 1 and 2) between eight and nine hundred lines without a single patently un-Shakespearian word, verse, or trait of any sort ; abounding in all the characteristics, good and bad, of his early " honey-tongued " period ; and containing a line ("Lilies that fester smell far worse than weeds") which he adopts and treats as his own at a conspicuous point in the most personal of his writings, his Sonnets. If this concurrence of probabilities do not constitute a practical certainty, we must abandon all arguments based upon style. Look at the scene between Edward and Lodowick—does it not give us a glimpse into the very workshop of the amatory poet ? Study the copious and somewhat frigid casuistry of Warwick's speeches to his daughter—is not this Shakespeare playing with his tools ? Have we not here the 'prentice-work of the pen which, some dozen years later, wrote the speeches of Ulysses in *Troilus and Cressida ?* What other poet had at his command such unchastened wealth of imagery, such well-nourished smoothness of style? If this be not Shakespeare's work, all I can say is that some nameless poet has out-Shakespeared Shakespeare. If I were asked to select a characteristic specimen of Shakespeare's style in the years antecedent to *Romeo and Juliet,* I verily believe I should choose the second act of *Edward III.*

The difference between *Arden of Feversham* and these scenes of *Edward III.* is simply this : in *Arden* there are a few lines (some fifty, perhaps, out of two thousand five hundred) which more or less strongly suggest Shakespeare, whereas in the Roxborough Castle episode there is scarcely a line that does *not* seem to bear his sign-manual. One or two expressions and cadences in *Arden* curiously foreshadow definite passages in Shakespeare. For instance, Mosbie's "Nay, if you ban, let me breathe curses forth," at once recalls Hamlet's "Nay, an thou'lt mouth, I'll rant as well as thou;" while Alice Arden's

"What! groans thou? Nay, then give me the weapon!" suggests Lady Macbeth's "Infirm of purpose! Give me the daggers!" In these cases one could almost imagine that Shakespeare, having been familiar with *Arden of Feversham* in his youth (perhaps having acted in it) remembered and deliberately reproduced, many years afterwards, two turns of phrase that had in their day proved notably effective. There are other passages in which the coincidence is one of style rather than of actual words; but they are very brief, and are separated by endless stretches of prosaic verse (with frequent *and unintentional* patches of sheer prose), from which the Shakespearian touch is conspicuously absent. If there were the slightest external evidence to bring Shakespeare into connection with the play, I should think it probable enough that he was interested in it, studied it, wrote in a few lines here and there (perhaps at rehearsal), and remembered some of its effects in later life. But all this is pure fantasy, innocent enough if we do not propound it as fact. On the other hand, my fantasy stops short at the effort to conceive that the pen which wrote *Romeo and Juliet* and *A Midsummer Night's Dream* could anywhere in the same century produce such lines as these:

ALICE.   In good time see where my husband comes.
Master Mosbie, ask him the question yourself.

MOSBIE. Master Arden, being at London yesternight,
        The Abbey lands, whereof you are now possessed,
        Were offered me on some occasion
        By Greene, one of Sir Antony Ager's men.

It would take a whole essay to show that the psychological style of *Arden* is as unlike Shakespeare's as the literary style. But the evidence of the literary style suffices. Even those brief passages which seem Shakespearian do not show the special characteristics, good or bad, of his early period, during which the play must have been written—those characteristics which mark every line of the *Edward III.* scenes. I know that this argument runs directly counter, in both particulars, to the authority of Mr. Swinburne; but, with all regret and respect, I cannot help it. I do not even find, with Mr. Swinburne, that *Arden* shows the hand of a young man. It strikes me as the work of a man of mature experience and singular talent, but an amateur in literature and drama. Even in Shakespeare's earliest work there is more of the craftsman, actual or potential. May not the play have been written by some local gentleman (like the Lord Cheiny introduced in it), who took a special interest in this particular theme, and made no other excursion into letters? This would account both for its anonymity (since play-writing was by no means a gentlemanly pursuit) and for its having been touched up by another hand—conceivably Shakespeare's.

XXXII.

"FOUR LITTLE GIRLS."

28th July.

ONE of the intellectual amusements of my schooldays was to make a formless scrabble of ink on a piece of paper, and, while the ink was still wet, to fold the paper together. When reopened, it exhibited a hideous blot, to which, however, its sheer symmetry imparted a semblance of design ; so that the eye of imagination could find in it a butterfly, or a dragon, or a spread-eagle, or some other bipennate and fantastic object. The composition of *Four Little Girls*,* a farce by Mr. W. S. Craven, now running at the Criterion, must have been just such an intellectual amusement. A mechanical and meaningless symmetry is the beginning and end of the author's art. In place of humour he gives us symmetry; in place of ingenuity—symmetry; in place of character—symmetry; in place of sense—symmetry. Two widower fathers, being about to marry their two widow housekeepers, want their two sons to marry the two housekeepers' two daughters. But the two sons have already married two wives of their own choosing, and the two housekeepers' two daughters

* July 17—August 7.

are already engaged to two other young men. Throw
in a tutor, out of *Betsy*, at the beginning of the cast,
and at the end a slavey out of *Our Boys* and seven
hundred and fifty other farces, and you have the
symmetry perfected. Every second scene takes the
form of a pair of compasses, with the tutor for its
pivot, thus :

Tutor

A. Father	Father B.
A. Son	Son B.
A. Son's Wife	Son's Wife B.
A. Housekeeper	Housekeeper B.
A. Housekeeper's	Housekeeper B.'s
Daughter	Daughter

I am not prepared to make affidavit that this precise
tableau ever occurs ; but this is the type towards which
every grouping tends. The stage-manager is for ever
constructing an isosceles triangle—building and de-
molishing the *pons asinorum*. If Housekeeper A's
daughter goes off with Father A's son into conservatory, R.U.E., we are sure that three minutes
will not have elapsed before Housekeeper B's daughter
will be flirting with Father B's son in conservatory,
L.U.E. No sooner has Son A's wife fainted down
stage L, than Son B's wife takes the opportunity of
swooning down stage R. I shall be told that this is
precisely the fun of the thing. It is the *only* fun of
the thing, I admit ; but the propositions are not

quite identical. People laughed at the farce, it is true, for Mr. James Welch, who played the tutor, is funny in the stupidest part, and Messrs. Barnes and Blakeley,* who played the fathers, are capital comedians. When I left the theatre, at the end of the second act, the piece promised to be a success; and for aught I know it may keep its promise. But I doubt it. The first-night audience, or rather a certain class of first-night audience, has a tolerance, if not an absolute taste, for the merely ignoble, which the great public, one hopes, does not really share. We critics are too apt to take a first-night audience, however composed, for the great public, and merely to shrug our shoulders at its imbecilities. We gloze over ineptitudes with conventional phrases, and it is only when a piece begins to have merit that we begin to be critical. This is a mistake—almost a betrayal of trust. For once, then, I am moved to be quite sincere, and to say that *Four Little Girls* is saddening and humiliating stuff. Apart from its geometrical variations of figure, its humour is sheer naught, consisting largely of such age-old quips as " He wants you to marry——" " The devil ! " " No, not the devil—Miss Middleage." Much of it, moreover, is highly mock-valentinish and unpleasing. Absolutely indecent the farce is not; it is merely vapid and ignoble. I cannot conceive any reason why people

* Mr. William Blakeley died December 8, 1897.

should seek entertainment in these "loves of the triangles," when they have such an intellectual master-piece (comparatively speaking) as *A Night Out* inviting them every evening.

XXXIII.

"THE SLEEPING PARTNER"—"AS YOU LIKE IT."

1st September.

PLAYGOERS who want but little here below, and want that little long, will find just what they require in *The Sleeping Partner* * at the Criterion. This farcico-sentimental play is an English version of an American adaptation (by Miss Martha Morton) of a German comedy. It is far too long for its substance, which is of the slenderest; but it is quite inoffensive, occasionally amusing, and very well acted. Mr. James Welch is excellent as the limpet father-in-law whose intrusive affection goes near to ruining his daughter's married life. He might put more movement, it seems to me, into the first act, especially at the close; but in the later acts he plays with most artistic sobriety and finish. Miss Lena Ashwell is skilful, natural, and charming as the too-devoted daughter; Mr. Fred Terry, Mr. F. H. Tyler, and Miss Ada Branson are

* August 17—September 25.

all good; and Mr. Richard Lambart contributes an eccentric character-sketch of some merit.

In Mr. George Alexander's provincial repertory, *As You Like It* naturally holds a prominent place, and he has found in Miss Fay Davis a delightful Rosalind. There is more in the character than Miss Davis as yet brings out of it, but she imports nothing into it that is foreign or inharmonious. She is graceful, spontaneous, intelligent. If here and there she slips or slurs a point, she is at least innocent of the much more destructive error of laborious point-making. One may say of Miss Davis what Mr. Arthur Symons says of Viola in his interesting *Studies in Two Literatures*, that she has not "the over-brimming life, the intense and dazzling vitality, of Rosalind." She has not yet penetrated to the depths of the part, but she presents its surface aspects with singular charm. The whole performance, at the Grand Theatre, Islington, seemed to me thoroughly enjoyable. Mr. Alexander's Orlando is manly and spirited, Mr. Vernon's Jaques is as admirable as ever, Miss Mabel Hackney makes a bright and pleasant Celia, Miss Julie Opp an imposing Phebe. No part, indeed, is less than efficiently filled, and everything is tuned to the right key.

XXXIV.

" DIE SCHMETTERLINGSCHLACHT "—" DIE VER-
SUNKENE GLOCKE."

8th September.

THE German drama has a peculiar interest for us,
inasmuch as it is running a sort of race with our own.
The present movement began almost simultaneously
in the two countries, and, although there is no deliberate competition between the two groups of playwrights, they may not unfairly or uninstructively be
measured against each other. The Germans had
some initial advantages not to be overlooked. In
the first place, the drama had never fallen so low in
Germany as in England. Friedrich Hebbel, Gutzkow,
Laube, Freytag, Anzengruber, were the contempor-
aries of our Knowles, Lytton, Reade, Taylor, and
Robertson—and the Germans were, individually and
collectively, a far stronger set of men. In the second
place, there is a much wider opening for artistic
work in Germany and Austria, with all their subsidised and unsubsidised theatres, than in—I was
going to say England, but for present purposes
England means simply the West End of London.
Notwithstanding these advantages, however, the German drama from 1870 to about 1885 had fallen, like

our own, almost entirely under the dominion of France. Original playwrights, so-called, produced either trivial farces or weak imitations of Sardou. There, as here, a new generation came to the front between 1885 and 1890. There, even more than here, the influence of Norway—of Björnson as well as Ibsen—helped to correct, or at least to supplement, the influence of France. It is this movement of the past decade that one inevitably compares with our own ; and I have been fortunate enough during the past month to see two characteristic plays by the two leaders of the movement, Sudermann and Hauptmann.

Let it not be supposed, however, that Sudermann and Hauptmann are the most popular playwrights of the Fatherland. No ! at the popular theatres, the Tivolis, Casinos, Stadtgartens, and so forth, the heroes of the hour are Messrs. Brandon Thomas and Harry Paulton. *Niobe* and *Charlies Tante* have only one serious competitor in public favour, and that is— *Trilby*. There must clearly be some element of universal appeal in this Anglo-Franco-American fairy tale, since it has made its barefoot pilgrimage, as Ouida would say, from Tobolsk to Tangier. In Germany, at any rate, Trilby figures in every book-shop and at every beer-garden. I did not pay my devoirs to her ; but somewhere or other—at Mann-heim, I think—I saw a photograph of the local Svengali, a sort of marionette ogre who would certainly have made Mr. Beerbohm Tree's flesh creep.

The play of Sudermann's which came in my way was not a favourable specimen of his manner. It was a four-act comedy, *Die Schmetterlingschlacht*, as who should say *The Battle of the Butterflies*. The butterflies in question are the three daughters of a deceased official, who have been brought up by their mother with the sole, and avowed, and carefully inculcated, design of making wealthy marriages. In the meantime, they earn a scanty sustenance by decorating fans; the youngest, Rosi, a girl of sixteen, having a genius for designing "butterfly battles," which the others paint. The action is in the highest degree sordid and uninviting. The miserly employer of this happy family has a son whom his hard usage has reduced almost to imbecility. The son, Max, falls in love with the eldest of the three girls, Else. Now Else is carrying on a flirtation, which seems to have gone to considerable lengths, with the chief traveller of the firm, a bouncing personage whose boast it is that when he travels second class people take him for an officer in mufti. Else has a hearty contempt for the ungainly and helpless Max; but she has been too carefully brought up not to know that, having hooked a millionaire's son, it is her duty to land him. At the same time, while officially betrothed to Max, she keeps up her relations with the fascinating bagman, using her sister, Rosi, as a screen to conceal them. Rosi, however, is not only the cleverest but the best of the family. She has an inborn sense of honour and decency which her mother's precepts and her sisters' example cannot altogether deaden. The upshot is that even the purblind Max discovers Else's unworthiness, and transfers his affections to Rosi, who has all the time loved him in secret. Thus the millions remain in the family; Else can, no doubt, marry her migratory Adonis; and the third sister, Laura, can angle at her ease for the middle-aged Graf on whom her mind is set. This ferocious satire on German middle-class life may or may not be just : all I know is that it makes a profoundly uninteresting play. There is merit in the character-drawing, especially in the figure of the genuinely devoted mother, to whom bitter poverty has made fortune-hunting appear in the light of a sacred duty ; but the dramatic invention is poor, the execution is heavy-handed, and the play, as a whole, seems hopelessly flat and uninspired. If Sudermann had written nothing else, he would be out of the running in the race aforesaid. But he has written the first and third acts of *Die Ehre*, *Heimat*, and, above all, *Teia* and *Fritzchen*, the first two playlets of that curious trilogy *Morituri:* these are the works that make him a really formidable competitor to our leading playwrights. The only feature of *Die Schmet-*

terlingschlacht to which I would invite their attention
is its frankly middle-class material. I think we have
of late given ourselves up too exclusively to studies
of a somewhat conventional upper-class, and of
"society" narrowly so called. Like Pooh Bah in
The Mikado, we have taken no notice of any one
under the rank of a stockbroker. The public, I
fancy, is a little tired of Mayfair, and would fain make
an occasional trip to Peckham or Canonbury. There
is a success in store for the playwright who shall be
daringly suburban, though his suburbanism need by
no means be so prosaic as Sudermann's.

The second play I saw—*Die versunkene Glocke*, by
Gerhart Hauptmann—is the reverse of prosaic. He
calls it a *Märchendrama*, and it is, in fact, something
like a mingling of *Tannhäuser* and *A Midsummer
Night's Dream*, with a touch of *Peer Gynt* thrown in.
The latest work of this as yet but half-ripe man of
genius—who began with ultra-naturalism in *Vor Son-
nenaufgang* only seven years ago—it has been a great
success at all the leading theatres of Germany, while
in the book-market it has gone through five-and-
twenty editions. Hauptmann is a real poet, of that
there is no doubt; there are exquisite passages in
this *Sunken Bell;* but it assuredly is not a work of
the first order. Its symbolism is obscure and elusive ;
but that may be said of other and greater works.
The fatal defect is, that neither scene by scene nor

in its general scheme is it really dramatic. Without any sacrifice of either poetry or symbolism, a man of truly dramatic genius might have made the same theme scenically absorbing. As it is, the effect of the scenes depends on their lyric beauty, not on their dramatic strength, and I own I was all the time yearning for the music which the author, or at any rate the management, sternly denied us. The story is this: Heinrich, a famous bell-founder, has made a great bell for a church which has been built at the top of a mountain. As it is being dragged up the mountain side, a malicious satyr upsets the cart, the bell rolls down into the depths of the lake, and the bell-founder either falls or throws himself after it. Not into the lake, however; he falls into the arms of Rautendelein, "an elfin creature," a sort of dryad or nixie, who lives with her witch-grandmother in the forest. The Priest, the Schoolmaster, and the Barber carry him off to his home in the valley, where his wife and two children await him; but he is on the point of dying when Rautendelein comes down and breathes new life into him. He follows her up to the mountain, and for some time flourishes greatly. He is full of vast plans for artistic effort and the regeneration of humanity; but somehow or other (one does not quite know why, for the machinery of the poem is as vague as its ethics) his plans all go wrong and he sickens of everything. The end comes when he sees his two

children toiling up the mountain carrying between
them a heavy pitcher:

HEINRICH. What bear ye in the pitcher, dear my children?
FIRST CHILD. Salt water.
SECOND CHILD.   Bitter water.
FIRST CHILD.   Mother's tears.

At the same moment the voice of the sunken bell
booms forth from the depths of the lake, and Heinrich
casts off Rautendelein with curses, and flees down
the mountain.   It is characteristic of Hauptmann's
seemingly deliberate carelessness of dramatic effect
that not till the next and last act do we learn (and
then in mere narrative) that the deserted wife has
drowned herself, and that it is her spirit which has
caused the bell to sound.   Heinrich, in this act,
comes back to seek Rautendelein and die, and the
play ends with a really exquisite lyrical colloquy
between them.   It is reported, I know not with what
truth, that there is an undercurrent of autobiographic
reference in *Die versunkene Glocke*, the bell itself
typifying Hauptmann's last great play, *Florian Geyer*,
which met with a disastrous fate.   Be this as it may,
the poem evidently allegorises the old story of genius
depressed by the dead air of the valley of domes-
ticity, and seeking new life and inspiration in the
freer atmosphere of the mountains—not to say the
" hill-tops."   But what, in this case, is the allegoric

function of the bell which gives the play its name?
There is no sign that before it fell Heinrich was
in the least dissatisfied with his life in the valley;
and the fact that the starting-point and turning-point of
the play seem both to lie outside the symbolic scheme
gives colour to the rumour that it took its rise in personal circumstances. The moral of the fable, as I
understand it, is that however fine an influence may
be in itself—and Rautendelein is, in the main, a
beautiful and benignant creature—it cannot be permanently helpful if it demand the sacrifice of fundamental affections and duties. This is no very original
doctrine, nor, I repeat, is it very clearly conveyed;
but the allegory and its moral would be of little
enough moment were the drama interesting and really
dramatic.   To my thinking, it is, on the contrary,
diffuse and wordy, though about a third of the printed
text is omitted in representation. The really dramatic
opportunities of the theme are either slurred or
entirely missed, while the poet poetises at large.   It
is only just to him to add that I saw the play under
most depressing circumstances at the Frankfort
Schauspielhaus—the mounting bad, the stage-management helpless, the acting third-rate. I suspect the
good people of Frankfort of starving their playhouse to feed their opera-house—an immoral proceeding.

XXXV.

"IN THE DAYS OF THE DUKE"—"MISS FRANCIS
OF YALE"—"A MARRIAGE OF CONVENIENCE"
—"HAMLET."

15th September.

IT seems as though *Secret Service* had put English
playwrights on their mettle, for its successor on the
Adelphi boards is by far the best home-made melodrama we have seen for many a day. Not that
Messrs. Haddon Chambers and Comyns Carr have
suddenly been seized with vaulting ambition. They
have attempted no departure from the beaten track.
Out of popular materials, and by popular methods,
they have concocted a popular play. The only novel
element they have introduced into the compound
is brains. They have shown ingenuity in conception,
tact in development. They have imagined a situation, a dilemma, of great emotional capacity; they
have worked it out through a series of picturesque
scenes and unexpected conjunctures; and they have
written a patriotic military drama without a single
passage of music-hall patriotism or vulgar bluster.
Though the title is *In the Days of the Duke*,* and the
main action lies between the Peninsula and Waterloo,
the play might be presented in Paris without seriously

* September 9—November 20.

wounding French susceptibilities. This dignity of
tone I applaud with both hands and with all my heart.
If we must fight our battles over again on the stage—
and Shakespeare, truly, set the precedent—let us try
to do so more or less like gentlemen, and not like a
set of swaggering, posturing, and often puling mounte-
banks. Of all ebullitions of patriotism I can remember on the stage, that which is least objectionable and
probably truest to nature is Major Tarver's reply, in
Dandy Dick, to Salome's inquiry, "What would you
do if the trumpet summoned you to battle?"—"Oh, I
suppose I should pack up a few charcoal biscuits and
toddle out, you know."

The story of *In the Days of the Duke* is really well
imagined. The Prologue, spirited and interesting in
itself, sets on foot a very nicely-balanced action,
adjusted with something of French inventiveness and
dexterity. According to the strict rules of the game,
the calumny against the hero's father should not have
leaked out through a chance utterance of the subordinate villain which the hero by chance overhears,
but should have been deliberately put abroad by the
villain-in-chief to serve his own wicked ends. Again,
the oath sworn by the hero's mother that she will
never let her son know of her shame is a feeble and
improbable expedient. Some other reason ought to
have been devised to reinforce her natural unwilling-
ness to disclose the truth to him. These details

excepted, the whole imbroglio of the letter (which makes it impossible to clear the father's honour in the son's eyes except at the expense of the mother's good name) is excellently conceived and developed. Scene after scene has the merit of carrying the emotion a step further, and higher, than one foresees at the outset—of superadding, as it were, a touch of fresh invention to the mere logical working-out of the given problem. The scene in Paris between Mrs. Aylmer and Colonel Lanson did not come out quite so strongly as it ought to have done, chiefly, I think, on account of a momentary failure of grip on the part of Miss Marion Terry, who, for the rest, acted with sincerity and charm. From the passage in the gaming-house onwards, the pictorial element rather took the upper hand of the dramatic; but the interest of the story was, on the whole, sustained with tolerable success. The duel-scene was highly picturesque, and one really regretted the untimely end of the subordinate villain, O'Hara, who, in the hands of Mr. J. D. Beveridge, was a very pleasant specimen of the good-humoured scoundrel. The Duchess of Richmond's ball was excellently put on the stage, but the Highland Reel struck me as curiously spiritless, the music seeming slow and the dancers self-conscious and embarrassed. As for the last act, at Hougomont after the battle, it was perhaps unnecessarily elegiac, but it brought the action to a fairly effective and satisfactory close.   The play, I repeat, is nothing but a spectacular, military melodrama of the most ordinary type; but it is conceived, constructed, and staged with far more than ordinary cleverness and care.

Professor Saintsbury is never tired of insisting that the only way to write historical romance is to make your leading characters entirely fictitious and keep your real personages on the second plane.   Messrs. Chambers and Carr have, by chance or design, acted on this principle with the happiest results.   It could only render the Duke of Wellington ridiculous to give him a prominent place, a personal interest, in an Adelphi melodrama.   Therefore they have kept him practically outside the action, in which he intervenes only as a sort of *deus ex machinâ ;* so that while we are always conscious of his presence in the background, his dignity is in no way sacrificed.   Mr. Charles Fulton looks the part admirably, and plays it with firmness and discretion.   Mr. Terriss plays both the Colonel Aylmer of the Prologue and the Captain Aylmer of the play, and looks equally well in both characters.   Miss Millward makes the most of a heroine who has very little to do ; and the comic relief, not over refined but now and then amusing, is in the hands of Mr. Harry Nicholls and Miss Vane Featherstone.

In *Miss Francis of Yale,** a farce by Mr. Michael

* September 7—October 30.

Morton, at the Globe, we plod through two acts of unamusing and unpleasing buffoonery, in order to reach a third act in which the horseplay becomes really entertaining in its boisterous fashion. *Miss Francis* is evidently a direct descendant of *Charlie's Aunt*. In other words, she is *Charlie's Cousin*, a great many times removed—indeed,

> " No more like to Charlie
> Than he to Hercules."

Mr. Weedon Grossmith is far too able a comedian for such a part as Frank Stayner, but all that can be made of it he makes. Other parts are well played by Mr. H. Reeves-Smith, Mr. Arthur Playfair, Mr. C. P. Little, Mr. Mark Kinghorne, Miss May Palfrey, and Miss Ethel Hope; and the first-night audience seemed, on the whole, to relish the farce.

In the reproduction of *A Marriage of Convenience** at the Haymarket, Mr. Frederick Harrison takes the part of the Comte de Candale, originally played by Mr. Terriss. Mr. Harrison was naturally nervous on the first night, and had not quite recovered the habit of the stage, which rusts in disuse like any other habit. By this time his performance will no doubt have acquired the ease which was what it chiefly lacked. The cast was otherwise unaltered, and the play went well. It was preceded by *The Tarantula*,†

* See p. 166.   † September 4—November 4.

a farce by Miss (or Mrs.) Mary Affleck Scott—innocent, but elementary in its humour.   It showed us
Mr. Brandon Thomas as a crazy Scotch entomologist,
a line of character in which he is always amusing.

First-night applause may be roughly classified under
three heads.   There is first the applause due to mere
politeness, friendship, and thoughtless good-nature,
proceeding from people who do not ask themselves
whether a piece of acting is good or bad, whether it
has or has not given them pleasure, but simply clap
because it is expected of them and because it is
pleasanter to approve than disapprove.   Secondly,
we have the applause of personal fanatics (often quite
disinterested in their mania) who think this actor or
that the greatest genius that ever lived, and bellow
themselves hoarse whatever he does and however he
does it.   The third and rarest sort of applause, easily
distinguishable from the other two, is that in which
the spontaneous and irrepressible delight of the whole
audience finds utterance; in which intelligent appreciation chimes in with fanaticism and good-nature; in
which the actor, if he have any delicacy of ear, can
detect the tribute of the few amid the facile plaudits
of the many.   Such was the applause which at many
points greeted Mr. Forbes Robertson's Hamlet on
Saturday night*—notably at the end of the second act,
and at the close of the play.   It was indeed an admir-

* Lyceum, September 11—December 18.

able performance, falling short in only one respect of
what may be called a reasonable ideal. The grace
and distinction of Hamlet, his affability (to use a
needlessly degraded word), his melancholy, his intellectual discursiveness—all these aspects of the
many-sided character Mr. Robertson brought out
to perfection. He shone especially in the mono-
logues. I have never heard any similar passage of
Shakespeare better delivered than the "Oh, what
a rogue and peasant slave am I" soliloquy, as treated
by Mr. Robertson. His method of introducing it,
while conning a prompt-book of the play handed him
by the First Actor, is at once ingenious and unforced;
and the way in which he graduates and varies it is
quite masterly. He makes it a little drama in itself.
Not quite so happy is his treatment of the "To be or
not to be" speech. His face seems to light up at the
phrase "To sleep—perchance to dream!"—whereas
the thought should clearly overcloud the momentary
serenity with which Hamlet has been contemplating
the "consummation devoutly to be wished." On the
whole, however, Mr. Robertson's handling of the
meditative passages could scarcely have been improved. It was so good that one doubly regretted
the omission of the "Now could I do it pat"* speech.
Having restored Fortinbras at the close, moreover,
Mr. Robertson might surely have managed to get in

* Afterwards restored.

the soliloquy " How all occasions do inform against
me," hitherto omitted along with the " occasion "
which inspires it.   As it is, the introduction of Fortinbras lends dignity and picturesqueness to the final
scene, but is of no literary value.   The only point
in which Mr. Robertson's performance is notably
defective happens, unfortunately, to be a rather important one : he slurs and almost ignores that
nervous excitability on Hamlet's part which merges
so naturally, nay, almost indistinguishably, into his
pretended madness.   We do not nowadays waste
time in arguments about Hamlet's sanity.   If Hamlet
is mad, which of us shall 'scape Hanwell?   He
deliberately puts on an "antic disposition " to serve
him at once as a mask and a weapon—to protect him
from his uncle's malice and at the same time to
further his revenge.   But there can be no doubt that
the assumption of lunacy is congenial to him, and
that he uses it as a safety-valve for pent-up emotion.
He is in a state of nervous overstrain which finds
relief in fantastic ejaculations, scathing ironies, wild
and whirling words of every sort, quite apart from
their calculated effect upon others.   Now Mr. Forbes
Robertson makes, one may almost say, as little as
possible of Hamlet's assumed lunacy and real hysteria.
It was probably this side of the character that chiefly
appealed both to actors and audiences, in Shakespeare's own day.   Our forefathers took a delight in

the contemplation of insanity which we no longer feel, and it is evident that their actors revelled in exhibitions of mopping, mowing, and gibbering, such as would merely inspire us with disgust. But the very fact that Hamlet's madness is assumed makes it quite endurable even to modern nerves, and I can conceive no reason, whether of art or expediency, for the exceeding tameness of Mr. Forbes Robertson's acting in such passages as the end of the first act (after the departure of the Ghost) and the great scene with Ophelia. He omits a good many of the wild and whirling words, and he puts no force or gusto into those he utters. Such a phrase, for instance, as "Aha, boy, art thou there!" addressed to the Ghost "in the cellarage," he speaks with respectful melancholy, instead of the feverish freakishness which is surely the keynote of this scene. I cannot but hope that Mr. Robertson will reconsider these scenes, which are certainly well within his compass. Artistic self-restraint is a very good thing, but in this case it verges on timidity. One or two individual readings I would gladly discuss with Mr. Robertson if space permitted. As it is, I can only refer him to *Dramatic Essays*, by George Henry Lewes (ed. 1896, p. 176), for proof that the strain by which "Neméan" can be got into the metre is not only uncalled-for but positively wrong. Shakespeare scanned the word as Virgil did— "Némean."

The other parts are not very fortunately cast. Mrs. Patrick Campbell's Ophelia cannot rank among her successes; Mr. Barnes is a far too robust and stolid Polonius; Miss Granville, as the Queen, looks absurdly young, and shows a total lack of experience in this class of work; no one, in short, except Mr. Forbes Robertson, rises above mediocrity. But he rises so far above it as to make the revival interesting and memorable.*

* _Letter to the Editor of the "Daily Chronicle."_

Sir,—May I beg you to reconsider the judgment expressed in your leading article of to-day that Mr. Forbes Robertson and the Lyceum company in general take _Hamlet_ in too quick time? The bane of almost all recent Shakespearian acting has been its torturing slowness; and if the Lyceum performance does indeed mark the setting-in of a reaction against this evil habit, criticism ought to encourage instead of checking it. Mr. Forbes Robertson happens to be an actor with a voice and a competent method of elocution. He is thus in a position to attempt, and often (as I think you will agree) to compass, the effects of fluent and impetuous diction which Shakespeare obviously intended. He is not compelled to cast about for subtleties of meaning which Shakespeare obviously did _not_ intend, in order to mask and excuse the breathing-spaces required by deficient physical power, and lack of skill in the management of the voice. He seeks his effects in Shakespeare's words, not in his own pauses; and that is what makes his performance, in spite of evident limitations, so vivid, fresh, and interesting as it is on all hands admitted to be. For my part, I was at no point conscious of any undue haste; but that, you

XXXVI.

"ONE SUMMER'S DAY"—"THE WHITE HEATHER" —"THE PURSER."

22nd September.

WHY, Mr. Esmond, oh, why did you kill "the Kiddy"? This is out-Heroding Herod with a ven-

will say, is merely a personal impression. Well, I appeal to Shakespeare, who probably knew at what speed his scenes could be most effectively taken. We know that the normal duration of a performance in Shakespeare's day (probably without entr'actes) was from two hours to two hours and a half. At the Lyceum, with very brief entr'actes, and with no time wasted on mere show and spectacle, the performance lasted nearly three hours and a half. We may safely say, I think, that the curtain was actually up and the play proceeding for full three hours; yet immense cuts were made, a good half of the fourth act being entirely omitted, and long scenes and speeches dropped out at many other points. We can scarcely suppose, indeed, that the whole text, as it stands in the Folio or the 1604 Quarto, was spoken even in Shakespeare's time; but there is no reason to assume that the cuts were anything like so heroic as those which are nowadays thought necessary. Even admitting that half as much was cut at the Globe as at the Lyceum (a very large admission), and supposing the time of performance extended, in the case of so popular a play, to three hours, it would still follow that Burbage, Shakespeare, and their fellow-actors must have spoken their words a good deal more rapidly than Mr. Forbes Robertson and his comrades, and given less time to "business" Let us pause,

geance. A more wanton and indefensible child-murder was never committed on any stage. It is worse than inhuman—it is inartistic. Don't tell me of extenuating circumstances. It is true we hadn't seen him in the flesh, but that makes it all the harder. Perhaps if we had seen him we shouldn't have minded so much. He was mirrored for us in Dick Rudyard's love and pride—untainted by the egoism of parentage—and his little figure irradiated the background of your play. It is equally useless to allege that his death affords you a novel and striking "curtain," and secures for Mr. Hawtrey a fine opportunity of proving that there is a pathetic side to his talent. All this is true enough. I am not aware that any one before you has ended a comedy in a flood of tears, and Mr. Hawtrey plays the scene exceedingly well. If we felt that there was any necessity for the child's death, or even that it had been adequately prepared and led up to, that flood of tears would be a stroke of genius. As it is, the effect is too cheaply—and therefore too dearly—bought. On second thoughts, I am inclined to regard it as a

then, before urging Mr. Robertson to prolong his pauses and substitute for the vigorous smoothness of his delivery the spasmodic languor which has so long wrought havoc on our stage.— I am, Sir, your obedient servant,

WILLIAM ARCHER.

LONDON, *Sept.* 13*th*.

stroke of genius all the same, however inexpertly delivered; but on the whole I resent more than I admire it.

This resentment, as I hope Mr. Esmond will perceive, is merely the recoil of overstrained sympathy. It is the Nemesis attendant on a too direct and too successful appeal to sentiment. We cannot have our affections trifled with. I, for one, had become so attached to that foolish and delightful couple, Major Dick Rudyard and Maysie, that all through the second act I found distinct comfort in remembering the title of the play, *One Summer's Day*,* and clinging to its (alas! fallacious) assurance that though the sun might go down on misunderstanding in the second act, happiness must rise with the moon in the third. Of course we all foresaw the misunderstanding from afar, though we could not foresee the incredible density with which Dick allows, or rather forces, Maysie to glide into it. This is a fault, and a regrettable one. It is also a fault, I think, that Maysie should instantly consent to marry Phil Marsden, merely because she is disappointed in Dick Rudyard. It is only on the stage that these lightning revulsions happen. In real life, no sane woman would thus make a shuttlecock of herself, behaving as if there were only two men in the world and she were bound by law to marry one of them before the clock strikes

* Comedy Theatre, September 15—still running.

twelve. To a woman of sense and sound instincts, a loveless marriage is not such a simple matter as our playwrights seem to think. Women have been known, indeed, to marry the wrong man in order to spite the right one; but, in this instance, not even that elevated motive comes in. Maysie's instantaneous acceptance of Phil is simply a stage convention. It might be defended as one of those mere compressions of time which are sometimes necessary on the stage; but the answer is that here it is not necessary at all. There is no sufficient reason why, in the last act, Phil should be actually engaged to Maysie. It is quite enough that he should think her finally estranged from Dick. His hope being thus revived, he would still be under the temptation to foment instead of removing their misunderstanding, which forms the dramatic mainspring of the last act; and, the hope being less definite, we should feel his ultimate disappointment less discordant with the tone of pleasant comedy which is, or ought to be, dominant in the play. It will be gathered from all this that construction is not the strong point of *One Summer's Day*. Truth to tell, Mr. Esmond has taken an old and sufficiently commonplace theme, and has expended no particular skill on the mere framework of his play. What renders it delightful—and thoroughly delightful, up to the point where the author takes to harrowing our feelings—is the kindly, original humour that permeates it, and especially the indefinable, irresistible lovableness of Dick Rudyard and Maysie. In conceiving the relation between them, and in writing the scenes in which it is developed, Mr. Esmond proves himself a true and delicate artist.

This is Mr. Esmond's first unqualified success— I say unqualified, for the audience apparently did not take "Kiddy's" death so much to heart as I did. Moreover, it is his most accomplished and evenly able piece of work. Yet it is still *The Divided Way*,* tentative and ill-starred as it was, that gives one assurance of his future. *One Summer's Day* is excellent Albery, or, perhaps more precisely, a capital piece of immature Pinero. Now Albery and immature Pinero are all very well in their way, but we want to know if a man can go further; and on that point the new comedy might leave us in doubt. Fortunately *The Divided Way* has disposed of this doubt in advance, and we can accept its successor as welcome evidence of fecundity and flexibility of talent. Mr. Esmond is pursuing a quite normal course of development, and rapidly disengaging his individuality. Amid all that is conventional in this play, and a good deal that is technically careless—for example, the free use of the soliloquy, and even of that prehistoric barbarism the soliloquy overheard— we are always conscious of the workings of an artistic,

* *Theatrical World of 1895*, p. 353.

a creative, will and temperament. The only thing
that remains to be seen with regard to Mr. Esmond's
talent is whether he has the capacity for acquiring
and (so to speak) assimilating real, intimate, first-
hand knowledge of life. Imagination he has, scenic
instinct he has; he has wit, humour, and at least the
makings of a style. In a word, he has plenty of
faculty—but has he vision? Can he put off the
distorting spectacles of theatrical tradition, and look
life straight in the face, catching shades and subtleties
of expression, and fixing them in the medium of his
art? Has he thought, and thought competently, on
human nature and human destinies? And has he
the gift of illustrating his thought by means of his
observation? In more general terms, has he an
adequate criticism of life, and the power of enforcing
it dramatically? The longer I live, the more am I
impressed by the inexhaustible wealth of dramatic
material in the everyday world around us. Our lot is
cast in a fabulously auriferous region; we every day
tread the richest " pockets " and " placers" under
foot, if only we had the gift of divining and the
power of working them. Every now and then there
comes a man who has this gift and power, and we
hail him a dramatist. He works his vein and makes
his pile, while others flock around to sift and re-sift
his dross and leavings. It is not yet quite clear
whether Mr. Esmond has really struck a lode of his

own, or is merely crushing and winnowing, with unusual skill, the slag of others. It is not quite clear,
indeed; but remembering *The Divided Way*, and
putting this and that together, we have every reason
to hope for the best.

Odd as it may appear, the one thing that inclines
me to distrust my judgment of Mr. Esmond's comedy
is the extraordinary charm of Miss Eva Moore's
acting in it. I cannot imagine Maysie played by
any one else; wherefore I begin to wonder whether
the author has created a character or only fitted
an actress to perfection. But the dilemma—the
"whether . . . . or"—is really gratuitous. There is
not the slightest reason why he should not have done
both, and that is the theory I propose to adopt.
Mr. Hawtrey, as Major Rudyard, proved himself as
convincing in sincerity as in mendacity, and that is
saying a great deal. I cannot quite make up my
mind whether Mr. Cosmo Stuart's curiously unsympathetic voice was a gain or a drawback to the
character of Phil Marsden. It certainly chilled one's
compassion for the luckless lover; but perhaps it is
as well that our sensibilities were not tortured on this
side also. Mr. Kemble, Mrs. Charles Calvert, Mr.
Kenneth Douglas, and Miss Lettice Fairfax were all
good, and Miss Constance Collier, as the gipsy
Chiara, looked imposing and played cleverly, but, as
it seemed to me, with rather too much refinement of

voice and accent. And now I bethink me that I have all this time said nothing of "the Urchin," marvellously acted by Master J. Bottomley, who was beyond a doubt the chief success of the play. He is an original conception, this Puck of the gutter, this precocious Flibbertigibbet, who flits like an imp of mischief through the comedy. Several of his sayings kindled throughout the house that "sudden glory" of irresistible laughter which is as rare as it is refreshing. But though, like every one else, I enjoyed the Urchin, it was somewhat against my better judgment. I felt that in this case Mr. Esmond's fantasy was rather too unconditioned, too remote from any foundation of fact. But I am ashamed of taking so churlish a view of the matter. The audience, more philosophical than I, showed no disposition to cross-examine the pleasure which this quaint creation afforded them.

No one realises more clearly than Messrs. Cecil Raleigh and Henry Hamilton, authors of *The White Heather*,* at Drury Lane, "the wealth of dramatic material in the everyday world around us." Life is all material to them, just as it is to the editor of an illustrated paper. Drury Lane, in fact, in the autumn season, has become a sort of "magnified and non-natural" *Illustrated London News*, the manager playing the part of editor, while the authors, rushing

* September 16—December 15.

around with their note-books, sketching-blocks and
kodaks, from Throgmorton Street to Boulter's Lock,
from Battersea Park to the bottom of the sea, are
indistinguishable from reporters and special artists.
And as, in the up-to-date illustrated journal, there is
always a section headed "In Lighter Vein," "In Merry
Mood," or what not, so the judicious editor of the
Drury Lane Budget takes care to make his young
men introduce "comic cuts" on every second page,
enlivened with all the slang, topical allusions and
wheezes of the day and of the year. Although the
staff works strenuously to keep abreast of the times,
an annual publication is doomed to have somewhat
the air of a back number. I cannot but foresee in
the near future a drama of such elastic framework
that one or two scenes, at least, can be placed in a
different setting from week to week or from month to
month, according as public interest shifts from place
to place. In *The White Heather*, for example, why
should not the villain's henchman have left the
missing marriage-certificate in the safe custody of
his foster-brother, an Afridi chief? We could thus
get in a realistic tableau of the siege and relief of Fort
Gulistan, with hand-to-hand combats, first between
the villain and the Afridi, then between the hero and
the villain. Or the precious document might have
been eaten by a transport-camel employed in the Nile
Expedition, so that we could make a little detour to

Berber on the way from Battersea to Boulter's Lock.
Far be it from me, however, to pit my ingenuity
against that of Messrs. Raleigh and Hamilton. I
merely suggest the idea of an adjustable kinemato-
graphic drama, going through a new edition every
week—the details I leave in their experienced hands.

Meanwhile, Mr. Arthur Collins is to be congratulated on having opened his campaign with an exceedingly amusing and spirited production of its class.
It is entertaining in its very absurdity; without pretending to refinement, it is at no point brutal or
offensive; and it is excellently mounted and put on
the stage. The opening scene, "The Moor," is a
striking and imaginative piece of scene-painting; I am
assured that the representation of the Stock Exchange
is marvellously faithful; Battersea Park and Boulter's
Lock are gay and animated tableaux; and if the
Duchess's Ball is more sumptuous than amusing—
well, I am not without a suspicion that this too may
be true to nature. On one point, however, the kine-
matograph still distances its emulators—its people are
so much better made-up. A little more care in
making scalps join and moustaches seem reasonably
plausible would not be thrown away in these repro-
ductions of the giddy whirl of the aristocracy. As for
the combat of the divers at the bottom of the sea,
with the fishes gambolling round them, it is presented
with a great deal of ingenuity, and stirred the audi-

ence to enthusiasm. Of the actors, Mrs. John Wood holds indubitably the most important position. She is the life and soul of the entertainment, and her part, a very long one, may fairly be described as a treasury of social philosophy adjusted to the meridian of Drury Lane. What a pity that *Madame Sans-Gêne* was not written some twenty years ago! Mrs. John Wood was born to play the part, but, unfortunately, born a little too early. The other comic parts are all sacrificed to Lady Janet McClintock, but Miss Pattie Browne and Mr. De Lange are as amusing as they have any chance of being. Miss Kate Rorke plays the heroine very pleasantly, Mr. Henry Neville is an emphatic and effective villain, and Mr. Dawson Milward shows tact and sincerity in the part of a poor apology for a hero. Minor characters are well played by Mr. J. B. Gordon, Mr. Robert Loraine, Mr. C. M. Lowne, and Miss Beatrice Lamb.

There is a comic idea in Mr. John T. Day's farce *The Purser*,* at the Strand Theatre, and the writing is not without cleverness. Unfortunately Mr. Day shows no power of carrying a story forward, but keeps the same situation afoot, without development or any essential change, throughout his three acts. Therefore our amusement, mild from the first, waned steadily towards the end. The farce was played with plenty of spirit by Miss Kate Phillips and Miss Adie

* September 13—October 16.

Burt, Mr. Edmund Gurney, Mr. J. G. Grahame, Mr. Righton, Mr. Charles Troode, and Mr. Stuart Champion. Its scene is the deck of a P. and O. liner, very ingeniously and prettily staged by Mr. Hemsley.

XXXVII.

"FRANCILLON."

29th September.

OF Mrs. Brown Potter's performance of *Francillon** I can only say, as I said of *The Sign of the Cross* on its production : this thing is outside the sphere of art—criticism has nothing to do with it. Yet I gather from the advertisement-columns of the daily papers that some critics—two at least—actually accepted it, not only as art, but as good art. "Mrs. Potter can now take her place among our leading actresses," one of these gentlemen is represented as saying ; while the second is of opinion that "Mrs. Potter proved by her acting of ever-varying lights and shades how accomplished she has become in her art." Other oracles are quoted, but they are equivocal, as oracles are apt to be—commenting upon her "eccentricity" and her fondness for "the unexpected." The unexpected she certainly achieves ;

* Duke of York's Theatre, September 18—November 6.

but the acme of the unexpected to me is that any one should be found to praise such unexpectedness. One is always prepared for difference of opinion, within certain limits; but here the question is not simply between good and bad, but between art and its negation. Dumas's comedy is very stiffly and clumsily translated—"mœurs" is always rendered "morals" ("other times, other morals"), "hommes d'esprit" becomes "men of spirit," and so forth. Yet it is not hopelessly stultified as it would be by "adaptation." In order to strengthen the part of the husband, he, instead of the Baronne Smith, is made to lay the trap for Francine which brings the action to an end; but up to that point the play, though much abbreviated, is not seriously deformed. Mr. Kyrle Bellew is well fitted for the part of Lucien de Riverolles, and plays it effectively; Mr. Beauchamp and Mr. Elwood are good as the Marquis and Henri de Symieux; Mr. Charles Thursby plays the notary's clerk with valuable discretion; Miss Helen Vane makes a pleasant Baronne Smith; and Miss Grace Noble plays Annette with sincerity, simplicity, and charm. But oh! the Francillon!

XXXVIII.

"The Baron's Wager"—"My Lady's Orchard"
—"The Mermaids."

6th October.

Only one item in the new Triple Bill* at the Avenue
Theatre calls for serious notice.   The other two
may serve their purpose or they may not ; they are
insubstantial, impalpable ; soap-bubbles without the
iridescence. If you are a very candid and unseasoned
playgoer, you may be amused by the late Sir Charles
Young's duologue *The Baron's Wager ;* if, on the
other hand, you seem to have seen it a score of
times already, and executed, moreover, with very
different ingenuity and sparkle, you are, I fear, an
impossible curmudgeon like myself.   It is Scribe
in the *n*th dilution. In *The Mermaids*, again, a
"submarine musical fantasy" by Mr. Gayer Mackay,
the fantasy remained conscientiously submarine, and
never for a moment came to the surface.   It is a
common error to confound the merely grotesque
with the fantastic—Caliban with Ariel.   Not that
there was anything brutal or particularly displeasing
in *The Mermaids ;* its worst fault was precisely its
lack of fantasy, its poverty of invention, its nullity

* October 2—15. See p. 289.

of idea. There were some fairly clever verses in it, set to very obvious rhythms by Mr. Claud Nugent. It did not appear which of the verses were by Mr. Mackay and which by Mr. Charles Brookfield, who was stated on the playbill to have contributed "additional lyrics." Mr. Frank Wyatt contrived to be amusing as a Merman, and Miss Lottie Venne, as Lady Barker, made really brilliant use of her scanty opportunities. The "fantasy" of these two genuine comedians kept the piece going, but their task was hard and thankless.

Remains *My Lady's Orchard*, by Mrs. Oscar Beringer, a drama of poetry and passion, blood and tears. If its accomplishment were equal to its ambition, and if it were acted with reasonable skill, it might redeem the programme from utter triviality ; but unfortunately these are very large "ifs." The theme is dramatic enough—indeed, it might be described as a tragic parody-in-advance of Mr. Bernard Shaw's *Candida*. John of Courtenay, "a Saxon Seigneur of Romani," has a young wife, Azalais, and a troubadour friend, Bertrand of Auvergne, professionally known as "the Wild Nightingale." The Romani Rye is a little more Saxon—that is to say, phlegmatic and inarticulate— than a husband, under such conditions, ought to be ; the lady is innocently, but recklessly, coquettish ; and the Wild Nightingale tries, in the phrase of his

brother lyrist Burns, to play the Old Hawk. The
Nightingale sulks and glooms and chants passionate
dawn-songs, until "friend John" can stand it no
longer. Scratch a Saxon and you find a Tartar;
the husband and the lover fight in presence of the
lady, who thinks it is all in fun; the lover is run
through the body, and "friend John" walks off
with Azalais, who still believes that Bertrand is
only keeping up the joke and pretending to be in
the agonies of death. We here touch one main
fault of the play—the inconceivable and exasperating
silliness of Azalais. The Nightingale must indeed
be hard up for inspiration who can warble to such
a goose. No Saxon husband of the twelfth century,
I am sure, would have drawn sword in such a case.
He would have regarded his wife as what she is—
an unbearably naughty child—and applied the classic
remedies. The stupidity of the lady reacts upon her
husband and lover, so that the whole trio remain
entirely uninteresting and unsympathetic. Moreover, they all talk a terrible pseudo-archaic jargon,
which it would be quite inadequate to describe as
"Wardour Street." There is good Wardour-Street
and bad Wardour-Street; and this is not good.
Mrs. Beringer is a lady who has shown a good deal
of dramatic talent; but she has here undertaken a
task which demands, in addition, a very much rarer
quality—consummate literary tact. Mr. Brookfield as

"friend John" looked, and no doubt felt, supremely uncomfortable — like a man who hates children, compelled, very much against his will, to dress up and take part in some nursery charade. Miss Vera Beringer played Azalais with all the nods and becks and wreathëd smiles traditionally supposed to belong to such a part, emphasising every second speech with a toss of her mane or a sweeping curtsey. This young lady has still much to learn, and to unlearn. Miss Esmé Beringer, arrayed in chain armour, enacted Bertrand "the Wild Nightingale." Her performance did not appeal to me; but I confess myself incapable of taking any interest in a male character played by a lady, whether the lady's name be Beringer or Bernhardt.

XXXIX.

"THE LIARS"—"OH! SUSANNAH!"

13th October.

THE merest tyro in criticism can point to the technical faults of Mr. Henry Arthur Jones's new play at the Criterion. They are too patent to be worth dwelling on for a moment, and they do not make the comedy a whit less agreeable. *The Liars** is bright and interesting from first to last, and the third act

* October 6—still running.

is most skilfully elaborated.   It is true that the hero
is outside the action, a mere confidant and chorus,
like the De Ryons or the Thouvenin of Dumas.   It
is true that the construction of the second act is
audaciously haphazard, the characters dropping in
without rhyme or reason, in the friendliest manner
possible, just when Mr. Jones requires them.   It is
true that even the third act, though it justifies the
title of the play, does not strictly belong to the
subject, since all the lying merely retards, without
affecting, the decision of the main question at issue :
the question whether passion or worldly wisdom is
to carry the day.   It is true that no one seems to
remark a glaring inconsistency on the very surface
of the story ultimately told to George and Gilbert
Nepean : if it was Dolly and not Rosamund who
dined with Jessica at the Shepperford Hotel, how
came it that Rosamund and not Dolly wrote to
George Nepean on the hotel paper, and posted the
letter at Shepperford ? *   It is true that we get a

---

* With reference to this remark Mr. Charles Wyndham wrote
to me : " I must correct a serious mistake on your part.   There
is no suggestion whatever that Lady Rosamund pretended to dine
at the hotel.   Perhaps you have forgotten that in the third act it
is expressly told that George Nepean was aware of the fact that
Lady Rosamund had dined with Mrs. Crespin in the neighbour-
hood."   I had not forgotten this fact.   It is this fact which
forces the conspirators to abandon the lie they originally intended
to tell—the lie which Falkner ultimately *does* tell—to wit, that

little tired of the perpetual allusions to eating and drinking, and that we are but moderately interested in the question where Gilbert Nepean and his wife are going to sup and what is to be their bill of fare. All this is true; and if the piece had any claims to rank as an enduring masterpiece, a perennial glory of English literature, all this would be of more or less importance. But the piece makes no such pretensions. It is a lively, entertaining, vigorously-written comedy of the day, which will have its day (a long one I doubt not), but will scarcely go down to posterity.

Let no one be deterred from going to see *The Liars* by the idea that it is a " problem play." It is nothing of the sort. In order to keep to the key of comedy, Mr. Jones has deliberately shirked the problem which might have arisen had the heroine been a woman with any strength of character. You cannot solve or even help to elucidate a problem by presenting a self-evident case. Mr. Jones propounds

Lady Rosamund dined with Lady Jessica. The inconsistency, or oversight, or improbability, which I point out is this : when the original lie is abandoned, and Dolly Coke, instead of Lady Rosamund, is put forward as Lady Jessica's companion, it is apparently forgotten that Lady Rosamund, as her letter proves, was also at the hotel, and the circumstance is not alluded to by either party, until Falkner, at the very end, blurts out the whole story. The matter is trifling in the extreme ; but I was under no misapprehension as to the facts.

a question and discusses it, with much vivacity, in abstract terms; but the concrete example he places before us does not in reality raise that question, or indeed any other. Here is the enunciation of what might have been the problem:

SIR CHRISTOPHER (*to* FALKNER). Come, old boy, there's no need for us to take this tone. Let's talk it over calmly, as old friends and men of the world.

FALKNER. Men of the world! If there is one beast in all the loathsome fauna of civilisation that I hate and despise, it is a man of the world! Good heaven, what men! What a world!

SIR CHRISTOPHER. Quite so, old fellow. It is a beastly bad world—a lying, selfish, treacherous world! A rascally bad world, every way. But, bad as it is, this old world hasn't lived all these thousands of years without getting a little common-sense into its wicked old noddle—especially with regard to its love affairs. And, speaking as an average bad citizen of this blackguardly old world, I want to ask you, Ned Falkner, what you mean by making love to a married woman, and what good or happiness you expect to get for yourself or her? Where does it lead? What's to be the end of it?

Now here is a problem, a very old problem, and one which has been discussed a thousand times in every tone and in every tongue. There is no reason why it should not be thrashed out again and yet again, with appropriate examples. But in *The Liars* the example is not in the least appropriate. There may be some question as to "what good or happiness

a man can expect" if he runs away with a married
woman who loves him; but if the woman does not
love him, does not even think she does, and is
incapable of entering into a single one of his ideas,
aspirations, or habits, it is manifest that his only
rational course is to steer clear of her. This is
exactly the case of Lady Jessica and Falkner. Had
she been ever so free, it would have been rank
lunacy on his part to marry her; much more evidently, then, is he mad to think of leading her
through the divorce court to the altar, or casting in
his lot with her in any way. That such infatuations
occur we all know, and this one makes a capital
comedy; but it has not the remotest bearing upon the
question whether it is ever possible to defy with impunity the canons and conventions of the existing
social order. Had Mr. Jones really wanted to argue
out this question, he would have chosen a case in
which the passion was not all on one side, and in
which there was at least some semblance of mutual
fitness between the man and woman concerned. As
it is, Sir Christopher Deering's homily in the last act,
amusing and effective though it be, never really
touches the point. Dramatically it is all right, for
even in such a conjuncture politeness puts a certain
curb upon sincerity; but logically it is all wrong,
circling round and glozing over the essential facts of
the case. Had Sir Christopher spoken his whole

mind, his harangue would evidently have taken something like this form: " I needn't enter into the
general question whether the divorce court is ever
the gateway to happiness. If you could point to fifty
couples who had passed through it into Elysium, I
should still say ' Don't follow in their footsteps ! '
You, Lady Jessica, are the last woman in the world
who can possibly set society at defiance. Society is
your element ; apart from it you do not exist. You
are a creature of frocks, frills, and furbelows. The
interests of your life centre entirely in dress and the
pastimes and tittle-tattle of your set. You have no
resources, intellectual or moral. Your mind is a
tissue of second-hand cynicisms ; you have no heart,
and even your senses are poverty-stricken. You are
not, cannot be, and do not want to be, anything like
the woman Ned Falkner sees in you. He, poor
fellow, though no longer young in years, is a boy
in simplicity of heart and power of idealisation. His
love is the frantic illusion of a strong and earnest
man who has hitherto starved that side of his nature.
Even if all outward circumstances were propitious,
you could not for a single week live up to his conception of you. But `outward circumstances are in
fact as unpropitious as they make 'em. He is not an
ordinary man who can be obscurely happy or un-
happy, as the case may be. He has a high character,
a great position. He is eager to sacrifice them for

the woman he thinks you; but you know as well
as I do that he thinks you very different from the
woman you are. Do not imagine for a moment
that the pain of disillusionment will be all his; however generous he may be in recognising that the error
was his own, and that you had no intention of de-
ceiving him, the misery of his situation will inevitably
react upon you. You will chafe each other to death
in solitude, in idleness, in ennui; or you will leave
him, and—I needn't tell you the rest. If you were
another woman, I might (or might not) preach in
another key. If you were capable of the love for
which the world is well lost, I might bid you, as
Francis Thompson puts it, 'shake off the bur o' the
world' with confident serenity. I might tell you that
your present marriage—your subjection to that gross
brute of a husband, for whom you cannot feel even
esteem or kindness—was more immoral than any
licence, more degrading than any scandal. I might
even urge you to take Ned Falkner's hand in faith
and hope, and let him drag you out of that slough.
But since you do not yourself feel the degradation,
it does not exist for you. You are bored and irritated,
not shame-stricken; and I cannot allow you to ruin
my friend's life out of mere boredom. Come now—
you are a shallow but not hitherto a noxious little
creature. In this case the responsibility rests upon
you, for you are sane and Ned Falkner is not. You

are not, you don't pretend to be, blinded by passion : show that you are capable of acting wisely and kindly for yourself and for him. Prove by resolutely rejecting him that there is something in you, after all, of the woman he imagines." It is clear enough that Sir Christopher could not make this speech, or anything like it; but this is what is in his mind, and the speech he does make is almost entirely beside the question. If Mr. Jones had wanted really to raise the problem, he would have chosen another object-lesson by which to illustrate it. But he did not want to raise the problem; he wanted to write a gay, insubstantial comedy, in which the Criterion public should find a pleasant relaxation after the painful tensity of *The Physician.* Therefore he chose a case which excluded from the outset all difference of opinion ; since it is abundantly evident that a woman who is congenitally unfitted to make a man happy or to be happy with him, does not become better fitted by the mere fact of being married to another man.

Mr. Wyndham, as an actor, has one great fault from the critic's point of view—he is too persistently good. Now that he has renounced the ultra-sentimental line of characters for which he at one time had a passing fancy, it is impossible to find anything but praise for him. There was a short passage near the beginning of the fourth act, in which I thought his delivery became a little monotonous and sing-

song ; otherwise he rendered the character to absolute
perfection. Here is a little problem for the aspiring
actor : a piano is heard, off the stage, there is a pause
in the conversation, a lady asks "Is that Mrs.
Ebernoe?" and a gentleman answers " Yes "—how is
the gentleman to convey to us in that one word
" Yes" the fact that he is devotedly, chivalrously,
adoringly in love with this Mrs. Ebernoe, whom, be it
observed, we have not seen and of whom we know
nothing? Don't ask me how it is done, but go to
the Criterion and see Mr. Wyndham do it. This
" Yes " certainly deserves to rank with Lord Burleigh's
nod in point of concentrated expressiveness. Mr.
Thalberg plays Falkner earnestly and with feeling,
but has not quite the personality of the part ; he is
too light a weight. Miss Mary Moore is agreeable as
ever, but puts into the part of Lady Jessica even less
reality of feeling than the author intended. Mr. Vane
Tempest is excellent as Freddie Tatton, the most
amusing character in the play ; Mr. Alfred Bishop is
good as Coke; and Miss Sarah Brooke plays very
cleverly the scene of Dolly Coke's disinterested mendacity. Mr. Standing and Mr. Leslie Kenyon play
the odious Brothers Nepean with valuable discretion.

The authors of *Oh ! Susannah !** at the Royalty
Theatre (Messrs. Mark Ambient, A. Atwood, and R.
Vaun) are to be congratulated on having provided

* October 5. Still running.

Miss Louie Freear with a congenial part. Miss Freear is not merely a comic personality, but a genuine artist. Her Aurora is a creation in its way and extremely amusing. She ought to make an incomparable " Marchioness," if only she could find a Dick Swiveller of equal talent. But for Miss Freear, there would be nothing worthy of comment either in the farce or in the acting.

XL.

" THE CHILDREN OF THE KING "—" NEVER AGAIN "—" THE LADY BURGLAR "—" MORE THAN EVER."

October 20th.

THE historian of the future may possibly be able to assign some reason for the sudden efflorescence of the fairy-tale on the German stage during the past five or six years. Is this nursery romanticism a reaction from the realism of Hauptmann, Sudermann, Max Halbe, and the little group of playwrights which gathered around the Berlin " Freie Bühne"? Or has the phenomenon a social rather than a purely literary origin? Is it the lowering aspect of the real world under the iron rule of the drill-sergeant that makes people look to the theatre for the solace of an idyllic "dreamery," as the Germans themselves would call it? Be this as it may, the fact is clear

that the *Märchen* is for the moment the popular art-
form in Germany.   Perhaps Hauptmann's *Hannele*
may be taken as a sort of connecting-link between the
realistic drama and the nursery-tale ; while his latest
work, *Die versunkene Glocke*, takes us to the very
heart of the elemental spirit-world.   Fulda's plays—
The Talisman (which had a brief run at the Haymarket) and *The Son of the Caliph*—are in effect
children's stories, the one borrowed from Hans
Andersen, the other suggested by, if not absolutely
founded on, the *Arabian Nights*.   Von Schönthan's
Renaissance, that charming comedy which the company of the Vienna Volkstheater acted at Daly's last
summer, though it does not actually trench on the
supernatural, is in truth nothing but a fairy-tale.   The
popularity of *Hänsel und Gretel* is still unexhausted ;
and here we have the author-composer of that fireside
legend providing a musical accompaniment—*mélodrame* is the technical term in Germany—to a fairy-
tale by "Ernest Rosmer" which, under the title of
Die Königskinder, has made the round of the German-
speaking world with universal applause.

In principle, I am with the Germans in their taste
for fairy lore.   I wish one or other of our own authors
—why not Mr. John Davidson ?—would follow their
lead, and give us a nursery legend for big and little
children.   But I would not propose for imitation their
treatment of their themes.   It is apt to be decidedly

heavy-handed. *The Children of the King*,* translated by Mr. Carl Armbruster, "revised" by Mr. John Davidson, and produced last week at the Court Theatre, would be very charming if it did not happen, by ill-luck, to be decidedly tedious. The story (and in a work of this class the story is everything) seemed to me obscure, the action languid, and the moral imperceptible. A moral there was somewhere; of that there could be no doubt. There was always an allegoric meaning lurking round the corner, but it never came out into the light of day. Whether the fault lay with the author, with the translators, with the actors, or simply with my own density and slowness of spiritual apprehension, the melancholy fact remains that I could make neither head nor tail of the thing. It almost seemed as though "Ernest Rosmer" assumed on the part of his audience a previous familiarity with the story, just as the Attic dramatists and our pantomime librettists (thus do extremes meet) assume in their audiences a general knowledge of the legends with which they deal. If the German public is prepared for the incidents, and takes them and their inter-connections for granted, it may have leisure to follow out the workings of the moral destiny, so to speak, which seems to preside over the fortunes of the Prince, the Minstrel, and the

* October 13—30. (Reproduced at twelve afternoon performances between December 4 and January 1, 1898.)

Goose Girl. An audience, on the other hand, to whom the incidents are quite new, is too much occupied in speculating (generally in vain) upon their why and wherefore, to have any attention to spare for their spiritual significance. I felt throughout, in a word—and I don't think I was alone in the feeling —that some key or clue was lacking, without which the story seemed motiveless and tantalising. The music, charming in itself, did not greatly enhance my personal pleasure, since it was ambitious enough to demand the undivided attention which one could not possibly accord to it. The German mind, it is to be supposed, can work at full pressure on two planes at once, else this system of *mélodrame* would not be so popular. My faculties are otherwise constructed. Where words and music blend or run parallel, as in a song or recitative, they can be taken in by one mental process ; but where the actors are saying one thing and the orchestra another, we can follow only by dint of "this way and that dividing the swift mind" in a sense not contemplated by the poet. The "slow music" of sentimental drama, though a sufficiently inartistic device, is not open to the same objection. It is a mere murmur of sound, an insidious crooning, designed to steal almost unperceived upon the hearer's sense, and predispose him to tender emotion. It "whispers the o'erwrought heart," without laying any claim on the intelligence or even the attention. But

Humperdinck's music is no such discreet susurrus. It is complex in suggestion and fairly elaborate in structure. We must either listen to it and lose the dialogue, or listen to the dialogue and do our best to ignore the running commentary of the orchestra. Frankly, I should prefer the play without the music and the music without the play. This only means, perhaps, that I am an unmusical person; but is the average English audience much better endowed in that respect? Observe, I do not despise or dislike the music; on the contrary, I am annoyed by the feeling that I should probably enjoy it keenly if my attention were not diverted from it by the sayings and doings of the actors.

When one imperfectly comprehends the author's intention in a play, one is scarcely in a position to judge of the acting. Mr. Martin Harvey did not seem to me quite the romantic young prince the story required; his performance was intelligent rather than poetic. Miss Cissie Loftus as the Goose-Girl was graceful, unaffected, childlike, and acted with a sort of appealing helplessness not inappropriate to the character. Mr. Dion Boucicault played the Minstrel with abundant spirit; Miss Isabel Bateman made an impressive Witch; Miss Hilda Spong, Miss Neilson, and Miss Lotta Linthicum acted with agreeable vivacity in the scene at the city gate; and Miss Lina Verdi was delightful as the Broombinder's little daughter. The piece is beautifully mounted, and the stage-management is excellent.

"Ernest Rosmer," it would appear, is a pseudonym. Am I wrong in guessing that the author chose it in order to suggest a certain affinity to Ibsen's *Rosmersholm*? I seemed to catch glimpses in the last act of Rosmer's idea of "ennobling" humanity. In what way the fable illustrated this idea I do not pretend to divine; but the intention was tolerably evident.

At the Vaudeville, *A Night Out* has given place to another Franco-American buffoonery, entitled *Never Again*.* It has all the sordid extravagance of its predecessor, with none of its ingenuity. It is a mechanical monstrosity, utterly ignoble in tone, which extorts laughter from a puerile public by sheer violence of horseplay. The clockwork system of stage-management so prevalent in America, which did something to mar the effect even of *Secret Service,* is here carried to a positively irritating pitch. Mr. Ferdinand Gottschalk, one of the original American company, played a German musician very cleverly indeed. The other actors scrambled through the play with remarkable agility and staying power.

The programme at the Avenue † is certainly strengthened by the substitution of *The Lady Burglar* for *The Baron's Wager* and *More than Ever* for *My Lady's*

* October 11—February 5, 1898.

† October 16. The theatre closed almost immediately.

Orchard. There is an ingeniously fantastic idea in *The Lady Burglar*, but Messrs. Malyon and James have treated it very slightly and perfunctorily. It passed the first half-hour agreeably enough, however, thanks to the bright and easy humour of Miss Julie Ring, who plays the title-part. Arthur Matthison's burlesque melodrama, *More than Ever*, amused the audience exceedingly, though a good deal of it must have seemed rather motiveless to those who do not remember the particular transpontine blood-curdler which suggested it. The actors, indeed, scarcely entered into the spirit of the thing, except Mr. Brookfield, who was excellent as Shambles, the faithful but fury-haunted major-domo. Mr. H. Stephenson was quite colourless as Sir Crimson Fluid, Bart., a personage who, in the hands of the late John Clayton, became a symbolic incarnation of sanguinary turpitude. Mr. Frank Wyatt, too, made little of the Man-Kangaroo, originally played by Mr. G. W. Anson, as a parody of Mr. George Conquest's then famous, now forgotten, Man-Monkey. *The Mermaids*, by Mr. Gayer Mackay, is still the main item in the programme, and seems to please the audience mightily.

XLI.

"THE FANATIC"—"THE VAGABOND KING."

27th October.

FROM the comments, articulate and inarticulate, which reached my ear in the theatre, I gathered that Mr. John T. Day's four-act play, *The Fanatic,** produced at the Strand last week, was regarded as a commonplace and rather stupid failure. In my opinion it was nothing of the sort. On the contrary, it showed not only intelligence, but dramatic intelligence. The idea of the play was original and excellent, and one could discern, through the veil of a very inadequate performance, several ably invented details. The author's inexperience was manifest in every scene, almost in every line. To make the play a good one, it would have to be written over again from first to last, with only here and there a phrase or a fragment of dialogue retained. The characters would have to be more delicately and more definitely drawn, the situations otherwise prepared and otherwise developed. But my own mental comment throughout, far from being contemptuous or derisive, was, "This is good— this is ingenious—this is even subtle—if only the author knew how to handle it!"

Mr. Day starts from a just observation, simple

* October 21—25.

enough, but, to all intents and purposes, new to the
English stage. We all know that the fanatic is not
necessarily, or indeed normally, a hypocrite ; but
it has been a tradition among our playwrights to
ignore the fact. Here again Puritanism has been
the curse of our theatre, in this case from the literary
point of view. It made itself so hated in the seven-
teenth century that the dramatists (whether before
or after the Civil War) did not dream of studying
it seriously and fairly. By a summary process of
polemical psychology, they made "zealot" synonymous with "rascal"; and the half-deliberate error,
the superficial and narrow convention, has come
down uncorrected to our own times. Through all
these three centuries the Puritan class—the class
which was capable of social, moral, or spiritual
idealism—has held aloof from the theatre, and has
left unthinking playwrights to babble over the old,
unmeaning commonplaces of character to equally
unthinking audiences. There has been no effective
demand from without for the correction of these
traditionary truisms and libels ; and for two at least
out of the three centuries we have had no playwright
of sufficient insight and originality to set about
correcting them of his own motive. Now the case
is altered. Whatever the defects and limitations of
our present school of playwrights, they are looking
at life for themselves, and gradually getting rid of

the old stereotypes of character. Following in the
wake of fiction—of Balzac, of George Eliot, of Mr.
Meredith and Mr. Hardy — they are acquiring a
psychological competence undreamt of by even the
most brilliant masters of the comedy of manners.
But the hypocrite-zealot is a conception so ingrained
in the popular mind that no one has ventured
formally to impugn it, until Mr. Day, with the
courage of inexperience, advanced to the attack.
Mr. Henry Arthur Jones, indeed, had got the length
of showing us fanatics who were sincere enough in
their convictions; but he has always (if I remember
rightly) made them break down notoriously in their
practice. Now this is not the typical, not the
essential, aspect of the case. It throws little light
on the real nature or secret of fanaticism to show
a temperance orator suffering from dipsomania, or
a social-purity zealot enthralled by a French demirep.
Mr. Jorgan, of *The Triumph of the Philistines*,* is a
direct descendant of Angelo in *Measure for Measure*
(though no doubt he has "diablement changé en
route"), and neither is a typical zealot. The fanatic
who is best worth studying is he who is sincere
in theory, benevolent in intention, consistent in
practice. This is the man Mr. Day has sought to
present to us; wherefore I say that in his choice
of subject he showed real insight and intelligence.

* *Theatrical World of 1895*, p. 152.

Nay, more, the main lines of his play are far from ill-conceived. He sets forth his design with amiable simplicity in a note on the back of the programme, the gist of which is as follows :—

"Your true hypocrite is a man with a very wide knowledge of the world indeed, and the wider his knowledge, the greater his success. Your fanatic, on the other hand, is essentially ill-informed. His outlook is narrow, and he is at bottom credulous and simple-minded as a child. Indeed, Credulity— which runs in double harness with Ignorance—seems to be the basis of fanaticism. And in the earlier portion of the play I contrive some amusing situations arising out of the credulity which is so conspicuous a feature of the zealot type.

"The comedy scenes take place in the early days of Isaiah Baxter's second marriage, to a woman younger than himself, who does not share his ideals. But, as time elapses, and the play advances, the pathos of incongruous union becomes apparent. Comedy gives way to serious drama, and the strain reaches the breaking-point when the husband deliberately affirms that he would rather see his wife in her grave than she should take a glass of wine ordered by her doctor !

"Improbable as this situation may seem, I wish to place on record my personal assurance that it arose on two separate occasions in real life to my own knowledge, and medical friends have told me that the experience is by no means rare."

This preface is not the work of a skilled writer, any more than the play is the work of a skilled dramatist. For one thing, Mr. Day should clearly have left his audience to determine whether his situations are "amusing"; but, as a matter of fact, the conception of Mr. Lincoln B. Flagg, with his non-alcoholic beverages which are absolutely indistinguishable from whisky, brandy, and sherry, is not only amusing, but ingenious and dramatic. The swindle is eminently plausible, and has the further advantage of fitting into the scheme of the play and becoming, potentially at least, a factor in the development of character. What more natural than that the strict teetotaller, betrayed into drinking the accursed thing, and even appearing in public more or less under the influence of alcohol, should become doubly embittered against it? So helplessly does Mr. Day work out his theme that I am not quite sure whether this is his intention. The situation at the end of the second act is a mere meaningless scramble. We cannot tell whether Mr. Baxter has found out for himself that Mr. Flagg's patent whisky resembles the genuine article not only in its taste but in its other properties; nor is it clear whether this incident affects his subsequent mental attitude and conduct. Had this been made clear, it would have done more than the testimony of any number of doctors, quoted on the programme, to prepare us for the situation in which Baxter declares that he would rather see his wife dead than suffer her to drink a glass of wine. There is nothing incredible in this trait, if only it were worked up to with reasonable skill. As it is, Mr. Day jerks it out so crudely as to make it, not precisely incredible, but simply (along with the whole scene in which it occurs) unnatural and unconvincing. He has yet to learn that if an effect is not carefully prepared for in the play, no amount of preparation on the programme will be of any avail.

On the whole, Mr. Day has carried out his unconventional idea by conventional methods, in which he is, moreover, quite inexpert. Not one of his leading characters is ever real to us; and, though this was partly the fault of the actors, the author was in the main to blame. I think he made an initial mistake in assuming such a disparity of age between the husband and wife. He was thus enabled, it is true, to give the Fanatic a son by a former marriage, and to show the young man kicking over the traces of parental severity; but this very obvious effect was dearly bought. It would have been much better to have made the Fanatic a man in the prime of life, and his wife not much his junior. We could then have understood (what is now a mystery to us) how she came to marry him, in spite of her total lack of sympathy with his ideas and habits. Either love or pecuniary interest is required to explain such a marriage as this; but it does not appear that Mrs. Baxter is very much in love with her middle-aged husband, while the nobility of her nature forbids us even to consider the alternative. Given a man of thirty-five and a woman not more than ten years his junior, there would be nothing easier than to conceive that her romantic admiration for idealism in general might reinforce her love, and tempt her to underrate the strength of her distaste for the particular idealisms of her husband's creed. Fanaticism, indeed, is almost unthinkable to the person who is by nature disinclined to it, so that the woman, in this case, would have no doubt of her ability gradually to soften and laugh away her husband's "fads," as she would call them. He, on his side, the more he loved her, would be the more distressed, and finally exasperated, by her inability to place herself for a moment at his point of view. His bigotry would become at once indurated and aggressive; he would find a perverse consolation in exaggerating the asperities of his creed; and, outward circumstances contributing (as in Mr. Day's play), he might easily be worked up to the pitch of gross inhumanity in the assertion of his principles. This is probably, in the main, the story Mr. Day designed to tell; but he has failed to lay down its outlines with any distinctness.

Observe that I accept without criticism Mr. Day's choice of the subjects on which his Fanatic is fanatical. In doing so I commit myself to no opinion on vegetarianism, teetotalism, anti-vivisectionism, or any other "ism." The dramatist's business is to study a particular habit of mind, not to discuss the absolute merits of any opinion or set of opinions; and we are bound to let him select topics on which he may safely assume a pretty general consensus among his audience. Were I to insist on quarrelling with Mr. Day because he does not happen to stand at my particular point of view, I should prove myself as great a fanatic as Mr. Isaiah Baxter. Perhaps at heart I am; perhaps at heart we all are; only that some of us happen to be fanatical with the majority, others with more or less insignificant minorities. Frankly, on almost all the points on which Mr. Day touches, I am, if not a fanatic myself, at least heartily in sympathy with the fanatics, and ashamed of myself for not taking active part with them. But the man who erects a matter of expediency into a matter of religion is, no doubt, logically indefensible. On the basis of that admission I can meet Mr. Day, and look at the tragi-comedy of fanaticism from his point of view. At the same time, I cannot but whisper in his ear that some of the greatest benefactors of their kind have been precisely the men who committed this logical error. The blighting fanatics are those whose religion is *in*expediency.

Mr. Louis Parker's play, *The Vagabond King*,* produced last week at the commodious Camberwell Theatre, is a bright and agreeable piece of what, for

* October 18—23. Reproduced, Court Theatre, November 4—27.

want of a preciser term, I may call Zendaism. The subject is possibly suggested by Daudet, but the manner is the manner of Anthony Hope. (Let me hasten to add that, beyond the mere subject, there is no resemblance between Mr. Parker's play and Daudet's *Rois en Exil.*) The first two acts are off-hand in their technique and a trifle languid, but the third act is a strong and ingenious piece of drama. In the fourth act Mr. Parker lets a question-able morality get the better of the spirit of irre-sponsible romance, in which the rest is conceived. With all respect for the Gospel of Work, one can scarcely see King Pedro and Stella " living happy for ever afterwards " on the two pounds a week which he is to earn as a fencing-master's assistant. Miss Bateman was excellent as the Queen Dowager, and Miss Lena Ashwell played her great scene in the third act with such sincerity and quiet power that the action of the play was interrupted by round on round of spontaneous applause. Mr. Murray Carson had not quite the grace and fascination demanded by the part of Don Pedro ; Mr. George Grossmith, jun., showed real ability as the other " king in exile " ; and Mr. Sidney Brough and Miss Phyllis Broughton were good in the not very plausible characters of an adventurer and adventuress.

XLII.

"THE TREE OF KNOWLEDGE."

3rd November.

SOME critics, I understand, when they sit down to write an article, always know exactly what they are going to say, and say it.   That is hardly ever my experience.   There are plays, indeed—such plays as *The Sign of the Cross* and *Never Again*—with regard to which I know exactly what I want to say, and say it, in so far as it is fit for publication.   But such plays, thank Heaven! are not of everyday occurrence. Whenever my impression is not absolutely single and simple—whenever I want to praise with reservations or condemn with extenuating circumstances—it is largely a matter of chance whether the praise or the reservations get the upper hand; and as a rule, such is the ill-conditioned doom of criticism, the betting is rather on the reservations.   Therefore, as the ultimate colour of an article is not quite within my control, I like to convey at the outset, before it has taken colour at all, the answer to the one essential question with regard to any play or performance: "Did it, or did it not, give you pleasure?"   In the case of Mr. Carton's new play at the St. James's the answer is most emphatically in the affirmative.   *The Tree of Know-*

*ledge**** is thoroughly interesting and entertaining. I did not find a dull moment or a seriously jarring word in it. One merit, and that no slight one, it possesses throughout—the writing, the mere wording of the dialogue, is extremely skilful. Other dramatists may be more terse, more eloquent, or more scrupulously natural than Mr. Carton, but no one, to my thinking, writes more gracefully than he. Whatever he wants to say, he says well. It may not always be the profoundest, the subtlest, or the most dramatic thing conceivable in the situation; but it is always charmingly turned. Mr. Carton has this time been almost entirely successful in subduing his tendency to florid ornamentation and metaphor-hunting. Just enough of it is still traceable to constitute a pleasant individuality of manner. In a word, Mr. Carton has now gained thorough control of his wit and fancy. His literary faculty is very considerable and very agreeable. He knows how to give his work a highly attractive surface-polish.

On looking below the surface, what do we find? Not a great drama, certainly — not a searching character-study, not a finely conceived situation of tragic intensity, not even a closely observed picture of manners. *The Tree of Knowledge* is rather a novel in dialogue than a well-knit drama. I say this merely by way of description, not of disparagement.

* October 25—February 10, 1898.

The novel in dialogue, if conducted, scene by scene, with spirit and skill, has its legitimate place on the stage.   In this instance we have two love-stories, presented simultaneously, but not in any real sense connected with each other.   Mr. Carton may very likely protest; in his mind, I daresay, the connection between them seems very close.   But let us look into it for a moment.   Nigil Stanyon and Monica Blayne (Story No. 1) are silently devoted to each other; but Nigil thinks he can never marry Monica because he can never tell her that in bygone years he had an unfortunate love-affair with a woman of deplorable character.   He did not deceive her, but she him; he wanted to marry her, but she declined, and ultimately left him.   Whether this is a substantial enough obstacle to keep the lovers apart through five acts I do not here inquire; in any case, it is the sole obstacle between them.   Presently (Story No. 2) the other woman herself appears on the scene, in the character of the adored wife of Nigil's bosom friend, Brian Hollingworth.   Nigil is thus placed, no doubt, in a highly embarrassing position, but his relation to Monica is, and remains, entirely unaffected.   He tells her in the last act what he might just as well have told her in the first; and she, so far as we can understand, is as fully prepared in the first act as in the last to take the common-sense view of the situation.   The two stories might quite well have been brought into

vital contact had the author been so minded.
Character might have been made to influence
character, for good or ill. For example, Monica
might have failed to realise, until she came to know
Belle, that Nigil had indeed been more sinned against
than sinning. At the very least, events might have
brought to Monica's knowledge the facts which Nigil,
of his own motive, might never have summoned
up courage to reveal to her. The two stories, in
short, could have been made to interact in a dozen
different ways; but, as a matter of fact, Mr. Carton
has chosen none of them. Monica's character and
attitude of mind remain absolutely the same throughout.
Events, perhaps, render it a trifle easier for Nigil to
make a clean breast of things to her, but the revelation is in no way forced upon him. And if Belle
has no influence on Monica, Monica has just as little
on Belle. The Belle-Brian story would have been
essentially the same if Monica and Nigil had been
at the Antipodes. The one practical result of all
Nigil's writhing and agonising in his (doubtless
unpleasant) predicament is the postponement by
about twenty minutes of Belle's midnight flitting with
Roupell. The play, then, has no dramatic unity or
coherence. It presents two distinct stories, con-
tiguous, but in no sense interdependent. In the first
of these stories—that on which our sympathetic interest
is concentrated—there is no progress, no development.

It contains matter for one act, not for five. The second story provides the real substance of the play, and lengthens it out by interrupting, without in any way influencing, the first story. Such a juxtaposition of two actions which barely touch each other is all very well in a novel, but sins against a fundamental canon of drama. The fact that, in spite of the canon, Mr. Carton has produced an attractive and even absorbing play, proves that, if a dramatist possesses a reasonable amount of scenic skill, he may (within limits) subordinate his main scheme to his details, and trust rather to the immediate interest of each individual scene, than to the general effect of the whole design. He may, to adapt the proverb, take care of the minutes, and let the hours take care of themselves. He may—but it is at his peril.

And now let us note that in the very fact of its resemblance to a novel this play brings home to us the radical difference between the arts of the novelist and of the dramatist. If *The Tree of Knowledge* were indeed a novel, it would be a poor and commonplace one. The characters are purely conventional. They may be simply and exhaustively classified as absolutely good and irredeemably bad, in the proportion of six to two. There is no theme, no idea in the play. We never touch for a moment upon that debatable land of conduct, that spacious realm of casuistry, in which resides the moral, as opposed to the merely spectacular, interest of life. The two villains, for example—Belle and Roupell—are simply noxious creatures, patently anti-social, the concentrated essence of the heartless adventuress and the cynical scoundrel. There is not a thought to be wasted on them, not a word to be said for them. We are vouchsafed no glimpse of either their social or their natural history. We have simply to take them for granted, as the mediæval public took for granted the Satan of the Mysteries, with his horns and tail. And the goodness of the good people is equally unconditioned. Nigil acts foolishly, sentimentally, even brutally, but he is intended to carry our unmixed sympathy throughout. His threat to kill Belle is not, in Mr. Carton's mind, a trait of folly, but of heroism. The character and the situation are alike unreal. Men have killed women for many reasons, but where in the criminal annals of England is the record of the man who, out of pure, disinterested friendship, killed his friend's wife in order to prevent her from eloping with another man? Mr. Carton had probably in mind vague reminiscences of French drama—of the pistol-shot in *Le Mariage d'Olympe*, and the sanguinary doctrines exemplified by Dumas in *La Femme de Claude* and *L'Affaire Clémenceau*. But the murderer in Augier's play conceived himself to be performing a social duty as the head of an ancient house threatened with irretrievable degradation; while the "Tue-la!"

of Dumas merely gave a certain extension to a right
already placed by French law, custom, and social
sentiment in the hands of an injured husband—not a
casual friend.   Nigil's threat, in fact, is a melodramatic
absurdity which, if carried out, would have made bad
worse for Brian, and involved himself and all who
loved him in hopeless misery.   True, he does not
carry it out, but that is nothing to the purpose.   If
he is merely vapouring, his position is contemptible.
But it is evident that he is not merely vapouring; his
intention is perfectly genuine, and we are supposed
to sympathise with it.   The incident, I repeat, and
the character from which it springs, are conventional
and unrealised.   Monica, again, is absolute goodness,
just as Belle is absolute turpitude.   The title of the
play seems to portend a certain struggle in her mind,
a more or less painful development, in the realisation
that life is not all buttermilk and roses.   One expects
her to have some difficulty in swallowing that wedge
of the apple of knowledge which her lover hands on
to her in the story of his past.   But not a bit of it!
In her demure way, she is evidently prepared from
the first for something of the sort.   Her wisdom is
throughout as perfect as her sweetness.   In other
words, she is a product of rather shallow idealism, a
vision, not a study.   Far be it from me to maintain,
with the late John Gabriel Borkman, that the Perfect
Woman nowhere exists.   What I mean is, that in this

play Mr. Carton has not really studied her, but has simply (like Foldal) drawn on his own idealistic imagination, and made a direct appeal to ours.

These characters, then, would make but a fifth- or sixth-rate novel—how comes it that they make, if not a first-rate play, at all events one which stands high in the second class? Some will reply, "Because the standard of playwriting is so much lower than that of novel-writing." But this is not the true answer to the conundrum. Playwriting—here is the point—is so much more difficult than novel-writing that matter which in the looser form would be practically worthless, may attain real artistic value when cast in the stricter form. There is ten times the thought, talent, and skill in Mr. Carton's play that would go to the making of a novel out of the same material. Compression generates power, and even these characters, deficient though they be in true vitality, are drawn with a crispness and brilliancy of touch that make them telling enough during their little span of life upon the stage. Monica is a delightful conception, full of humour and freshness; Nigil is a good fellow in his way, in spite of his determination to be a hero at all hazards; Mrs. Stanyon is amiable and amusing; the Hollingworths, father and son, are pleasantly sketched; there is a superficial air of novelty about the wickedness of Belle and Roupell that makes them highly entertaining; Major Blencoe is an agreeable eccentric; and as for Mr. Sweadle and his daughter, they are real creations, as good as the old housekeeper in Mr. Carton's *White Elephant.* In brief, there is every sort of ability in *The Tree of Knowledge*, except an eye for complexities of character, a sense for ethical half-shades, and a penetrating criticism of life. It contains enough wit, humour, technical accomplishment, and literary power to furnish forth a dozen commonplace novelists.

It was unusually well acted all round. Mr. Alexander, as Nigil, manly, forcible, sympathetic; Mr. H. B. Irving, as Roupell, original, incisive, subtle; Mr. Esmond highly entertaining as the Major; Mr. Vernon and Mr. Fred Terry quite satisfactory as the two Hollingworths; and Mr. George Shelton exceedingly clever as the egregious Sweadle. Miss Julia Neilson made a really memorable figure of the baleful Belle; Miss Carlotta Addison was perfect as Nigil's devoted mother; and Miss Fay Davis played Monica so charmingly that I should not wonder if this particular type of quaintly self-possessed and humorously tender heroine became, for some seasons, a stereotype, and no comedy were reckoned complete without a Fay Davis character.

XLIII.

"THE LITTLE MINISTER"—"THE CAT AND THE
    CHERUB"—"THE FIRST-BORN"—"KATHERINE
    AND PETRUCHIO"—"THE VAGABOND KING"—
    "THE TEMPEST."

November 10*th.*

IT is a pleasure—a pleasure too long delayed—to
have nothing but "high commendation, true applause,
and love" for a play by Mr. J. M. Barrie.   His
comedy founded on, and entitled, *The Little Minister,**
is in no sense a great, nor even in every sense a
good, play; but it is amiable, original, sincere, and
thoroughly entertaining.   Mr. Barrie is indubitably
a man of genius, a man whom it would be the
grossest injustice to confound with the imitators who
have vulgarised his method.   In this play some
savour of his genius, as distinct from the commoner
part of his talent, gets across the footlights.   We feel
ourselves in contact with a perceptive faculty, narrow
perhaps, but, within its limits, intense, an extraordinary gift of sympathetic humour, and—somewhat
to our surprise—a real adroitness of dramatic invention.   The first two acts are a trifle sketchy.   Those
who do not know the book can form but a faint
conception of the characters of Gavin and Babbie.

* November 6—still running.

I cannot help thinking that a single more or less
serious scene between them in the second act would
be greatly to the advantage of the play. It would
make them both a little more real to us, and enhance
the sympathy with which we follow their fortunes in
the third act. This third act, and the fourth, are
ingenious and entirely delightful scenes of pure
comedy. The audience enjoyed them hugely, and
no one more than I. They assured the success, and
doubtless the lasting success, of the play. Oddly
enough, the two leading parts were not the most
fortunately treated. Mr. Cyril Maude has a difficult
task in the Rev. Gavin Dishart, because nine-tenths
of his character are left behind in the book and have
to be taken on trust. Mr. Maude did his best under
the circumstances, but was never quite convincing.
Miss Winifred Emery was a charming but scarcely
an ideal Babbie. Some of her effects were a little
too obvious. The Auld Licht elders were admirably
played by Mr. Brandon Thomas, Mr. Mark Kinghorne, and Mr. F. H. Tyler; Mr. Sydney Valentine
made a forcible and picturesque Rob Dow ; Miss
Sydney Fairbrother played with spirit and grace as
his son, Micah; and Mrs. E. H. Brooke was perfect
as Nannie Webster, her Scotch being especially rich
and racy. The Scotch is surprisingly good all round,
except in the case of Mr. Holman Clark (one of the
Elders), who ought to take lessons from Mrs. Brooke.

Is it possible that there was any real competition in America between the two sketches of life in China-town which were last week bidding against each other for the favour of London? On the question of precedency I have no information, nor do I know which of them stands in the closer relation to the story or group of stories on which they are both founded. All I know is that one of them, *The Cat and the Cherub*,* by Chester Bailey Fernald (at the Lyric), is amusing, touching, and in its way artistic; while the other, *The First-Born*,† by Francis Powers (at the Globe), is crude, undramatic, and tedious. In *The Cat and the Cherub* an interesting story is clearly and rapidly told, the incidental illustrations of Chinese manners and habits of thought being not unskilfully embroidered on the action. A constructed play, in our Western sense of the word, it is not, but rather a tragic incident, which, for my part, I found curiously impressive in its very simplicity. I shall not soon forget the "learned Doctor," Wing Shee, impassive and dignified as ever, seeking out and slaying the murderer of his son, while we hear the voice of the mad girl, within doors, wailing from time to time the name of her murdered lover. The "learned Doctor" is from first to last a delightful

* October 30—November 27. Reproduced at Royalty (before *Oh! Susannah!*), December 4—still running.

† November 1—6.

and memorable character, and, in executing his
vendetta, he makes murder such a fine art that the
horror of the scene is lost in the sense of intellectual
superiority with which it impresses us. The effect
may leave something to be desired in point of
morality, but in point of art it is original and fine.
In *The First-Born* the "learned Doctor" becomes
a subsidiary and uninteresting personage, though he
has one delightful speech, to a compatriot newly
arrived in San Francisco: "The vice of curiosity
compels me to ask from what province you come."
In this play the person originally killed is not the
child's would-be rescuer, but the child himself. The
method of his death is obscure, but the body is
displayed on the stage; and even in Chinese drama
I object to the massacre of innocents, unless the
artistic design absolutely requires it. In this case it
manifestly does not, since in the other and much
more effective version of the same story not a hair
of the child's pig-tail is harmed. Then, at the
beginning of the second act or scene, the story is
absolutely discontinued for some time, while more or
less uninteresting episodes of street-life in Chinatown
are presented. About five minutes before the end,
the story is taken up again, and the concluding
incident is the same as in the other play — the
murderer propping up his victim's body so as to
make him pass for a living man, while the Caucasian

policeman (the "street god") saunters past unsuspecting. The incident is the same, indeed, in both plays; but in *The Cat and the Cherub* it is most skilfully managed, in *The First-Born* clumsily and ineffectively. Another curiously inartistic feature of the latter play is the mixture of languages. We have passages of Chinese, then passages of broad, unadulterated American (supposed to be spoken by Chinamen and China-women), and then again low-comedy scenes in the pidgin-English used by Celestials in communicating with "foreign devils." The real Chinese and the pidgin-English, far from heightening the illusion, utterly ruin it. How much more rational the convention adopted in *The Cat and the Cherub*, in which the characters (who are all Chinese with the exception of the silent "street god") are throughout made to translate their thoughts, as it were, into pure, though of course quaintly formal, English! Mr. Holbrook Blinn, at the Lyric, is excellent as the Learned Doctor; Mr. Richard Ganthony is grim and effective as the villain, Chim Fang; and the heroine, Ah Yoi, and the Cherub's nurse, Hwah Kwee, are cleverly played by Miss Ruth Benson and Miss Alethea Luce respectively. The Globe performance was altogether rougher and more melodramatic, but I fancy there was merit in the acting of Miss May Buckley and Mr. Francis Powers.

Mr. Beerbohm Tree, in reproducing the Grundy-

Dumas *Silver Key* at Her Majesty's, has eked it out with Garrick's *Katherine and Petruchio*,* or, in other words, a compressed version of the purely farcical scenes in *The Taming of the Shrew.* It is marvellous to me that two such artists as Mr. and Mrs. Tree should find any satisfaction in scrambling through this archaic tomfoolery, rendered tolerable only by what is here suppressed — the graceful and even poetical setting in which Shakespeare contrived to enchase it. But their taste seemed to coincide with that of the audience, who were highly amused. Mrs. Tree looked charming as Katherine, and played the part very brightly, while Mr. Tree did not fail to put vigour and movement into Petruchio.

From Camberwell, *The Vagabond King*† has been transferred to Chelsea, and was last Thursday received with much favour at the Court Theatre. Though the performance was in some respects improved, my first impression of the play remained unaltered—the idea is excellent, but the execution is not quite successful except at one point, the third act. This act is remarkably strong and interesting; in the rest of the play Mr. Parker gives too much licence to his fantasy, and sacrifices plausibility to crude and immediate effect. Mr. Herbert Ross makes King Pandolfo of Sardinia a little less grotesque than he was in the hands of Mr. Grossmith,

* November 1—26. See p. 226. † See p. 298.

junior, and somewhat heightens the effect of his one strong scene in the third act. Miss Ellis Jeffreys takes the Princess Zea a good deal more seriously than did Miss Phyllis Broughton. Mr. Murray Carson and Miss Bateman throw themselves heart and soul into the characters of King Pedro and his terrible mother; Mr. Sydney Brough is amusing as the Chevalier Moffat; and Miss Lena Ashwell, as Stella, repeats the striking success she made on the first night.

In the performance of *The Tempest* by the Elizabethan Stage Society at the Mansion House,* there was diligence, enthusiasm, even talent—everything, in fact, except common sense. This quality one has long ceased to hope for in the otherwise meritorious efforts of Mr. Poel and his comrades. Whatever the ancient Elizabethans obviously did *not* do—whatever contradicts the text and flies in the face of reason — that the modern Elizabethans conscientiously set themselves to achieve. Their choice of a play is this time beyond criticism. Nothing could have been more curious than an endeavour to realise the original presentment of *The Tempest*. But what is the first thing our Elizabethans do? They choose a side gallery or balcony, cut in the very cornice of the lofty hall, to represent the ship at sea, and they make Miranda watch the wreck from the stage, some

* November 5.

thirty or forty feet below! Now if Shakespeare
intended Miranda to be visible during the shipwreck,
he would clearly place her on the raised platform at
the back of the scene, looking down, as though from
some headland, upon the main stage, which would
represent the deck of the ship. It seems to me more
probable, however, that Shakespeare intended both
the lower and the upper stage to be used as parts
of the ship, representing the main deck and some
poop or fo'c's'le. The boatswain and mariners would
appear aloft, the passengers below, and they would
hail each other at some distance through the howling
of the storm. This is simply my own conjecture,
which must be taken for what it is worth. All we
can say with absolute assurance is that Shakespeare
did not picture Miranda gazing skywards, as though
at Tennyson's vision of "navies grappling in the
central blue." He depicts a shipwreck, not a balloon
catastrophe. Then Prospero and Miranda appear,
both speaking with a slow and plaintive drawl which
is precisely the reverse of what must have been the
method of elocution on the Shakespearian stage:
crisp in attack, rapid, sonorous, and compelling
attention. Prospero breaks his long speech some
half-dozen times by saying to Miranda, "Dost thou
hear?" or "Thou attend'st not," evidently implying
that Miranda is so placed that she can turn away
her head from him. Therefore, in the E.S.S. arrange-

ment, she is made to stand directly opposite him, her eyes riveted upon him, and obviously intent on every syllable he utters. At the end of the narration Shakespeare makes Prospero say "Now I arise"; but Mr. Poel, disdaining the old superstition about suiting the action to the word, has had him on his feet for several minutes, and pacing about the stage. It was in the first apparition of Ariel, however, that the Society achieved its triumph of wrongheadedness. The dress (from a contemporary print) was plausible enough; but imagine a curate - Ariel mechanically intoning his rote-learnt lines, with his eyes fixed on the ceiling, motionless, expressionless, like one in a dream! Was ever perversity more elaborately destructive! The other incarnations of Ariel, the Sea-Nymph and the Harpy, were played by different performers— a most unsatisfactory device. It is not quite clear, of course, how the character was treated in Shakespeare's day, but the probable, or at any rate the safe, thing would be to assign it to a clever and well-grown boy, and let him simply change his costumes. It would be tedious to go through the play and enumerate the absurdities of grouping, stage - arrangement, and "business." The upper stage was never brought into use at all, though it stood there ready, and though the stage-direction in the folio (Act III., Sc. 3) says expressly: *Prospero on the top (invisible).* The "shapes" were well habited, but their action was slow and spiritless; the music, under the direction of Mr. Dolmetsch, and with Miss Louise Macpherson as vocalist, was delightfully rendered, but no attempt was made to suggest its supernatural origin. The actors spoke the text with tolerable accuracy, but with no feeling for the metrical quality of the elusively exquisite verse. Of individual performers the best were Mr. A. Broughton as Stephano, and Mr. Hodges as Caliban, effectively got-up after the fashion of the Bayreuth Alberich or Mime. Mr. E. Playford was good as the Boatswain, and Miss Hilda Swan made a very graceful Miranda.

XLIV.

MR. VEZIN AS A READER.

November 17th.

MR. HERMANN VEZIN has struck quite a new vein as a Shakespearian reciter. Nothing could have been better than his rendering of *Hamlet** at Steinway Hall on Thursday last. The only fault was a slight uncertainty of memory (for Mr. Vezin used no book) in the minor parts. Otherwise the recital was a model of taste and skill. There was no ranting, no mouthing, no grotesque mimicking of the different char-

* Mr. Vezin also read *Julius Cæsar, Othello, The Merchant of Venice,* and *Macbeth.*

acters. Mr. Vezin realised the limits of the effect to
be aimed at, and the result was that he never missed
it. His gestures and attitudes were graceful without
a touch of pose ; his voice resonant and finely modu-
lated ; his English perfect in its purity and refinement ;
and his sensitive features expressive without grimace.
It is a pleasure to see anything done with such easy
mastery.

XLV.

"ADMIRAL GUINEA."

November 24th.

FOR one reason or another, the managers are giving
us a holiday. There has been no production or
revival for more than a fortnight. This means, I take
it, that the season is a prosperous one ; most of our
leading theatres are in possession of successes which
will carry them to Christmas or beyond it. On the
other hand, an unusual number of theatres are closed
—a circumstance, no doubt, which partly results from,
partly contributes to, the prosperity of the others.

I take advantage of this lull to say a few words as
to *Admiral Guinea*, to be produced next week by the
New Century Theatre. Its dramatic, or at any rate
its theatrical, merit remains to be proved, and I am
far too superstitious to venture any forecast on that

point. As one of the committee of the New Century
Theatre, and as a warm admirer—even, if I may say
so, a friend—of both the authors, I naturally wish the
play to succeed. Far be it from me, then, to chal-
lenge Nemesis by one over-confident word. Wreaths
and "floral offerings" prepared in advance are the
unerring harbingers of failure. When I see the acting-manager handing them to the attendants, and the
attendants passing them on to the leader of the
orchestra, I always think of the flowers on a coffin,
and know that the play or performance is, to use an
obsolete but expressive vulgarism, "corpsed." I am
twining no wreath, then, for *Admiral Guinea* as an
acting play. Its fate is on the knees of the gods.
But it is assuredly not one of the plays which exist
for the stage or not at all. Its place in literature is in
no way dependent on the event of Monday next. It
seems to me, however, that the very fact of its
dramatic form has in some measure blinded us to its
literary qualities. We are so unaccustomed to look for
style in modern drama that we do not recognise it
when we see it. What I would here suggest is that
this play, written by our master of romance in collaboration with a poet, who happened to be at the
same time an adept in the literature of picturesque
scoundrelism, may claim no insignificant place among
Stevenson's works, but rather shows one side of his
talent at its very best.

Who does not remember the blind beggar Pew in *Treasure Island*? Who does not, at the mention of his name, think at once of the tap-tapping of his stick on the frozen road, while Jim Hawkins and his mother are sifting the guineas from the doubloons in the buccaneer's chest? No other figure in latter-day romance (figure, be it noted, as distinct from character) has so vividly impressed itself on the popular imagination. Readers of *Treasure Island* may more easily forget Long John Silver himself. We must go back to Dickens to find a personage projected in such lurid relief as David Pew. And yet— here we have the extraordinary art of the thing—Pew appears and is gone like a flash of lightning He is scarcely drawn at all, but only suggested. In nine short pages he is out of the saga; the words he utters (I have counted them) would just about fill this page. With touches incredibly few and infallibly just, Stevenson has etched this arch-miscreant upon the reader's memory, and made him seem no less familiar than terrible. But the fact remains that he is only a rapid outline. There was not room between the covers of a single book for the full development of two such scoundrels as Long John and Pew, and the lines of the story demanded that Long John should hold the field. Stevenson, however, knew all about Pew—fifty times more than he could tell in *Treasure Island*. He could draw

him in outline because he saw him in detail; and it
would have been a thousand pities to let the detail
perish unrecorded.   Accordingly, he took counsel
with Mr. Henley, like himself an ardent amateur of
maritime. tradition and romance; and between them
they invented a fable in which Pew should have
ample room to develop his genius and display the
engaging qualities of his head and heart.   In *Admiral
Guinea*, then, we can study at our leisure the figure
which, seen by a lightning-flash in *Treasure Island*,
had haunted us ever since.

And he surpasses our fondest expectation.   Losing
nothing in grimness, he gains enormously in variety,
ingenuity, humour, and resourceful audacity.   He
touches the sublime of scoundrelism.   Fearless and
ruthless, he taps his way through the world with such
keenness of instinct and readiness of wit that we
admire as much as we detest him.   He is one of
those creatures of intense vitality who put to shame
our moral commonplaces.   For he is a happy man, if
ever there was one.   His needs are few, his sensibilities none.   Rum is his nectar and nepenthe
("Ah, rum!   That's my sheet anchor, ma'am; rum
and the blessed Gospel;" and again, to himself—
"Rum! ah, rum, you're a lovely creature; they
haven't never done you justice"); and he keeps
himself amply supplied with the "lovely creature"
by the constant exercise of the overbearing cruelty

and cynical hypocrisy which are his heart's delight. He revels in his cleverness; he chuckles over it with an unholy glee. He has all the self-complacency of the man whom Destiny has cruelly mishandled, but who, in virtue of his inborn greatness of spirit, sets Destiny at defiance.

> " Though fallen on evil days,
> On evil days though fallen, and evil tongues,*
> In darkness, and with dangers compassed round,
> And solitude "—

yet he neither repines, despairs, nor seeks to propitiate the hostile powers, but ever and in all extremities proves himself "the master of his fate, the captain of his soul." Only once does he show a trace of fear—when, in the last act, he finds himself in a situation which baffles his intelligence, which his mind's eye cannot penetrate, and which therefore strikes him as mysterious, supernatural, and ghastly, "the horrors come alive." Danger known and understood never gives him a moment's pause; and though he clings to life, as to a hostelry where the rum is to his taste, yet he has no real dread of death. Who is the Happy Warrior if this be not he? To have no fear, no conscience, no compassion, and an

---

* MRS. DRAKE. Well, sailor, people talk, you know.

PEW. I know, ma'am; I'd have been rolling in my coach if they'd have held their tongues.—*Act II.*, *Sc. I.*

ever-welling spring of animal spirits—this is to be
impregnably bastioned against all the assaults of
Fate.

Here, then, we have one of the heroic scoundrels of
literature, an English and a nautical Macaire   Yet
the general impression made by the little play is not
cynical, not even painful, so delightfully are the other
characters touched in.   The story is of no particular
account, save for one highly ingenious situation in the
last act, the theatrical effect of which has yet to be
gauged.   There is just enough plot, or rather incident,
to bring the characters into vigorous action and contrast.   Captain Gaunt, the ex-slaver, now, as Pew
phrases it, "bearing away for the New Jerusalem,"
is as vivid as Pew himself—a type of self-torturing
other-worldliness, opposed to a type of light-hearted
ruffianly paganism.   He is suggested by Cowper's
John Newton, and is a masterly study of the bitter
fanaticism begotten of remorse.   His eloquence is
nothing less than superb.   It has all the full-blooded
alertness of Stevenson's style, with an added something—one is tempted to call it Miltonic—in which
we may trace, not doubtfully, the touch of the singer
of *London Voluntaries.*   How admirable, for instance,
is the phrasing of this retort upon Kit French !

"You speak of me ? In the true balances we both weigh
nothing.   But two things I know: the depth of iniquity, how
foul it is; and the agony with which a man repents.   Not until

seven devils were cast out of me did I awake; each rent me as
it passed. Ay, that was repentance. Christopher, Christopher,
you have sailed before the wind since first you weighed your
anchor, and now you think to sail upon a bowline? You do
not know your ship, young man; you will go to le'ward like a
sheet of paper; I tell you so that know—I tell you so that
have tried, and failed, and wrestled in the sweat of prayer, and
at last, at last, have tasted grace."

And again:

"Heaven forbid that I should be hard, Christopher. It is
not I, it is God's law that is of iron. Think! if the blow were
to fall now, some cord to snap within you, some enemy to plunge
a knife into your heart; this room, with its poor taper light, to
vanish; this world to disappear like a drowning man into the
great ocean; and you, your brain still whirling, to be snatched
into the presence of the eternal Judge: Christopher French, what
answer would you make? For these gifts wasted, for this rich
mercy scorned, for these high-handed bravings of your better
angel—what have you to say?"

It is a pleasure to copy from the printed page such
English as this: simple, Saxon, characteristic, even to
its nautical technicalities, yet so exquisite in its poise
and cadence that if a word were altered or displaced
one would feel it with a shock: a prose no more to
be tampered with than the most delicate verse.   Kit
French and Arethusa, again, are in essence the conventional hero and heroine of nautical drama, trans-
figured, however, by the sheer vitality and beauty of
their diction.   Never a phrase is strained or unnatural,

yet never a phrase is common.   Take, for example,
Kit's outburst in the second act:

"Prayers? Now I tell you freely, Captain Gaunt, I don't
value your prayers. Deeds are what I ask; kind deeds and
words—that's the true-blue piety, to hope the best, and do the
best, and speak the kindest. As for you, you insult me to my
face; and then you'll pray for me? What's that? Insult
behind my back is what I call it! No, sir; you're out of the
course; you're no good man to my view, be you who you may.
. . . You spoke just now of a devil; well, I'll tell you the devil
you have; the devil of judging others. And, as for me, I'll get
as drunk as Bacchus."

Or listen to Arethusa's soliloquy after Kit has been
dismissed by her father:

"I thought the time dragged long and weary when I knew
that Kit was homeward bound, all the white sails a-blow-
ing out towards England, and my Kit's face turned this
way! . . . Ah, there is no parting but the grave! And Kit
and I both live and both love each other; and here am I cast
down? O Arethusa, shame! And your love home from the
deep seas, and loving you still; and the sun shining and the
world all full of hope? O Hope, you're a good word!"

If any one still imagines that it is impossible to
combine naturalness with distinction in prose dialogue, *Admiral Guinea* will quickly convince him of
his error.

Sticklers for the literal veracity of *Treasure Island*
inquire how it comes to pass that after being trampled
to death by Supervisor Dance's horse in Chapter V.

of that history, Pew should, in *Admiral Guinea*, meet
with a second and somewhat less inglorious death.
This ambiguity troubles me not a jot.   Jim Hawkins
says nothing about his burial, and until you had seen
such a man safely battened under hatches, you could
never feel secure from the tap-tapping of his stick.
It is not to be conceived that a mere horse's hoofs
should trample the life out of David Pew; a steam-
roller might pass over him and he would come up
smiling.   One has scant faith even in the quietus
given him by Kit French's cutlass—but "oh, for the
touch of the vanished hand" that could have resus-
citated him!

XLVI.

"A MAN'S SHADOW."

1st December.

IN regard to the managers, we critics occupy the
position, vaunted by Lucretius, of onlookers standing
at their ease on dry land, and watching storm-tossed
vessels labouring within sound of the breakers on a
lee shore.   A particularly "gurly sea," as the ballad
has it, and reef-strewn and treacherous withal, is the
West-End theatrical world.   Many must be the
anxious hours of the skipper who embarks upon it.
Night by night, in tempestuous seasons, he must

look ahead with haggard eyes, and listen with straining ears for the voice of his mate (the acting-manager)
heaving the lead in shoaling waters of Popularity,
and reporting the "returns." Meanwhile we, high
and dry in irresponsible safety, shout down to him
confident and for the most part contradictory advice,
one bidding him spread all canvas and scud before
the gale, another reproaching him with cowardice
or incapacity because he cannot sail right in the
teeth of the wind, a third bidding him lay an ideal
course and stick to it, even if it lead straight to
wreck and ruin. The metaphor may indeed be
carried too far. It can scarcely be pretended that
all our managers are masters of the art of theatrical
navigation, or that they always take the very best
advantage of wind and tide. But no doubt they
are more fully alive to the complexities of their
position than we can possibly be, and it must now
and then try their tempers to find themselves bitterly
reproached for pursuing a course which is (or at
least which they believe to be) imposed on them
by dire necessity.

It is certainly not exhilarating to see the finest
playhouse in London, under the direction of one
of the ablest and most energetic of actor-managers,
given up, even temporarily, to such work as *A Man's
Shadow* (*Roger La Honte*).* A third-rate French

* November 27—January 15, 1898.

melodrama, such as no Parisian theatre of the
smallest literary pretensions would dream of offering
to its public, this play would be quite in place at
the Adelphi, the Princess's, or the Pavilion. There
is no harm in it, and it even shows a certain
mechanical cleverness; but it is devoid of that vein
of genuine humanity which places such a piece as
Two Little Vagabonds (*Les Deux Gosses*) in a
distinctly higher class. It is sad, I say, that Mr.
Beerbohm Tree should have to condescend upon
such work, even as a stop-gap; but I say it in a
tone of condolence, not of reproach. It can be no
pleasure to him, personally, to play this very inferior
Dubosc and Lesurques, nor, I am sure, can Mrs.
Tree find any scope for her intelligence or her
executive powers in such a conventional nonentity
as Henriette Laroque. But from the clamorously
cordial reception of the play on Saturday evening,
I cannot but conclude that as a piece of managerial
policy the revival will amply justify itself. The pit
and gallery loved it, and nowadays, as we see on
all hands, the stalls half-cynically, half-obsequiously,
take their cue from the pit. The acting, too, is good
in its way. Mr. Tree's performance has the fault which
seems inevitable in all "dual" impersonations—he
makes his Laroque and Luversan (like Sir Henry
Irving's Lesurques and Dubosc) so utterly dissimilar
that no one could for a moment mistake the one

for the other. They are as different as Dr. Jekyll
and Mr. Hyde. When Julie, three minutes after
Laroque-Jekyll has left the stage, looks up from her
writing and unhesitatingly addresses Luversan-Hyde
as "Lucien," our powers of make-believe are strained
to the snapping-point. Luversan, however, is an
admirable piece of purely external character-acting,
and the whole performance shows Mr. Tree's
remarkable power of refashioning and disguising
his personality. This is what, in strict logic, it
ought *not* to show; but melodrama laughs at logic.
Mrs. Tree's performance of Henriette is pleasant
and pathetic, and Miss Lily Hanbury is good as
the traitress Julie. Mr. Lewis Waller made a great
success as De Noirville, the gallery imperiously
raising him from the dead after the trial scene to
bow his acknowledgments. Little Miss Dorrie Harris
was a delightful Suzanne, no less charming, I think,
than Miss Minnie Terry, who played the part at the
Haymarket. Messrs. Lionel Brough and E. M.
Robson made the comic soldiers very popular, and
Mr. F. Perceval Stevens was clever as the police-
officer. Altogether, the revival promised to serve
its purpose well; but I am sure Mr. Tree will forgive
me for hoping that it may not be *too* long before we
meet again at Philippi.

XLVII.

"ADMIRAL GUINEA"—"HONESTY."

December 8th.

IN writing of *Admiral Guinea** before it had stood
the test of performance, I was careful to express no
opinion of its merits as an acting play. This
reticence seems to have been interpreted in some
quarters as a confession of scepticism. It was not so
intended. I trusted that the reader would discern
between the lines my ardent belief in the acting
qualities of the play—a belief which the experience
of last week has absolutely confirmed. Most of the
critics—all, I think, who did not come to the theatre
with an inveterate prejudice against everything that
savoured of "literature"—have admitted its acting
qualities, with reservations. Knowing the piece more
familiarly than they, and therefore, I believe, discerning its possibilities more clearly, I venture to suggest
that these reservations were for the most part—not
unfounded, but—misdirected. The critics could not
help feeling that several passages dragged a good
deal; at the same time they saw (and have emphatically stated) that the actors engaged were individually
excellent; whence they concluded that, where they

* November 29—December 3 (afternoon performances).

felt their interest flag, the play must be at fault. The mistake was very natural, but a mistake none the less. No one with any knowledge of the stage will think it a paradox to assert that, in a play of five characters, five excellent pieces of acting do not necessarily make a perfect representation. Without attributing the slightest blame to any individual artist, I think it only fair to the authors to say that the first performance was altogether too slow. The time of representation might have been reduced by a quarter of an hour, perhaps even twenty minutes, without the omission of a single word; and this quarter of an hour would have made all the difference in the general effect. No one was to blame, or if any one, I myself. I attended several rehearsals, and found all the actors most courteous and cordial in accepting such suggestions as I was able to offer. Since, then, this slowness remained uncorrected, the fault must be in some measure mine. There it was, at any rate; and it went a good way to mar a performance which, for the rest, has on all hands been recognised as admirable. Mr. Sydney Valentine's Pew was the powerful, picturesque and humorous embodiment which was only to be expected of one of the very best of our character-comedians. Mr. William Mollison, less known to the London public, made an equally profound impression in the part of John Gaunt. His fine voice, his vigorous and fervid delivery, and his stern countenance,

softening at times into the truest tenderness, were
precisely what the character required. I am much
mistaken if this creation does not mark a step in Mr.
Mollison's career. Mr. Robert Loraine, who played
Kit, is a young actor of whom we shall hear much in the
future. He has a good voice, a striking presence, and
abundant intelligence and feeling. As yet, perhaps,
he is a little over-eager, and apt to be too much
carried away by the spirit of a scene. This is a good
fault, and one which will correct itself. In Miss
Cissie Loftus's exceedingly simple, graceful, and unaffected Arethusa, there were moments which betrayed
inexperience; but there were many other moments
which revealed genuine and unmistakable talent.
Her first greeting of Kit, for instance, was perfect;
one could not wish to see such a passage more
delightfully treated; and this was only one out of
many equally charming touches. The part of Mrs.
Drake—small but far from insignificant—was admirably filled by Miss Dolores Drummond, an artist in
all she undertakes. I have always the greatest
diffidence in criticising a performance in the preparation of which I have had any hand; but here
I am only re-wording, with absolute sincerity, the
general opinion of critics and public alike.

To return, then, to the play. A very favourably-
disposed and even enthusiastic critic sums up his
judgment in the phrase "Not drama, but something

almost better;" and several others have said the same thing in different words. This is the view against which I most strenuously protest. On the question which other critics have discussed with some warmth —whether *Admiral Guinea* is or is not to be classed as a melodrama—I have no definite opinion. Questions of classification are always rather idle. If every play be a melodrama in which the action turns upon rascality and violence and the characters are synthetically, not analytically, presented, then so much the better for melodrama—it may certainly claim *Admiral Guinea* for its own. The "melo" is neither here nor there; it is the "drama" on which I insist. Take any definition you please of drama, and this play— this simple, old-fashioned, nautical "yarn"—fulfils it to the letter. The most popular definition at the present moment is, I understand, a conflict of will with will. Others prefer to put it that the essence of drama lies in an Obstacle which the leading personages must overcome, or against which they must shatter themselves. What have we here but a conflict of will with will, and an Obstacle overcome? Let us put aside for the moment all charm of style, and suppose the language that of the sorriest hack playwright. We start with the prime element of half the dramas in existence—a Lover and his Lass. Between them stands the girl's stern and bigoted father, determined that his child shall not make an "ungodly" marriage. That is the initial situation; it is briefly, vigorously presented; and then comes the crisis—the drama—in the course of which the stern parent's heart is softened and his self-righteousness rebuked. An associate of his old and evil days has sought him out, in the belief that he hoards untold doubloons in his brass-bound sea-chest. This visitant from the past is none other than that gorgeous and incomparable villain, Pew; but we have agreed to reduce the thing to its simplest terms; let us suppose him any the most commonplace ruffian. In the great scene which ends the first act, the Penitent and Impenitent Thieves are confronted and contrasted with each other, their histories sketched, their characters posited, and the interest carried forward in the blind man's threat of vengeance. If this be not drama, what is? In the next act, the lover, smarting under the bigot's scorn, has been drowning his sorrows in liquor. His sweetheart seeks him out, their meeting is interrupted by her father, and the lover, goaded beyond all self-control, retorts upon the bigot in such stinging terms that he is fairly silenced and driven from the field. The blind man has listened unseen to this passage at arms; he thinks to find in the exasperated lover the seeing accomplice whom he requires in his attack upon the sea-chest, and plies him with flattery and drink in order to deaden his scruples. If this be not drama, what is? Meanwhile the father and

daughter have returned home. The father, much
moved and somewhat shaken by the scene he has just
gone through, tries to justify himself in his daughter's
eyes by telling her the tragedy of his life and of her
mother's death, and showing her that the supposed
bullion-chest contains nothing but a few trinkets of
her mother's, which are the treasures of his remorseful soul. Be it well written or ill, I say this scene
is of the very essence of drama, and furthermore
that it is rightly motived, rightly placed, and rightly
developed; for the daughter, with exquisite feminine
dexterity, turns her father's avowals against himself,
and succeeds in half-softening him towards her lover.
They go to bed, and the housebreakers appear on the
scene. As soon as he realises Pew's design, Kit,
drunk as he is, cries off; whereupon Pew leaps at
him like a tiger, rouses the house and completely
turns the tables against him, by making up a tale
more consistent and less improbable than his. At
Arethusa's intercession, however, Captain Gaunt con-
sents to let her lover go free; but Kit will not accept
the benefit of the doubt, and constitutes himself the
Captain's prisoner. Though they were couched in
the fustian of a Pettitt or a Fitzball, these scenes would
still be essentially dramatic. There is no need to
go in detail into the very short last act—the situation
of the sleep-walker, the blind man and the lighted
candle. Its function in the scheme of the play is to

vindicate Kit's honour as against Pew, and to complete the breach in Gaunt's pharisaism. Every one admits its ingenuity, though some—Mr. Walkley, for instance—argue that it is "one of those situations which are more thrilling to *think out* than to see in action." This may possibly be so; the description certainly applies to many other scenes of elaborate ingenuity, and indicates the rock on which they tend to split. My own belief is that had the actors been able to get every movement accurately timed, every gesture and expression under thorough control, Mr. Walkley's judgment of it would have been different. This, however, is only an opinion, which may one day, perhaps, be proved or disproved. I am willing to set down as doubtful the theatrical value of the last scene, though of its imaginative strength there can be no doubt. It is not on this act, but on the other three, that I found my faith in the distinctively theatrical quality of the play. I have tried to show that it states and works out a definite theme, simple but very human, and that, even were it written in transpontine jargon, its scenes and incidents would be eminently dramatic. But as a matter of fact it is written in a nimble, delicate, nervous, and harmonious English that gives (to my ear) a keener joy on the tenth hearing than on the first. Every speech, while strictly true to character, is yet a little masterpiece either of racy ruffianism or of grace, or tenderness, or manly vehemence, or thrilling sonority. This is not "literature" inappropriately dragged upon the stage. It is the perfection of dramatic writing as applied to such a semi-conventional subject—a glorified nautical drama, just as *Treasure Island* was a glorified nautical romance. If *Admiral Guinea*, now that it has made its way to the footlights, is not heard again and yet again for many a year to come, it can only be because the conditions of the English theatre are invincibly hostile to anything like distinction in theatrical art.

I have no space left, unfortunately, to do justice to the opening piece, *Honesty—a Cottage Flower*, by Miss Margaret Young. It has been generally, but not adequately, praised; its commonplace exterior having in some measure obscured its delicate and ingenious humour. Miss Young is a writer of real talent, who will certainly make her mark. The part of Clorinda Anne was brilliantly played by Miss Kate Rorke, with able assistance from Mr. S. A. Cookson, Miss Una Cockerell, and Mr. Ridgwood Barrie.

XLVIII.

"THE HAPPY LIFE"—"DANDY DAN."

15th December.

MR. PINERO, according to the paragraphists, intends to call his forthcoming play "a comedietta in four

acts." Mr. Louis Parker has been beforehand with
him. He has not appropriated the phrase, but he has
produced the thing. *The Happy Life**** is a comedietta in four acts, and if you like your comediettas in
four acts, you will enjoy *The Happy Life*. Seriously,
it is quite enjoyable—alert, entertaining, amiable,
humorous, and very fairly acted. You will not be
bored, and, if you resolutely tell yourself from the
outset "This is a comedietta, and nothing more,"
you will not be disappointed. I, unfortunately, was
not thus forewarned. Mr. Parker had neglected
Mr. Pinero's precaution, and called his play on the
programme, not a comedietta, but a comedy. Consequently I was taken in by his first act, which seemed
to promise a serious, almost tragic, romance, and had
to readjust my expectations (always a disagreeable
process) between the second act and the third.

Mr. Parker's first act is, indeed, a singularly skilful
and even poetical prologue—to a different drama.
We are introduced to an æsthetic quietist, who thinks
to evade the common lot of men by shutting himself
up in a "brazen tower" of indifferentism, and looking on at the shifting pageant of existence without
ever sallying forth and taking part in it. One Christmas Eve, in his "brazen tower" (situated, by the
way, in Fig Tree Court, Temple) he vaunts this
philosophy, over the walnuts and the wine, as the

* Duke of York's Theatre, December 6—January 29, 1898.

secret of the Happy Life. One of his guests, a Pole, warns him of the danger of such boasting. According to a Polish superstition, the man who ventures to declare himself unassailably happy will presently hear the knock of a Figure at the Door, bringing "the Unexpected Gift: to the merry, sorrow; to the idle, toil; to the unambitious, a great task." This is simply our old friend Nemesis in Sarmatian attire; but the disguise is effective. With delicate skill, Mr. Parker parodies in advance the incident which we all foresee, and thus masks its conventionality. Scarcely has the Pole given his warning when the expected knock is heard at the door—and behold! it is only the waiter, who has been sent out in search of a corkscrew. Yet even the waiter, in a sense, is an emissary of Nemesis; for the news he brings, that the whole house is absolutely deserted, has a determining influence on the sequel. Our philosopher's guests disperse, and he sinks into his easy-chair by the fireside, to doze luxuriously over Omar Khayyam. Suddenly he hears a fall on the staircase outside, then a wail, then a moan. He opens the door, and there, on his threshold, lies a young and beautiful woman, in rich evening dress, senseless, and bleeding from a wound in the forehead. Now, I say this is a bit of excellent romance; and it is ingeniously heightened, when he has carried her into his room, by the symbolism of the Sword of Severance—a detail which it

would take too long to explain. I do not even cavil
at the stage-arrangement by which the philosopher is
compelled to pass the night watching over his unconscious charge. It is not, in fact, very convincing ;
even at the cost of leaving her alone for a few minutes,
he ought clearly to have gone out and summoned aid,
medical and other. But this is a trifle; a little re-
adjustment (some trick of a door-lock) would make
the thing plausible enough; and one ought never to
quarrel with an initial postulate which is not grotesquely and foolishly impossible. The situation at
the end of the first act, in short, is to my thinking
novel, imaginative, appetising.

But what comes of it? Why, nothing but that most
commonplace thing in the world, that true comedietta-
catastrophe, a happy marriage. The remaining three
acts serve only to hasten the marriage and to retard
the happiness—in each case with no adequate reason.
The second act, indeed, with its picture of the
Pettigrew-Smith household, is exceedingly entertaining. The story stands absolutely still during three-
fourths of it, but the character-drawing is so clever
and vivacious that we are in no hurry for the thread
to be resumed. And when at last it is taken up
again, what do we find? A problem of convention
where we had looked for a crisis of passion. Was it
unreasonable to expect that the Figure at the Door,
so solemnly, so impressively introduced, was destined

to bring a gust of tragedy into "the Happy Life"? For my part, I had no doubt that the lady in the syncope had been knocked downstairs by a brute of a husband, and that the drama was to lie in the seemingly hopeless, though no doubt ultimately victorious, passion that should spring up between her and her rescuer. Or she might have been a lady with a past (or even a present), and the barrier between them might have lain, not in any outward bond, but in her own character. It seemed perfectly evident, at any rate, that the Figure at the Door must bring, as her Unexpected Gift, temptation, agony, despair, an emotional cyclone of some sort. But not a bit of it! The Unexpected Gift is love at first sight; there is no sort of barrier between the parties; and the only thing that retards the happiness which we see to be inevitable is the philosopher's preposterous Quixotism in persuading himself and others that a marriage of mutual inclination is a marriage of chivalrous duty, forced by cruel fate upon two unwilling victims. It may be a nice question of casuistry what a gentleman ought to do if a lady is compelled by circumstances over which neither of them has any control to pass a night in his chambers; but it is absolutely certain that, unless they love each other, the very worst thing he can do is to marry her. It is not quite clear whether Mr. Parker would have us understand that Cyril Charteris's Quixotism is only his love in disguise; but this was not what I gathered. Cyril, I take it, would have felt equally bound to marry any lady, however unamiable and unattractive, to whom he had rendered a compromising service; and I suspect, moreover, that in this he has Mr. Parker's approval. If so, I must gently but firmly protest. People don't do these things; and if they did, the drama would be much better employed in "smiling such chivalry away" than in celebrating and rewarding it. Accepting Cyril, however, as a veritable Don Quixote—that is to say, a gentleman of the best intentions who ought to be placed under legal restraint—one could see a drama in the passionate repugnance of a sane and right-minded girl to a marriage proposed by this benevolent madman, and forced upon her by her rapacious relations, who jump at the absurd pretext of a "compromising" adventure, in order to get a millionaire's son into the family. Some such drama seems to have hovered before Mr. Parker's mind, but he has not grasped and presented it. We see nothing of Evelyn's character until the marriage is over, and very little even then. The real drama takes place in the interval between the second and third acts, and is left entirely to the imagination. The third and fourth acts are devoted to the leisurely and conventional working out of the old comedietta situation of two people really and evidently loving each other, but each mistaking the other's feeling and too proud to make the first advance. There is some ingenuity, of an old-fashioned sort, in the details, and the writing is throughout agreeable enough. But one resents the dwindling of the passionate romance foreshadowed in Act I. into the trivial domestic comedy of Acts III. and IV. There is nothing more exasperating in drama than the deliberate and elaborate avoidance of an explanation which is trembling, so to speak, on the tip of the tongue, but must be postponed because it is only 10.30 and the final tableau is not due till 11.

Mr. Frederick Kerr did wonders with a part which was obviously designed rather on the Forbes-Robertson model. It would be hard to imagine any one less Quixote-like in appearance and manner; but he played with such tact and pleasant sincerity that the audience accepted him without misgiving. It was with some amusement that, in reading the play after the performance, I came upon this stage-direction: "Cyril reads from the open book on his knees; and, as he reads, his right hand unconsciously closes on the handle of the sword, so that he realises the well-known Doré picture of Don Quixote." The blame may rest with my sluggishness of perception, but Mr. Kerr, at this point, stirred in me no faintest reminiscence either of Cervantes or of Doré. Miss Dorothea Baird had to struggle with a practically non-existent character; for Evelyn has nothing to do

but to look haggard and speak querulously. Miss
Baird got through the ungrateful part with credit—
the greatest genius could scarcely have made it
effective. Mr. Hermann Vezin was admirable as the
poor old hack who lives by "gutting" masterpieces.
The scene of his disillusionment, in the fourth act,
was warmly and justly applauded. Miss Frances
Ivor was very clever as Mrs. Pettigrew-Smith; Miss
Henrietta Watson as Maggie showed really remarkable talent in the second act, where alone she has
any opportunity; and Miss Carlotta Nillson was
bright and agreeable as Don Quixote's practical-
minded sister. Other parts were well played by
Mr. John Beauchamp, Mr. Arthur Elwood, Mr.
Sidney Brough, Mr. Scott Buist, and Mr. Aubrey
Fitzgerald.

At the Lyric Theatre the devotees of Mr. Arthur
Roberts may study him in his latest avatar, *Dandy
Dan, the Lifeguardsman;** for whom words have been
concocted by Mr. Basil Hood and music by Mr.
Walter Slaughter. The piece is absolutely chaotic;
it exists in and for Mr. Arthur Roberts, who gambols
through it at his own sweet will, no one for a moment
inquiring into the why or wherefore of any of his
fantastic proceedings. We may say of Mr. Roberts,
as Matthew Arnold said of an earlier actor-manager:
"Others abide our question; thou art free." There

* December 4—still running.

is a good deal of cleverness in some of the disguises which Mr. Roberts assumes in the second act; but his fundamental disguise, that of the Lifeguardsman, is too far beyond the limits of conceivable caricature to be at all funny.   Mr. W. H. Denny's performance of a melancholy policeman was a piece of genuine comedy; otherwise there was nothing in the acting to call for special note.

XLIX.

WILLIAM TERRISS.

22nd December.

THE death of Mr. William Terriss * is one of those occurrences on which no comment seems possible save an almost inarticulate cry of horror and regret. It is a meaningless brutality of chance before which one can only stand aghast.   There is no moral to be drawn, no consolation to be suggested.   It is impossible to discern any sort of " poetic justice " or tragic significance in the event.   The crudest material accident has generally its lesson—points to some common danger that can be abated, or conveys a warning against some form of recklessness.   But the psychological accident to which (so far as we can see)

---

* Mr. Terriss was assassinated at the stage-door of the Adelphi Theatre on the evening of December 16.

Mr. Terriss fell a victim is a thing which no policy can prevent, no caution avert. Society—humanity—stands helpless before a malignant caprice of fate. The loss to melodrama is great ; for of our heroes of melodrama Mr. Terriss was not only the most popular, but also by far the most agreeable. In some of the parts which lately came in his way, he acted with real sincerity and impressiveness. In work of a higher order, a lack of sincerity was his stumbling-block. His " fatal gift of beauty " hampered him as an artist. He was always self-conscious and always cold. When we think, however, of his rivals in the melodramatic field, and ask ourselves who is to succeed him, we realise that even those who care least for the form of art in which he excelled have ample reason to deplore his loss.

L.

PLAYS FROM HANS ANDERSEN—"A SHEEP IN WOLF'S CLOTHING."

29th December.

UNLESS the children of to-day, like their elders, have been corrupted by a surfeit of spectacle, the afternoon entertainment* at Terry's Theatre ought to be popular

* December 23—January 29, 1898

during the holidays. It consists of three, or rather four, of Hans Andersen's stories arranged for the stage by Mr. Basil Hood, with music by Mr. Walter Slaughter. Mr. Hood has shown real ingenuity in compressing his themes so as to secure that unity of time and place which is quite as essential in nursery extravaganza as in classic tragedy—where, by the way, it is not essential at all. He first deals with *Little Claus and Big Claus*, which he treats as a rapid and rattling farce—almost too summarily, perhaps, for clear comprehension. Mr. Hood no doubt felt, quite justly, that the incidents of this delectable "droll" would not bear leisurely examination. There is a fine mediæval heartlessness about it which would be a little trying to modern susceptibilities if we were given time to think about and realise it. Children, however, are thoroughly mediæval in their ethics, and accept the slaughter of the grandmother, the drowning of Big Claus, and all the ingenious villainies of Little Claus, without turning a hair. I am not sure that the juvenile members of the audience, who were many, did not enjoy this hasty sketch as much as the more elaborate entertainments which followed. The longest of these was a cleverly interwoven version of *The Princess and the Swineherd* and *The Emperor's New Clothes*. From first to last it was highly diverting. The musical entry of the Emperor and his household (modelled on "The House that Jack

Built ") was not unworthy of Gilbert and Sullivan ; the Princess's gambols with her dolls and her doctors were full of spirit and enjoyment ; and the more sentimental element in the action, mainly represented by the swineherd-Prince, was marked by genuine feeling, yet remained well on the hither side of the didactic and the goody-goody. Mr. H. O. Clarey made an amusingly fantastic Emperor, Miss Kitty Loftus a sprightly and merry Princess, and Miss Louie Pounds a picturesque Prince. The third place in the bill was occupied by a brief and bright version of *The Soldier and the Tinder-Box*, which was even more successful than its predecessors. Nothing could be better than Mr. Eric Lewis's portraiture of the nincompoop King, a masterly piece of quiet humour. The duet between the two Toy Soldiers (Mr. Windham Guise and Mr. J. W. Macdonald) was exceedingly funny ; Mr. Murray King, as the Witch, was perhaps the uncanniest beldame ever seen on any stage ; and Mr. Joseph Wilson and Miss Louie Pounds were very pleasant as the Soldier and the Princess. Altogether the "triple bill" may be cordially commended to parents and guardians. Their charges will be delighted with it, and they themselves will not be bored—or, if they are, they should be ashamed to confess it.

Mrs. Bernard Beere, happily restored to health, has made her reappearance in the part of Anne Carew in *A Sheep in Wolf's Clothing** at the Comedy Theatre. Her performance showed no decline either in charm or in power, and was greeted with enthusiasm by the audience. It is remarkable, indeed, that after so long a period of enforced retirement, Mrs. Beere's talent should show no sign of even a momentary faltering. Mr. Henry Neville played Jasper Carew with his unfailing vigour and decision, and Mr. Kemble was picturesque and amusing, though less truculent than might have been desired, in the part of Colonel Kirke. The comedietta precedes Mr. Esmond's delightful comedy *One Summer's Day*, which has fulfilled the promise of its first night and is now well past its hundredth.

* December 4—still running.

EPILOGUE STATISTICAL.

—— •◦• ——

THE present volume contains the fifth yearly in-
gathering of my criticisms of the London stage.   As
some five-and-twenty theatres in the West End of
London are practically the only places in the British
Empire where new plays of any importance are produced,* it follows that whoever keeps a constant
watch on these theatres passes in review the whole
of the living English drama, in so far as it approaches,
however remotely, to the confines of literature.   The
Provinces and the Colonies are supplied either with
plays which have stood the test of a London production, or with melodramas, farces, and variety-
plays even lower than the lowest of those which
we see at the West End theatres.   These volumes,
then, may be said to contain, not only the record
of the five-and-twenty play-houses aforesaid, but the
history of the English Drama for the past five years,

* The recent fashion of provincial "trial trips" does not
invalidate this statement.   Within the five years in question, at
any rate, no play of any moment has been produced in the
Provinces or Colonies and not seen in London.

from the point of view of one fairly diligent observer.

History, however, is too large a word. Let us rather say annals—the materials for history. Fifty years hence the history of these five years may be written — perhaps in five lines. If the historian of 1950 makes any mention of the volumes in which so many hours of my life are buried, it will probably be to chuckle over some delectable ineptitude of criticism or forecast, as in this volume (p. 189) I smile at George Henry Lewes's criticism of, and forecast concerning, " La Dame aux Camélias." Ungrateful historian ! I forgive you in advance, and even propose, out of the magnanimity of my nature, to heap anticipatory coals of fire upon your as yet unborn head. I propose to give you, what no one, to my knowledge, has hitherto essayed : a statistical summary, a quantitative analysis, of the five years' output of the five-and-twenty theatres. You shall learn from the following pages, not in vague guesses and rash generalisations, but in tolerably accurate figures, what forms of drama had the greatest vogue, how native English work bulked in proportion to adaptations, what authors were the most popular, with several other facts of more or less significance. You can then compare the like statistics for your own age, and wonder (I hope) how we could manage to support existence in the theatrical world of the far-off and almost fabulous nineteenth century.

But I do not write solely for this conjectural historian or antiquary. The enquiry, I take it, is of living interest to ourselves. Without it, we do not really know what has been passing before our eyes. We have only vague impressions as to the preponderance of this or that style of play, the popularity of this or that author. For example, the belief that the English theatre subsists almost entirely on adaptations from the French still lingers on in several quarters— mainly, indeed, in Paris, but also among those superior persons in England who, because they dislike, think it necessary also to despise, the stage. The figures to be given presently will once for all dispose of this illusion. We have still far too many adaptations from the French, but they form considerably less than one-fifth of the theatrical fare consumed by the London public during these five years.

A distinctive feature of my annual record has been, from the first, the registering of the length of run attained by each play. What I am now doing, then, is to systematise and bring to a focus the information contained in the footnotes scattered throughout these volumes. A summing up of the events of one year is of very little practical use. The period is too short to afford any basis for a valid generalisation.

But a conspectus of five years is a different matter. It may not lead to any very definite or profitable result; but the experiment is at least worth trying. The lustrum in question will, I think, be recognised as pretty distinctly marked off from the years which preceded it.* Whatever its value, a new literary movement set in with the production of "The Second Mrs. Tanqueray" in May 1893; and it was about the same time, or a little earlier, that the all-conquering "musical farce" began its triumphal progress. There is surely something to be learnt, then, from what I have called a quantitative analysis of the theatrical entertainments of this period.

My "perlustration" begins with January 1st, 1893, and ends with December 31st, 1897. I take no cognisance of anything outside these fixed points. If a play was produced in 1891 or 1892 and ran on into 1893, I count those weeks only which fell within the latter year; and similarly "The Little Minister" (to take one example), produced November 6th, 1897, counts for eight weeks only in my reckoning, though it may be destined

---

* It is perhaps worth noting that at the beginning of the period (in January 1893) "Our Boys" was running at the Vaudeville Theatre. It disappeared after four weeks, and with it H. J. Byron, the most popular author of the previous twenty years, vanished from the scene. Nor has any play by James Albery been revived during the years under review.

to outrun the century. I have made my calculations in weeks, partly because this unit gave me more manageable figures to deal with, mainly because it would have involved intolerable and quite unnecessary labour to reckon the actual number of performances of each play. At some theatres only occasional matinées are given, at some there is a weekly matinée, at others two matinées a week. No human industry could have grappled with all these details; so I contented myself with counting the weeks of a run, and leaving the matinées to take care of themselves. Odd days I struck off my reckoning, unless they came within one of the complete week; thus a play which ran six weeks and three days counts for six weeks only, whereas one which ran six weeks and five days counts for seven weeks. This may seem an arbitrary rule, but the inexactness it involves is very trifling. In a few cases in which plays, after a certain steady run, have been played two or three times a week, in alternation with other plays, I have reckoned the total number of such intermittent performances and reduced it to weeks. I have tried to take into account every production * at the recognised West End theatres that ran for a week or more, except pantomimes, operas (whether serious or comic), and plays

* One-act pieces are not included in my calculations, but only such plays as have formed the staple of an evening's entertainment.

in foreign languages.   The boundary between comic opera and musical farce is not very clearly defined, but in practice I have found little difficulty in making the distinction.   In a comic opera, I take it, the music and the plot are of prime importance; in a musical farce there is nothing that can be called a plot, and yet the libretto, the "gags," and the "comic business" are of more importance than the music.   As I shall print in full my list of musical farces, there can at least be no doubt as to where I have (rightly or wrongly) drawn the line.   Let me add that at the Princess's and the Opera Comique the entertainments presented have occasionally been so distinctly of the East End or provincial order that I felt they did not come within my critical province ; wherefore my record as regards these theatres is not quite complete.   It is possible that at other theatres I may have overlooked unimportant and brief revivals; and, as I am no great arithmetician, I may perhaps have fallen into some errors of mere computation.   I am confident, however, that no such oversight or inaccuracy is sufficient seriously to invalidate the statistics I am about to present.

One more word of preface.   It would of course be idle to suppose that the comparative popularity of two plays is exactly indicated by the length of their respective runs.   For one thing, theatres differ greatly in size, and Drury Lane, for example, will seat about three times as many people as the Haymarket or the St. James's. It might have been possible, no doubt, to allow for differences of size and reckon one week at Drury Lane as equivalent to three weeks at the Haymarket. But even this would not give anything like an exact and conclusive result, since the audience in a theatre (and especially the paying audience) is not always, or even generally, commensurate with its capacity. At a theatre of moderate rent, worked by an inexpensive company, plays can be acted for months and years to audiences that at another theatre would mean speedy bankruptcy. Moreover, many plays are run for weeks and months either at a constant loss, or at so small a profit that two or three weeks of bad "business" will swallow it all up, and leave a deficit on the whole enterprise. It is impossible, in short, without access to the books of the management, to measure with absolute precision the power of attraction exercised by any particular play. My counting of weeks yields only an approximate indication of popularity, but an indication which, in the mass, will not lead us far astray. Three provisos are, however, worth making —(1) As musical farce and spectacular melodrama are usually played at large theatres, and by large and expensive companies, a long run, for plays of these two classes, may safely be taken as indicating very great (though not necessarily very remunerative) popularity. (2) Our comedy theatres, where the works of such writers as Mr. Pinero, Mr. Jones, and Mr. Grundy are usually acted, do not differ very greatly in capacity, so that, within this particular class, comparative length of run forms a pretty trustworthy indication of comparative power of attraction. (3) The effect of the bogus run—the sham success, carried on week after week at a steady loss, either to salve some one's vanity, or in the gambler's frenzied hope that the luck must turn, or to give the play a good start in the provinces—the effect of the bogus run is to lend a false air of popularity to the lowest forms of entertainment, and especially to worthless farces, whether home-made or imported. A serious play at a leading theatre cannot be run for long to empty or profusely "papered" houses—the loss would be too great. Thus where the works of our leading authors are concerned, apparent success may be taken to mean real success ; whereas if one dared strike off the bogus successes (most of them notorious to every one who is at all behind the scenes) the figures for farce and adaptations from the French would be significantly reduced.

My scheme of classification has been as follows :—

A. ENGLISH PLAYS—

    i. Shakespeare.

    ii. Old Plays, other than Shakespeare's.

    iii. Modern Plays.

      1. Dramas, comedies, and serious prose plays
          in general.

      2. Poetical plays.

      3. Melodramas.

      4. Farces.

      5. Burlesques.

      6. Musical farces.

B. AMERICAN PLAYS.

C. FOREIGN PLAYS—

      i. From the French.

      ii. From the German.

      iii. From the Norwegian.

      iv. From other languages.

Here, then, are the results of my enumeration:—

A. ENGLISH PLAYS—

i. Shakespeare—

          1893.   Weeks.

King Lear   .   .   .   . 4 (after Jan. 1, 1893).

The Taming of the Shrew   . 2

Occasional performances of The Merchant of Venice, Much Ado about Nothing, and Henry VIII. were given at the Lyceum; and Measure for Measure was acted by the amateurs who afterwards became the Elizabethan Stage Society.

          1894.   Weeks.

Twelfth Night   16

As You Like It was performed once; The Merchant of Venice, once; The Merry Wives of Windsor, twice; and Hamlet, twice.

          1895.   Weeks.

The Two Gentlemen of Verona .   .   . 1

A Midsummer Night's Dream .   .   . 3

Romeo and Juliet   13

Occasional performances of The Merchant of Venice, Much Ado, and Macbeth were given at the Lyceum. The Elizabethan Stage Society performed Twelfth Night and The Comedy of Errors.

	1896.	Weeks.
King Henry IV. (Part I.)	. . . .	4
Cymbeline	. . . . . .	13
As You Like It	. . . . .	15

Sir Henry Irving played Richard III. once, the run being cut short by an accident. The Elizabethan Stage Society acted The Two Gentlemen of Verona.

	1897.	Weeks.
Richard III.	. . . . .	5
Hamlet (Olympic)	. . . .	2
Othello	. . . . .	1
Merchant of Venice	. . . .	1
Antony and Cleopatra	. . . .	2
Macbeth	. . . . .	1
Hamlet (Lyceum)	. . . .	14

Two performances of Hamlet were given at Her Majesty's, and the Elizabethan Stage Society acted Twelfth Night, the Shakespearian scenes from Edward III., and The Tempest.

Detached performances apart, Shakespeare has occupied the stage for 97 weeks. Twenty of his plays (including those produced by the Elizabethan Stage Society) have at one time or another been performed.

ii. Old Plays, other than Shakespeare's.

		Weeks.
1893. The Hunchback (Sheridan Knowles)	.	1
The School for Scandal (Sheridan)	.	5

Weeks.

1894.	Caste (Robertson)	.	.	.	.	8
	Money (Lytton)	.	.	.	.	15
1895.	The Rivals (Sheridan)	.	.	.	.	6
1896.	The School for Scandal	.	.	.	.	5
	The Liar (Foote)	.	.	.	.	1
	Black Ey'd Susan (Jerrold)		.	.	.	19
1897.	David Garrick (Robertson)		.	.	.	4
	Virginius (Knowles) .	.	.	.	.	2
	Caste	.	.	.	.	4

70

High Life Below Stairs was played for eight weeks as a curtain-raiser at Terry's. The Elizabethan Stage Society has given single performances of Dr. Faustus and Arden of Feversham.

iii. Modern Plays.

1. DRAMAS, COMEDIES, AND SERIOUS PROSE PLAYS IN GENERAL.

I need not print the full list of the plays which come under this heading. All the more important ones will be enumerated in separate tables, showing the number of weeks during which each of our leading dramatists has held the stage. Suffice it to say that I include in this class 88 plays, which occupied in all 740 weeks.

2. POETICAL PLAYS.

Weeks.

Hypatia (Ogilvie)	.	.	.	.	15
Becket (Tennyson)	.	.	.	.	13*
The Tempter (Jones)	.	.	.	10

* Including revival.

Weeks.

The Foresters (Tennyson)	. . .	2
King Arthur (Carr) . . .	. .	16
The Sin of St. Hulda (Ogilvie) .	. .	2
The Pilgrim's Progress (Collingham)	.	3

7 plays, occupying 61 weeks.

3. MELODRAMAS.

	The Prodigal Daughter	. . . .	2
1893.	The Black Domino .	. . . .	8
	A Woman's Revenge	. . . .	35
	A Life of Pleasure .	. . . .	20
1894.*	The World .	. . . .	7
	The Cotton King .	. . . .	8
	Shall we Forgive Her	. . . .	8
	The Fatal Card .	. . . .	27
	The Derby Winner .	. . . .	19
	Robbery Under Arms	. . . .	2
1895.	Cheer, Boys, Cheer .	. . . .	22
	One of the Best .	. . . .	24
1896.	Tommy Atkins . .	. . . .	1
	The Sign of the Cross	. . .	62†
	True Blue . .	. . . .	5
	The Star of India .	. . . .	6
	Boys Together . .	. . . .	14
	The Duchess of Coolgardie	. .	10
1897.	The Free Pardon . .	. . .	3
	The Daughters of Babylon	. .	9
	The Mariners of England .	. .	4
	The Days of the Duke .	. . .	10
	The White Heather .	. . .	13

23 plays, occupying 319 weeks.

* Revival.   † Including revival in 1897.

4. FARCES.

Here, again, the list is too long to print in full. It amounts to 51 plays, occupying 657 weeks. It should be stated, however, that nearly a third of this tale of weeks is furnished by " Charlie's Aunt " alone, which, produced before the period under review, ran for 206 weeks within it.

5. BURLESQUES.

Burlesques, as distinct from the all-absorbing musical farces, cut a very poor figure :

	Weeks.
The Babble Shop	2
Jaunty Jane Shore	6
*Little Jack Sheppard	6
Under the Clock	7
All my Eye-Vanhoe	I
A Model Trilby	II

6 plays, occupying 33 weeks.

6. MUSICAL FARCES.

	Weeks.	
In Town	33	after Jan. 1, 1893.
1893. Morocco Bound . . .	43	
A Modern Don Quixote .	3	
The Gaiety Girl . . .	61	
Don Juan	33 = 173 weeks.	
1894. Go-Bang	24	
King Kodak . . .	8	
Claude Duval . . .	20	

* Revival.

Weeks.

The Lady Slavey . . .	13	
Little Christopher Columbus .	61	
The Shop Girl	78 = 204 weeks.	
1895. The Artist's Model . . .	57	
Gentleman Joe	56	
All Abroad	15 = 128 weeks.	
1896. The New Barmaid . . .	20	
Biarritz	10	
The Geisha	87	
On the March	11	
My Girl	26	
Monte Carlo	10	
Lord Tom Noddy . . .	8	
The White Silk Dress . .	20	
The Belle of Cairo . . .	10	
The Gay Parisienne . . .	50	
The Circus Girl	55 = 307 weeks.	
1897. The Man about Town . .	3	
The French Maid . . .	36	
The Maid of Athens . . .	4	
Dandy Dan	3 = 46 weeks.	

29 plays, occupying 858 weeks.

It thus appears that musical farce has occupied 118 more weeks than serious prose plays, 57 more weeks than serious prose plays and poetical plays put together, and 201 more weeks than non-musical farce. Were we to reckon along with musical farce the cognate forms of entertainment, pantomime and comic opera, the preponderance would be altogether overwhelming.

B. AMERICAN PLAYS.†

		Weeks.
	The Lost Paradise . . .	10⎫ after Jan. 1,
	The Silent Battle . . .	3⎭ 1893.
1893.	Man and Woman . . .	7
	The Silver Shell	7
	A Trip to Chicago . . .	11
	(A) Love in Tandem . . .	2
	(A) Dollars and Sense . . .	2
	(A) The Last Word	1
	(A) The Orient Express . . .	2 = 45 weeks.
1894.	The Trip to Chinatown . .	15 = 15 weeks.
1895.	That Terrible Girl . . .	2
	The Girl I Left Behind Me .	17
	(A) The Railroad of Love . . .	1
	A New York Divorce . . .	3
	Alabama	6 = 29 weeks.
1896.	Jedbury Junior	20
	(A) The Countess Gucki . . .	2
	(A) Love on Crutches . . .	2 = 24 weeks.
1897.	My Friend the Prince . .	25
	The Prodigal Father . . .	9
	Lost, Stolen, or Strayed . .	10
	Secret Service	20
	The County Fair . . .	2
	The Cat and the Cherub . .	4
	The First-Born	1
	The Sleeping Partner	5
	Miss Francis of Yale . . .	7 = 83 weeks.

27 plays, occupying 196 weeks.

† Including adaptations (marked with an A) from the French and German, produced by the Daly Company.

C. FOREIGN PLAYS.

i. From the French.   Weeks.

Trooper Clairette . . .	3 } after Jan. 1,
To-day	1 } 1893.
1893. The Sportsman	12
* Diplomacy	27
* The Ironmaster . . .	6
* Forbidden Fruit . . .	9
The Great Unpaid . . .	2
The Other Fellow . .	11
The Two Johnnies . .	1
The Lady Killer . . .	4
Mrs. Othello . . .	8=84 weeks.
1894. An Aristocratic Alliance .	8
* Frou-Frou . . .	11
* A Bunch of Violets . .	16
Jean Mayeux (pantomime) .	1
* The Two Orphans . .	5
* The Candidate . . .	11
* Hot Water	4
* Odette · . . .	2
The Gay Widow . . .	6
* Dr. Bill	4=68 weeks.
1895. *A Pair of Spectacles . .	7
Delia Harding . . .	4
* Fédora	8
The Swordsman's Daughter	13
The Chili Widow . .	30
Mrs. Ponderbury's Past .	26
The Squire of Dames . .	20=108 weeks.

* Revival.

Weeks.

1896.	For the Crown	13
	A Night Out	75
	The Queen's Proctor	15
	My Artful Valet	6
	Two Little Vagabonds	46
	His Little Dodge	12=167 weeks.
1897.	*Betsy	6
	A Pierrot's Life (pantomime)	17
	Saucy Sally	16
	Madame Sans-Gêne	15
	* The Bells	1
	On Leave	2
	A Marriage of Convenience	16
	All Alive, oh !	3
	The Silver Key	8
	* A Man's Shadow	5
	Francillon	7
	Never Again	11 = 107 weeks.

46 plays, occupying 534 weeks.

Adrienne Lecouvreur was played three or four times at the Royalty. A few isolated performances of The Bells, The Lyons Mail, Louis XI., and The Corsican Brothers have been given at the Lyceum. Mr. Beerbohm Tree has frequently appeared in The Ballad-Monger (one act).

ii. From the German.

Weeks.

1893.	Alexandra	1
	Clever Alice	2
1894.	Once upon a Time	3
	* Faust	12
1896.	*On 'Change	4

* Revival.

Weeks.

1896. The New Baby   2
     Magda   2
1897. The Children of the King .   .   4 = 30 weeks.
         8 plays, occupying 30 weeks.

iii. From the Norwegian.

Here we must reckon, not by weeks, but by single performances.

1893. IBSEN : The Master Builder   .   37 times.
          A Doll's House   .   .   . 14 ,,
          Hedda Gabler .   .   .   . 4 ,,
          Rosmersholm .   .   .   . 4 ,,
          An Enemy of the People   . 7 ,,
1894. IBSEN : An Enemy of the People   .   once.
          The Wild Duck   .   .   . 3 times.
    BJÖRNSON : A Gauntlet   .   .   . 4 ,,
1896. IBSEN : Little Eyolf   .   .   .   . 24 ,,
1897.   John Gabriel Borkman .   . 5 ,,
          A Doll's House   .   .   . 5 ,,
          The Wild Duck   .   .   . 5 ,,
         9 plays, occupying 19 weeks.

The fourth act of Brand was played four times along with The Master Builder in 1893.

iv. From other Languages.

    SPANISH : Mariana (Echegaray) .   . 5 times.
    DUTCH : Leida (Josine Holland) .   . once.
         A Man's Love (J. C. de Vos) . twice.

Now for a general summing-up of results ; and first for a comparison of the time occupied by English and non-English plays respectively :—

ENGLISH.		NON-ENGLISH.	
	Weeks		Weeks
Shakespeare . .	97	American . .	. 196
Old plays other than		French . .	. 534
Shakespeare's .	70	German . .	. 30
Modern dramas, come-		Norwegian . .	. 19
dies, etc. .	. 740	Other languages	. 1
Modern poetical plays	61		
Melodramas .	. 319		
Farces . .	. 657		
Burlesques . .	. 33		
Musical Farces .	. 858		
Total	2835	Total	780

We see, then, that the time given to home manufactures exceeds the time given to imported products by 2055 weeks, or by nearly four to one. But though American plays are imported products, they spring from the same root as our own, and are nourished by the same sap of tradition. A juster comparison would lie between plays written in English and plays translated or adapted from foreign languages; in which case we should have 3031 weeks to set against 584, or more than five to one.

As for the alleged preponderance of adaptations from the French, we find it a mere superstition. Each of the three main classes of English plays (modern dramas, farces, and musical farces) largely outstrips the total of adaptations from the French. We have had 801 weeks of serious modern plays in

24

prose and verse, 657 weeks of farce, 858 weeks of musical farce, as against 534 weeks of " Parisian confections."   Or, to take the matter from another point of view, if we exclude musical farce and burlesque, and compare the total time given to English non-musical plays, old and new, with the time given to English versions of French plays, we have to set 1944 weeks against 534 weeks, or nearly 4 to 1.   Our dramatic life will never be thoroughly healthy until the time given to plays from the French is reduced by at least one half; but it is absurd to speak as though London to-day were, in theatrical matters, a mere suburb of Paris.

Let us now see for what space of time, during these five years, each of our leading playwrights has held the stage.   I marshal them alphabetically :—

MR. J. M. BARRIE.

Weeks.

Walker, London	27 } after Jan. 1, 1893.
1894. The Professor's Love Story	17
1895.*The Professor's Love Story	1
1897. The Little Minister	8 = 53 weeks.

A one-act play by Mr. Barrie named Becky Sharp (an episode from "Vanity Fair") was played 5 or 6 times in 1893.

MR. R. C. CARTON.

Weeks.

Liberty Hall	20 } after Jan. 1, 1893.
1893. Robin Goodfellow	

* Revival.

Weeks.

1895. The Home Secretary . . . 14
1896. The White Elephant . . . 15
1897. The Tree of Knowledge . . 9 = 63 weeks.

MR. H. V. ESMOND.

1895. Bogey 2
      The Divided Way . . . 3
1897. One Summer's Day . . . 15 = 20 weeks.

MR. SYDNEY GRUNDY.†

1893. A White Lie 7
      Sowing the Wind . . . 17
1894. An Old Jew 4
      The New Woman . . . 22
1895. Slaves of the Ring . . . 2
      *Sowing the Wind . . . 4
1896. The Late Mr. Castello . . 7
      The Greatest of These— . . 6 = 69 weeks.

MR. HENRY ARTHUR JONES.

1893. The Bauble Shop . . . 20
      The Tempter 10
1894. The Masqueraders . . . 19
      *The Middleman 1
      The Case of Rebellious Susan . 22

---

* Revival.
† Mr. Grundy's adaptations from the French :—

Weeks.

A Bunch of Violets . . . 16
A Pair of Spectacles . . . 7
A Marriage of Convenience . . 16
The Silver Key . . . . 8 = 47 weeks.

Weeks.

1895. The Triumph of the Philistines .   5
1896. Michael and his Lost Angel   .   1
The Rogue's Comedy.   .   .   5
1897. The Physician   12
The Liars   .   .   .   .   12 = 107 weeks.

MR. LOUIS N. PARKER.

1893. Gudgeons†   8
1895. The Blue Boar†   4
1896. Rosemary†   27
Love in Idleness‡   .   .   .   12
1897. The Vagabond King .   .   .   4
The Happy Life .   .   .   .   3 = 58 weeks.

The Man in the Street, a one-act play by Mr. Parker,
has been frequently performed at several theatres.

MR. A. W. PINERO.

Weeks.

1893. The Amazons   17
The Second Mrs. Tanqueray   .   32
1895. The Notorious Mrs. Ebbsmith .   13
*The Second Mrs. Tanqueray   .   2
The Benefit of the Doubt .   .   10
1897. The Princess and the Butterfly .   13
*The Hobby-Horse   .   .   .   3 = 90 weeks.

LORD TENNYSON.

1893. Becket   11
The Foresters   2
1893.* Becket   .   .   .   .   2 = 15 weeks.

* Revival.

† With Mr. Murray Carson.   ‡ With Mr. E. J. Goodman.

Mr. George Bernard Shaw.

1894. Arms and the Man . . . 11 weeks.

Mr. Oscar Wilde.

1893. A Woman of No Importance . 16
1895. An Ideal Husband . . . 16
    The Importance of being Earnest 12=44 weeks.

It may be noted that these 10 authors have occupied among them 530 weeks, just 4 weeks less than have been devoted to adaptations from the French. It also appears that Mr. Henry Arthur Jones has held the stage for 10 weeks more than Shakespeare, while the author of "The Second Mrs. Tanqueray" comes in 7 weeks behind the author of "Hamlet."

Let me now present a summary of

PLAYS ADAPTED FROM NOVELS.*

		Weeks.
Trilby	.	34
Manxman (2 versions)	.	4
The Prisoner of Zenda	.	33
Under the Red Robe .	.	32
The Sorrows of Satan	.	7
The Seats of the Mighty	.	5
The Little Minister .	.	8 = 123 weeks.

Of our leading novelists, Mr. Meredith has contributed nothing to the stage, either during these five years or at any other time, though it is rumoured that he has more than one comedy in his desk. A one-act play of Mr. Thomas Hardy's, "The Wayfarers,"

---

* These are all included in Class A, iii. 1.

was produced by Mr. Charrington in 1893, and repeated some five or six times; Mr. Henry James's "Guy Domville" had a run of four weeks at the St. James's in 1895; Mr. George Moore has written a four-act play, "The Strike at Arlingford," which was performed once by the Independent Theatre in 1893;* "Admiral Guinea," by William Ernest Henley and Robert Louis Stevenson, was performed five times by the New Century Theatre in 1897 ; and Mr. Conan Doyle has written two one-act plays, "Foreign Policy," performed along with Mr. Hardy's "Wayfarers" in 1893, and "A Story of Waterloo," frequently acted by Sir Henry Irving. Mr. Barrie alone, as we have seen above, has largely and successfully contributed to the acted drama.

I have said that absolute certainty as to the attractive power of any given production cannot be attained unless one has access to the accounts of the management. At the same time, no one who keeps his eyes and ears open, and has any knowledge of the ways of the theatrical world, is likely to be very much deceived as to the real fortunes of a play. Apart from actual information (which must, of course, be taken for what it is worth), there are many symptoms by which a sham success may be distinguished from

* He has also adapted from the French, in collaboration with "John Oliver Hobbes," a one-act play, "Journeys end in Lovers meeting."

a real one. I have gone through my lists of modern plays, melodramas, farces, musical farces, American plays, and adaptations from the French (in each case excluding revivals), and have marked them off, according to the best of my knowledge and judgment, into three classes: (*a*) Genuine successes; (*b*) Doubtful successes—plays which had a considerable run, but probably did little, if anything, more than pay their expenses; (*c*) Indubitable failures. To give particulars under each of these heads would be to involve myself in endless controversies, if not in actions for libel. Therefore I can only state general results, to which the reader must attach what credence he thinks fit. If my estimate is at all to be trusted, it fully bears out my remark on p. 140 as to the amount of money wasted month by month and year by year on theatrical enterprises which have not, from the outset, the remotest chance of success. Of the indubitable failures (especially in the department of farce) there is probably not one in ten for which any competent critic, on merely reading the manuscript, would not have predicted disaster with cheerful confidence. Here, then, is my estimate :—

MODERN PLAYS.

(In prose and verse : revivals excluded.)

(A) Successes	.	.		.	. 25
(B) Doubtful	.	.	.	.	. 12
(C) Failures	.	.	.	.	. 45

MELODRAMAS.

(A) Successes	.	.	.	.	.	9
(C) Failures	.	.	.	.	.	13

FARCES.

(A) Successes	.	.	.	.	.	8
(B) Doubtful	.	.	.	.	.	14
(C) Failures	.	.	.	.	.	29

MUSICAL FARCES.

(A) Successes	.	.	.	.	.	14
(B) Doubtful	.	.	.	.	.	9
(C) Failures	.	.	.	.	.	6

AMERICAN PLAYS.*

(A) Successes	.	.	.	.	.	4
(B) Doubtful	.	.	.	.	.	6
(C) Failures	.	.	.	.	.	10

ADAPTATIONS FROM THE FRENCH.

(A) Successes	.	.	.	.	.	5
(B) Doubtful	.	.	.	.	.	13
(C) Failures	.	.	.	.	.	13

In sum, then, we have 65 successes, 54 doubtful cases, and 116 failures; and as at least half of the doubtful cases must have been in reality failures more or less expensively disguised, we may safely conclude that failures have out-numbered successes in the proportion of two to one. There have been, on an average (let

* Exclusive of Mr. Daly's productions, which have almost all been revivals put on for a limited number of nights.

me repeat that I am speaking of new plays only), 13 indubitable successes in each year, as opposed to 23 indubitable failures. In the department of what I have called serious modern plays, there have been, on an average, 5 distinct successes per annum, and 9 manifest failures. Of plays written in the English language 60, in all, have achieved marked successes, as against 5 adaptations from the French—an average of 12 per annum, as against one. The neatness with which these averages work out may seem suspicious; but I give my word of honour that I have in no way "cooked" my calculations.

Here I bring to a close my statistical survey of the past five years. Having presented the facts, marshalling and co-ordinating them to the best of my ability, I leave the reader to reflect upon them and deduce whatever moral or morals he pleases. Their full significance can hardly be discerned until, in 1903, we can place beside them a similar statistical statement for the coming lustrum. Some one, I trust, will undertake this task, even if, as is not improbable, my own record should in the meantime be discontinued.

February 5th, 1898.

SYNOPSIS OF PLAYBILLS,

1897.

BY HENRY GEORGE HIBBERT.

———◆◆———

JANUARY.

2. A MAN ABOUT TOWN: Musical Farce in Three Acts, by "Huan Mee"; Music by Alfred Carpenter. **Avenue.** Cast: *Frank Ennesleigh*, Mr. E. J. Lonnen; *Ralph Fenton*, Mr. Charles Cherry; *Lucius Light*, Mr. E. Dagnall; *Henri Lavelle*, Mr. Sidney Howard; *Robert Jansen*, Mr. Littledale Power; *Gwendoline Grova*, Miss Alma Stanley; *Edith*, Miss May Edouin; *Kate Derwent*, Miss Grace Hamond; *Nora Ennesleigh*, Miss Alice Lethbridge. Withdrawn 22nd January.

8. A PIERROT'S LIFE: Play without Words in Three Acts, by F. Beissier; Music by M. Costa. **Prince of Wales's.** Cast: *Pierrot*, Mdlle. Litini; *Louisette*, Madame Germaine Ety; *Fifine*, Mdlle. G. Faurens; *Pochinet*, Signor Egidio Rossi; *Julot*, M. Jacquinet; *Petit Pierrot*, La Petite Gaudry. Withdrawn 11th May. Afternoon performances, but one evening performance was given on 20th February.

9. THE SORROWS OF SATAN: Play in Four Acts, adapted by Herbert Woodgate and Paul M. Berton from the novel by Marie Corelli. **Shaftesbury.** Cast: *Prince Lucio Rimanez*, Mr. Lewis Waller; *Geoffrey Tempest*, Mr. Yorke Stephens; *The Earl of Elton*, Mr. John Beauchamp; *Viscount Lynton*, Mr. Tripp Edgar; *Duke of Launceston*, Mr. C. W. Garthorne; *Sir Thomas Tenby*, Mr. George Rollit; *Morgeson*, Mr. L. F. Chapuy; *Bentham*, Mr. George Humphrey; *Ellis*, Mr. Compton Coutts; *Amiel*, Mr. Edward

O'Neil; *Two Servants*, Mr. Philip Darwin and Mr. Lennox; *Lady Sybil*, Miss Granville; *Duchess of Launceston*, Mrs. Saker; *Mavis Clare*, Miss E. B. Sheridan; *Diana Chesney*, Miss Rose Dupre; *Miss Charlotte Fitzroy*, Miss Charlotte Morland; *Lady Mary Spencer*, Miss Alleyn; *Simmons*, Miss Alice Johnson. Withdrawn 27th February.

11. DELICATE GROUND: Comedietta by Charles Dance, revived at **Terry's Theatre** in association with **THE EIDER-DOWN QUILT.** Cast: *Citizen Sangfroid*, Mr. Arthur Playfair; *Pauline*, Miss Lena Ashwell; *Alphonse de Grandier*, Mr. Cosmo Stuart.

18. The Carl Rosa Opera Company began a three weeks' season at the **Garrick,** producing **Tannhäuser, Romeo and Juliet, The Vivandiere,** an Opera in Three Acts, French words by Henri Cain, English translation by George Whyte; Music by Benjamin Goddard (first time in London), **Faust, The Meistersingers, Mignon, Cavalleria Rusticana** and **I Pagliacci, Carmen, Lohengrin, The Valkyrie** (English version, the first time in London), and **The Bohemian Girl.**

22. SOCIETY. An afternoon performance for the benefit of Edward Hastings, at the **Criterion.** Cast: *Lord Ptarmigant*, Mr. Edward Righton; *Lord Cloudwrays*, Mr. C. W. Garthorne; *Sydney Daryl*, Mr. Scott Buist; *John Chodd, Sen.*, Mr. Kemble; *John Chodd, Jun.*, Mr. Ernest Cosham; *Tom Stylus*, Mr. Gerald Maxwell; *O'Sullivan*, Mr. Charles Brookfield; *M'Usquebaugh*, Mr. J. Carne; *Dr. Macvicz*, Mr. W. Wyes; *Bradley*, Mr. Fuller Mellish; *Scargill*, Mr. Eric Lewis; *Sam Stunner*, Mr. Valentine; *Shamheart*, Mr. Gilbert Farquhar; *Reporter*, Mr. Lennox; *Doddles*, Mr. L. F. Chapuy; *Moses Aaron*, Mr. E. Dagnall; *Trodnon*, Mr. George Temple; *Sam*, Mr. Compton Coutts; *Soldier*, Mr. Rupert Lister; *Printer's Boy*, Mr. Robert Earle; *Lady Ptarmigant*, Miss Rose Leclercq; *Maud Hetherington*, Miss Laura Graves; *Little Maud*, Miss Beatrice Murray; *Mrs. Churton*, Miss Morland; *Servant*, Miss Thompson.

28. THE FREE PARDON: Domestic Drama in Four Acts, by F. C. Phillips and Leonard Merrick. **Olympic.** Cast: *Webster P. Washington,* Mr. W. L. Abingdon; *Eric Annesley,* Mr. Harrison Hunter; *Colonel Philip Annesley,* Mr. Courtenay Thorpe; *Sergeant Twentyman,* Mr. George Cockburn; *Julian Annesley,* Mr. Edward O'Neil; *Inspector Pennyquick,* Mr. A. T. Hilton; *Mr. Bunter,* Mr. Leslie Thomson; *Aitken,* Mr. H. Delplanque; *Taylor,* Mr. John Webb; *Toomy,* Mr. C. Dudley; *Bates,* Mr. J. Cole; *George,* Mr. Webster; *Algy Fanshawe,* Mr. T. Leslie; *Reynolds,* Mr. Dudley Clinton; *Steve Pringle,* Mr. C. Lismaine; *Ethel Wynyard,* Miss Esme Beringer; *Miss Peggy Flitters,* Miss Cicely Richards; *Pansey Esmond,* Miss Carleton; *Mrs. Flitters,* Miss Grosvenor; *Polly,* Miss Merriman; *Louise Murray,* Miss Vane. Withdrawn 20th February.

30. OLIVIA: Play in Four Acts, by W. G. Wills. Originally produced at the Court Theatre, 28th March 1878; now revived at the **Lyceum.** Cast: *Dr. Primrose,* Mr. Hermann Vezin; *Squire Thornhill,* Mr. Frank Cooper; *Mr. Burchell,* Mr. F. H. Macklin; *Moses,* Mr. Martin Harvey; *Farmer Flamborough,* Mr. S. Johnson; *Leigh,* Mr. Tyars; *Dick,* Master Stewart Dawson; *Bill,* Miss Valli Valli; *Polly Flamborough,* Miss Brenda Gibson; *Phœbe,* Miss Foster; *Gipsy Woman,* Miss Edith Craig; *Mrs. Primrose,* Miss Maud Milton; *Sophia,* Miss Julia Arthur; *Olivia,* Miss Ellen Terry.*

FEBRUARY.

1. THE PRODIGAL FATHER: An Extravagant Farce in Three Acts, by Glen MacDonough. Tentatively played at the New Theatre, Oxford, 25th January; now reproduced at the **Strand.** Cast: *Dodge,* Mr. Harry Paulton; *Catesby Duff,*

---

* *Cymbeline,* reproduced in the emergency of Sir Henry Irving's accident on 26th December 1896, was played a few times only, then withdrawn till 23rd January, and again played a few nights. On 27th February Sir Henry Irving resumed performances of *Richard III.* Withdrawn 7th April.

Mr. Charles Collette; *Tom Breeze*, Mr. Charles Weir; *Smith*, Mr. William Hargreaves; *Percy Dodge*, Mr. Alex. Bradley; *Smile*, Mr. C. Garth; *Kate*, Miss May Palfrey; *Birdikins*, Miss Lulu Valli, Dollie Bond, Miss Florence Gerard. Withdrawn 20th March.—Preceded by **A MERRY CHRISTMAS,** an adaptation by an anonymous playwright of the old French comedietta, "Je Dine chez ma Mere." Cast: *The Duke of Maresfield*, Mr. Alex. Bradley; *Sir Ralph Treherne*, Mr. C. Garth; *Frank Little*, Mr. Charles Weir; *Marion*, Miss Agnes Paulton; *Rose Darling*, Miss Florence Gerard.

6. THE DAUGHTERS OF BABYLON: Play in Four Acts, by Wilson Barrett. **Lyric.** Cast: *Zoar*, Mr. Alfred Brydone; *Lemuel*, Mr. Wilson Barrett; *Jediah*, Mr. Franklyn M'Leay; *Sabaal*, Mr. Charles Hudson; *Ahira*, Mr. Edward Irwin; *Arad*, Mr. James Barber; *Hezron*, Mr. George Wensleydale; *Adoram*, Mr. Reginald Dance; *Elymas*, Mr. Horace Hodges; *Elkanus*, Mr. Stafford Smith; *Naomi*, Miss Helen Bancroft; *Elna*, Miss Maud Jeffries; *Cozbi*, Miss Rose Pendennis; *Tirzah*, Miss Nora O'Brien; *Heldia*, Miss Ross-Selwicke; *Judith*, Miss May Yates; *Kiturah*, Miss Vere St. Clair; *Alorus*, Mr. Ambrose Manning; *Mananahim*, Mr. Percy Foster; *Gazabar*, Mr. Charles Derwood; *Parnach*, Mr. George Bernage; *Sechen*, Mr. Norman Jeffries; *Hachmoni*, Mr. Marcus St. John; *Migdapal*, Mr. George Howard; *Jael*, Mr. Henry Ludlow; *Laban*, Mr. Ernest Mayne; *Elcia*, Miss Lily Hanbury; *Meraioth*, Miss Constance Collier; *Sarepta*, Miss Daisy Belmore; *Melkina*, Miss Harrietta Polini; *Ibleanna*, Miss Alice Gambier; *Genetho*, Miss Marie Towning; *Zephathah*, Miss Ellen Goss. Withdrawn 10th April.

8. SWEET NANCY: An adaptation, by Robert Buchanan, of Rhoda Broughton's novel of the same name. Originally produced at the Lyric Theatre, 12th July 1890. **Court.** Cast: *Sir Roger Tempest*, Mr. Edmund Maurice; *Mr. Gray*, Mr. George Canninge; *Algernon*, Mr. Martin Harvey; *Bobby*, Mr. Hubert Short; *The Brat*, Mr. Trebel; *Frank Musgrave*, Mr. C. M. Hallard; *Butler*, Mr. Williams;

Nancy Gray, Miss Annie Hughes; *Barbara Gray,* Miss Beryl Faber; *Teresa Gray,* Miss Beatrice Ferrar; *Mrs. Gray,* Miss Henrietta Cowen; *Mrs. Pemberton,* Miss Campbell Bradley; *Mrs. Huntley,* Miss Helen Ferrars.   Withdrawn 8th May.— Preceded by **A BIT OF OLD CHELSEA :** Play in One Act, by Mrs. Oscar Beringer. Cast : *Jack Hillier,* Mr. Edmund Maurice; *Phil M'Donnell,* Mr. Martin Harvey; *Jim Dixon,* Mr. E. W. Tarver; *Paul Raymond,* Mr. Cosmo Hamilton; *Alexandra Victoria Belchamber,* Miss Annie Hughes.

11. NELSON'S ENCHANTRESS : Play in Four Acts, by Risden Home. **Avenue.** Cast : *Ferdinand,* Mr. Charles Goodhart; *Sir William Hamilton,* Mr. Nutcombe Gould; *Sir John Trevor,* Mr. Sydney Brough; *Captain Horatio Nelson,* Mr. Forbes Robertson; *The Hon. Charles Greville,* Mr. A. Elwood; *George Romney,* Mr. P. Ben Greet; *Captain the Hon. H. Blackwood,* Mr. C. M. Lowne; *Captain Hardy,* Mr. Frank Dyall; *Lieutenant Lapenotiere,* Mr. Clifford Soames; *Dr. Beatty,* Mr. W. Pilling; *Lieutenant Nisbet,* Mr. E. H. Brooke; *John,* Mr. A. Somerville; *James,* Mr. Leslie Norman; *Servant to Romney,* Mr. J. Willes; *Servant to Greville,* Mr. R. Bottomley; *Servant to Nelson,* Mr. H. Evelyn; *Queen of Naples,* Miss Clara Denman; *Mrs. Cadogan,* Mrs. E. H. Brooke; *Bridget,* Miss Marianne Caldwell; *Miss Emma Hart,* Mrs. Patrick Campbell.   Withdrawn 20th March.

13. MY FRIEND THE PRINCE : Play in Three Acts, by Justin Huntley M'Carthy (suggested by the American farce, "My Friend from India"). **Garrick.** Cast : *Prince Maurice of Pannonia,* Mr. Percy Lyndal; *The Hon. Peto Godolphin,* Mr. Paul Arthur; *Matthew Jannaway,* Mr. Fred Kaye; *Pink Jannaway,* Mr. Aubrey Boucicault; *Baron Hertzlein,* Mr. Herbert Ross; *Shottery,* Mr. E. Dagnall; *Ambrose Pinning,* Mr. James Welch; *Princess Brunehilde,* Miss Miriam Clements; *Poppy Jannaway,* Miss Sybil Carlisle; *Pansy Jannaway,* Miss Blanche Massey; *Bennett,* Miss Toby Claude; *Mdlle. Gilberte Picard,* Miss Juliette Nesville.   Withdrawn 6th August.—Preceded by **THE MAN IN THE**

STREET: A Play in One Act, by Louis N. Parker. Cast: *Philip Adare*, Mr. E. C. Lovat-Fraser; *Minnie Adare*, Miss May Marshall; *Jabez Gover*, Mr. James Welch.

16. **IL MAESTRO DI CAPPELLA:** Opera-buffa in One Act, in Italian; Music by Ferdinande Paër. **Prince of Wales's.** Cast: *Gertrude*, Miss Pauline Joran; *Barnaba*, Signor G. Maggi; *Benetto*, Mr. Austin Boyd. Produced in association with **A PIERROT'S LIFE** (afternoon performances).

16. **OTHELLO.** An afternoon performance, at the **Avenue,** for the exploitation of Mrs. Loftus as *Desdemona;* *Othello*, Mrs. Charles Whitley. — Preceded by **MARY,** a comedietta, by H. J. Wynter. Cast: *The Rev. Edward Selwyn*, Mr. Frank Dyall; *Sir Jasper Trevelyan*, Mr. Leslie Norman; *Jack Sinclair*, Mr. Clifford Soames; *Mrs. Ferguson*, Miss Marianne Caldwell; *Mary Selwyn*, Miss Edyth Olive; *Fanny*, Miss M. Aschdale Vicars.

20. **HIS MAJESTY; OR, THE COURT OF VIGNOLIA:** Comic Opera by F. C. Burnand and R. C. Lehmann; Music by Sir A. C. Mackenzie. **Savoy.** Cast: *Ferdinand the Fifth*, Mr. George Grossmith; *Count Cosmo*, Mr. Scott Russell; *Baron Vincentius*, Mr. Jones Hewson; *Baron Michael*, Mr. Earldom; *Prince Max*, Mr. Charles Kenningham; *Mopolio VII.*, Mr. Fred Billington; *Boodel*, Mr. Walter Passmore; *Herr Schnippentrimmer*, Mr. Bryan; *Chevalier Klarkstein De Frise*, Mr. H. Charles; *Adam*, Mr. Herbert Workman; *Princess Lucilla Chloris*, Miss Florence Perry; *Felice*, Madame Ilka Palmay; *Duchess Gonzara*, Miss Macaulay; *Dame Gertrude*, Miss Bessie Bonsall; *Helena*, Miss Jessie Rose; *Dorothea*, Miss Ruth Vincent; *Claudina*, Miss Mildred Baker. Withdrawn 24th April.

22. **MARIANA:** Drama in Four Acts, translated from José Echegaray's drama of the same name, by James Graham. **Court.** An afternoon performance. Cast: *Daniel De Montoya*, Mr. H. B. Irving; *Don Felipe*, Mr. Hermann

Vezin ; *Don Pablo*, Mr. Edward O'Neil; *Don Castulo*, Mr. James Welch ; *Arturo*, Mr. Martin Harvey; *Ramon*, Mr. George Bancroft; *Dona Clara*, Miss B. Sitgreaves ; *Dona Luisa*, Miss Mary Keegan ; *Claudia*, Miss Mabel Hackney; *Mariana*, Miss Elizabeth Robins.

24. LA POUPÉE : Comic Opera in Three Acts (originally produced at the Gaité, Paris, 21st October 1896), by Maurice Ordonneau ; Music by Edmond Audran ; English adaptation by Arthur Sturgess. **Prince of Wales's.** Cast : *Lancelot*, Mr. Courtice Pounds; *Father Maxime*, Mr. Norman Salmond ; *Chanterelle*, Mr. Charles Wibrow ; *Loremois*, Mr. Eric Thorne; *Balthazar*, Mr. W. Cheesman; *Agnelet*, Mr. Arthur Deane ; *Benoit*, Mr. Conway Dixon; *Basilique*, Mr. W. Walshe ; *Hilarius*, Mr. Willie Edouin ; *Madame Hilarius*, Miss Kate Mills ; *Guduline*, Miss Stella Gastelle ; *Henri*, Miss Ellas Dee ; *Pierre*, Miss Carrie Benton; *Jacques*, Miss Pierrette Amella ; *Marie*, Miss Kate Hermann ; *Alesia*, Mdlle. Alice Favier. Still running.

25. THE MACHAGGIS : Farce in Three Acts, by Jerome K. Jerome and Eden Phillpotts. Tentatively produced at the Theatre Royal, Peterborough, 22nd February; now reproduced at the **Globe.** Cast : *James Grant*, Mr. Weedon Grossmith ; *Gregory Drake*, Mr. H. Reeves-Smith ; *The Mac Gillie Cuddie*, Mr. Blake Adams ; *Mr. Tadshaw*, Mr. Sydney Paxton ; *Bull*, Mr. George Shelton ; *Black Hamish*, Mr. Duncan Tovey; *Pansy Verrinder*, Miss Annie L. Aumonier; *Mrs. Verrinder*, Miss Claire Pauncefort ; *Eweretta*, Miss Laura Johnson ; *Jennie Fergusson*, Miss Beatrice Ferrar. Withdrawn 24th April.—Preceded by **CONFEDERATES :** a Drama in One Act, by Henry Woodville. Cast : *Amos Hansen*, Mr. Sydney Paxton ; *Dick Burton*, Mr. Wilton Heriot; *Henry Leigh*, Mr. Harry Farmer ; *Sergeant Doughty*, Mr. Duncan Tovey ; *Nora Hansen*, Miss Mabel Lane.

MARCH.

1. THE PILGRIM'S PROGRESS. Revival for one week at the **Olympic.** Cast : *Apollyon*, Mr. Courtenay Thorpe;

Fairspeech, Mr. Lance Holt; *Holdworld*, Mr. Henry Lesmere; *Thankless*, Mr. Roland Atwood; *Vainhope*, Mr. W. E. Sauter; *Dives*, Mr. Jack Cole; *Pamper*, Mr. Frank Macrae; *Graspall*, Mr. P. C. Beverley; *First Slave*, Mr. T. Leslie; *Second Slave*, Mr. Alleyn Hylton; *Speranza*, Miss Anne Beaufort; *Madame Bubble*, Miss Ffolliott Paget; *Florimonde*, Miss Marjorie Christmas; *Isolde*, Miss Stuart Innes; *Malignity*, Miss Calharm; *Mistress Timorous*, Miss Audrey Littleton; *Raphael*, Mr. H. W. Varna; *Faithful*, Mr. Howard Russell; *Death*, Mr. Lesly Thomson; *Giant Despair*, Mr. W. Vernon; *Bertram*, Mr. F. Mansell; *Simple*, Mr. J. Paul; *Mammon*, Mr. Ben Field; *Timeserver*, Mr. Reginald Forbes; *Presumption*, Mr. Wm. Montford; *Sloth*, Mr. Wm. Farrar; *Melusina*, Miss Jennie D. Eustace; *Crafty*, Miss Georgie Grantley; *Dame Gossip*, Miss Beatrice Grosvenor; *Page*, Miss Helen Beverley; *Christian*, Miss Grace Hawthorne.

8. THE LADY LAWYER: Operetta in One Act, by G. D. Lynch, composed by J. W. Ivimey. **Garrick.** Cast: *Justitia Temple,* Miss Mary Collette; *Sylvia Golding*, Miss K. Adams; *Dick Temple*, Mr. Shallard; *Eugene Tripp*, Mr. F. Walsh.—Played in association with **MY FRIEND THE PRINCE.**

9. THE MARINERS OF ENGLAND: Nautical Drama in Four Acts and Ten Tableaux, by Robert Buchanan and Charles Marlowe. Originally produced at the Grand Theatre, Nottingham, 1st March 1897. **Olympic.** Cast: *Lord Nelson and Bronté,* Mr. W. L. Abingdon; *Admiral Talbot*, Mr. Frederick Stanley; *Admiral Collingwood*, Mr. W. H. Brougham; *Admiral White*, Mr. Geoffrey Weedall; *Captain Hardy*, Mr. Adam Alexander; *Captain Lebaudy*, Mr. Herbert Sleath; *Lieutenant Portland*, Mr. Ernest Mainwaring; *Mr. Lestrange*, Mr. Gilbert Wemys; *Mr. Beaumont*, Mr. Cyril Catley; *Tom Trip*, Mr. E. M. Robson; *Old Trip*, Mr. Julius Royston; *John Marston*, Mr. Tom Taylor; *Bill Bucket*, Mr. Charles H. Fenton; *Joe Appleyard*, Mr. Geo. Hareton; *Officer of Coastguard*, Mr. Frank Stribly; *Harry Dell*, Mr. Charles

Glenney; *Mabel Talbot*, Miss Keith Wakeman ; *Nelly Dell*, Miss Florence Tanner ; *Polly Appleyard*, Miss Edith Bruce. Withdrawn 3rd April.

10. **SAUCY SALLY :** Comedy in Three Acts, adapted by F. C. Burnand from Maurice Hennequin's *La Flamboyante*. **Comedy.** Cast : *Herbert Jocelyn*, Mr. Charles H. Hawtrey ; *Captain Jocelyn*, Mr. W. T. Lovell ; *Percival Chudleigh*, Mr. F. Volpe ; *Ulysses Jeffson*, Mr. Wilfred Draycott ; *Evan Evans*, Mr. Ernest Cosham ; *Jack Buncombe*, Mr. Ernest Hendrie ; *Perkins*, Mr. H. Deane ; *Mrs. Lambert*, Mrs. Charles Calvert; *Rosie Jocelyn*, Miss Jessie Bateman ; *Hannah*, Miss Doris Templeton ; *Jane*, Miss Violet Craven ; *Cecile*, Miss Maud Abbott. Withdrawn 4th June; revived 26th July; withdrawn 20th August.—Preceded by **BYEWAYS :** a Comedy in One Act, by George S. Payne. Cast: *Sir Eustace Carroll*, Mr. W. T. Lovell; *Ebenezer Higgs*, Mr. F. Volpe; *Lady Spilsby*, Miss Gheen ; *Sophie*, Miss Gwynne Herbert ; *Martha Higgs*, Miss Florence Haydon.

25. **THE PHYSICIAN :** Play in Four Acts, by Henry Arthur Jones. **Criterion.** Cast : *Dr. Lewin Carey*, Mr. Charles Wyndham ; *The Rev. Peregrine Hinde*, Mr. Alfred Bishop; *Walter Amphiel*, Mr. T. B. Thalberg ; *Dr. Brooker*, Mr. Leslie Kenyon ; *Stephen Gurdon*, Mr. J. G. Taylor ; *James Hebbings*, Mr. Kenneth Douglas; *John Dibley*, Mr. A. E. George; *Viccars*, Mr. F. H. Tyler ; *Postman*, Mr. F. Vigay ; *Lady Valerie Camville*, Miss Marion Terry ; *Mrs. Bowden*, Miss E. Vining ; *Mrs. Dibley*, Miss Carlotta Addison ; *Louisa Pack*, Miss Jocelyn ; *Marah*, Miss Valli Valli ; *Lizzie*, Miss M. Clayton ; *Saunders*, Miss D. Fellowes ; *Edana Hinde*, Miss Mary Moore. Withdrawn 15th June.

29. **THE PRINCESS AND THE BUTTERFLY ; OR, THE FANTASTICS :** Comedy in Five Acts, by Arthur W. Pinero. **St. James's.** Cast : *Sir George Lamorant, Bart.*, Mr. George Alexander ; *Edward Oriel*, Mr. H. B. Irving ; *Mr. St. Roche*, Mr. H. V. Esmond ; *Lieut.-Colonel Arthur Eave*, Mr. C. Aubrey Smith ; *Hon. Charles Denstroude*, Mr. Ivo

Dawson; *Sir James Velleret*, Mr. R. Dalton; *Mr. Adrian Mylls*, Mr. George Bancroft; *Mr. Bartley Levan*, Mr. Gerald Gurney; *Mr. Perceval Ord*, Mr. A. Vane-Tempest; *Maxime Demailly*, Mr. Arthur Royston; *Major-General Sir R. Chichele*, Mr. H. H. Vincent; *Count Vladislaus Reviczky*, Mr. S. Hamilton; *General Yanokoff*, Mr. Richards; *Kara Pasha*, Mr. Robert Soutar; *Col. the Hon. R. Ughbrook*, Mr. C. Stafford; *Faulding*, Mr. A. W. Munro; *Princess Pannonia*, Miss Julia Neilson; *Mrs. Marsh*, Mrs. Kemmis; *Annis Marsh*, Miss Dorothy Hammond; *Lady Ringstead*, Miss Rose Leclercq; *Lady Chichele*, Miss Pattie Bell; *Mrs. Sabiston*, Mrs. Cecil Raleigh; *Mrs. St. Roche*, Miss Granville; *Blanche Oriel*, Miss M. Hackney; *Mrs. Ware*, Miss Julie Opp; *Madame Yanakoff*, Miss Ellen Standing; *Mrs. Ughbrook*, Miss Leila Repton; *Catherine*, Miss Eleanor Aickin; *Fay Zuliani*, Miss Fay Davis. Withdrawn 30th June.

31. THE YASHMAK: A STORY OF THE EAST: Musical Play in Two Acts. Libretto by Cecil Raleigh and Seymour Hicks; Music composed and arranged by Napoleon Lambelet. Cast: *Smudge*, Mr. John Le Hay; *Owen Moore*, Mr. Lionel Mackinder; *The Hon. Fitzroy Lende*, Mr. Lawrence D'Orsay; *Mr. Dingley*, Mr. Fred Emney; *Sir Andrew Drummond*, Mr. Charles Ryley; *Bustapha Pasha*, Mr. E. Dagnall; *The Sultan of Shelock*, Mr. Arthur Nelstone; *The Vizier*, Mr. Sidney Howard; *Dr. Cathcart*, Mr. J. G. Wigley; *Captain Murad*, Mr. H. Foster; *Mr. Marshall*, Mr. George Humphery; *Zillah*, Miss Aileen d'Orme; *Mary Montressor De Coursey*, Miss Mabel Love; *Dot Sinclair*, Miss Marie Yorke; *Violet Delmere*, Miss Edith Johnston; *Noormahal*, Miss Topsy Sinden; *Balroubadour*, Miss Maggie Ripley; *Hetty*, Miss E. Maurice; *Florrie*, Miss Helene Sevier; *Corrie*, Miss D. Temple; *Irene*, Miss M. Temple; *Connie*, Miss Blanche Wallace; *Gwendoline*, Miss Nelson; *Mabel*, Miss Wallis; *Capt. Hassan*, Miss Dudley; *Capt. Calid*, Miss Georgie Lennard; *Capt. Ali*, Miss Budd; *Zorah*, Miss May; *Lalah*, Miss Davenant: *Medora*, Miss Cameron; *Haidee*, Miss Erskine; *Dora Selwyn*, Miss Kitty Loftus. Withdrawn 30th July.

APRIL.

10. MADAME SANS=GÊNE: Comedy, in a Prologue and Three Acts, adapted by J. Comyns Carr from the piece by MM. Victorien Sardou and Emile Moreau (Paris Vaudeville, 27th October 1893). **Lyceum.** Cast: *Napoleon,* Henry Irving; *Lefebvre,* Mr. Frank Cooper; *Fouche,* Mr. Mackintosh; *Comte de Neipperg,* Mr. Ben Webster; *Savary, Duc de Rovigo,* Mr. F. H. Macklin; *Despreaux,* Mr. Norman Forbes; *Saint-Marsan,* Mr. H. Cooper Cliffe; *Roustan,* Mr. Tyars; *Jasmin,* Mr. Lacy; *Leroy,* Mr. William Farren, Jun.; *Cop,* Mr. Archer; *The Chevalier Corso,* Mr. Clarence Hague; *Canouville,* Mr. Mellish; *De Brigode,* Mr. Belmore; *Vabontrain,* Mr. S. Johnson; *Jolicœur,* Mr. James; *Rissout,* Mr. Marion; *Vinaigre,* Mr. Reynolds; *Jardin,* Mr. Jones; *De Mortemart,* Mr. Passmore; *Duroc,* Mr. Tabb; *Junot,* Mr. Widdicombe; *De Lauriston,* Mr. Rivington; *Constant,* Mr. Howard; *Arnault,* Mr. Innes; *Raynouard,* Mr. Grahame; *Fontanes,* Mr. Porter; *Mathurin,* Master Hayes; *Caroline, Queen of Naples,* Miss Gertrude Kingston; *Elisa, Princess of Piombino,* Miss Julia Arthur; *Madame de Rovigo,* Miss Mary Rorke; *La Roussotte,* Miss Maud Milton; *Julie,* Miss Brenda Gibson; *Toinon,* Miss Edith Craig; *Madame de Bulow,* Mrs. Tyars; *Madame de Mortemart,* Miss Dayne; *Madame de Talhouet,* Miss Vynor; *Madame de Canisy,* Miss Crichton; *Madame de Brignolles,* Miss Yeolande; *Madame d'Aldebrandini,* Miss Wilmour; *A Neighbour,* Miss Leslie; *Lady-in-Waiting,* Miss Davis; *Catherine, Madame Sans-Gêne,* Miss Ellen Terry. Withdrawn 23rd July.

10. EAST LYNNE. Revived for a few performances at the **Opera Comique.** Cast: *Archibald Carlyle,* Mr. Alfred B. Cross; *Captain Levison,* Mr. H. Gomer May; *Lord Mount Severn,* Mr. James Carral; *Richard Hare,* Mr. W. E. Sauter; *Mr. Dill,* Mr. H. C. Morton; *Mr. Justice Hare,* Mr. Charles Wilcox; *Cornelia Carlyle,* Mrs. Stanislaus Calhaem; *Barbara Hare,* Miss Ffolliott Page; *Wilson,* Miss Blanche Whittier; *Joyce,* Miss Edith Penrose; *Susanne,* Miss Lena Roth; *Willie Carlyle,* Miss Lily Kildare; *Lady Isabel,* Miss Jennie A.

Eustace.— Preceded by **POLLY'S STRATAGEM:** a
Sketch by Malcolm Watson, previously played on the Variety
stage. Miss Lottie Elliott appeared as *Polly*.

17. ON LEAVE: Farce in Three Acts, adapted by Fred
Horner from *Le Sursis* of **MM.** Sylvane and Gascogne.
Avenue. Cast: *Mr. Bernard Vaughan*, Mr. Arthur
Playfair; *Mr. Lecky Dobson*, Mr. W. H. Denny; *Lieut.
Colonel Embleton*, Mr. John Beauchamp; *Captain Charles
Berkeley*, Mr. Charles Cherry; *Surgeon-Major Neale*, Mr.
Gilbert Farquhar; *Major Pomeroy*, Mr. F. J. Arlton;
Lieutenant Rivers, Mr. E. Covington; *Private John Dixon*,
Mr. G. E. Bellamy; *Mr. Jackson*, Mr. Harry Ford; *Mrs.
Vaughan*, Miss Kate Phillips; *Miss Phyllis Henderson*, Miss
May Palfrey; *Amelia Bond*, Miss Alice Carlton; *Jenny Rogers*,
Miss Clara Jecks; *Miss Kathleen Metcalf*, Miss Esme Beringer.
Withdrawn 1st May.

17. THE MANXMAN: Melodrama founded on Hall
Caine's novel, by Wilson Barrett. Revival at the **Lyric**, with
Mr. Barrett as *Pete Quillam;* Miss Maud Jeffries as *Kate
Cregeen;* Mr. T. Wigney Percival as *Philip Christian;* and
Mr. Ambrose Manning as *Cæsar Cregeen*. Withdrawn 7th May.

17. THE QUEEN'S PROCTOR: Comedy adapted
by Herman Merivale from *Divorçons*, by Victorien Sardou.
Originally produced at the Royalty, 2nd June 1896; now
revived at the **Strand.** Cast: *Sir Victor Crofton, M.F.H.*,
Mr. Arthur Bourchier; *The O'Paque, M.P.*, Mr. Charles
Weir; *Cæsar Borgia*, Mr. Charles Troode; *Joseph Popplecombe*,
Mr. Fred Thorne; *Reddie*, Mr. Mark Kinghorne; *Thompson*,
Mr. F. W. Permain; *Stokes*, Mr. Willoughby West; *Gardener*,
Mr. Herbert Maule; *Boy*, Mr. Claude Agnew; *Lady Crofton*,
Miss Violet Vanbrugh; *Lady Roller*, Miss Ada Sentance; *The
Hon. Mrs. Pilkington*, Miss Helen Rous; *Mrs. Maydew*,
Miss Gethyn Darragh; *Williams*, Miss Katharine Stewart.
Withdrawn 21st May. — Preceded by **KITTY CLIVE,**

ACTRESS: Comedy in One Act, by Frankfort Moore. Cast: *Kitty Clive*, Miss Irene Vanbrugh; *Jack Bates*, Mr. Charles Weir; *Landlord*, Mr. Herbert Maule.

23. DR. JOHNSON: Episode in One Act, by Leo Trevor. Originally produced at the Theatre Royal, Richmond, 11th May 1896; now reproduced in association with **THE QUEEN'S PROCTOR** at the **Strand.** Cast: *Samuel Johnson, LL.D.*, Mr. Arthur Bourchier; *James Boswell*, Mr. Fred Thorne; *Captain Alan M'Kenzie*, Mr. Charles Weir; *Mrs. Boswell*, Miss Sidney Crowe.

24. THE FRENCH MAID: Musical Comedy in Two Acts, by Basil Hood; Music by Walter Slaughter. Originally produced in London at the Metropole, Camberwell, on 6th May 1896. **Terry's.** Cast: *Admiral Sir Hercules Hawser*, Mr. H. O. Clarey; *General Sir Drummond Fife*, Mr. Windham Guise; *Lieut. Harry Fife, R.N.*, Mr. Richard Green; *Paul Lecuire*, Mr. Herbert Standing; *Mons. Camembert*, Mr. Eric Lewis; *The Maharajah of Punkapore*, Mr. Percy Percival; *Charles Brown*, Mr. Murray King; *Jack Brown*, Mr. Joseph Wilson; *Alphonse*, Mr. J. W. MacDonald; *Dorothy Travers*, Miss Louie Pounds; *Lady Hawser*, Miss Kate Talby; *Violet Travers*, Miss Hilda Jeffries; *Madame Camembert*, Miss Lillie Pounds; *Suzette*, Miss Kate Cutler. Still running.

27. AN AMATEUR WIFE: Farcical Comedy in Three Acts, by Mrs. Lancaster Wallis. Tentative afternoon performance. **Criterion.** Cast: *Benjamin Barker*, Mr. Sydney Harcourt; *M. Castelle*, Mr. Athol Ford; *Captain Giffy*, Mr. W. Granville Blake; *The Hon. Percy Franks*, Mr. F. Newton Lindo; *Tom Heavysides*, Mr. Fewlass Llewellyn; *Lieut. Charles Younghusband*, Mr. Arnold Lucy; *Mr. Potton*, Mr. Fred Epitaux; *Stevens*, Mr. C. Edmonds; *Binny*, Mr. Harry Buss; *Miss Halliday*, Miss Lucy Roche; *Mrs. Binny*, Miss Henrietta Cowen; *Miss Smythe*, Miss Cicely Richards.

27. LOST, STOLEN, OR STRAYED : Musical Farce in Three Acts, adapted by J. Cheever Goodwin from the French; Music by Woolson Morse. **Duke of York's.** Cast: *Bidart*, Mr. Frank Wheeler ; *Chaconne*, Mr. J. H. Barnes ; *Roquefort*, Mr. Robb Harwood ; *Godard*, Mr. H. De Lange ; *Gaston*, Mr. Arthur Appleby ; *Pacheco*, Mr. Arthur Styan ; *Honorine*, Miss Ethel Sydney ; *Catherine*, Miss Elsie Cross ; *Julie*, Miss Nina Martino ; *Rose d'Ete*, Miss Decima Moore ; *Jolivet*, Mr. Hubert Willis ; *Captain Latour*, Mr. Akerman May ; *Corporal Bridoux*, Mr. Harry Kilburn ; *Achille*, Mr. W. Butler ; *Françoise*, Miss Annie Godfrey ; *Louise*, Miss Beatrice Grenville ; *Eileen*, Miss Nora Neville ; *Madame Delacour*, Miss Edith Stuart ; *Delphine*, Miss Violet Ellicot ; *Georgette*, Miss Ethel Bartlett ; *Lisette*, Miss Florence Glynn ; *Rosalie*, Miss Maud Foss ; *Vivienne*, Miss Florence Hamer ; *Celestine*, Miss Mabel Daymond ; *Balloon Girl*, Miss Beatrice Hart ; *Balloon Man*, Mr. Charles Crook. Revised and renamed **A DAY IN PARIS.** Withdrawn 10th July.

27. LEAH ; OR, THE JEWISH MAIDEN : Adapted from Mosenthal's German play *Deborah*. Produced originally in America at the Howard Athenæum, Boston, 9th December 1862 ; first presented to a London audience at the Adelphi on 1st October 1863 ; revived at the Lyceum with Miss Bateman in her celebrated impersonation of the title-part on 18th May 1872 ; now revived for a few performances at the **Opera Comique.** Cast : *Rudolf*, Mr. E. H. Vanderfelt ; *Nathan*, Mr. Charles Lander ; *Lorenz*, Mr. Aubrey Fitzgerald ; *Father Herman*, Mr. H. Gray Dolby ; *Jacob*, Mr. Ernest Bertram ; *Grophen*, Mr. William Bent ; *Ludwig*, Mr. H. C. Morton ; *Fritz*, Mr. Robert Earle ; *Johann*, Mr. Robert Farquharson ; *Kapellmeister*, Mr. Renton Wills ; *Abraham*, Mr. Graham Heath ; *Rosel*, Miss Blanche Whittier ; *Sarah*, Miss Stuart Innes ; *Hannah*, Miss Vera Norman ; *Madalena*, Miss Jennie A. Eustace ; *Leah*, Miss Ethel Rayner ; *Dame Gertrude*, Miss Violet Hunt ; *Mother Groschen*, Mr. Stanislaus Calhaem ; *Leah*, Miss Grace Hawthorne.

28. THE SEATS OF THE MIGHTY: Adaptation, in a Prologue and Three Acts, by Gilbert Parker of his novel of the same name. Opening of the new **Her Majesty's** by Mr. Beerbohm Tree. Cast: *Louis XV.*, Mr. Charles Brookfield; *Tinoir Doltaire*, Mr. Tree; *Captain Moray*, Mr. Lewis Waller; *M. François Bigot*, Mr. Murray Carson; *Sergeant Gabord*, Mr. Lionel Brough; *Voban*, Mr. William Mollison; *The Seigneur Duvarney*, Mr. Charles Allan; *M. Vendome*, Mr. Henry Arncliffe; *Comte de Chauvelin*, Mr. Gayer Mackay; *Sartine*, Mr. H. W. Varna; *Colonel Lancy*, Mr. Arthur Holmes-Gore; *Lieut. Ferney*, Mr. Gerald Du Maurier; *The Prince Soubise*, Mr. Cookson; *The Bishop of Orleans*, Mr. D. J. Willia..is; *The Bishop of Quebec*, Mr. Arthur Coe; *Renard*, Mr. F. Percival Stevens; *Corporal Labrouk*, Mr. F. Macvicars; *Mr. Wainfleet*, Mr. Berte Thomas; *The Marquise de Pompadour*, Miss Janette Steer; *Madame Cournal*, Mrs. Tree; *Mathilde*, Miss Edith Ostlere; *Babette*, Miss Winifred Leon; *Mdlle. Alixe Duvarney*, Miss Kate Rorke. Withdrawn Saturday, 5th June.

MAY.

1. MR. SYMPKYN: Farce in Three Acts, by A. J. Flaxman and William Young. **Globe.** Cast: *Jasper Selwyn*, Mr. Sydney Paxton; *Mark Humboldt*, Mr. Cecil H. Thornbury; *Mr. Sympkyn*, Mr. George Shelton; *Mrs. Selwyn*, Miss Mabel Lane; *Mrs. Strickley*, Miss Madge Johnstone; *Hannah*, Miss Blanche Wolseley. Withdrawn 21st May. — Preceded by **CONFEDERATES:** Drama in One Act, by Henry Woodville. Cast: *Amos Hansen*, Mr. Sydney Paxton; *Dick Burton*, Mr. Wilton Heriot; *Henry Leigh*, Mr. Harry Farmer; *Sergeant Doughty*, Mr. Duncan Tovey; *Nora Hansen*, Miss Mabel Lane.

3. JOHN GABRIEL BORKMAN: Play in Four Acts, a translation by William Archer of Ibsen's Play. A short series of afternoon performances. **Strand.** Cast: *John Gabriel Borkman*, Mr. W. H. Vernon; *Mrs. Borkman*, Miss Genevieve

Ward; *Erhart Borkman*, Mr. Martin Harvey; *Ella Rentheim*, Miss Elizabeth Robins; *Mrs. Wilton*, Mrs. Beerbohm Tree; *Vilhelm Foldal*, Mr. James Welch; *Frida Foldal*, Miss Dora Barton; *Maid*, Miss Marianne Caldwell.

5. THE YEOMEN OF THE GUARD: Comic Opera, written by W. S. Gilbert, composed by Arthur Sullivan. Revived at the **Savoy Theatre.** Cast: *Sir Richard Cholmondeley*, Mr. Jones Hewson; *Colonel Fairfax*, Mr. Charles Kenningham; *Sergeant Meryll*, Mr. Richard Temple; *Leonard Meryll*, Mr. Scott Russell; *Jack Point*, Mr. Walter Passmore; *Wilfred Shadbolt*, Mr. Henry A. Lytton; *The Headsman*, Mr. Richards; *First Yeoman*, Mr. Cory Thomas; *Second Yeoman*, Mr. H. Gordon; *First Citizen*, Mr. C. H. Workman; *Second Citizen*, Mr. E. Byran; *Elsie Maynard*, Madame Ilka Palmay; *Phœbe*, Miss Florence Perry; *Dame Carruthers*, Miss Rosina Brandram; *Kate*, Miss Ruth Vincent. Withdrawn 20th November; an intermission in August.

8. 'CHAND D'HABITS: Musical Play, without words, in One Act and Three Scenes, by Catulle Mendes; Music by Jules Bouval. **Her Majesty's.** Cast: *Pierrot*, M. Severin; *'Chand d'Habits*, Mr. Charles Lauri; *The Viscount*, Mr. Enrico Zanfretta; *A Coiffeur*, M. D. Philippe; *A Coachman*, M. B. Tito; *A Valet*, M. H. Kitchen; *Musidora*, Madame F. Zanfretta.—Played in association with THE SEATS OF THE MIGHTY.

8. VIRGINIUS: Tragedy by Sheridan Knowles. Revival at the **Lyric.** Cast: *Virginius*, Mr. Wilson Barrett; *Icilius*, Mr. Edward Irwin; *Appius Claudius*, Mr. Alfred Brydone; *Caius Claudius*, Mr. T. Wigney Percival; *Dentatus*, Mr. Franklin M'Leay; *Numitorius*, Mr. Horace Hodges; *Lucius*, Mr. Stafford Smith; *Marcus*, Mr. Marcus St. John; *Titus*, Mr. George Howard; *Servius*, Mr. Percy Foster; *Oppius*, Mr. C. Derwood; *Vibulanus*, Mr. George Markley; *Cenius*, Mr. H. Barber; *Virginia*, Miss Maud Jeffries; *Servia*, Miss Frances Ivor; *Female Slave*, Miss Alice Gambier. Withdrawn 21st May.

10. HAMLET. Revival at the **Olympic.** Cast : *Claudius*, Mr. Frank Dyall ; *Hamlet*, Mr. Nutcombe Gould ; *Polonius*, Mr. Ben Greet ; *Laertes*, Mr. George R. Foss ; *Horatio*, Mr. Alfred Kendrick ; *Rosencrantz*, Mr. E. H. Brooke ; *Guildenstern*, Mr. Roland Atwood ; *Osric*, Mr. Michael Dure ; *Marcellus*, Mr. C. Goodhart ; *Bernardo*, Mr. Harold Mead ; *Francisco*, Mr. W. Pilling ; *Priest*, Mr. H. Willis ; *First Gravedigger*, Mr. Arthur Wood ; *Second Gravedigger*, Mr. Maurice Robinson ; *Players*, Mr. W. R. Staveley, Mr. Lorton, Mr. Field, Miss Mary C. Mackenzie ; *Ghost of Hamlet's Father*, Mr. Courtenay Thorpe ; *Gertrude*, Miss Mary Allestree ; *Ophelia*, Miss Lily Hanbury. Ben Greet season, of five weeks duration ; see also **THE MERCHANT OF VENICE** and **MACBETH** below.

10. A DOLL'S HOUSE : Play by Henrik Ibsen. Revival for six nights at the **Globe.** Cast : *Torwald Helmer*, Mr. Courtenay Thorpe ; *Nils Krogstad*, Mr. Charles Fulton ; *Doctor Rank*, Mr. Charles Charrington ; *A Porter*, Mr. H. Davis ; *Mrs. Linden*, Miss Vane Featherston ; *Anna*, Miss Mary Stuart ; *Ellen*, Miss Florence Ashton ; *Einar*, Miss Ethel Rayner ; *Bob*, Miss Maud Evelyn ; *Emmie*, Miss Alice Scott ; *Nora Helmer*, Miss Janet Achurch.

11. SOLOMON'S TWINS : Farcical Comedy in Three Acts, by F. Kinsey Peile. A tentative afternoon performance. **Vaudeville.** Cast : *Ralph Osborne*, Mr. George Giddens ; *Solomon Sweeting*, Mr. James Welch ; *Major Lawledge*, Mr. Charles Collette ; *Mr. Pilkington*, Mr. William Blakeley ; *Mr. Honeybun*, Mr. William Wyes ; *Rudolph*, Mr. Aubrey Fitzgerald ; *An Organ-grinder*, Mr. H. Barker ; *A Policeman*, Mr. W. K. Jones ; *Mrs. Pomona Sweeting*, Miss Gladys Homfrey ; *Mrs. Lawledge*, Mrs. Edmund Phelps ; *Nora Lawledge*, Miss Phyllis Broughton ; *Miss Primrose*, Miss Charlotte Morland ; *Nurse Edith*, Miss Sybil Grey ; *Eliza*, Miss Alice Beet.

15. SECRET SERVICE : Drama in Four Acts, by William Gillette. **Adelphi.** Cast : *Brigadier-General Nelson*

Randolph, Mr. Joseph Brennan; *Mrs. General Varney*, Miss Ida Waterman; *Edith Varney*, Miss Blanche Walsh; *Wilfred Varney*, Mr. Henry Woodruff; *Caroline Mitford*, Miss Odette Tyler; *Lewis Dumont*, Mr. William Gillette; *Henry Dumont*, Mr. M. L. Alsop; *Mr. Benton Arrelsford*, Mr. Campbell Gollan; *Miss Kittridge*, Miss Ethel Barrymore; *Lieutenant Maxwell*, Mr. Francis Neilson; *Martha*, Miss Alice Leigh; *Jonas*, Mr. H. D. James; *Lieutenant Foray*, Mr. W. B. Smith; *Lieutenant Allison*, Mr. Louis Duval; *Sergeant Wilson*, Mr. I. N. Drew; *Sergeant Ellington*, Mr. Henry Wilton; *Corporal Matson*, Mr. H. A. Morey; *Lieutenant Tyree*, Mr. Lyon Adams; *Lieutenant Ensing*, Mr. Martin Schultz; *Cavalry Orderly*, Mr. Frederick Maynard; *Artillery Orderly*, Mr. Raymond Buchan; *Messenger from the Hospital*, Mr. Ira Hards; *First War Messenger*, Mr. J. W. Warterbury; *Second War Messenger*, Mr. Chas. W. Giblin; *Third War Messenger*, Mr. W. E. Hyde; *Fourth War Messenger*, Mr. Albert Perry; *Messenger A.*, Mr. G. A. Hatch; *Messenger B.*, Mr. Walter Brown; *Eddinger*, Mr. James Rickard. Transferred to the **Comedy**, 14th June; restored to the **Adelphi**, 15th July; last performance by the American Company, 4th August.

15. THE HOBBY-HORSE: Comedy in Three Acts, by A. W. Pinero. Produced at the St. James's, 25th October 1886; now revived at the **Court.** Cast: *The Rev. Noel Brice*, Mr. Frank Gillmore; *Mr. Spencer Jermyn*, Mr. John Hare; *Mr. Pinching*, Mr. Frederick Kerr; *Mr. Shattock*, Mr. Charles Groves; *Mr. Pews*, Mr. Charles Goold; *Mr. Lyman*, Mr. William Cathcart; *Mr. Moulter*, Mr. Thomas; *Tom Clarke*, Mr. Gilbert Hare; *Hewitt*, Mr. E. Vivian Reynolds; *Tiny Landon*, Master Atkinson; *Mrs. Spencer Jermyn*, Miss May Harvey; *Mrs. Porcher*, Miss Susie Vaughan; *Miss Moxon*, Miss Mona K. Oram; *Bertha*, Miss Nellie Thorne; *Mrs. Landon*, Miss Leila Carford. Withdrawn 5th June.

17. THE WILD DUCK: Play in Five Acts, by Henrik Ibsen. Revived for a series of five afternoon performances. **Globe.** Cast: *Werle*, Mr. Leonard Outram; *Gregers Werle*, Mr. Courtenay Thorpe; *Old Ekdal*, Mr. James Welch; *Hialmar*

Ekdal, Mr. Lawrence Irving; *Gina Ekdal*, Miss Kate Phillips; *Hedvig*, Miss Winifred Fraser; *Mrs. Sorby*, Miss Ffolliott Paget; *Relling*, Mr. Charles Charrington; *Molvik*, Mr. Leonard Calvert; *Graberg*, Mr. G. Edmond; *Pettersen*, Mr. J. Bertram; *Jensen*, Mr. Alfred Wyn; *A Flabby Gentleman*, Mr. G. Nix Webber; *A Thin-Haired Gentleman*, Mr. Farquharson; *A Short-Sighted Gentleman*, Mr. Ronald Bagnall.

17. Mdlle. Jane May's season at the **Royalty** (afternoon performances) began. Productions: **La Petite Fadette, À ce Soir, Comme elles sont toutes, Un Mari dans du Coton, Le Monde où l'on s'ennuie, Monsieur et Madame Pierrot, Le Pauvre Petit, Les Amours de Cléopatre, Les Premiers Armes de Pierrot.**

18. A COURT OF HONOUR: Play in Three Acts, by John Lart and Chas. Dickinson. **Royalty.** Cast: *Captain Neville Norway*, Mr. Fred Terry; *Kenrick Fector*, Mr. W. L. Abingdon; *Lord Beldon*, Mr. Charles Fulton; *Dr. Ashby*, Mr. Fred Grove; *Hon. Tom d'Arcy*, Mr. E. H. Kelly; *Algie Leigh*, Mr. Patrick Evans; *Dick Marsden*, Mr. Walter Head; *Mr. Brankston*, Mr. Jarvis Widdicombe; *Mr. Craik*, Mr. Graham Wentworth; *Mr. Hayter*, Mr. Hubert Evelyn; *Sarney*, Mr. Stanley Grahame; *Soldier Servant*, Mr. William Brandon; *Servant*, Mr. Orlando Barnett; *Cora Favarger*, Miss Eleanor Calhoun; *Lady Meryon*, Miss Alice De Winton; *Violet Leigh*, Miss Nina Boucicault; *Mrs. Carlisle*, Miss Marion Bishop; *Mrs. Boldershaw*, Miss Florence Hermann; *Miss Pope*, Miss Vera Schlesinger. Withdrawn 4th June.

19. BELLE BELAIR: Play in Four Acts, by Ralph Lumley. **Avenue.** Cast: *Hamilton Pigeon*, Mr. Weedon Grossmith; *Sir Barnaby Bullingham*, Mr. Gilbert Farquhar; *Garnet Tracey*, Mr. John Beauchamp; *V. Francis Strange*, Mr. Martin Harvey; *Jessop*, Mr. Athol Ford; *Tipman*, Mr. J. Byron; *Bunting's Man*, Mr. Aubrey Fitzgerald; *Hopwood Tattenham*, Mr. E. W. Tarver; *Shillam*, Mr. F. M'Donnell; *Lady Bullingham*, Miss Louise Moodie; *Vivian*, Miss Irene

Vanbrugh ; *Lady Poltower*, Miss Emily Fitzroy; *Miss Harringay*, Miss Constance Cross ; *Miss Gertrude Harringay*, Miss Violet Ley; *Mrs. Jessop*, Mrs. Campbell Bradley; *The Hon. Mrs. Belair*, Mrs. John Wood. Withdrawn 29th May.

22. OTHELLO: Shakespeare's Tragedy. Mr. Wilson Barrett's season. **Lyric.** Cast : *Othello*, Mr. Wilson Barrett ; *Iago*, Mr. Franklin M'Leay; *Cassio*, Mr. T. Wigney Percyval ; *Roderigo*, Mr. Ambrose Manning ; *Duke*, Mr. Alfred Brydone ; *Brabantio*, Mr. Horace Hodges ; *Montano*, Mr. Edward Irwin ; *Lodovico*, Mr. Stafford Smith ; *Gratiano*, Mr. Percy Foster ; *Julio*, Mr. C. Derwood ; *Messenger*, Mr. Marcus St. John ; *Desdemona*, Miss Maud Jeffries ; *Emilia*, Miss Frances Ivor. Withdrawn 29th May.

24. ANTONY AND CLEOPATRA. Independent Theatre series of five afternoon performances. **Olympic.** Cast : *Marc Antony*, Mr. Louis Calvert ; *Octavius Cæsar*, Mr. Alfred Kendrick ; *Marcus Emilius Lepidus*, Mr. Leonard Calvert ; *Sextus Pompeius*, Mr. Frank H. Westerton ; *Domitius Enobarbus*, Mr. Carter Edwards ; *Eros*, Mr. Michael Dure ; *Scarus*, Mr. H. Mead ; *Philo*, Mr. H. Hollins ; *Agrippa*, Mr. Jerrold Robertshaw ; *Thyreus*, Mr. T. Homewood ; *Menas*, Mr. W. Pilling ; *Canidius*, Mr. E. H. Brooke ; *A Soothsayer*, Mr. Heselwood ; *Mardian*, Mr. Leonard Buttress ; *Diomedes*, Mr. Croker-King ; *A Clown*, Mr. H. Stansfield ; *Octavia*, Miss Margaret Halstan ; *Charmian*, Miss Ada Mellon ; *Iras*, Miss Marie Fauvet ; *Cleopatra*, Miss Janet Achurch.

26. THE MERCHANT OF VENICE. Revival at the **Olympic.** Ben Greet season. Cast : *Duke of Venice*, Mr. Frank Dyall; *Prince of Morocco*, Mr. Louis Calvert ; *Antonio*, Mr. George R. Foss; *Bassanio*, Mr. Alfred Kendrick ; *Gratiano*, Mr. Frank H. Westerton ; *Lorenzo*, Mr. Michael Dure ; *Salanio*, Mr. E. H. Brooke ; *Salarino*, Mr. C. Goodhart ; *Shylock*, Mr. Nutcombe Gould ; *Tubal*, Mr. H. Mead ; *Balthazar*, Mr. H. Bottomley; *Stephano*, Mr. Field ; *Gobbo*, Mr. W. R. Staveley; *Launcelot*, Mr. Ben Greet ; *Jessica*, Miss Hilda Hanbury; *Nerissa*, Miss Mary C. Mackenzie ; *Portia*, Miss Lily Hanbury.

31. MACBETH. Revival at the **Olympic.** Ben Greet season. Cast: *Duncan,* Mr. W. R. Staveley; *Malcolm,* Mr. Alfred Kendrick; *Donalbain,* Mr. H. Bottomley; *Macbeth,* Mr. Louis Calvert; *Macduff,* Mr. Frank Rodney; *Banquo,* Mr. Frank H. Westerton; *Fleance,* Master Bottomley; *Lennox,* Mr. E. H. Brooke; *Ross,* Mr. Jerrold Robertshaw; *Siward,* Mr. T. Homewood; *Seyton,* Mr. W. Pilling; *Physician,* Mr. H. Willis; *Bleeding Officer,* Mr. H. Mead; *First Murderer,* Mr. Leonard Buttress; *Second Murderer,* Mr. H. Hollins; *Third Murderer,* Mr. H. Thomson; *First Witch,* Mr. Heselwood; *Second Witch,* Mr. Croker-King; *Third Witch,* Mr. Michael Dure; *Gentlewoman,* Miss Eleanor Tanner; *Lady Macbeth,* Miss Laura Johnson.

JUNE.

1. PYGMALION AND GALATEA. Afternoon performance for a charity, at the **Prince of Wales's.** Cast: *Pygmalion,* Miss Esme Beringer; *Cynisca,* Mrs. Clement Scott.

3. THE MAID OF ATHENS: Musical Play in Two Acts; Libretto by Charles Edmund and Henry Chance Newton; Music by F. Osmond Carr. **Opera Comique.** Cast: *The O'Grady,* Mr. E. J. Lonnen; *Major Treherne,* Mr. W. Elton; *Seymour,* Mr. Charles Weir; *Marlow,* Mr. Percy Brough; *O'Rigger,* Mr. Edward Morehen; *Lord Alfred Fitz Clarence,* Mr. Cecil Ramsey; *Branks,* Mr. St. John Hamund; *Sergeant,* Mr. W. C. Newton; *De Belvidere,* Mr. Fred Storey; *Ambrosia,* Miss Cicely Richards; *Ina,* Miss Claire Romaine; *Maid of Athens,* Miss Constance Collier; *Chloris,* Miss Ettie Williams; *Medea,* Miss Esme Gordon; *Hebe,* Miss Lily Forsythe; *Daphne,* Miss Dolly Douglas; *Merope,* Miss Florence Wilson; *Topsy St. Ledger,* Mdlle. Louise Beaudet.

3. SETTLED OUT OF COURT: Play in Four Acts, by Estelle Burney. Tentative afternoon performance. **Globe.** Cast: *Sir Gerald Delacourt,* Mr. Lewis Waller; *Lord Mottram of the Peak,* Mr. Charles Fulton; *The Hon. Bobby Haigh,* Mr.

Sidney Brough; *Morris*, Mr. Holmes-Gore; *François*, Mr.
Wilton Meriot; *Mrs. Alleyn*, Miss Granville; *Lady Helena St.
Quentin*, Miss Frances Ivor; *Moyra*, Miss Janette Steer.

5. THE COUNTY FAIR: Comedy-Drama in Four
Acts, by Charles Barnard. Originally produced in America;
first played in England at the Opera House, Brixton,
12th April 1897. **Princess's.** Cast: *Abigail Prue*, Mr.
Neil Burgess; *Otis Tucker*, Mr. Edward S. Metcalfe; *Solon
Hammerhead*, Mr. Cecil Elgar; *Tim the Tanner*, Mr. Ridge-
wood Barrie; *Joel Bartlett*, Mr. Laurence Cautley; *Bill
Parker*, Mr. James A. Leahy; *Cold Molasses*, Running Treacle;
Sally Greenaway, Miss Essex Dane; *Maria Perkins*, Miss Ray
Scott; *Little Tony*, Mr. W. Painter; *Markham*, Mr. Henry
Walters; *Fredericks*, Mr. Charles Daintry; *Taggs*, Miss Emma
Pollock. Withdrawn 18th June.

5. A MARRIAGE OF CONVENIENCE: Play in
Four Acts, adapted by Sydney Grundy from Alexandre Dumas's
Comedy, in Four Acts, *Un Mariage sous Louis Quinze.*
Haymarket. Cast: *Comte de Candale*, Mr. William Terriss;
Chevalier de Valclos, Mr. Cyril Maude; *The General*, Mr.
Sydney Valentine; *Jasmin*, Mr. Holman Clark; *An Officer*,
Clarence Blakiston; *A Suisse*, Mr. H. H. Welch; *A Footman*,
Mr. Sutton Barnes; *Marton*, Miss Adrienne Dairolles; *Com-
tesse de Candale*, Miss Winifred Emery. Withdrawn 24th
July; reproduced 4th September; withdrawn 4th November.

7. TRILBY: Play in Four Acts, by Paul M. Potter,
dramatised from George Du Maurier's novel. Revival at
Her Majesty's. Cast: *Svengali*, Mr. Tree; *Talbot Wynne*,
Mr. J. H. Barnes; *Alexander M‘Alister*, Mr. Lionel Brough;
William Bagot, Mr. Henry Arncliffe; *Gecko*, Mr. F. Percival
Stevens; *Zouzou*, Mr. Gerald Du Maurier; *Dodor*, Mr. Gayer
Mackay; *Lorimer*, Mr. Berte Thomas; *Oliver*, Mr. S. A. Cook-
son; *Rev. Thomas Bagot*, Mr. Charles Allan; *Manager Kaw*,
Mr. Arthur Holmes-Gore; *Trilby O'Ferrell*, Miss Dorothea
Baird; *Mrs. Bagot*, Miss Jessie Warner; *Madame Vinard*, Miss
Rosina Filippi; *Angele*, Miss Winifred Leon; *Honorine*, Miss

Somerset; *Musette*, Miss Courtfield; *La Petite Noisette*, Miss Wigley; *Hortense*, Miss Langton; *Desiree*, Miss Graeme; *Mimi*, Miss Lovell. Withdrawn 11th June.

9. AN IRISH GENTLEMAN: Play in Three Acts, by David Christie Murray and John L. Shine. **Globe.** Cast: *Gerald Dorsay*, Mr. John L. Shine; *Dorsay Dillon*, Mr. H. Reeves Smith; *Mr. MacQuarrie*, Mr. J. B. Gordon; *Tim Kelly*, Mr. Richard Purdon; *Lord Avon*, Mr. T. Kingston; *Jim Darcy*, Mr. E. Fitzdavis; *Daley Doyle*, Mr. J. L. Mackay; *Bill Horsley*, Mr. Howard Russell; *Ellaleen Dunrayne*, Miss Eva Moore; *Mrs. Dunrayne*, Mrs. George Canninge; *Constance*, Miss Lilian Menelly; *Katty*, Miss Kate Kearney. Withdrawn 12th June.

10. DAVID GARRICK. Revived at the **Criterion,** for the benefit of the Prince of Wales's Hospital Fund; put in the evening bill on 16th June. Mr. Charles Wyndham as *Garrick;* among his "supporters" Miss Mary Moore, Mr. William Farren, Mr. Sydney Brough, Mr. W. Blakeley, and Mr. Akerman May. Withdrawn 16th July.

10. FOR THE HONOUR OF THE FAMILY: Comedy-Drama in Three Acts, adapted from Emile Augier's *Mariage d'Olympe* (Paris Vaudeville, 17th July 1855). Tentative afternoon performance. **Comedy.** Cast: *Duke of MacIlvray*, Mr. Edmund Gurney; *Lord Ullswater*, Mr. Laurence Cautley; *Sir Vincent Griesdale*, Mr. Bell; *Tommy Wickslow*, Mr. Willis Searle; *Cyril-Percy*, Mr. Cairns James; *Captain Nevins*, Mr. Leighton Leigh; *Lieut. Forsdyke*, Mr. Stephen Bond; *Stuart*, Mr. R. Curtis; *Charles*, Mr. A. Furnival; *Duchess of MacIlvray*, Mrs. Theodore Wright; *Lady Hilda*, Miss Lena Dene; *Mrs. Ritchie*, Mrs. Rose Vernon-Paget; *Lady Ullswater*, Miss Eleanor Lane.

10. APRON STRINGS: Duologue by Basil Hood. **Terry's.** Cast: *Edwin*, Mr. Eric Lewis; *Angelina*, Miss Louie Pounds. An afternoon performance for a benefit; put in the evening bill, 9th October.

10.   CASTE : Comedy in Three Acts, by T.W. Robertson. Revival at the **Court.** Cast: *Hon. George D'Alroy*, Mr. Frank Gillmore ; *Captain Hawtree*, Mr. Frederick Kerr ; *Eccles*, Mr. John Hare ; *Sam Gerridge*, Mr. Gilbert Hare ; *Dixon*, Mr. E. Vivian Reynolds ; *Marquise De St. Maur*, Miss Susie Vaughan; *Esther Eccles*, Miss Mona K. Oram ; *Polly*, Miss May Harvey. Withdrawn 9th July.

12.   THE RED LAMP : Play in Four Acts, by W. Outram Tristram.   Revival at **Her Majesty's.**   Cast : *Paul Demetrius*, Mr. Tree ; *General Morakoff*, Mr. F. Percival Stevens ; *Allan Villiers*, Mr. J. H. Barnes ; *Prince Alexis Valerian*, Mr. Lewis Waller ; *Ivan Zazzulic*, Mr. C. H. Brookfield ; *Kertch*, Mr. Charles Allan ; *Count Bohrenheim*, Mr. George Du Maurier ; *Turgan*, Mr. S. A. Cookson ; *Rheinveck*, Mr. Gayer Mackay ; *Tolstoi*, Mr. Berte Thomas ; *Officer of Police*, Mr. Montague ; *Servant*, Mr. Varna ; *Princess Claudia Morakoff*, Mrs. Tree ; *Olga Morakoff*, Miss Kate Rorke ; *Felise*, Miss Gigia Filippi ; *Madame Dannenberg*, Miss Laura Graves ; *Countess Voelcker*, Miss Winifred Leon.   Withdrawn 9th July.— Preceded by **THE BALLAD-MONGER :** an adaptation of De Banville's *Gringoire*, by Walter Besant and Walter Herries Pollock.   Cast : *Louis XI.*, Mr. C. H. Brookfield ; *Gringoire*, Mr. Tree ; *Olivier*, Mr. Charles Allan ; *Simon*, Mr. F. Percival Stevens ; *Loyse*, Miss Dorothea Baird; *Nicole*, Miss Laura Graves.   A few afternoon performances of **TRILBY** intervened.

16.   ALL ALIVE, OH ! Farce in Three Acts, adapted from Alexandre Bisson and Andre Sylvane's *Disparu* (Gymnasse, Paris, 19th March 1896).   **Strand.**   Cast : *Chetwynd Green*, Mr. Arthur Bourchier ; *Judge Bordle*, Mr. Fred Thorne ; *Sir George Burlington*, Mr. Gerald Biron ; *John Drake*, Mr. Mark Kinghorne ; *Stupples*, Mr. James Leigh ; *William Crebbin*, Mr. Compton Coutts ; *Jacob Caratstein*, Mr. Coventry Davies ; *James*, Mr. Herbert Maule ; *William*, Mr. Charles Garth ; *Abrahams*, Mr. Claude Agnew ; *Clerk*, Mr. Percy Greenwood ; *Mrs. Bordle*, Miss Phyllis Broughton ; *Mrs.*

Crozier, Miss Ada Sentance ; *Myra Wensleydale*, Miss May Palfrey ; *Andromeda Drake*, Miss Helen Rous. Withdrawn 9th July.

17. Sarah Bernhardt's season at the **Adelphi** began. It lasted until 14th July, and included **Lorenzaccio**, Drama in Five Acts, by Alfred de Musset, adapted by Armand D'Artois (first time in London), **La Dame aux Camélias, Magda, Frou Frou, Fédora, Spiritisme** (first time in London), **La Tosca,** and **L'Etrangere.**—Madame Bernhardt gave an " extra farewell " performance at Her Majesty's on 24th July.

17. OLD SARAH : Operetta in One Act, words by Harry Greenbank, music by François Cellier. **Savoy.** Cast : *The Right Hon. Claud Newcastle*, Mr. Jones-Hewson ; *Archibald Jones*, Mr. Charles Childerstone ; *Simon the Smuggler*, Mr. C. Herbert Workman ; *Margery*, Miss Jessie Rose ; *Old Sarah*, Miss Louie Henri.—Done in association with **THE YEOMEN OF THE GUARD.**

26. IN SIGHT OF ST. PAUL'S : Drama in Five Acts. Originally produced at the Princess's on 1st August 1896. **Princess's.** Cast : *Mr. Chichester*, Mr. Alec Franks ; *Tom Chichester*, Mr. Ernest Leicester ; *Harry Chichester*, Mr. George Hippisley ; *John Gridston*, Mr. J. B. Gordon ; *Fretley Burnside*, Mr. Gerald Kennedy ; *Gillie Fletcher*, Mr. Ernest Wood ; *Dennis Sheridan*, Mr. Chris. Waller ; *Robert Treacher*, Mr. E. Carter Livesey ; *Jim Palfrey*, Mr. Geo. T. Minshull ; *Inspector Clarkson*, Mr. Campbell Browne ; *Prescott*, Mr. A. Rymon ; *Amos*, Mr. C. Astley ; *A Chelsea Pensioner*, Mr. S. Foley ; *A Drummer Boy*, Master H. Bottomley ; *Cynthia Dell*, Miss Hettie Chattell ; *Beatrice Moreland*, Miss Beatrice Selwyn ; *The Countess Fellstar*, Miss Flora Wills ; *Mrs. Burlington March*, Miss Mary Batey ; *Lady Snow*, Miss Lilian Jones ; *Rose*, Miss Winifred Eldred ; *Becky Vetch*, Miss Florrie Millington ; *Gracie Chichester*, Miss Lillie Richards ; *Aileen Millar*, Miss Kate Tyndall. Withdrawn 17th July.

28. Madame Rejane's season began at the **Lyric.** It included **La Douloureuse,** Four-Act Play by Maurice Donnay (first time in London), **Frou Frou,** and **Madame Sans Gêne.**

28. Vienna Volkstheater Company's season. **Daly's.** The productions included **Untreu** (from the Italian of Roberto Bracco, by Otto Eisenschutz), **Die Goldene Eva,** by F. von Schönthan and Frantz Koppell-Ellfeld, and **Renaissance** (by the same authors).

JULY.

1. THE PRISONER OF ZENDA: Romantic Play in a Prologue and Four Acts, adapted from Anthony Hope's story by Edward Rose. Revival for eight nights at the **St. James's Theatre.** Cast—Prologue: *Prince Rudolf,* Mr. George Alexander; *Duke Wolfgang,* Mr. C. Aubery Smith; *Gilbert, Earl of Rassendyll,* Mr. H. H. Vincent; *Horace Glyn,* Mr. Vincent Sternroyd; *Jeffries,* Mr. Henry Boyce; *Giffen,* Mr. F. Stone; *Amelia, Countess Rassendyll,* Miss Mabel Hackney. Play: *Rudolf the Fifth—Rudolf Rassendyll,* Mr. George Alexander; *Michael, Duke of Strelsau,* Mr. C. Aubery Smith; *Colonel Sapt,* Mr. W. H. Vernon; *Fritz Von Tarlenheim,* Mr. Arthur Royston; *Captain Hentzau,* Mr. Robert Lorraine; *Detchard,* Mr. James Wheeler; *Bertram Bertrand,* Mr. Ivo Dawson; *Marshal Strakencz,* Mr. Henry Lorraine; *Lorenz Teppich,* Mr. R. Dalton; *Franz Teppich,* Mr. R. G. Legge; *Lord Topham,* Mr. George Croft; *Ludwig,* Mr. S. Hamilton; *Toni,* Mr. A. W. Munro; *Josef,* Mr. Frank Dall; *Princess Flavia,* Miss Fay Davis; *Antoinette de Mauban,* Miss Julie Opp; *Frau Teppich,* Miss Kate Darvill.

5. THE GOLDEN AGE; OR, PIERROT'S SACRIFICE: Musical Romance, Libretto by Henry Byatt; Music by Florian Pascal. Afternoon performance for a "benefit." **Savoy.** Cast: *Pierrot,* Mr. W. L. Abingdon; *Troubadour,* Mr. Charles Kenningham; *Rosemary,* Miss Ruth Vincent.

10. **THE SILVER KEY:** Version in Four Acts, by Sydney Grundy, of *Mademoiselle de Belle-Isle*, by the elder Dumas. **Her Majesty's.** Cast: *Duc de Richelieu*, Mr. Tree; *Chevalier d'Aubigny*, Mr. Lewis Waller; *Duc d'Aumont*, Mr. Charles Allan; *Chevalier d'Auvray*, Mr. Lionel Brough; *Chamillac*, Mr. Gerald Du Maurier; *Germain*, Mr. Arthur Coe; *Lackey*, Mr. Gayer Mackay; *Lackey*, Mr. S. A. Cookson; *Marquise de Prie*, Mrs. Tree; *Mariette*, Miss Gigia Filippi; *Mdlle. de Belle-Isle*, Miss Evelyn Millard. Withdrawn 11th August; reproduced, after a provincial tour, 1st November; withdrawn 26th November.

17. **FOUR LITTLE GIRLS:** Farce in Three Acts, by Walter Stokes Craven. **Criterion.** Cast: *Jakel Muggeridge, M.A.*, Mr. James Welch; *Robert Raddlestone*, Mr. J. H. Barnes; *Thomas Tyndal*, Mr. W. Blakeley; *Dick Raddlestone*, Mr. Richard Lambart; *Percy Tyndal*, Mr. Kenneth Douglas; *Mrs. Humbleton*, Mrs. M. A. Victor; *Mrs. Middleage*, Miss Emily Miller; *Lillie Raddlestone*, Miss Violet Lyster; *Florence Tyndal*, Miss Mabel Beardsley; *Polly Humbleton*, Miss Dora Barton; *Ethel Middleage*, Miss Audrey Ford; *Charlotte*, Miss Sidney Fairbrother. Withdrawn 7th August.—Preceded by **BEFORE THE DAWN:** One Act Play, by Henry Byatt. Cast: *Sir John Radley, Bart.*, Mr. Henry Arncliffe; *Policeman*, Mr. Akerman May; *Coachman*, Mr. C. Edmonds; *Lena*, Miss Mabel Beardsley; *Sally Glibbery*, Miss Sidney Fairbrother.

26. **A LABOUR OF LOVE:** One Act Piece by Horace W. C. Newte. **Comedy.** Cast: *Captain Lord Gayne*, Mr. Wilfred Draycott; *Captain Gerald Laird*, Mr. Cosmo Stuart; *Sergeant Phipps*, Mr. H. Deane; *Private Hinks*, Mr. Harry Ford; *Pearson*, Mr. Fred Thorne; *Violet Trent*, Miss Maud Abbot.—Played in conjunction with **SAUCY SALLY,** now revived.

31. **TOMMY ATKINS:** Melodrama in Four Acts, by Arthur Shirley and Ben Landeck. Originally produced at the

Pavilion; now revived at the **Princess's.** Cast: *Harold Wilson*, Mr. Ernest Leicester; *Colonel Hardwick*, Mr. G. L. Eveson; *Captain Richard Maitland*, Mr. Oscar Adye; *Captain Robert Sparrow*, Mr. Royston Keith; *Colour-Sergeant Paddy Molloy*, Mr. John F. Lambe; *Private Mason*, Mr. George W. Cockburn; *Private Harris*, Mr. Fred Boustead; *Ebenezer Skindle*, Mr. Fred Coyne; *Stephen Raymond*, Mr. Frank Harding; *Thomas Trotman*, Mr. Arthur Reede; *Sir Simon Redgrave*, *J.P.*, Mr. George Yates; *Perkins*, Mr. Charles Cecil; *Jack*, Little Miss May; *Arab Chief*, Mr. C. Ferry; *Ruth Raymond*, Miss Kate Tyndall; *Elsie Wilson*, Miss Marie Polini; *Margaret Maitland*, Miss Ethel Sarjient; *Kate Perkins*, Miss Fanny Selby; *Martha*, Miss Edith Camm; *Rose Selwyn*, Miss Lily Tweed. Withdrawn 2nd October.

AUGUST.

5. SECRET SERVICE. Now reproduced at the **Adelphi,** with an English cast: *Brigadier-General Nelson Randolph*, Mr. Harry Nicholls; *Mrs. General Varney*, Miss Bella Pateman; *Edith Varney*, Miss Millward; *Wilfred Varney*, Mr. Marsh Allen; *Caroline Mitford*, Miss Georgie Esmond; *Lewis Dumont*, Mr. William Terriss; *Henry Dumont*, Mr. Charles Weir; *Mr. Benton Arrelsford*, Mr. Creagh Henry; *Miss Kittridge*, Miss Mabel Hardy; *Lieut. Maxwell*, Mr. Leslie; *Martha*, Miss Lestrange; *Jonas*, Mr. Maurice Drew; *Lieut. Foray*, Mr. Carter Bligh; *Lieut. Allison*, Mr. T. E. Buxton; *Sergeant Wilson*, Mr. F. G. Strickland; *Sergeant Ellington*, Mr. T. Warrener; *Corporal Matson*, Mr. Gaylord; *Lieut. Tyree*, Mr. Maule Cole; *Lieut. Ensing*, Mr. C. Wallis; *Cavalry Orderly*, Mr. W. Powell; *Artillery Orderly*, Mr. R. Lovell; *Messenger from the Winder Hospital*, Mr. S. Wade; *First War Department Messenger*, Mr. A. Bliss; *Second War Department Messenger*, Mr. H. Hadfield; *Third War Department Messenger*, Mr. P. West; *Fourth War Department Messenger*, Mr. A. Kingsley; *Messenger A*, Mr. J. Wilson; *Messenger B*, Mr. C. Crowe; *Eddinger*, Mr. M. Mori. Withdrawn 4th September.

9. IN TOWN: Musical Comedy, by Adrian Ross and James T. Tanner; Music by Osmond Carr. Originally produced at the Prince of Wales's Theatre, 15th October 1892; now revived at the **Garrick.** Cast: *Captain Arthur Coddington,* Mr. W. Louis Bradfield; *The Duke of Duffshire,* Mr. Lawrence Caird; *Lord Clanside,* Miss Florence Lloyd; *The Rev. Samuel Hopkins, M.A.,* Mr. Leedham Bantock; *Shrimp,* Miss Claire Romaine; *Hoffman,* Mr. Fritz Rimma; *Benoli,* Mr. Arthur Hope; *Bloggins,* Mr. E. G. Woodhouse; *The Duchess of Duffshire,* Mrs. Edmund Phelps; *Lady Gwendoline Kincaddie,* Miss Marie Studholme; *Kitty Hatherton,* Miss Minnie Hunt; *Maud Montressor,* Miss Maud Hobson; *Flo Fanshawe,* Miss Rosie Roots; *Lottie,* Miss Kitty Adams; *Lillie,* Miss Marjorie Prior; *Ethel,* Miss Lottie Williams; *Rose,* Miss Dora Nelson; *Edith,* Miss Violet Trelawney; *May,* Miss Daisy Jackson; *Juliette Belleville,* Miss Juliette Nesville. Withdrawn 27th August.

12. HAMLET. Revival at **Her Majesty's,** for two performances only. Cast: *Hamlet,* Mr. Tree; *Claudius,* Mr. S. A. Cookson; *Polonius,* Mr. E. Holman Clark; *Horatio,* Mr. Otho Stuart; *Laertes,* Mr. Lewis Waller; *Rosencrantz,* Mr. Gerald Du Maurier; *Guildenstern,* Mr. H. W. Varna; *Marcellus,* Mr. Gayer Mackay; *Bernardo,* Mr. A. Lincoln; *Francisco,* Mr. Arthur Coe; *Priest,* Mr. Percival; *Ghost of Hamlet's Father,* Mr. F. Percival Stevens; *First Gravedigger,* Mr. Lionel Brough; *Second Gravedigger,* Mr. D. J. Williams; *First Actor,* Mr. Charles G. Allan; *Second Actor,* Mr. E. Murray; *Osric,* Mr. A. Mansfield; *Court Jester,* Master Croxon; *Gertrude,* Miss Francis Ivor; *Player Queen,* Miss Raymond; *Ophelia,* Mrs. Tree.

17. THE SLEEPING PARTNER: An English version of Miss Martha Morton's Comedy, "His Wife's Father," first done in America, founded on a German Play by L'Arronge. **Criterion.** Cast: *Henry Bassett,* Mr. James Welch; *John Temple,* Mr. Fred Terry; *Montague Brabazon,* Mr. Lawrence D'Orsay; *Byron Brabazon,* Mr. Richard Lambart; *Mason,*

Mr. F. H. Tyler; *Mrs. Torrington*, Miss Ffolliott Paget; *Kitty Torrington*, Miss Audrey Ford; *Aunt Janet*, Mrs. E. H. Brooke; *Maid*, Miss Dora Barton; *Nellie Bassett*, Miss Lena Ashwell. Withdrawn 25th September.

21. THE SIGN OF THE CROSS: Play in Four Acts, by Wilson Barrett. Revival at the **Lyric.** Cast: Pagans—*Marcus*, Mr. Wilson Barrett; *Nero*, Mr. Franklyn M'Leay; *Tigellinus*, Mr. Carter Edwards; *Licinius*, Mr. Edward Irwin; *Glabrio*, Mr. Ambrose Manning; *Philodemus*, Mr. George Howard; *Metellus*, Mr. P. Belmore; *Signius*, Mr. D. M'Carthy; *Servillius*, Mr. Horace Hodges; *Strabo*, Mr. Marcus St. John; *Viturius*, Mr. C. Derwood; *Berenis*, Miss Lillah M'Carthy; *Dacia*, Miss Daisy Belmore; *Poppea*, Miss Grace Warner; *Ancaria*, Miss Alida Cortelyon; *Daones*, Miss Rose Pendennis; *Julia*, Miss Cecilia Wilman; *Cyrene*, Miss Lawrence; *Edoni*, Miss Alice Gambier; *Zona*, Miss Bessie Elma; *Catia*, Miss Nellie Steele; *Mytelene*, Miss M. Brierly. Christians—*Favius*, Mr. T. Wigney Percyval; *Titus*, Mr. Stafford Smith; *Melos*, Mr. Percy Foster; *Stephanus*, Miss Haidee Wright; *Mercia*, Miss Maud Jeffries. Withdrawn 23rd October.

SEPTEMBER.

4. RIP VAN WINKLE: Romantic Opera by William Akerman and Franco Leoni. **Her Majesty's.*** Cast: *Rip Van Winkle*, Mr. Hedmondt; *Nick Vedder, Young Vedder*, Mr. Arthur Winckworth; *The Burgomaster*, Mr. Arthur Percival;

---

* Mr. Hedmondt's season of opera in English, terminating 2nd October; also produced: — **THE PRENTICE PILLAR,** on 24th September (*q. v.*), and **HANSEL AND GRETEL.** Cast: *Hansel*, Miss Marie Elba; *Gretel*, Miss Margaret Ormerod; *Gertrude*, Madame Julia Lennox; *Sandman, Dewman*, Miss Ada Davies; *The Witch*, Miss Edith Millar; *Peter*, Mr. William Paull.

Derrick von Slous, Mr. Homer Lind; *Knickerbocker,* Mr. Herbert Linwood; *Gretchen,* Miss Attalie Claire; *Alice,* Miss Ada Davies; *Katrina,* Miss Isa M'Cusker; *Gnome,* Miss Nellie Reed; *Spirit of the Mountains,* Miss Ross-Selwicke.

4. THE TARANTULA: Comedietta by Mary Affleck Scott. **Haymarket.** Cast: *Professor McBeastie,* Mr. Brandon Thomas; *Algy Golightly,* Mr. Clarence Blakiston; *Maud Golightly,* Miss Beryl Faber.—Played in conjunction with a **MARRIAGE OF CONVENIENCE,** now revived after a vacation.

6. THE WIZARD OF THE NILE; OR, THE EGYPTIAN BEAUTY: Libretto by Harry B. Smith; Music by Victor Herbert. **Shaftesbury.** Cast: *Kibosh,* Mr. J. J. Dallas; *Ptolemy,* Mr. Charles Rock; *Ptarmigan,* Mr. Harrison Brockbank; *Cheops,* Mr. E. Dagnall; *Captain of the Royal Guards,* Mr. Cecil Bevington; *M'Ibis,* Mr. Court; *O'Pasht,* Mr. Birtly; *Chop-Chop,* Mr. Tate; *Chopum,* Mr. Capet; *Simoona,* Miss Amy Augarde; *Abydos,* Miss Clara Thropp; *Myrza,* Miss Dorothy Hanbury; *Elmina,* Miss Alice Burke; *Odaliska,* Miss Ileene Howard; *Nitocris,* Miss Da Costa; *Cleopatra,* Miss Adele Ritchie. Withdrawn 1st October.

7. MISS FRANCIS OF YALE: Farce in Three Acts, by Michael Morton. **Globe.** Cast: *Frank Staynor,* Mr. Weedon Grossmith; *Fred Anderson,* Mr. Harry Reeves-Smith; *Byron M'Stuff,* Mr. Arthur Playfair; *James FitzAllen,* Mr. C. P. Little; *Soaper,* Mr. Mark Kinghorne; *Vesta FitzAllen,* Miss Spencer-Brunton; *Edna FitzAllen,* Miss May Palfrey; *Miss Mann,* Miss Ethel Hope; *Mrs. Chetwynd,* Miss Helen Ferrers; *Cosette,* Miss Beatrice Ferrar. Withdrawn 30th October.

9. IN THE DAYS OF THE DUKE: Drama in a Prologue and Four Acts, by Haddon Chambers and Comyns Carr. **Adelphi.** Cast: Characters in Prologue—*Colonel Aylmer,* Mr. William Terriss; *Laurence Aylmer,* Little Marie;

Captain Lanson, Mr. Charles Cartwright ; *Captain Maine*, Mr. Henry Vibart ; *Mr. O'Hara*, Mr. J. D. Beveridge ; *Sergeant Bunder*, Mr. Harry Nicholls ; *Lieut.-Colonel Arthur Wellesley*, Mr. Charles Fulton ; *A Native Soldier*, Mr. Cyril Melton ; *Mrs. Aylmer*, Miss Marion Terry ; *Mrs. Maine*, Miss Eily Desmond ; *Dorothy Maine*, Little Dorrie ; *An Ayah*, Miss Burdett. Characters in Play—*Laurence Aylmer*, Mr. William Terriss ; *Colonel Lanson*, Mr. Charles Cartwright ; *Mr. O'Hara*, Mr. J. D. Beveridge ; *Sergeant Bunder*, Mr. Harry Nicholls ; *Captain Clinton*, Mr. Laurence Cautley ; *F.M. The Duke of Wellington, K.G.*, Mr. Chas. Fulton ; *Lieut.-Colonel Sir Alexander Gordon*, Mr. Grahame Stewart ; *General Muffing*, Mr. Albert Sims ; *Captain Rudorf*, Mr. F. Strickland ; *Lieut.-Colonel Sir G. H. F. Berkeley*, Mr. Bulckley ; *Dr. Clarke*, Mr. Stanley Gordon ; *French Doctor*, Mr. Leonard Shepherd ; *Major Bertram*, Mr. Charles D. Cox ; *Captain Clifford*, Mr. H. Arnold ; *Lieut. Orpington*, Mr. Sauter ; *Sergeant Drewitt*, Mr. Jarvis Widdicombe ; *Private Dale*, Mr. Arnold Lucy ; *Jacob Sparling*, Mr. Webb Darleigh ; *Dick Cropper*, Mr. Jackson ; *Pierre*, Mr. Leicester ; *Antoinette*, Miss Le Sage ; *William*, Mr. A. Cameron ; *François*, Mr. Smythe ; *Dorothy Maine*, Miss Millward ; *Mrs. Clinton*, Miss Millicent Barr ; *Mrs. Bunder*, Miss Vane Featherstone ; *Julie*, Miss Haygett ; *Mrs. Aylmer*, Miss Marion Terry. Withdrawn 20th November.

II. HAMLET. Revival at the **Lyceum.** Cast : *Claudius*, Mr. H. Cooper Cliffe ; *Hamlet*, Mr. Forbes Robertson ; *Horatio*, Mr. Harrison Hunter ; *Polonius*, Mr. J. H. Barnes ; *Laertes*, Mr. Bernard Gould ; *Ghost of Hamlet's Father*, Mr. Ian Robertson ; *Fortinbras*, Mr. Whitworth Jones ; *Rosencrantz*, Mr Grahame Browne ; *Guildenstern*, Mr. Frank Dyall ; *Osric*, Mr. Martin Harvey ; *Marcellus*, Mr. J. Fisher White ; *Bernardo*, Mr. Clifford Soames ; *Francisco*, Mr. Hubert Carter ; *Reynaldo*, Mr. Roland Bottomley ; *First Player*, Mr. James Hearne ; *Second Player*, Mr. Elliot Ball ; *First Grave-digger*, Mr. J. Willes ; *Second Gravedigger*, Mr. Leslie Victor ; *Priest*, Mr. Chris. Walker ; *A Messenger*, Mr. Harry Johnston ;

Gertrude, Miss Granville; *Player Queen,* Miss Sidney Crowe; *Ophelia,* Mrs. Patrick Campbell. Withdrawn 18th December.

13. THE PURSER: Nautical Farcical Comedy in Three Acts (produced at Portsmouth on 12th July 1897). **Strand.** Cast: *Captain Causton,* Mr. Edward Righton; *Reginald Temple,* Mr. J. G. Grahame; *Patrick Brady,* Mr. Edmund Gurney; *Fred Finchley,* Mr. Stuart Champion; *Dick Masters,* Mr. Charles Troode; *Powell,* Mr. J. Sebastian Smith; *Edith Somers,* Miss Adie Burt; *Mabel Viney,* Miss Lena Benson; *Mrs. Stanley,* Miss Kate Phillips. Withdrawn 16th October.— Preceded by **THE GREEK SOPRANO,** Comedy in One Act (produced at Portsmouth on 12th July 1897). Cast: *Harry Quintin,* Mr. H. Nye Chart; *Billy Thomson,* Mr. Gerald Biron; *Madame Larissa,* Miss Florence Fordyce; *Mabel J. Jones,* Miss Beatrix Mervin; *Letitia Jeffreys,* Miss Lena Benson.

14. LA PERICHOLE: Offenbach's Opera, new version by Alfred Murray, in Three Acts, of Meilhac and Halèvy's libretto. **Garrick.** Cast: *Don Andres De Ribiera,* Mr. John Le Hay; *Don Pedro,* Mr. Fred Kaye; *Don Gomez,* Mr. Wilfred Howard; *The Marquis De Santarem,* Mr. A. G. Poulton; *Pablo,* Mr. Tim Ryley; *Carlos,* Mr. G. Vere; *Miguel,* Mr. F. J. Vigay; *Piquillo,* Mr. Richard Clarke; *Anita,* Miss Emmie Owen; *Mannuelita,* Miss José Shalders; *Berginella,* Miss P. Fraser; *Donna Frasquinalla,* Miss Queenie Dudley; *Donna Violetta,* Miss Stuart Barker; *Donna Bambrilla,* Miss Maggie Roberts; *Donna Ninetta,* Miss F. Archer; *La Perichole,* Miss Florence St. John, who was replaced, during the last few nights of the "run," by Miss Helen Bertram. Withdrawn 4th December.

15. ONE SUMMER'S DAY: A Love Story in Three Acts, by H. V. Esmond. **Comedy.** Cast: *Major Dick Rudyard,* Mr. Charles H. Hawtrey; *Theodore Bendyshe,* Mr. Henry Kemble; *Phil Marsden,* Mr. Cosmo Stuart; *Robert Hoddesden,* Mr. Ernest Hendrie; *Tom,* Mr. Kenneth Douglas; *Seth,* Mr. Lyston Lyle; *The Urchin,* Master J. Bottomley;

Maysie, Miss Eva Moore; *Irene*, Miss Lettice Fairfax; *Bess*, Miss Lydia Rachel; *Chiara*, Miss Constance Collier; *Mrs. Theodore Bendyshe*, Mrs. Charles Calvert.   Still running.

16. THE WHITE HEATHER: Drama in Four Acts, by Cecil Raleigh and Henry Hamilton. **Drury Lane.** Cast: *Lady Janet Maclintock*, Mrs. John Wood; *Marion Hume*, Miss Kate Rorke; *Lady Molly Fanshaw*, Miss Pattie Browne; *Lady Hermione de Vaux*, Miss Beatrice Lamb; *The Hon. Blanche Rossitor*, Miss Lilian Menelly; *Donald*, Miss Valli Valli; *Lady Lumley*, Miss Mary Brough; *Lady Delroy*, Miss Margaret Brough; *Mrs. Andrews*, Mrs. E. Palmer; *Lord Angus Cameron*, Mr. Henry Neville; *Edgar Trefusis*, Mr. H. De Lange; *Captain Alec Maclintock*, Mr. Dawson Millward; *Dick Beach*, Mr. Robert Lorraine; *James Hume*, Mr. J. B. Gordon; *Captain Dewar Gay*, Mr. C. M. Lowne; *Horace Saxonby*, Mr. Ernest Lawford; *Jack Sadler*, Mr. Albert Mayer; *The Duke of Shetland*, Mr. J. Rosier; *Jackson*, Mr. Howard Russell; *Dr. Blake*, Mr. Akerman May; *Mr. Craven*, Mr. Edwin Palmer; *Hudson*, Mr. Edward Shrimton; *Turner*, Mr. Frank Damer; *Max Leclare*, Mr. Alfred Balfour; *William Smart*, Mr. R. A. Lyons.   Withdrawn 15th December.

18. FRANCILLON: Comedy in Three Acts, arranged from the French of Alexandre Dumas *fils*. **Duke of York's.** Cast: *Marquis de Riverolles*, Mr. John Beauchamp; *Lucien, Comte de Riverolles*, Mr. Bellew; *Stanislas de Grandredon*, Mr. J. L. Mackay; *Henri de Symieux*, Mr. Arthur Elwood; *Pinguet*, Mr. Charles Thursby; *Célestin*, Mr. Ernest Elton; *Simon*, Mr. George Slater; *Annette de Riverolles*, Miss Grace Noble; *Baroness Smith*, Miss Helen Vane; *Eliza*, Miss Marie Brooke; *Francillon, Comtesse de Riverolles*, Mrs. Potter. Withdrawn 6th November.

24. THE PRENTICE PILLAR: Romantic Opera in One Act; Words by Guy Eden; Scenario written and Music composed by Reginald Somerville. **Her Majesty's.** Cast: *Alan*, Mr. William Paull; *Brunone*, Mr. Homer Lind; *Vincenzo*, Mr. Arthur Winckworth; *Lisetta*, Miss Attalie Claire.

OCTOBER.

2. LA BOHEME: Romantic Opera in Four Acts, by Puccini. **Covent Garden.** Cast: *Rudolph*, Mr. Salvi; *Marcel*, Mr. Maggi; *Schaunard*, Mr. Charles Tilbury; *Colline*, Mr. William Dever; *Benoit*, Mr. Homer Lind; *Parpignol*, Mr. Jupp; *Musetta*, Miss Bessie Macdonald; *Mimi*, Miss Alice Esty. First night of the Carl Rosa season, ending 30th October. The productions included **Tannhäuser, Faust, Carmen, Romeo and Juliet, Lohengrin, Cavalleria Rusticana, I Pagliacci, The Meistersingers, Maritana, The Bohemian Girl, Diarmid** (*q. v.*, 23rd October).

2. THE BARON'S WAGER: Comedietta by Sir Charles Young. **Avenue.** Cast: *Baron Octave de Geraudot*, Mr. Sidney Warden; *Clothilde, Marquise de Marsay*, Miss Edith Ostlere.—Also **MY LADY'S ORCHARD:** Play in One Act, by Mrs. Oscar Beringer. Originally produced at the Theatre Royal, Glasgow, on 23rd August 1897. Cast: *John of Courtenay*, Mr. Charles Brookfield; *Dennis*, Mr. Frederick Volpe; *Pierre*, Mr. Sidney Warden; *Scrivener*, Mr. V. Brockbank; *Azalais*, Miss Vera Beringer; *Page*, Miss Laura Farrell; *Lisette*, Miss Katherine Stewart; *Bertrand of Auvergne*, Miss Esme Beringer.—And **THE MERMAIDS:** Submarine Fantasy by Gayer Mackay, music by Claud Nugent, with additional lyrics by Charles Brookfield. Originally produced as "In the Depths of the Sea," on 5th July 1894, at the same theatre. Cast: *John Doricus*, Mr. Frank Wyatt; *Rufus Mullet*, Mr. Cecil Lawrence; *Sylvia Whiting*, Miss Ruth Davenport; *Marina*, Miss Topsy Sinden; *Annie Chovey*, Miss May Marton; *Sir James Barker*, Mr. Arthur Helmore; *Algie Fitzroy*, Miss C. M. Hallard; *Maud Fitzroy*, Miss Julie Ring; *Lady Barker*, Miss Lottie Venne.—This triple bill was revised on 16th October by the substitution of "The Lady Burglar" and "More than Ever" (*q. v.*) for "The Baron's Wager" and "My Lady's Orchard," but the season then abruptly terminated.

4. TWO LITTLE VAGABONDS: Melodrama in Five Acts, adapted from Pierre Decourcelle's *Les Deux Gosses* by

George R. Sims and Arthur Shirley. Now revived at the **Princess's.** Cast: *George Thornton*, Mr. Ernest Leicester; *Captain Darville*, Mr. Clifton Alderson; *John Scarth*, Mr. M. Sabine Pasley; *Bill Mullins*, Mr. S. Major Jones; *Dido Bunce*, Mr. J. Gilston Carey; *The Cough Drop*, Mr. Harry Barford; *Leeson*, Mr. Herbert Vyvyan; *Hargitt*, Mr. Edward Warden; *Dr. Lynn*, Mr. C. Astley; *Job Gargoyle*, Mr. S. Foley; *Whiffin*, Mr. Thomas Kean; *Footman*, Mr. A. Rymon; *Marion Thornton*, Miss Geraldine Olliffe; *Barbara Scarth*, Miss Eva Williams; *Sister Randall*, Miss May Thorne; *Biddy Mullins*, Miss Blanche Stanley; *Maidservant*, Miss Ethel Rigby; *Wauy*, Miss Beryl Mercer; *Dick*, Miss Kate Tyndall. Withdrawn 18th December.

5. OH! SUSANNAH! Farcical Comedy in Three Acts, by Mark Ambient, Alban Atwood, and Russell Vaun. First played at the Eden, Brighton, on 6th September 1897. **Royalty.** Cast: *John Sheppard*, Mr. Charles Glenney; *Mr. Plant*, Mr. Alfred Maltby; *Lieut. Andrew Merry, R.N.*, Mr. L. Power; *The Hon. Waverly Vane*, Mr. Charles J. Bell; *Flora*, Miss Mary Milton; *Susannah Sheppard*, Miss Alice Mansfield; *Ruby*, Miss Bella Graves; *Pearl*, Miss Grace Vicat; *Mrs. O'Hara*, Miss Kate Kearney; *Tupper*, Miss Clara Jecks; *Aurora*, Miss Louie Freear. Still running.—Preceded by **A BIT OF OLD CHELSEA**, by Mrs. Oscar Beringer. Produced at the Court on 8th February 1897. Cast: *Jack Hillier*, Mr. C. J. Bell; *Phil M'Donnell*, Mr. L. Power; *Jim Dixon*, Mr. J. Curtice; *Paul Raymond*, Mr. R. Graeme; *Alex. Victoria Belchamber*, Miss Annie Hughes.

6. THE LIARS: Comedy in Four Acts, by Henry Arthur Jones. **Criterion.** Cast: *Colonel Sir Christopher Deering*, Mr. Charles Wyndham; *Edward Falkner*, Mr. T. B. Thalberg; *Gilbert Nepean*, Mr. Herbert Standing; *George Nepean*, Mr. Leslie Kenyon; *Freddie Tatton*, Mr. A. Vane-Tempest; *Archibald Coke*, Mr. Alfred Bishop; *Waiter at the Star and Garter*, Mr. Paul Berton; *Taplin*, Mr. R. Lambart; *Gadsby*, Mr. C. Terric; *Footman*, Mr. A. Eliot; *Mrs. Crespin*, Miss Janet Steer; *Beatrice Ebernoe*, Miss Cynthia Brooke;

Lady Rosamund Tatton, Miss Irene Vanbrugh ; *Dolly Coke*, Miss Sarah Brooke ; *Ferris*, Miss M. Barton ; *Lady Jessica Nepean*, Miss Mary Moore. Still running.

11. NEVER AGAIN : Farcical Comedy in Three Acts, adapted from *Le Truc d'Arthur* by Maurice Desvallieres and Anthony Mars. Originally produced at the Theatre Royal, Birmingham, on 4th October 1897. **Vaudeville.** Cast : *Ribot*, Mr. George Giddons ; *Vignon*, Mr. Allan Aynesworth ; *Planchette*, Mr. Hubert Willis ; *Katzenjammer*, Mr. Ferdinand Gottschalk ; *Lavrille*, Mr. Robb Harwood ; *Seraphin*, Mr. Cairns James ; *Chamnois*, Mr. Gus Danby ; *Madame Ribot*, Miss Maggie Holloway Fisher ; *Marceline*, Miss Mary Clayton ; *Octavie*, Miss Agnes Millar ; *Madame Lavrille*, Miss Helen Rous ; *Maud*, Miss Dorothy Drake ; *Desiree*, Miss Marion Wakeford ; *Victoire*, Miss Mat Marshall ; *Julie*, Miss Fanny Ladbrooke ; *Madame Prudence*, Miss Ellen Amery ; *Lucile*, Miss Clara Earle ; *Henriette*, Miss Madge Deane ; *Clairette*, Miss Madge Victoria ; *Blanche*, Miss Amy Kensington. Still running.—Preceded by **THE CAPE MAIL,** by Clement Scott. Originally produced at the St. James's Theatre on 27th October 1881. Cast : *Mrs. Preston*, Miss Helen Rous ; *Mrs. Frank Preston*, Miss Madge M'Intosh ; *Surgeon-Major Hugh Marsden, M.D.*, Mr. Neville Doone ; *Mary Preston*, Miss Lottie Sargent ; *Mr. Quicke*, Mr. Cairns James ; *Bartle*, Mr. William Benson ; *Mason*, Miss Helen Amery.

13. THE CHILDREN OF THE KING : Fairy Tale in Three Acts, translated by Carl Armbruster from the German of Ernest Rosmer, revised by John Davidson ; Music by Engelbert Humperdinck. **Court.** Cast : *The Prince*, Mr. Martin Harvey ; *The Minstrel*, Mr. Dion G. Boucicault ; *The Broombinder*, Mr. Herbert Ross ; *The Woodcutter*, Mr. Fred Thorne ; *The Elder of the Council*, Mr. Robert Soutar ; *The Innkeeper*, Mr. G. Bernage ; *The Ostler*, Mr. H. Short ; *The Gatekeeper*, Mr. W. H. Quinton ; *The Witch*, Miss Isabel Bateman ; *The Innkeeper's Daughter*, Miss Hilda Spong ; *The Table Maid*, Miss Lottie Linthicum ; *The Barmaid*, Miss Neilson ; *The*

Broombinder's Daughter, Miss Lina Verdi ; *The Goose-girl*, Miss Cissie Loftus. Withdrawn 30th October, but revived 4th December for a few afternoon performances.

16. THE LADY BURGLAR: Comedietta by E. J. Malyon and Charles James. Originally produced at the Theatre Royal, Kilburn, on 3rd May 1897. **Avenue.** Cast: *George Slumleigh*, Mr. Frederick Volpe ; *Hon. Fluffington*, Mr. Arthur Helmore ; *Miss Winthrope*, Miss Julie Ring.— Also **MORE THAN EVER:** Burlesque by the late Arthur Matthison. Cast: *Sir Crimson Fluid, Bart.*, Mr. H. Stephenson ; *Arsenico della Morte*, Mr. Cecil Ramsey ; *Kangy*, Mr. Frank Wyatt ; *Shambles*, Mr. C. H. E. Brookfield ; *The Avenger*, Mr. Brockbank ; *The Lady Aqua Toffeana*, Miss Edith Ostlere. Withdrawn after a single performance.

21. THE FANATIC: Dramatic Comedy in Four Acts, by John T. Day. Originally produced at the Theatre Royal, Margate, on 23rd July 1897. **Strand.** Cast: *Isaiah Baxter*, *M.P.*, Mr. Edmund Gurney ; *Wilfred Lawson Baxter*, Mr. Charles Troode ; *James Fanshawe, B.A.*, Mr. H. Nye Charte ; *Douglas Stirling, M.D.*, Mr. J. H. Grahame ; *Sir Barbour M'Pherson*, Mr. Lesly Thomson ; *Lincoln B. Flagg*, Mr. Stuart Champion ; *Boyden*, Mr. J. Sebastian Smith ; *Mrs. Baxter, née Mary Varley*, Miss Florence Fordyce ; *Janet M'Pherson*, Miss Beatrix Mervyn ; *Susan*, Miss Lena Benson ; *Matilda Maudsley*, Miss Kate Phillips. Withdrawn 25th October.

23. DIARMID: Grand Opera in Four Acts, founded on heroic Celtic legends, written by the Marquis of Lorne ; Music by Hamish M'Cunn. (Carl Rosa Opera season.) **Covent Garden.** Cast: *Diarmid*, Mr. Brozel ; *Fionn*, Mr. Maggi ; *Eragon*, Mr. Charles Tilbury ; *Granina*, Madame Marie Duma ; *Eila*, Miss Kirkby Lunn ; *Freya*, Miss Agnes Janson.

25. THE TREE OF KNOWLEDGE: Play in Five Acts, by R. G. Carton. **St. James's.** Cast: *Nigil Stanyon*, Mr. George Alexander ; *Sir Mostyn Hollingworth*, Mr. W. H. Vernon ; *Brian Hollingworth*, Mr. Fred Terry ; *Loftus*

Roupell, Mr. H. B. Irving; *Major Blencoe,* Mr. H. V. Esmond; *Sweadle,* Mr. George Shelton; *Royds,* Mr. H. Ives; *Mrs. Stanyon,* Miss Carlotta Addison; *Monica Blayne,* Miss Fay Davis; *Deborah Sweadle,* Miss Winifred Dolan; *Belle,* Miss Julia Neilson. Still running.

30. **THE CAT AND THE CHERUB:** Chinese Play by Chester Bailey Fernald. Originally produced in America. **Lyric.** Cast: *Wing Shee,* Mr. Holbrook Blinn; *Chim Fang,* Mr. Richard Ganthony; *Hoo King,* Mr. Fred Volpe; *Wing Sun Loey,* Mr. E. W. Morrison; *Ah Yoi,* Miss Ruth Benson; *Hwah Kwoe,* Miss Alethea Luce; *Hoo Cheo,* Miss Hilda Foster; *One Two,* By Himself. Withdrawn 27th November.—Preceded by **THE JUDGMENT OF PARIS:** Light Opera, founded on *Les Charbonniers;* Lyrics by W. G. Rothery. Cast: *Pierre Cargouniol,* Mr. Homer Lind; *Bidard,* Mr. A. S. Winckworth; *Tardivel,* Mr. Charles Raymond; *Marie,* Mdlle. Ada Marius; *Therese Valbrezegne,* Miss Marie Elba.

NOVEMBER.

1. **KATHERINE AND PETRUCHIO:** Version by Garrick, in One Act, of "The Taming of the Shrew." Revival at **Her Majesty's.** Cast: *Petruchio,* Mr. Tree; *Baptista,* Mr. Charles G. Allan; *Hortensio,* Mr. James R. Fagan; *Music Master,* Mr. F. Percival Stevens; *Tailor,* Mr. Gayer Mackay; *Biondello,* Mr. Gerald Du Maurier; *Pedro,* Mr. H. W. Varna; *Grumio,* Mr. Lionel Brough; *Curtis,* Miss Frances Ivor; *Bianca,* Miss Margaret Halstan; *Katherine,* Mrs. Tree.—Played in association with **THE SILVER KEY,** now reproduced after a provincial tour.

1. **THE FIRST=BORN:** Chinese Play in Two Acts, by Francis Powers. Originally produced in New York. **Globe.** Cast: *Loey Tsing,* Miss May Buckley; *Cho Pow,* Miss Nellie Cummins; *Chan Lee,* Miss Carrie E. Powers; *Doctor Pow Len,* Mr. George Osborne; *Chan Wang,* Mr. Francis Powers; *Hop Kee,* Mr. J. H. Benrimo; *Chum Woe,*

Mr. Harry Spear ; *Kwa Kee*, Mr. John Armstrong ; *Duck Low*, Mr. George Fullerton ; *Sum Chow*, Mr. Harry Levian ; *A Chinese Rag-picker*, Mr. Walter Belasco ; *A Provision Dealer*, Fong Get ; *Chan Toy*, Miss Vennie Wells ; *Way Get*, Mr. Joseph Silverstone ; *Tourists*, Ysobel Haskins, Florence Heverleigh, L. J. Fuller, Hugo Toland.   Withdrawn 6th November. —Preceded by **A NIGHT SESSION :** Farce, adapted from the French of Georges Feydeau. Cast : *Gentillac*, Mr. Percy Lyndal ; *Fauconnet*, Mr. J. R. Crauford ; *Joseph*, Mr. W. H. Day ; *Rigolin*, Mr. Robert Castleton ; *Clarisse*, Miss Helen Fordyce ; *Artemise*, Miss May Protheroe ; *Emelie Bonbouche*, Miss Maude Vernon ; *Emelie*, Miss Keith Kave.

4. THE VAGABOND KING : Play in Four Acts, by Louis N. Parker. First played at the Metropole, October ; now produced at the **Court.** Cast : *Don Pedro XIV.*, Mr. Murray Carson ; *Pandolfo*, Mr. Herbert H. Ross ; *Don Miguel de Santa Rosa y Paruro*, Mr. Gilbert Farquhar ; *Marchese di Castelverano*, Mr. Lawrence D'Orsay ; *Chevalier Moffat*, Mr. Sidney Brough ; *Monsiegneur*, Mr. Fred Grove ; *Benito*, Mr. Lewin Mannering ; *One-Eyed Sammy*, Mr. Athol Forde ; *Donna Pia*, Miss Bateman (Mrs. Crowe) ; *Stella Desmond*, Miss Lena Ashwell ; *Princess Zea of Santorin*, Miss Ellis Jeffreys ; *Lady Violet*, Miss Ethel Verne ; *Mrs. Wallis*, Mrs. Leigh. Withdrawn 27th November.

6. THE LITTLE MINISTER : Play in Four Acts, by J. M. Barrie ; founded on his novel of the same name. **Haymarket.**   Cast : *The Earl of Rintoul*, Mr. W. G. Elliot ; *The Rev. Gavin Dishart*, Mr. Cyril Maude ; *Captain Halliwell*, Mr. C. M. Hallard ; *Thomas Whamond*, Mr. Brandon Thomas ; *Snecky Hobart*, Mr. Mark Kinghorne ; *Silva Tosh*, Mr. F. H. Tyler ; *Andrew Mealmaker*, Mr. E. Holman Clark ; *Rob Dow*, Mr. Sidney Valentine ; *Micah Dow*, Miss Sidney Fairbrother ; *Jow Cruickshanks*, Mr. Eardley Turner ; *Sergeant Davidson*, Mr. Clarence Blakiston ; *Thwaites*, Mr. H. H. Welch ; *Nannie Webster*, Mrs. E. H. Brooke ; *Felice*, Miss Nina Cadiz ; *Jean*, Miss Mary Mackenzie ;

Lady Babbie (*Lord Rintoul's daughter*), Miss Winifred Emery. Still running.

11. THE OTHER WOMAN: Duologue, by Miss Ellis Kingsley. Afternoon performance for the benefit of the Actors' Association. **Her Majesty's.** Cast: *Silvia*, Miss Winifred Emery; *Enid*, Miss Esme Beringer.

16. IL PICCOLO HAYDN: Lyric Opera in One Act, by Antonio Cipollini; composed by Gaetano Cipollini. **Lyric.** Cast: *Guiseppe Haydn*, Miss Marie Elba; *Mariana*, Madame Julia Lennox; *Annoletta*, Miss Marie Titiens; *Nicolo Porpora*, Mr. W. H. Stevens; *Count Kaunitz*, Mr. A. S. Winckworth. — Played in association with **THE CAT AND THE CHERUB.**

17. THE SCARLET FEATHER: Comic Opera in Two Acts, adapted from *La Petite Mariee*, by MM. Leterrier and Vanloo, by Harry Greenbank; Music by Charles Lecocq. **Shaftesbury.** Cast: *Rudolph*, Mr. E. C. Hedmondt; *San Carlo*, Mr. Joseph Tapley; *The Marquis of Sassari*, Mr. G. H. Snazelle; *Dr. Alphonse*, Mr. Thos. Q. Seabrooke; *Grimaldi*, Mr. C. Lawrence; *Marie*, Miss Nellie Stewart; *Renee*, Miss Decima Moore; *Felicia*, Miss M. A. Victor; *Marcelle*, Miss Florence Young. Still running.

24. SECRET SERVICE: Drama in Four Acts, by William Gillette. Revived at the **Adelphi.** Cast: *General Nelson Randolph*, Mr. Harry Nicholls; *Mrs. General Varney*, Miss Bella Pateman; *Edith Varney*, Miss Millward; *Wilfred Varney*, Mr. Marsh Allan; *Caroline Mitford*, Miss Georgie Esmond; *Lewis Dumont*, Mr. William Terriss; *Henry Dumont*, Mr. Stanley Wade; *Mr. Benton Arrelsford*, Mr. Creagh Henry; *Miss Kittridge*, Miss Olive Haygate; *Lieut. Maxwell*, Mr. Frederick Lane; *Martha*, Miss Lestrange; *Jonas*, Mr. Maurice Drew; *Lieut. Foray*, Mr. Carter Bligh; *Lieut. Allison*, Mr. T. E. Buxton; *Sergeant Wilson*, Mr. F. G. Strickland; *Sergeant Ellington*, Mr. T. Warrener; *Corporal Matson*, Mr.

Gaylord; *Lieut. Tyree*, Mr. Maule Cole; *Lieut. Ensing*, Mr. C. Wallis; *Cavalry Orderly*, Mr. W. Powell; *Artillery Orderly*, Mr. R. Lovell; *Messenger from Hospital*, Mr. Wilkinson; *First War Messenger*, Mr. A. Bliss; *Second War Messenger*, Mr. H. Hadfield; *Third War Messenger*, Mr. Pollard; *Fourth War Messenger*, Mr. A. Kingsley; *Messenger A.*, Mr. J. Wilson; *Messenger B.*, Mr. C. Crowe; *Eddinger*, Mr. M. Mori. Withdrawn 16th December (when Mr. William Terriss was murdered).

25. FROLICSOME FANNY: Farce in Three Acts, by Alfred C. Calmour. Tentative afternoon performance. **Gaiety.** Cast: *Samuel Hazzard*, Mr. Arthur Williams; *Saville Erskine*, Mr. L. Mackinder; *Paul Trench*, Mr. Edmund Gurney; *Lord Harold Craven*, Mr. E. H. Kelly; *The Rev. Matthew Marrydew*, Mr. Robert Nainby; *Warrant Officer*, Mr. A. C. Hardie; *Bowker*, Master J. Bottomley; *Caroline Hazzard*, Miss Emily Thorne; *Muriel Erskine*, Miss Nina Boucicault; *Zamora Hastings*, Miss Rose Dearing; *Penelope Quelch*, Miss Sophie Larkin.

27. A MAN'S SHADOW: Play adapted by Robert Buchanan from *Roger la Honte*, by Jules Mary and Georges Grisier. Originally produced at the Haymarket on 12th September 1889; now revived at **Her Majesty's.** Cast: *Lucien Laroque* and *Luversan*, Mr. Tree; *Raymond de Noirville*, Mr. Lewis Waller; *M. Gerbier*, Mr. S. A. Cookson; *Picolet*, Mr. Lionel Brough; *Tristot*, Mr. E. M. Robson; *Jean Ricordot*, Mr. Gerald Du Maurier; *President of the Court*, Mr. Charles G. Allan; *Advocate-General*, Mr. Gayer Mackay; *Lacroix*, Mr. F. Percival Stevens; *Usher*, Mr. James B. Favan; *Valet*, Mr. H. W. Varna; *Officer*, Mr. D. J. Williams; *Henriette*, Mrs. Tree; *Suzanne*, Miss Dorrie Harris; *Victoire*, Miss Winifred Leon; *Julie*, Miss Lily Hanbury. Still running.

29. ADMIRAL GUINEA: Play in Four Acts, by William Ernest Henley and Robert Louis Stevenson. Five afternoon performances organised by the New Century Theatre.

Avenue. Cast : *John Gaunt*, Mr. William Mollison ; *Arethusa Gaunt*, Miss Cissie Loftus ; *David Pew*, Mr. Sidney Valentine ; *Kit French*, Mr. Robert Lorraine ; *Mrs. Drake*, Miss Dolores Drummond. — Preceded by **HONESTY, A COTTAGE FLOWER:** Play in One Act, by Margaret Young. Cast : *Clorinda Anne*, Miss Kate Rorke ; *Wentworth*, Mr. S. A. Cookson ; *Lucy Kingston*, Miss Una Cockerell ; *Tom*, Mr. Ridgewood Barrie.

30. **A NEW LEAF:** Domestic Play in One Act, by Herbert Darnley. **Royalty.** Cast : *Lord Annerly*, Mr. Charles J. Bell ; *Lady Annerly*, Miss Grace Vicat ; *Tottie Evans*, Miss Mabel Beardsley ; *Parker*, Mr. Harry Parker. —Produced in association with **OH! SUSANNAH!** but only played a few times.

DECEMBER.

4. THE GRAND DUCHESS: Comic Opera, Lyrics by Adrian Ross ; Dialogue by Charles H. Brookfield ; Composed by Offenbach. Originally produced in Paris in 1867. **Savoy.** Cast: *The Grand Duchess of Gerolstein*, Miss Florence St. John ; *Wanda*, Miss Florence Perry ; *Fritz*, Mr. Charles Kenningham ; *Prince Paul*, Mr. Henry A. Lytton ; *Baron Puck*, Mr. William Elton ; *Nepomuc*, Mr. George Humphery ; *General Boom*, Mr. Walter Passmore ; *Baron Grog*, Mr. C. H. E. Brookfield ; *Carl*, Mr. C. H. Workman ; *Col. Marcobrunner*, Mr. Scott Fishe ; *Capt. Hocheim*, Mr. Jones Hewson ; *Lieut. Nierstein*, Mr. Cory James ; *Iza*, Miss Ruth Vincent ; *Olga*, Miss Mildred Baker ; *Amelie*, Miss Jessie Rose ; *Charlotte*, Miss Beatrice Perry. Still running.

4. DANDY DAN, THE LIFEGUARDSMAN: Musical Comedy in Two Acts, by Basil Hood ; Music by Walter Slaughter. Originally produced at the Opera House, Belfast, 23rd August 1897 ; now reproduced at the **Lyric.** Cast : *Dandy Dan*, Mr. Arthur Roberts ; *The Earl of Capercailzie*, Mr. Blake Adams ; *Roderick Ptarmigan*, Mr. Frank Barclay;

Robert White, Mr. W. H. Denny, *Mr. Wheeler*, Mr. Arnold Lucy; *Ben Smith*, Mr. Steve Blamphin; *Trumpeter Tom*, Miss Rose Seymour; *Donald*, Mr. F. Cremlin; *Colin*, Mr. George E. Bellamy; *James*, Mr. George A. Hoghland; *Henry*, Miss Maud Mason; *Inspector Grigg*, Mr. William Birch; *Drummer Jones*, Miss Elsie Lanoma; *Lady Margaret Ptarmigan*, Miss Kate Erskine; *Lady Cicely Ptarmigan*, Miss Mabel Hensey; *Lady Mabel Ptarmigan*, Miss Maud Stanley; *Lady Letty Ptarmigan*, Miss Frances Balfour; *Mrs. Smith*, Miss Jane Grey; *Lady Bulwarke*, Miss Ella Essington; *The Hon. Madeleine Lee-Scupper*, Miss Hilda Trevernor; *The Hon. Muriel Lee-Scupper*, Miss Violet Foulton; *Kate*, Miss Hilda Crosse; *Barbara*, Miss Violet Dalrymple; *Mary*, Miss Isa Bowman; *Lady Catherine Wheeler*, Miss Phyllis Broughton. Still running.

6. THE HAPPY LIFE: Comedy in Three Acts, by Louis N. Parker. **Duke of York's.** Cast: *Cyril Charteris*, Mr. Frederick Kerr; *John Charteris*, Mr. John Beauchamp; *Prince Szczepanowski*, Mr. Arthur Elwood; *Dicky Smith*, Mr. Hermann Vezin; *Jimmy Pastor*, Mr. Sydney Brough; *Harold Boughton*, Mr. W. Scott Buist; *Vyvyan Pettigrew-Smith*, Mr. Aubrey Fitzgerald; *A Waiter*, Mr. W. P. Warren-Smith; *Carter*, Mr. John W. Laurence; *Mrs. Pettigrew-Smith*, Miss Frances Ivor; *Maggie*, Miss Henrietta Watson; *Halcyon Charteris*, Miss Carlotta Nillson; *Plunkett*, Miss Campbell-Bradley; *A Temple Laundress*, Miss Henrietta Cowen; *Evelyn*, Miss Dorothea Baird. Still running.

6. THE TRIPLE ALLIANCE: Farcical Comedy in Three Acts, by W. S. Beadle. Originally produced at the Opera House, Chatham, on 26th April 1897, under the title of "Poor Tommy"; now reproduced (a tentative afternoon performance) at the **Strand.** Cast: *Colonel Hobbes*, Mr. Thomas Thorne; *Jack Walmesley*, Mr. Charles Thursby; *Fred Walker*, Mr. Frank Gillmore; *Thomas Eversleigh*, Mr. Fred Thorne; *Hector Popple*, Mr. George Thorne; *Shadrack*, Mr. Douglas Berry; *Henry*, Mr. Algernon Newark; *Policeman*, Mr. Graham Herington; *Miss Matilda Rowley*, Miss Kate Phillips; *Edith*,

Miss Mary Allestree; *Cicely*, Miss Alice De Winton; *Miss Popple*, Miss Emily Thorne.

23. BIG CLAUS AND LITTLE CLAUS, THE PRINCESS AND THE SWINEHERD, and THE SOLDIER AND THE TINDER BOX: Three Fairy Tales from Hans Andersen arranged for the stage by Basil Hood; Music by Walter Slaughter. Afternoon performances at **Terry's.** Casts: **Big Claus**—*Big Claus*, Mr. Wyndham Guise; *The Sexton*, Mr. Eric Lewis; *The Drover*, Mr. J. W. MacDonald; *The Farmer's Wife*, Miss Alice Barth; *Little Claus*, Mr. Murray King; *The Farmer*, Mr. Metcalfe; *The Old Grandmother*, Mr. Bert Sinden; *Gretchen*, Miss Rowena Curtice.—**The Princess**— *The Emperor*, Mr. H. O. Clarey; *The Lord Chamberlain*, Mr. Barton De Solla; *The Royal Footman*, Mr. Percy Percival; *The Royal Tailor*, Mr. Murray King; *The Royal Physician*, Mr. J. W. MacDonald; *Professor of the Ologies*, Mr. Alfred Vine; *The Royal Governess*, Miss Alice Barth; *The Prince*, Miss Louie Pounds; *The Royal Butler*, Mr. Sterling; *The Royal Buttons*, Miss May Yates; *The Royal Valet*, Mr. Oades; *The Chief Swineherd*, Mr. Metcalfe; *Professor of the Ographies*, Mr. Bert Sinden; *The New Nurse*, Miss Louie West; *The Princess*, Miss Kitty Loftus.—**The Soldier**— *His Majesty the King*, Mr. Eric Lewis; *Her Majesty the Queen*, Miss Lillie Pounds; *The Prime Minister*, Mr. Percy Percival; *The Soldier*, Mr. Joseph Wilson; *The Mayor*, Mr. H. O. Clarey; *The Witch*, Mr. Murray King; *The Dog with the Great Big Eyes*, Mr. Henry E. Garrod; *The Dog with Greater Bigger Eyes*, Mr. Bert Sinden; *The Dog with the Greatest Biggest Eyes*, Mr. Alfred Vine; *The Mechanical Soldiers*, Mr. Wyndham Guise, Mr. J. W. MacDonald; *The Executioner*, Mr. Garton; *The Herald*, Mr. Sterling; *H.R.H. The Princess*, Miss Louie Pounds. Still running.

23. A SHEEP IN WOLF'S CLOTHING: Drama by Tom Taylor. Revived at the **Comedy.** Cast: *Colonel Percy Kirke*, Mr. Henry Kemble; *Colonel Lord Churchill*, Mr. Wilfred Draycott; *Kester Chedzoy*, Mr. Ernest Hendrie;

John Zoyland, Mr. Ernest Cosham; *Corporal Flintoff*, Mr. H. Stephenson; *Hackett*, Mr. H. Ford; *Master Jasper Carew*, Mr. Henry Neville; *Dame Carew*, Miss Florence Hayden; *Sibyl*, Miss Dorothy Raymonde; *Keziah Mapletoft*, Miss Beatrice Ferrar; *Anne Carew*, Mrs. Bernard Beere.—Produced in association with **ONE SUMMER'S DAY.**

27. HOW LONDON LIVES: Melodrama in Five Acts, adapted by Martyn Field and Arthur Shirley from *Le Camelot* of Paul Andry, Max Maurey, and Georges Jubin. **Princess's.** Cast: *Jack Ferrers*, Mr. Charles Warner; *Col. Sir George Ferrers, Bart.*, Mr. Charles Garry; *Stephen Grainger*, Mr. Oscar Adye; *Lieutenant Harry Maxwell*, Mr. Stephen T. Ewart; *Billy Tigser*, Mr. Herbert Vyvyan; *Crumpets*, Mr. F. Walford; *Snitch*, Mr. Chris Walker; *The Microbe*, Mr. J. H. Bishop; *Benson*, Mr. Alfred Phillips; *Sergeant of Police*, Mr. A. Rymon; *Pawnbroker*, Mr. S. Major Jones; *Sandy M'Grab*, Mr. W. Getston Carey; *Inspector of Police*, Mr. Thomas Kean; *Bertie*, Mr. Harry Barford; *Gussie*, Mr. E. Warden; *First Reporter*, Mr. C. Astley; *Second Reporter*, Mr. S. Foley; *Drunken Gent*, Mr. Sam Fearney; *Boy*, Master Alfred Rose; *Police Constable*, Mr. Aubrey; *Lady Ferrers*, Miss Geraldine Olliffe; *Molly Crockett*, Miss Mary Duggan; *Mrs. Delaney*, Miss Blanche Stanley; *Maud Vere De Vere*, Miss Millicent Barr; *Maid*, Miss Helen Vincent; *Katie*, Little Garnet Vane; *Gladys*, Miss Kate Tyndall. Still running.

27. CINDERELLA: Pantomime by Geoffrey Thorne. **Garrick.** Cast: *Cinderella*, Miss Grace Dudley; *Thisbe*, Mr. Harry Nicholls; *Clorinda*, Mr. J. Le Hay; *Baron Pumpolino*, Mr. William Lugg; *Baroness*, Miss Kate Phillips; *Pedro*, Mr. Fred Kaye; *Prince Felix*, Miss Helen Bertram; *Dandini*, Miss Florrie Harmon; *Fernando*, Miss Lillie Thurlow; *Alidoro*, Mr. Guy Barrett; *The Grand Chamberlain*, Mr. C. Thornburn; *The Fairy Godmother*, Miss Cicely Richards; *The Black Cat*, Mr. O. E. Lennon; *The Wood Pigeon*, Miss Louie Loveday; *The Fox*, Miss E. Hoby; *Modiste*, Miss Violet Darrell; *Fancy*, Miss Georgina Leno. Still running.

27. BABES IN THE WOOD: Pantomime by Arthur Sturgess and Arthur Collins. **Drury Lane.** Cast: *Prince Paragon*, Miss Ada Blanche; *Marian*, Miss Violet Robinson; *Miss Gertie Girton*, Miss Alice Barnett; *The Spirit of Youth*, Miss Kate Graves; *Queen Humming-Bird*, Madame Grigolati; *Reggie*, Mr. Dan Leno; *Chrissie*, Mr. Herbert Campbell; *The Baron Banbury*, Mr. John A. Warden; *Bill*, Mr. Griffin; *Will*, Mr. Dubois; *Spirit of Indigestion*, Mr. Charles Angelo; *Spirit of Castigation*, Mr. Alfred Balfour; *King Frog*, Mr. Ernest D'Auban; *Showman*, Mr. A. T. Hendon. Still running.

OTHER LONDON AND SUBURBAN PANTOMIMES.

Alexandra, Stoke Newington, Dick Whittington; *Artillery, Woolwich*, The Babes in the Wood; *Balham*, Cinderella; *Britannia*, Will o' the Wisp; *Broadway, Deptford*, Cinderella; *Brixton*, Robinson Crusoe; *County, Kingston - on - Thames*, Beauty and the Beast; *Elephant and Castle*, Aladdin; *Edmonton*, Cinderella; *Grand, Croydon*, Cinderella; *Grand, Fulham*, Aladdin; *Grand, Islington*, Dick Whittington; *Lyric, Hammersmith*, Cinderella; *Metropole, Camberwell*, Red Riding Hood; *Morton's, Greenwich*, Red Riding Hood; *Parkhurst*, Cinderella; *Pavilion*, Jack and the Beanstalk; *Queen's, Crouch End*, Ali Baba, or the Forty Thieves; *Richmond*, Robinson Crusoe; *Shakespeare, Clapham*, Dick Whittington; *Standard*, Sinbad; *Surrey*, The Yellow Dwarf; *West London*, Dick Whittington; *Walthamstowe*, Robinson Crusoe.

Note.—Throughout this Synopsis "still running" means on 31st December 1897.

Corrigenda.—"A Man about Town" was withdrawn from the Avenue on 23rd January; "The Manxman" was played at the Lyric for the last time on 5th May; "The Maid of Athens" was withdrawn from the Opera Comique on 1st July.

Outlying and Suburban Theatres.

JANUARY.

4. THE CITY OUTCAST: Drama in a Prologue and Three Acts. Originally produced in the provinces. **Theatre Royal,** Stratford.

25. RICHARD WHITTINGTON AND HIS CAT: Pantomime by Victor Stevens. **Theatre Royal,** Kilburn.

FEBRUARY.

13. TRICKY ESMERALDA; OR, A WOMAN'S WIT: Musical Sketch by W. E. Bailey and Edgar Ward; Music by Edgar Ward. **West London.**

22. THE SLEDGE-HAMMER: Drama in Four Acts, by Nestor Le Theirs; adapted to the English stage by Wilson Barrett. **Theatre Royal,** Kilburn. Cast : *Matthew Derrick,* Mr. Alfred Northway; *Jacob Derrick,* Mr. Ronald Bayne; *Simon Derrick,* Mr. Arthur Skelton; *Everard Derrick,* Mr. Frank Lindo; *John Merlo,* Mr. Fred S. Majur; *Cornelius Derrick,* Mr. Littleton Eyre ; *Bob Merlo,* Mr. Richard H. Lindo; *Tom Walker,* Mr. Harry Elliston; *Dr. Clark,* Mr. Frank Charles; *Ezra Walker,* Mr. Robert Mynton; *Anthony Hebblethwaite,* Mr. James Hennesey; *Sam Shaws,* Mr. Alfred Scott; *Martha Derrick,* Miss Susie Fradelle ; *Catherine Hennis,* Miss Marion Wakeford ; *Rose Maywell,* Miss Agnes B. Cahill.

MARCH.

1. THE DESTROYING ANGEL: Mystic Drama in Four Acts, by F. A. Scudamore. **Brixton Theatre.** Cast :

Cyril Aubrey, Mr. Edward Beecher; *Mr. Orcus*, Mr. Cyril Austin-Lee; *Lord Furnival Hestor*, Mr. Frank Harding; *Lord Algernon Blight*, Mr. Arthur Edmonds; *Sir Tony Vere*, Mr. Ernest Pope; *The Rev. Samuel Reeve*, Mr. John Ottoway; *Bill Hat*, Mr. Charles H. Stone; *Jim West*, Mr. W. Jackson; *Thomas*, Mr. J. J. Dallas, Jun.; *Scruggs*, Mr. Viner; *Nixus*, Mr. A. W. Draper; *Mrs. Hobbins*, Miss Emily Miller; *Lady Josephine Blight*, Miss May Fallows; *Sparkes*, Miss Viola March; *Evelyn West*, Miss Agnes Hewitt.

8. TAKEN BY FORCE: Drama in Five Acts, by Wilfred Rodgers; founded upon Kilsyth Stellier's novel of the same title. **Novelty.**

8. A DAUGHTER OF ISHMAEL: Drama in Four Acts, by W. J. Patmore. Originally produced at the St. James's Theatre, Manchester, as " Miriam Grey, or the Living Dead," 20th July 1896; played for the first time in London at the Lyric, Hammersmith, under its present title, 31st August 1896. **Surrey.** Cast: *Jack Winthorpe*, Mr. Ernest E. Norris; *Sir Richard Harcourt*, Mr. Charles Cruikshanks; *Stephen Holt*, Mr. John Webb; *Horatio Theophilus Bruce*, Mr. George Conquest, Jun.; *The Hon. Bertie Cross*, Mr. Arthur Conquest; *James Lee*, Mr. Frank Lister; *Daniello Mastarne*, Mr. Ernest Ball; *Pietro*, Miss Cissy Farrell; *Dawson*, Mr. Arthur Hall; *John Tramphard*, Mr. J. Miller; *Lady Harcourt*, Miss Cissy Percival; *Sally Pope*, Miss Mabel Luxmore; *Mrs. Boxer*, Miss Marian Hall; *Alice Harcourt, Miriam Grey*, Miss Kate Olga Vernon.

12. MRS. H—— WILL GIVE LESSONS IN LOVEMAKING: Comedietta by Allan Atwood and Russell Vaun. **Parkhurst.**

22. CATHARINE: Drama in One Act, by Cecil Fitzroy. **Novelty.**

29. THE CORONER: Drama in a Prologue and Four Acts, by J. W. Hemming and Cyril Harrison. **Novelty.**

APRIL.

5. SKIPPED BY THE LIGHT OF THE MOON:

Musical Comedy in Two Acts, by G. R. Sims; Lyrics by Percy Marshall; Music by George Pack and Henry Wm. May. Originally produced at the County Theatre, Reading, 24th August 1896. **Theatre Metropole**, Camberwell. Cast: *Obadiah Dingle,* Mr. George Walton; *Augustus Crackle,* Mr. Frank Lacy; *James Warfield,* Mr. Rudolph Lewis; *Frank Pelham,* Mr. Frank Barclay; *Garnishee M'Intyre,* Mr. John F. M'Ardle; *James Sharpleigh,* Mr. Trueman Towers; *Oysterman,* Mr. William Palmer; *Cabman,* Mr. Howard Law; *Postman,* Mr. Joe Shaw; *Mrs. Augustus Crackle,* Miss Alice Selwyn; *Mrs. Obadiah Dingle,* Miss Evelyn Shelley; *Millicent Warfield,* Miss Amu Farrell; *Madame Farleigh,* Miss Florence Melville; *Ethel,* Miss Violet Crossley; *Kitty,* Miss Rita Leslie; *Edith,* Miss Laura Farrell; *Amy,* Miss Daisy Cook; *Sarah,* Miss Isa Bowman.

5. OUR HOSTESS:

English version of Goldoni's *La Locandiera,* by A. O'D. Bartholeyns. **Theatre Royal,** Kilburn. Cast: *Mr. Anthony Oriel,* Mr. J. Herbert Beaumont; *Sir Boyle Overton,* Mr. Dallas Welford; *Captain Bendor,* Mr. Hubert Hope; *Farringham,* Mr. Herbert Maule; *Peter,* Mr. G. Bassett; *Bell Brighton,* Miss Joan Bartra; *Sal Larkins,* Miss Violet Royal; *Ellen Bracingdle,* Miss Irene Vanbrugh.

5. CAPTAIN FRITZ:

Musical Comedy-Drama in Five Acts, founded on "Rosedale," a well-known American play. **Lyric Theatre,** Hammersmith. Cast: *Captain Fritz,* Mr. Charles Arnold; *Sir Geoffrey Vereker, Bart.,* Miss May Douglas; *Colonel Vereker,* Mr. Kenneth Black; *Adrian Earle, M.D.,* Mr. W. S. Hartford; *Squire Studholm,* Mr. George Delaforce; *Simeon Lake,* Mr. H. M. Clifford; *Corporal Soyer,* Mr. James M'William; *Underwood,* Mr. William Aysom; *Rube,* Mr. C. Porter; *Amos,* Mr. W. Yeldham; *Lady Vereker,* Miss Leak Marlborough; *Sybil Errington,* Miss Dot Frederic; *Priscilla Gedge,* Miss Dorcas Corsbie; *Dina Wurzle,* Miss Marie Wright; *Mother Rook,* Mrs. Douglas.

5. **TRUE TO THE CORE: A STORY OF THE ARMADA:** Historical Prize Drama in Five Acts, by A. R. Slous.—Also **THE LAST TEMPTATION:** A Sketch by Percival H. T. Sykes. **Novelty.**

12. **THE SORROWS OF SATAN:** Play in Four Acts, founded on George Augustus Sala's story of " Margaret Forster " and Marie Corelli's novel, " Sorrows of Satan." **Shakespeare,** Clapham. Cast : *Prince Lucio Ahriman,* Mr. C. W. Somerset; *Paul Carruthers,* Mr. S. Herberte Basing; *Crafton Lyle,* Mr. J. Nelson Ramsey; *Lord Francis Wellington* and *John Burrows,* Mr. Harry Buss; *The Bishop of Beerborough,* Mr. Martin Wade; *Sir John Grabley,* Mr. R. Peningley; *Peter Wurrell,* Mr. Phipps Weston; *Alun Fox,* Mr. J. J. Fenton; *Margaret Forster,* Miss Alice De Winton; *Mary Forster,* Miss Hilda Foster; *Countess Draggnette,* Miss Maud Brennan; *The Hon. Ethel Cholmondeley* and *Vane Clartenax,* Miss Winifred Davies; *Mother Wurrell,* Miss Sydney Keith; *Lady Delila Draggnette,* Miss Grace Warner.

12. **THE COUNTY FAIR:** Drama in Four Acts, by Charles Bernard. Originally produced in America. **Brixton.** Cast : *Abigail Prue,* Mr. Neil Burgess; *Otis Tucker,* Mr. Bartley M'Callum; *Solon Hammerhead,* Mr. Cecil Elgar; *Tim the Tanner,* Mr. Ridgeway Barrie; *Joel Bartlett,* Mr. Laurence Cautley; *Bill Parker,* Mr. Charles Craig; *Taggs,* Miss Emma Pollock; *Sally Greenaway,* Miss May Taylor; *Maria Perkins,* Miss Ray Scott; *Jockeys,* Mr. W. A. Eastwood, Mr. J. B. Russell, Mr. M. Victor.

17. **LA REVANCHE DES CIGALES:** Pantomime Play; originally produced at the Cercle Funambulesque, Paris; performed for the first time in England.—Also **A ROYAL ROUNDHEAD:** Romantic Operetta in One Act, Libretto by Hugh Seton; Music by Denham Harrison. **Matinée.**

19. **SINBAD:** The Christmas Pantomime revived at the **Surrey.**

19. **A FRIEND IN NEED:** Comedietta by Frank Runciman. **Novelty.**

19. THE MONEY-SPIDER: Comic Opera in Two Acts, by Arthur Eliot; composed by Clarence Lucas. **Matinée.**

26. AT THE FERRY: Play in One Act, by Mrs. Fawcett. **Theatre Royal,** Kilburn.

26. AT DEAD OF NIGHT: Melodrama in Five Acts, by Harold Whyte. **Novelty.**

26. THE HUE AND CRY: Melodrama in Four Acts, by Arthur Shirley and Benjamin Landeck. **Pavilion.** Cast: *Cleve Ryley*, Mr. Ashley Page; *Inspector Lilson*, Mr. Charles Cecil; *Eustace Lee, alias Captain Nero*, Mr. Julian Cross; *Frank Dixon*, Mr. G. W. Cockburn; *William Coltson*, Mr. H. F. M'Clelland; *Dave Crowley*, Mr. James Elmore; *Rathburne*, Mr. F. Boustead; *Herbert Mason*, Mr. Russell Norrie; *Stephanie*, Miss Clara Nicholls; *George Slagg*, Mr. Maitland Marler; *Theophilus Timmins*, Mr. Lennox Pawle; *Christopher Coates*, Mr. George Yates; *Robert Fisher*, Mr. Charles Stuart; *Ned Ryley*, Little Ethel Rainforth; *Two Roughs*, Messrs. Godfrey and Sparkes; *Warder*, Mr. Johnson; *Matilda Timmins*, Miss Harriet Clifton; *Madeline*, Miss Marian Denvil; *Nancy*, Miss Rachel de Solla; *Bessie*, Miss Lilian Millward.

26. SHAMUS O'BRIEN, THE BOULD BOY OF GLENGALL: Melodrama in Four Acts, by F. Maeder and C. Vernon. **West London.**

26. A CAPITAL MATCH: Comedietta in One Act, by William Parker. **Theatre Royal,** Richmond.

MAY.

3. THE SORROWS OF SATAN: Play in Three Acts, adapted by S. Creagh Henry from Marie Corelli's novel. **Lyric,** Hammersmith. Cast: *Prince Lucius Rimani*, Mr. Frank Adair; *Godfrey Howard*, Mr. W. S. Hartford; *The*

Earl of Eldon, Mr. Kenneth Black; *Mr. Bentley*, Mr. George Delaforce; *Nonus Neil*, Mr. James M'William; *Peters*, Mr. W. Aysom; *Mrs. Pinch*, Miss Kate Vollaire; *The Countess of Eldon*, Miss Alice Ingram; *Lady Mabel Eldon*, Miss Leah Marlborough; *Phyllis Dare*, Miss Ruth M'Kay; *Anna Christy*, Miss Marie Wright.

3. THE LADY BURGLAR: Play in One Act, by E. J. Malyon and Charles James.—Also **CUPID FROM JEWRY:** Comedy in Three Acts, by J. A. Mason. **Theatre Royal,** Kilburn.

6. THE INSTITUTE ABROAD: An Adaptation of "The Celestial Institute," by Alfred Stallman and G. B. Carvill; Music by Leonard Butler. **Matinée.**

17. ALL FOR HER: by Palgrave Simpson and Herman Merivale. **Grand.** Cast: *Hugh Trevor*, Mr. Kendal; *Radford*, Mr. J. F. Graham; *Lord Edendale*, Mr. Frank Fenton; *Colonel Damer*, Mr. William Lugg; *Hamilton*, Mr. Rudge Harding; *Morris*, Mr. Alfred Brown; *Lindsay*, Mr. Rodney Edgcumbe; *Crake*, Mr. G. P. Polson; *Johnson*, Mr. A. Owens; *Greystone*, Mr. Charles Sennett; *Officer*, Mr. W. Arrowsmith; *Mary Rivers*, Miss Nellie Campbell; *Lady Marsden*, Mrs. Kendal.

17. THE AMERICAN BELLE: Musical Comedy in Two Acts, by Hugh Seton and Sydney Ward. Originally produced at the Opera House, Cheltenham, on 19th April 1897. **Theatre Metropole,** Camberwell. Cast: *Dick Beaumont*, Mr. Charles E. Stevens; *Jack Dunne*, Mr. Maurice Mancini; *Lord Pomeroy*, Mr. H. G. Dupres; *The Hon. Gussie Granby*, Mr. Harold Eden; *Shakespeare Middleman*, Mr. Arthur Alexander; *Mr. Peter*, Mr. Walter Westwood; *Bertie Brown*, Mr. O. E. Lennon; *Charles*, Mr. Frank Couch; *Prudence Beaumont*, Miss Cissy Saumarez; *Sadie Clay*, Miss Jenny Owen; *The Hon. Miss A. Youngbody*, Miss Clarissa Talbot; *Hannah*, Miss Marie Campbell.

17. THE BLACK BOARDER: Farce, by Horace Johnstone. **Theatre Royal,** Kilburn.

31. BIRTHRIGHT; OR, THE BRIGAND'S RANSOM: Drama in Four Acts, by John Douglass. **Lyric,** Hammersmith.

JUNE.

1. A LOST EDEN: Drama in One Act, by Miss Hammond Hills. **Novelty.**

7. THE CONSCIENTIOUS CONSTABLE: Farce, by Bernard Macdonald. **Theatre Royal,** Kilburn.

7. WINKHOPPER'S PLOT: Farce, by V. C. Rolfe. **Novelty.**

16. THE SYNDICATE: Farcical Comedy in Two Acts, by Adeline Votieri. — Also **THE BROKEN STRING:** Musical Episode, by Alfred C. Calmour. **Matinée.**

17. IN THE GOLDEN DAYS: Play in Four Acts, adapted from Edna Lyall's novel of the same name by Edwin Gilbert. **Matinée.**

19. SIR GORGER THE GIANT AND LITTLE BOY BLUE: Musical Fancy Play by Aveton Giffard. **Parkhurst.**

28. WHEN LONDON SLEEPS: Melodrama, by Charles Darrell (originally produced at the Theatre Royal, Darlington, on 18th May 1896). **Shakespeare,** Clapham.

JULY.

5. FALSELY ACCUSED: Drama in Four Acts, by Rita Carlyle. **Pavilion.** Cast: *Frank Palmer,* Mr. Tom Terriss ; *Colonel Sylvester,* Mr. George Yates ; *Reginald Harrington,* Mr. Frank Adair ; *Captain Faversham,* Mr. C. Yates ;

Brian O'Donohue, Mr. Robert Barton; *Charlie Deighton*, Mr. Bernard Leill; *Aquilipoota*, Mr. Charles Hermann; *Andy Casey*, Mr. E. O'C. Fitzsimon; *Running Fox*, Mr. W. H. Merton; *Sydney Palmer*, Master Charlie Clarke; *Clarice Harrington*, Miss Florence Hermann; *Mrs. Kittie O'Connor*, Miss Harriet Clifton; *Eileen O'Connor*, Miss Josie Danby; *Maranda*, Miss Maude St. John; *Mona*, Miss Lillie Thurlow; *Minnie Livingston*, Miss Marion Preston; *Vera Sylvester*, Miss Rita Carlyle.

5. THE SORROWS OF SATAN: Dramatic Version of Marie Corelli's novel, by Henry S. Dacre. **Britannia.** Cast: *Prince Lucio Rimanez*, Mr. Charles East; *Geoffrey Tempest*, Mr. Algernon Syms; *Amiel*, Mr. Harry Royce; *Lord Elton*, Mr. J. B. Howe; *Viscount Lynton*, Mr. William Garrett; *The Hon. Arthur Estcourt*, Mr. J. Dunlop; *Captain Marsden*, Mr. Edwin Fergusson; *Mr. Ellis*, Mr. Edward Leigh; *Morris*, Mr. F. Beaumont; *John*, Mr. Broughton; *William*, Mr. Gregory; *Policeman*, Mr. Barrett; *Man*, Mr. Atterton; *Lady Sybil Elton*, Miss East Robertson; *The Countess of Elton*, Mrs. Marion Arnold; *Mavis Clare*, Miss Louisa Peach; *The Duchess of Worldom*, Miss Julia Summers; *The Marchioness of Mayfair*, Miss Maggie Kelsey; *Diana Chesney*, Miss Marie Brian; *Mary*, Miss Florrie Kelsey; *Mrs. Hughes*, Miss Weston.

5. A NIGHT IN ARMOUR: Musical Comedy-Drama in Four Acts, by Walter Burnot and Harry Bruce; Music by Peter Wilson.   Originally produced as "A (K)Night in Armour" at Theatre Royal, Leigh, in August 1895. **Surrey.**

6. THE COLLABORATORS: Farce in One Act, by Lord Kilmarnock. **Matinée.**

9. ARDEN OF FEVERSHAM: Play ascribed to Shakespeare. Elizabethan Stage Society's performance.—Also **THE KING AND THE COUNTESS:** Episode in the Play of "King Edward the Third." Elizabethan Stage Society's performance. **Matinée.**

9. A MUSICAL DISCORD: Sketch in One Act, by Clay M. Greene. First time in London. **Borough,** Stratford.

12. THE CROSS FOR VALOUR: Military Drama in Four Acts, by John Douglas and Frank Bateman. **Brixton.**

15. THE MERRY MONK: Comic Opera in Two Acts, by Michael Dure and Malcolm Bell, composed by A. Llewellyn. **Matinée.**

19. THE KANGAROO GIRL: Musical Version of "Dr. Bill"; music by Oscar Barrett. Originally produced at the Pleasure Gardens Theatre, Folkestone, 12th July 1897. **Metropole,** Camberwell. Cast: *Dr. William Browne,* Mr. J. R. Crauford; *Mr. Firman,* Mr. George Raiemond; *George Webster,* Mr. Edward Morehen; *Mr. Horton,* Mr. Francis Horley; *Baggs,* Mr. John Pritchard; *Sergeant,* Mr. Charles Phillips; *Mrs. Horton,* Miss Nellie Ganthony; *Mrs. William Browne,* Miss May Cross; *Jennie Firman,* Miss Kate Dudley; *Mrs. Firman,* Miss Pattie Bell; *Ellen,* Miss E. Pryce; *Miss Kate Fauntleroy,* Miss Florrie Harmon.

19. THE SILENCE OF NIGHT: Drama in Four Acts, by John D. Saunders. **Shakespeare,** Clapham. Cast: *Jack Eversley,* Mr. John D. Saunders; *Sir William Alexander,* Mr. D. Lyn Harding; *Urban Flinton,* Mr. Henry Vibart; *Henry Valentine,* Mr. H. Gomer May; *Parker,* Mr. Harry Elliston; *Pipable,* Mr. Cecil Elgar; *The Hon. Drawley,* Mr. J. Warrington; *Lord Stiffenbache,* Mr. G. Stevens; *Frank Hustier,* Mr. Frank Beresford; *Jockster,* Mr. C. A. Morgan; *Jarvis,* Mr. Jarvis Widdicombe; *Old Billy,* Mr. H. B. Dunfield; *Hochmuth,* Mr. Clifford Tanner; *Inspector Quick,* Mr. T. H. Harrison; *Thomas,* Mr. Manners-Knight; *Murdoch,* Mr. C. F. Rochford; *Harriet Valentine,* Miss Laura Johnson; *Kitty Spencer,* Miss Emile Ormesby; *Miss Violet Snellgrove,* Miss Maud Thompson; *Miss Moneylove,* Miss Ruby Desmond;

Lady Stiffenbache, Miss Ada Palmer; *Winifred Alexander,* Miss Dora De Winton.

22. BROKEN FETTERS: Play in One Act, by Charles Thursby. **Matinée.**

26. THE VICTORIA CROSS: Drama by J. W. Whitbread. Originally produced at the Queen's Theatre, Dublin, 6th September 1896. **Pavilion.**

AUGUST.

2. THE HAND OF PROVIDENCE: Drama in Four Acts, by T. Gideon Warren. **Surrey.** Cast: *James Ventnor,* Mr. Charles Cruikshanks; *Harold Ventnor,* Mr. Ernest E. Norris; *Stephen Gale,* Mr. John Webb; *Champion Bragge,* Mr. George Conquest, Jun.; *Ben Brayling,* Mr. Frank Lister; *Fred Denvil,* Mr. Fred Conquest; *Nat Blacket,* Mr. Ernest E. Ball; *Joe Goss,* Mr. Arthur Hall; *Colley,* Mr. Arthur Conquest; *Judge Parkes,* Mr. H. Saunders; *Inspector of Police,* Mr. J. Millar; *Wilson,* Mr. H. Evans; *Rose Raeburn,* Miss Kate Olga Vernon; *Lady Pagnell,* Miss Florence E. Florence; *Eleanor Pagnell,* Miss Laura Dyson; *Kate Brayling,* Miss Cissie Farrell; *Madame Klein,* Miss Cissy Percival; *Miss Frogmore,* Miss Amy Dyson.

2. THE BALLET GIRL: Musical Comedy in Two Acts, by James T. Tanner; Lyrics by Adrian Ross; Music by Carl Kiefert. First played at the Grand Theatre, Wolverhampton, 15th March 1897. **Brixton.**

9. STIRRING TIMES: Musical Play by Frank H. Celli and Brian Daly. Originally produced, 2nd August 1897, at the Opera House, Southport. **Shakespeare,** Clapham.

30. A BIT OF DRAPERY: Comedietta by Preston Hope. **Metropole,** Camberwell.

30. NORAH: Comedy in One Act, by Re Henry. **Grand.**

30. OH, MY WIFE! Duologue by Daphne De Rohan. **Lyric,** Ealing.

SEPTEMBER.

20. TOTO AND TATA: Operetta in Three Acts, by MM. Paul Bilhaud and Albert Barre ; Music by Antoine Banes. Originally produced as " Toto " at the Menus-Plaisirs, Paris, 10th June 1892 ; English version by A. M. Thompson ; Lyrics by Boyd Jones and J. J. Wood. First played at the Grand Theatre, Leeds, 23rd August 1897. **Metropole.** Cast : *Cabestan,* Mr. E. J. Lonnen ; *Gaston Manners,* Mr. Roland Cunningham ; *Bernard,* Mr. Walter Groves ; *Dupalet,* Mr. Richard Blunt ; *Captain Victor Hanotaux,* Mr. Bert. Haslem ; *Riebert,* Mr. Frank James ; *Gendarme,* Mr. Charles Usher ; *Foulard,* Mr. Frederick Rix ; *Waiter,* Mr. James Francis ; *Fireman,* Mr. J. G. Shuter ; *Policeman,* Mr. F. Finch ; *Cesarine,* Miss Alys Rees ; *Aurilie,* Miss Emily Millar ; *Suzanne,* Miss Maud Hoppe ; *Marie,* Miss Edith Armstrong ; *Madame Hanotaux,* Miss Ruth Mackay ; *Paul,* Miss Violet Dacre ; *Anatole,* Miss Florence Wykes ; *Emile,* Miss M. Gathorne ; *Erneste,* Miss E. Maynard ; *Mdlle. Corinne,* Miss Dorothy Dean ; *Charlot,* Miss M. Bell ; *Etienne,* Miss Esme Gordon ; *Toto and Tata,* Miss Marie Montrose.

20. THE PERILS OF PARIS: Domestic Drama in a Prologue and Three Acts, adapted by Arthur Shirley from *La Porteuse de Pain* of MM. De Montepin and Dournay. Produced at the Paris Ambigu on 11th January 1889. **Lyric,** Hammersmith.

27. FROM SCOTLAND-YARD: Drama in a Prologue and Four Acts, by John Douglas and Frank Bateman. Originally produced at Accrington, 16th August 1897. **Parkhurst.**

OCTOBER.

4. THE NEW MEPHISTO: Musical Comedy in Two Acts. Originally produced as the " New Mephistopheles " at the Grand Theatre, Leeds, 29th March 1897. **Brixton.**

11. WOMAN AND WINE: Drama in Four Acts, by Ben Landeck and Arthur Shirley. **Pavilion.** Cast : *Dick Seymour*, Mr. Ashley Page; *Hugh Seymour*, Mr. G. W. Cockburn; *Alphonse Beaudet*, Mr. Oscar Adye; *Pierre Crucru*, Mr. Albert Marsh; *Professor Sawter*, Mr. Fred Coyne; *Charles Sawter*, Mr. Lennox Pawle; *Phineas Collins*, Mr. H. F. M'Clelland; *Mark Parkins*, Mr. A. W. Fitzgerald; *Duc d'Arnac*, Mr. Russell Norrie; *Bob Tipton*, Mr. Fred Boustead; *President of the Court*, Mr. Charles Cecil; *Carlo*, Mr. Ferry; *Joseph*, Mr. Adams; *Foreman of the Jury*, Mr. Godfrey; *An Advocate*, Mr. R. Collins; *Mary Andrews*, Miss Marion Denvil; *Marcel Rigadout*, Miss V. St. Lawrence; *Janet Marlow*, Miss E. Brinsley Sheridan; *La Colombe*, Miss Rachel De Solla; *Madame Perinet*, Miss Iona Robertson; *Susanne*, Miss Edith Chapman.

11. KITTY : Comic Opera in Two Acts, by Walter Parke and Henry Parker. First played at the Opera House, Cheltenham, 30th August 1897. **Theatre Royal,** Kilburn.

18. THE FORTUNE-HUNTER : Play in Three Acts, by W. S. Gilbert. Originally produced at the Theatre Royal, Birmingham, 27th September 1897. **Queen's Opera House,** Crouch End. Cast : *The Duke of Dundee*, Mr. C. B. Clarence; *Sir Cuthbert Jameson*, Mr. Edmund Maurice; *The Marquis De Breville*, Mr. Arthur Nerton; *Vicomte Armand De Breville*, Mr. Luigi Lablache; *M. Lachaud*, Mr. George P. Hawtrey; *Mr. Dudley Coxe*, Mr. Compton Coutts; *Mr. Barker*, Mr. W. R. Staveley; *Mr. Taylor*, Mr. C. Butt; *Mr. Paillard*, Mr. C. O. Axton; *Mr. M'Quarris*, Mr. Vivian Stenhouse; *Pollard*, Mr. A. Clay; *Captain Munroe*, Mr. Charles Howe; *Mr. M'Fie*, Mr. Howard Sturge; *Quartermaster*, Mr. Charles Leighton; *The Duchess of Dundee*, Miss Cicely Richards; *The Marquise De Breville*, Miss Adelina Baird; *Mrs. Dudley Coxe*, Miss Nora O'Neil; *Miss Somerton*, Miss Regina Repton; *Miss Bailey*, Miss A. Beauchamp; *Diana Caverel*, Miss Fortescue.

18.   SPORTING LIFE : Drama in Four Acts, by Cecil Raleigh and Seymour Hicks. **Shakespeare Theatre,** Clapham Junction.   Cast : *John, Earl of Woodstock,* Mr. Leonard Boyne ; *Sir Charles Braybourne,* Mr. Sam Sothern ; *The Hon. Dudley Stanhope,* Mr. Edward Sillward ; *Gen. Reginald Molyneux, V.C.,* Mr. Walter M'Ewen ; *Isidore Andreade,* Mr. G. R. Foss ; *Sergeant Dan Doxey,* Mr. Fred Emney ; *Geoffrey Pilgrim,* Mr. Hardie ; *Joe Lee,* Mr. George Flood ; *Malet De Carteret,* Mr. Julian Royce ; *Jordan,* Mr. F. Dark ; *George Gale,* Mr. D. Holcroft ; *Lucas,* Mr. John Grant ; *Mason,* Mr. H. Daly ; *Mavor,* Mr. T. H. Elsworthy ; *Saunders,* Mr. W. W. Watson ; *A Beggar,* Mr. Frank Hilton ; *Cleary,* Mr. George Claremont ; *Barney,* Mr. A. B. Fielding ; *Red Mike,* Mr. J. E. Manning ; *Burton,* Mr. T. B. Malling ; *Willmot,* Mr. C. J. Fairleigh ; *Gelland,* Mr. G. H. Oliver ; *Cabmen,* Mr. H. Peters ; *Referee,* Mr. Harry De Lacy ; *Policeman,* Mr. Thompson Long ; *Timekeeper,* Mr. Frank Davey ; *Master of the Ceremonies,* Mr. C. Francis ; *Crake,* Mr. H. A. Millar ; *Newsboy,* Mr. T. C. Aubrey ; *Joe Spratt,* Mr. Thiel ; *Jim,* Mr. George Dauncy; *First Rustic,* Mr. E. C. Owen ; *Second Rustic,* Mr. George Davison ; *Miles Cavanagh,* Mr. W. J. Robertson ; *Philip,* Mr. E. H. Brooke ; *Norah,* Miss Denman ; *Kitty,* Miss Kathleen Deene ; *Clara,* Miss Madge Merry ; *Jessie,* Miss Beresford ; *Nursemaid,* Miss Bonheur ; *First Lady,* Miss Helen Rowley ; *Olive De Carteret,* Mrs. Raleigh.

18.   THE VAGABOND KING : Play in Four Acts, by Louis N. Parker. **Metropole,** Camberwell.   Cast : *Don Pedro XIV.,* Mr. Murray Carson ; *Pandolfo,* Mr. George Grossmith, Jun.; *Don Miguel de Santa Rosa y Paruro,* Mr. Gilbert Farquhar ; *Marchese de Castelverano,* Mr. Lawrence D'Orsay ; *Chevalier Moffat,* Mr. Sidney Brough ; *Monseigneur,* Mr. Fred Grove ; *Benito,* Mr. D. L. Mannering ; *One-eyed Sammy,* Mr. Charles Mordan ; *Donna Pia,* Miss Bateman ; *Stella Desmond,* Miss Lena Ashwell ; *Princess Zea of Santorin,* Miss Phyllis Broughton ; *Lady Violet,* Miss Ethel Verne ; *Mrs. Wallis,* Mrs. Leigh.

25. AT THE FOOT OF THE ALTAR: Drama in Four Acts, by Frederick Jarman. Originally produced at the Opera House, Londonderry, 20th September 1897. **Theatre Royal**, Stratford.

27. THE BURGLAR'S BABY: Comedy-Drama in Three Acts, by John Douglas and Charles Williams. **Lyric**, Ealing.

NOVEMBER.

1. THE DUCHESS OF DIJON: Comic Opera in Two Acts; Book by Basil Hood; Music by Walter Slaughter. First played at the Theatre Royal, Portsmouth, 20th September 1897. **Metropole.**

15. THE GOLDEN SERPENT: Drama in Four Acts, by T. N. Walter. **Theatre Royal**, Stratford.

22. WHEN THE LAMPS ARE LIGHTED: Drama in Four Acts, by George R. Sims and Leonard Merrick. Produced at the Regent Theatre, Salford, 11th October 1897. **Grand.** Cast: *Dan Rafferty*, Mr. John F. Sheridan; *Paul Wayland*, Mr. Nelson Ramsey; *Frank Amory*, Mr. Maurice Mancini; *Stephen Lyle*, Mr. William Devereux; *Jim Radley*, Mr. Wm. Brandon; *Richard Draycott*, Mr. Frederick Annerly; *Beauty*, Mr. George T. Minshull; *Tommy Bloss*, Mr. Bert Williams; *Charley Scraggs*, Mr. Douglas Miller; *Policeman*, Mr. Fred Fentiman; *Dosser No.* 1, Mr. Charles Denham; *Dosser No.* 2, Mr. Louis Hatch; *Frankie*, Master Bertie; *Margaret Draycott*, Miss Mena Le Bert; *Ruth*, Miss Marie Polini; *Loo Enderby*, Miss Helena Head; *Semolina*, Miss Ida Laurence; *Tilly Fitzfotheringay*, Miss Gracie Whiteford.

26. HENRY ESMOND: Play, adapted by T. Edgar Pemberton from Thackeray's novel. Originally produced at the Lyceum, Edinburgh, 5th March 1897. **Queen's Opera House,** Crouch End.

DECEMBER.

2. SOCIAL DEBTS: Farcical Comedy in Three Acts, founded on a German Play, by Barton White. **County,** Kingston-on-Thames.

6. THE COURTSHIP OF MORRICE BUCKLER: Play in Four Acts, adapted by the author and Miss Isabel Bateman from Mr. A. E. W. Mason's novel of the same name. **Grand.** Cast: *Morrice Buckler*, Mr. Yorke Stephens; *Count Lukstein*, Mr. W. L. Abingdon; *Lord Elmscott*, Mr. Henry Vibart; *Sir Julian Harnwood*, Mr. Charles Fulton; *Lord Culverton*, Mr. E. H. Kelly; *Hugh Marston*, Mr. Herbert Parcy; *Cuthbert Cliffe*, Mr. Fred Parr; *Charles Aglionby*, Mr. William Luff; *Father Spaur*, Mr. Frederick Powell; *Otto Krax*, Mr. Charles Levey; *A Gaoler*, Mr. Gerald Godfrey; *Servant*, Mr. W. Goodner; *Ilga Lukstein*, Miss Esme Beringer; *Betty Marston*, Miss Helen Leyton; *Clemence Durette*, Miss Furtado Clarke.

13. CHARLOTTE CORDAY: Play in Four Acts. **Grand,** Islington. Cast: *Marat*, Mr. Bellew; *Francis De Corday D'Armont*, Mr. Frederick Everill; *Abbe Fleuriot*, Mr. Arthur Wood; *Adam Luse*, Mr. A. Bawtree; *David*, Mr. Henry Lee; *Potin*, Mr. W. St. John; *Drouet*, Mr. Lyons; *Chabot*, Mr. Edmunds; *Chevause De La Garde*, Mr. Walter Gay; *Rebullet*, Mr. A. Harding; *Cannut*, Mr. Ernest Elton; *A Frinter*, Mr. Athelstone; *A Gendarme*, Mr. Lyons; *A Jailor*, Mr. E. J. Norris; *Rose De Corday D'Armont*, Mrs. Harding; *Simmone Everad*, Miss Ailsa Craig; *Marianne*, Miss Mabel Hackney; *Madame Richard*, Mrs. Crofton; *Marie*, Miss Brooke; *Concierge*, Miss Wilmer; *Charlotte Corday*, Mrs. Potter.

17. BANTRY BAY: Play in One Act, by Stephen Bond. **Surrey.**

17. A WOMAN'S HEART: Play in One Act, by R. S. Warren Bell. **Surrey.**

INDEX.

---◆---

THEATRES, Etc.

PLAYS.

AUTHORS.

ACTORS.

ACTRESSES.